T0247813

REAP THE
WHIRLWIND

ALSO BY PETER HOULAHAN

Norco '80: The True Story of the Most Spectacular Bank Robbery in American History

REAP THE WHIRLWIND

Violence, Race, Justice,
and the Story of Sagon Penn

PETER HOULAHAN

COUNTERPOINT / CALIFORNIA

First Counterpoint edition: 2024

Library of Congress Cataloging-in-Publication Data
Names: Houlahan, Peter, 1961- author.
Title: Reap the whirlwind : violence, race, justice, and the story of Sagon Penn / Peter Houlahan.
Description: San Francisco, CA : Counterpoint, [2024]
Identifiers: LCCN 2024010045 | ISBN 9781640094512 (hardcover) | ISBN 9781640094529 (ebook)
Subjects: LCSH: Police—Violence against—California—San Diego. | African Americans—Violence against—California—San Diego. | Racism in law enforcement—California—San Diego. | Traffic stops (Law enforcement—California—San Diego. | Penn, Sagon, 1962-2002—Trials, litigation, etc. | Encanto (San Diego, Calif.)—Social conditions.
Classification: LCC HV8148.S32 H58 2024 | DDC 363.209794/985—dc23/eng/20240419
LC record available at https://lccn.loc.gov/2024010045

Jacket design by Farjana Yasmin
Jacket images of cop car © Shutterstock/PhotoJuli86,
palm trees © iStock/skodonnell
Book design by Laura Berry

COUNTERPOINT
Los Angeles and San Francisco, CA
www.counterpointpress.com

Printed in the United States of America

10 9 8 7 6 5 4 3 2 1

For my mother,
who has always given more love and support than
any writer or son could ever ask for

For they have sown the wind, and they shall reap the whirlwind.

—Hosea 8:7

The day was bright, and everything was smooth, and the sun beamed down on the City of Blues.

—Anthony "Cold Doc Tee" Lovett

CONTENTS

REAP THE
WHIRLWIND

PROLOGUE

I N 1917, THE SEVENTY THOUSAND RESIDENTS OF SAN DIEGO had a decision to make: "Smokestacks versus Geraniums." Few cities have the chance to define their future, but the candidates in the 1917 election for mayor made the two possibilities clear. Gilded Age banker-type Louis J. Wilde—for whom no industrial project was too big to finance—marketed himself as "The Smokestack Candidate," promising good jobs and good wages through the development of the city's deep-water harbor into a center for shipping and manufacturing. Depart-ment store owner "Geranium George" Marston—champion of Balboa Park and organizer of the wildly successful 1915 Panama-California Exposition—saw the city's welcoming climate and natural beauty as its greatest assets, promising a prosperous future in real estate and tourism through beautification and carefully managed growth.

Wilde had money and charisma, and he won the election with the backing of labor unions and business but soon got into a scandal, fled to Los Angeles, and died. Marston stuck around, lived to age ninety-five, and, through persistence and persuasion, brought the rest of San Diego around to his vision for their future. Geraniums it would be.

San Diegans never regretted their chosen path. With the well-established United States Navy anchoring the local economy alongside their Pacific fleet, and a post–World War II housing market flooded with VA-loan-eligible buyers, the residential real estate developers be-came the power brokers of the city. The tourism and hospitality indus-tries loved the place, leveraging the white sand beaches, ocean sunsets, pleasant-year-round climate, and a rollicking Mexican border town that had become a tourist attraction itself into a major vacation destination. The city adjusted its zoning laws and dedicated its resources accordingly.

By 1985, the population of the greater San Diego metropolitan area had topped two million and moved onto the list of the ten most populous in the country. But San Diegans simply refused to believe it. In their minds, they were still a beach town, all fun in the sun, blue skies, and perfect waves, with a steady stream of tourists eager to spend their money to be there, even if only for a few days. "America's Finest City" was what they called the place to outsiders, but among themselves they had a different slogan: "We are not L.A."

Los Angeles, one hundred miles to the north, was increasingly plagued with murderous street gangs, guns, violent crime, and hard drugs. San Diego had none of these, right? They even elected a mayor in 1983 on a promise to stop the "L.A.-ification" of their city, and so far, it looked like the guy was living up to his campaign slogan. At least as far as they could see. But that was only because they were not looking in the right place.

WHEN SAN DIEGO chose geraniums, the railroad tracks and freight trains that hauled products and raw materials across the country turned north, destined for the smokestacks and deepwater commercial port of Los Angeles instead. With them went the industrial and manufacturing demand for unskilled and low-skilled labor that attracted so many Black workers from the southern states and northeastern urban centers. The result was that the Black community in San Diego remained the smallest and least politically powerful among those of any major American city. As the rest of the city grew, the usual forces conspired to segregate and concentrate the Black population into a single area of the city, the Southeast, where it was guaranteed to be neglected and underserved.

The federal Home Owners' Loan Corporation redlined the entire area of Southeast San Diego into the lowest Grade D-4 rating, recommending that mortgage lenders "refuse to make loans in these areas or only on a conservative basis," due to "detrimental influences and an undesirable population or an infiltration of it." With mortgages all but impossible to obtain, the community was denied home ownership and the accumulation of intergenerational wealth that went with it. The construction of elevated freeways carved up neighborhoods and commercial districts and allowed San Diegans to pass through the Southeast without ever knowing it was there. Suburban mega-malls doomed local retailers, and a 1978 statewide taxpayer revolt starved the area of the bonds and tax measures needed to maintain existing infrastructure and fund area improvements.

Southeast San Diego nevertheless developed into a vibrant, culturally rich, socially active community with strong religious and civic organizations. But it remained economically disadvantaged and vulnerable. By 1985, PCP, crystal meth, and crack cocaine had joined heroin in ruining lives, spiking burglaries and robberies by addicts, and flooding the area with guns. Street gangs became bigger, bolder, meaner, and more heavily armed as meaningless turf wars over the color of a bandana became open warfare for control of lucrative street corner drug markets. As things got progressively worse, the residents and community leaders of Southeast San Diego seemed unable get the rest of the San Diego to recognize it had become a big city with big-city problems.

That is, until March 31, 1985, when two white San Diego Police officers followed a pickup truck with seven young Black men up a long dirt driveway in the Southeast neighborhood of Encanto. Minutes later, something terrible happened.

THE SOUND OF a terrified woman's voice coming over the San Diego Police Department radio frequency was chilling: "We need help. We need help." Police racing through the streets in response to the desperate cry for help barely took notice of the police cruiser that passed them going the opposite direction, its light bar whirling blue and red. Behind the wheel, a police revolver on the seat beside him, was a twenty-three-year-old named Sagon Penn.

In the aftermath of the horrifying incident, the city of San Diego was left wondering how a police force considered one of the most progressive in the country when it came to issues of race and use of force could see two of its rising stars pull over a truck full of innocent young men on their way back from a day at the park, and still have everything go so terribly wrong. Sagon Penn, a soft-spoken and idealistic young man who believed his Buddhist chants could bring about the oneness of humanity, never disputed the violent events that occurred on that driveway in Encanto. San Diego was left to decide: Was there anything that could possibly justify such an act? For the city's older, white establishment with their deep military traditions and rigid ideas of law and order, there could be no conceivable justification. But the Black community, numbering less than 7 percent of the population, had no trouble conceiving of such a scenario.

HAD THE STORY of Sagon Penn happened today, it would be a national media sensation, transfixing and dividing the country with its shocking developments and riveting courtroom drama. But in 1985, San Diego, California, was still young enough not to have discovered a national obsession with true crime, and it did not yet have access to the internet and twenty-four-hour news channels to deliver stories of crime and punishment into every home at all hours of the day. Nor had the majority-white population awoken to the historically difficult relationship between the Black community and the authorities charged with policing them.

For over two years, the city was forced to confront these uncomfortable truths about itself as it struggled with the realization that America's Finest City had always been two cities living separate lives.

PART 1

1

BALBOA PARK CLOSES AT DUSK, BUT ON MARCH 31, 1985, dusk came early to the area known as Pepper Grove. "Sorry, fellas, it's closed," a San Diego police officer manning a barricade told the driver of the old pickup truck when it pulled up to the busy parking area. There were lots of spots to kick back, throw a football around, or just soak up the sun in the sprawling park, but the only place the five young men in the pickup truck wanted to go was Pepper Grove. It was not the most beautiful part of what is called "The Jewel of San Diego," just an area of lawn and picnic benches, with scattered shade trees. But Pepper Grove was the area of Balboa Park where the young Black citizens of San Diego went on a Sunday afternoon.

Sagon Penn looked past the police officer to the groups of young people sitting together on the lawn, the families at picnic tables, and others checking out the customized lowriders and street racers lined up in a row. He scanned the parking lot and pointed to an empty spot a few spaces beyond the barricade. "Couldn't I take one of those, sir?" he asked. The officer shook his head. "I didn't say it was full, I said it was closed." Sagon heard groans of disappointment from his teenage brother and two friends riding in the back of the pickup. "What do you mean, closed?" he asked, genuinely confused. "Closes at dusk," said the officer, less polite than the first time. Sagon looked up at the late-afternoon sun arcing through a clear blue sky on its way toward the western horizon. He didn't get it. "Yeah, but it's still a couple—"

"All right, thank you, officer," Sagon's best friend Bryan Ross called out from the passenger seat, before the officer had to repeat it a fourth time. Sagon was twenty-three and Bryan only twenty, but Bryan seemed to understand how these things worked. For a kid who grew up in Southeast San Diego, Sagon was remarkably naive about the world around him. "Let's go," Bryan said. They drove off. Bryan smiled and shook his head. "Do you know anything?"

The young guys in the back of the pickup were disappointed to be turned away. At fifteen years old, Sagon's half brother, Sean Arkward, was the youngest, friendly but quiet, and seemingly getting taller by the day. The two were close, but there was a seven-year age difference, so they had different friends, went to different schools, and, for much of the time, lived in different homes. Nineteen-year-old DeWayne Holmes, who went by "Keno," was upbeat, fancied himself the neighborhood playboy, and never stopped talking. Eighteen-year-old Cedric Gregory was the organizer, always coming up with something for the group to do. Pepper Grove was his idea. "The place is off the hook; we gotta go!" he told them.

None of them owned cars, but Sagon and Sean's grandfather, Yusuf Abdullah, had an old pickup truck he used for hauling supplies for his popular Muslim cuisine restaurant on Imperial Avenue. At fifteen, Sean was definitely not on his grandfather's approved-driver list, but Sagon was. He had been living with his grandfather since high school and frequently helped at the restaurant. Yusuf would let him use the truck if he had a good reason for needing it. Abdullah had thirty grandchildren but a soft place in his heart for Sagon.

Cedric and Keno had never met Sagon prior to that weekend. There were only a few things Sean had ever told them about his older brother: don't smoke weed around him, he's not into any of that gang shit, and he knows how to fight. But with Sagon, it wasn't the usual type of fighting they had in the Southeast. "My karate brother," Sean called him.

SAGON BEGAN TRAINING in the Korean martial art of tae kwon do at age sixteen with an intense and charismatic sixth-degree black belt named Master James Wilson. Training sessions under Wilson were rigorous and demanding, three to four hours involving repetition of movements to sharpen skills and sparring with other students. If you engaged in an instructional demonstration with Wilson himself, you could count on ending up on the studio mat more than a few times. The first thing any tae kwon do student learned at Master Wilson's Southwestern Association of Martial Arts were the makki blocking techniques, using one's forearms to sweep incoming blows away from the body. Failure to learn that meant risking a broken rib or having your head taken off by a fist strike, side kick, or escrima stick.

Wilson's students were top performers, participating in state, national, and world-championship tournaments. None were more promising than Sagon Penn, who Wilson felt with continued training was talented enough to qualify for the debut of tae kwon do at the 1988 Seoul Olympics. But there was a problem with Sagon chasing any Olympic dream: money. After graduating high school, he realized he would never have the financial freedom to put in the training necessary to be an elite performer. He needed to get a job, maybe start a career. In mid-1983, at age twenty-one, Sagon walked away from Master Wilson's studio after four and a half years. He tried out Kempo karate and boxing, but never with the same intensity. He got out of the martial arts entirely shortly after he began practicing Buddhism. "Inflicting pain on a fellow human being went against the law of the fellow man," he said.

IT WAS NOT difficult to find another place to hang out in Balboa Park because no place other than Pepper Grove was "closed." The five young men got out of the truck and sat around at a picnic table in the sunshine. The temperature was in the seventies, as it always seemed to be in San Diego, with a soft ocean breeze coming in off the Pacific. Sagon began messing around with tae kwon do kicks and moves, trying to goad Bryan into a good-natured sparring match. "No way," Bryan said, shaking his head. Bryan's refusal to mix it up with Sagon made an impression on Cedric and Keno. They'd seen how good a street fighter Bryan Ross was at Mission Beach the day before.

Sean had talked Sagon into driving him to Mission Beach, along with his friends and their teenage twin cousins, Raphyal and Aarmayl. The seven young men walked along the boardwalk, lined with surf shops, hot dog stands, and outdoor restaurant bars, and down to the penny arcades, public pool, and old wooden roller coaster. Among the mostly white and Hispanic beachgoing crowd, a group of swaggering young Black men drew some second looks. Sean and his friends decided to sit on a low wall and check out the honeys, as Cedric called them, passing by in bikinis and Dolphin shorts. Across the sand, a shimmering blue ocean stretched out to the horizon, with nothing but azure skies above—The City of Blues.

Sagon decided to take a break from the teenagers and go for a walk. When he came back, he discovered they had gotten into some kind of shit with three muscled-up white guys in swim trunks. He didn't even bother to ask why. Probably just a sideways look, a scowl, or eye contact held a beat too long. Two groups of young men—one white, one Black—most likely throwing down for no good reason all. Bryan had gotten pulled into it and apparently fought so well he sent the three bigger men retreating down the boardwalk.

For the moment, the two sides were still separated, throwing tough looks at each other and working themselves up for another go. Sagon saw that there were bloody noses involved, eyebrows already beginning to swell. Beachgoers in swim trunks, bikinis, and flip-flops stood by waiting to see what would happen next.

Sagon Penn didn't want to fight. In addition to the rigorous physical regimen, Master Wilson had taught discipline and restraint. Sagon had faced hundreds of opponents and spent thousands of hours sparring, but the strict principles of Wilson and tae kwon do prohibited using one's skills outside the studio. The only exception was to defend oneself. "The absolute rule is a life-and-death situation," Wilson instructed.

"What are you doing?" Sagon asked, his eyes settling on each of the younger boys in turn. Nobody answered. They were just teenagers, still a bit scrawny and not as tough as they thought but fearless nonetheless. And they were Black kids from Southeast San Diego, so they all knew how to fight. "Then why are you doing it?" He looked down the board-walk at the three guys about forty feet away and amped up on anger and testosterone. He shook his head. "You're just letting them take your power away."

With the crowd of mostly white faces looking on, Sagon walked to the opposing three combatants. His physical presence did not make much of an impression at first sight. He was not especially big-–five feet eleven inches and a solid 170 pounds. He had an athletic build: strong, loose-jointed, and well-proportioned but not imposing. There was no pretense to his movements, nothing intended to project menace, as was often the case with young men from the Southeast. More likely to draw attention was his good looks. He was a strikingly handsome young man with sculpted, symmetrical features and large smokey-brown eyes. His wide, bright smile was genuine and disarming. He wore his hair close-cropped and had never grown facial hair. He rarely swore, used street slang, or took the Lord's name in vain. He sprinkled his vocabulary with nerdy expressions such as "golly" and "wow."

When he reached the other men, he could see there were cuts and contusions on them as well. Sagon was relaxed as he spoke, motioning back to his brother and the others at one point. Whatever he had to say, the three guys were listening. They said something back to Sagon and then turned and resumed their way down the boardwalk.

SAGON WAS WORRIED about the direction his brother seemed to be headed. He was starting to get in trouble at school and had had some run-ins with police. He suspected Sean was hanging out with members of the Bloods street gang. Sagon had already been planning to take him to the Buddhist temple he attended, but with this stupid fight over nothing, he decided he would take all of these kids right now.

Sagon's exposure to the Buddhist faith seemed to be the answer to a frenetic spiritual quest he began at a young age. He had tried the "traditionally Black" Christian churches in Southeast San Diego. "It was too segregated," he said. "The whole damn church had all Black people in it." He attended his grandfather's Muslim mosque but was turned off by what he felt was a hostility toward white people. "I just couldn't take all that negativity."

Then a friend brought him to a meeting of the Buddhist organization Nichiren Shoshu of America. "Everything was just like I wanted it—just like I always dreamed. We had Hispanics, African American Blacks, Caucasians, Orientals . . . all of us. We was all family and stuff." He was taught the path to enlightenment and inner peace was through daily meditations and repetitive chanting of a single phrase believed to contain the essence of truth: "nam myoho renge kyo." Sagon believed it had the power to change negativity to positivity, create a life force energy that could be projected to those around him, and alleviate the suffering of others. Collectively, they could achieve world peace by chanting.

But none of the guys in the truck were especially interested in their life force touching another's or in taking on the suffering of their fellow man. "Come on, just chant three times and you'll get benefits, it'll change your destiny," Sagon urged them when they balked at removing their shoes before entering. The whole thing was just too weird for a group of young men in the process of polishing up their street credentials. "Nah, I ain't doing this," one said, turning and walking back toward the truck. The others followed. "His negativity overpowered my positivity," Sagon later said, dispirited by the rejection. "They didn't even go inside. And that just kinda hurt me, because it really, really works."

IN BALBOA PARK, the sun was dipping low in the sky, and the younger boys were getting bored. This was no Pepper Grove. The real dusk, not the San Diego Police dusk, was approaching, anyhow. "Let's go," one of them said. They piled into the back of the truck while Bryan got into the cab with Sagon. They exited the south end of the park on the fringe of downtown and headed for the 94 freeway to take Cedric and Keno back to Encanto. After that, Sagon planned to drop off a completed job application at the Sunrise Market convenience store on Market Street on his way back to his grandfather's house in Mountain View. He had even dressed up a little to look presentable when he did, wearing a pair of nice jeans, a white long-sleeve button-down shirt he wore untucked, and stylish patent leather lace-up shoes.

But he did not care that much about the Sunrise Market job; it was just the same type of low-wage employment he'd had since he started working at age fifteen: at a shoe store, as a security guard, at another convenience store, bagging groceries and collecting shopping carts at a Safeway super-market. He worked the kitchen at Yusuf's, his grandfather's restaurant, and obtained a vendor's license to sell their locally famous bean pies to make a little extra money. He even had an idea for developing the recipe into a Betty Crocker–type instant pie mix but could not navigate the complicated federal patent process. At twenty-three, he was looking for a career, not just a job. Two years earlier, he had taken the entrance exams for the San Diego Police Department, passing the physical test but failing the reading-comprehension portion because he did not realize the test was timed. But he had recently put in another application with the department, this time to be a community service officer, and was looking forward to taking the entrance exam the coming Thursday, just four days away.

There was a sudden pounding on the roof of the cab of the pickup truck as they passed a McDonald's a couple blocks outside of the park. "Pull over," Sean shouted. Keno had spotted his older brother, Junius, walking with a young couple who lived in their neighborhood. Keno called out to his brother while Sagon pulled to the curb.

Twenty-one-year-old Junius Holmes just wanted to be a rapper. It was a relatively new aspiration of his. But then again, it was for anyone in San Diego. While established on the East Coast, the emergence of the West Coast rap scene was so new, few outside of the Southeast even knew there was one, if they had heard of the music at all. Junius went by the stage name "J.P." and had worked his way into a neighborhood rap group called the Mighty Key Gang.

The people walking with Junius were another rapper in the group named Ricky Clipper and his girlfriend, Doria Jones. The two were temporarily crashing on the couch of Anthony "Doc" Lovett, leader of the Mighty Key Gang, who lived in a small duplex one street over from Junius and Keno on Brooklyn Avenue. After an afternoon in Pepper Grove, they were walking to catch a bus. Keno recognized them because Ricky was wearing a green-and-black jacket with "Mighty Key Gang" written on the back. As they pulled away from the curb, Sean, Cedric, Keno, Junius, and Ricky were seated in the bed of the truck. Doria Jones sat in the cab between Sagon and Bryan Ross, after Sagon insisted he would never ask a lady to ride in the back of a truck.

It was 5:55 p.m. when the pickup entered the 94 freeway at Seventeenth Street headed in the direction of Encanto. The Sunday-evening traffic was light as they traveled the four and a half miles eastbound on 94, the wind whipping through the open windows of the cab as they went. They exited at Kelton Road and continued over to Old Memory Lane. The low sun threw the long shadows of palm trees across the small stucco and wood-frame houses of Encanto. In the back, Ricky Clipper began to freestyle some rhymes. Junius joined in, the two trading off lines.

> *Cold. It's a cold world y'all.*
> *It's cold, cold world we're living in.*
> *Cold world. Cold world.*
> *Brother can I trust you as a friend?*
> *Cold . . . Cold, Cold.*

Sagon turned down Sixtieth Street. To the right, the hillside fell away into Radio Canyon, the grass and scrub brush green from spring rains. After exchanging a few words at the start, the three in the front were mostly silent on the ride. A careful driver by nature, Sagon kept to the speed limit. Doria noticed he was always using his indicator at turns because she could hear it getting stuck each time. At Broadway, he took a left turn and headed east along the residential street curving through the hillsides. After a few blocks, someone directed him to turn right down Sixty-Fifth Street in the direction of Imperial Avenue, the main commercial roadway passing through the heart of the Southeast. The plan was to drop everyone except Bryan at a house at 6564 Brooklyn Avenue, where Clipper and Jones were staying with "Doc" Lovett and his girlfriend, Angie McKibben. Junius would stick around there for a Mighty Key Gang rehearsal, while Cedric and Sean were going to hang with Keno at his parents' house one street over.

They went down the steep hill on Sixty-Fifth Street, past the one-story Encanto Elementary School on the right and Encanto Recreation Center on the left. At the bottom of the hill, a San Diego Police car turned left out of Brooklyn and headed up Sixty-Fifth in the opposite direction. A second police car came out from Brooklyn Avenue a few seconds later and followed the first. The two cars passed the truck. Sagon paid little attention to them as he prepared to make a left turn onto Brooklyn. But in the bed of the truck, Junius and Ricky went quiet. They watched as one police car swept a hard U-turn at the recreation center. Seconds later, the other one used the entrance to Encanto Elementary School to swing around and fall in behind the first. As the two cop cars approached, Junius shook his head. "You know they're gonna stop us," he said.

2

S AN DIEGO POLICE AGENT DONOVAN JACOBS SAT BEHIND the wheel of his patrol unit surveying the scene through his front windshield. It was a typical late Sunday afternoon in the Southeast neighborhood of Encanto, with residents watering front lawns, fixing cars in driveways, or chatting with neighbors while children rode bikes and played in the street. It was the activity on the south side of the 6100 block of Brooklyn Avenue that drew his immediate attention. A young man in shorts and a matching sleeveless shirt was arguing with three teenage girls over a pair of sunglasses. The young man did not appear aggressive, just frustrated as the girls held the glasses away from him. All four were Black, which was common for Encanto. In the front yard of a house on the north side of the street, a barbecue smoked away with two men standing beside it. Two others sat on a retaining wall along the sidewalk. They were all watching Jacobs.

That was okay; he would wait a little longer, scan the scene for threats, until his backup unit was a little closer. With a half dozen years on the force, Donovan Jacobs was too experienced to let his guard down, especially on a "possible 417—person with a gun" call he was respond- ing to now. Intelligent and ambitious, Jacobs finished second in his class at the police academy, excelling particularly in anything involv- ing physical fitness. There, he mastered sleeper holds, take-down moves, the handling of the advanced PR-24 baton, and proficiency in the two department-issued firearms, the .38-caliber revolver and the Win- chester shotgun. His first assignment in 1978 was to the relatively quiet

Northern Division. He volunteered for as many special assignments as he could find, including those involving the most perilous situations a cop can face—warrant details, special enforcement teams, narcotics operations. He joined the department's SWAT team, learning additional weapons skills.

Jacobs was what cops call a "five-percenter," one of those who go the extra mile, actively search for bad guys, aggressively generate arrests, and work harder than the other 95 percent. In the field, he was confident and self-assured. He liked to go where the crime was, and for him that meant wherever there were street gangs and drug addicts. It was a strategy known as "proactive and aggressive policing," and it routinely landed him near the top of his division in contacts and arrests.

In 1981, Jacobs requested a transfer to Southeast Division. The Southeast was where the action was, where there were junkies and dusters, street gangs and property crimes, stabbings and drive-bys. It was where ambitious cops earned their credentials to move up the ladder, the same way ambitious military officers went to war to earn theirs.

AS AN AGENT, Jacobs was a uniformed officer in a marked police vehicle, one rank above patrol officer and one below sergeant. Being promoted to agent was a big deal; he was one of only ten to twelve officers in a field of 125 to 150 in the division singled out by superiors. It was considered the first step toward greater things in the department, and by all appearances that was where the twenty-eight-year-old Jacobs was headed.

Donovan Jacobs was his usual busy self in the field since coming on duty at 2:00 p.m. that day. Almost immediately, he and a young officer named Anne-Marie Tyler responded to a report of a teen walking on a residential street with a rifle. When they located fifteen-year-old Anthony Fields at his parents' house, he did not have a rifle, but they discovered that detectives wanted him picked up in connection with a robbery. Jacobs handcuffed the youth, and Tyler processed the arrest. Just after 4:30 p.m., he responded to a burglary call at Keiller Middle School and helped Officer Leroy McDowell arrest a suspect inside the building. Minutes after that, he was down the street for the report of a suspect leaving the scene of a petty theft. At 5:30 p.m., he was on the scene of another burglary on Euclid Avenue. At 5:51 p.m., there came the current dispatch for a possible 417, person with a gun, on the 6100 block of Brooklyn Avenue.

THE OTHER PATROL unit to sign on to the call was 414-Alpha, Agent Thomas Riggs. Less than a year apart in age and both recently promoted to agents in the Southeast, Tom Riggs and Donovan Jacobs were on similar career trajectories. Both were effective cops but with different styles. Jacobs succeeded through frenetic energy and raw intensity, was known to come on strong when first contacting individuals, and demanded strict compliance during interactions. Riggs excelled through steady policing, keeping situations calm while he worked to figure out what might be going on with an individual. His initial contact was likely to be a respectful exchange, with Riggs watching and listening carefully for anything that pinged his radar. Even his frequent-flier arrestees could not help but admire him on some level. "You keep arresting me, and I keep getting out," one repeat drug offender said to him. "Then you put me in jail, and I get out. I got to hand it to you, Riggs, you don't give up."

Riggs was just under six feet tall and weighed 185 pounds with enough muscle to have been a lineman on the local Sweetwater High School football team. He was well liked, with an easy smile and dark brown eyes that communicated an intensity that belied his laid-back personality. He carried himself with an unassuming confidence that came along with other natural leadership qualities.

Tommy, as most called him, was the middle child of seven in an Irish Catholic family with deep roots in law enforcement. His father, Charles, retired from the San Diego Police Department as a sergeant, and his sister had married a cop on the force. After attending some college and considering other career choices, Riggs settled on a career in law enforcement too, a job he grew to love.

Tom met Coleen Wibe shortly after high school while taking classes at a local junior college. They fell in love but waited until they were twenty-one to get married. She was also from a law enforcement family. Her father was a sergeant with the San Diego County Sheriff's Department, and her sister married a San Diego Police officer. They bought a two-bedroom starter home just off the busy Interstate 8 free-way in the east-county city of El Cajon. Their son, Adam, was just over two years old.

Riggs arrived at the Southeast substation just before the three o'clock shift start, gathered up his gear, and signed out a radio and his usual patrol unit 785, one of the new Ford LTDs. "You got a ride-along," Sergeant John Wray informed him at the shift briefing. The department liked to put ride-alongs of all types with Riggs. With journalists, community representatives, or politicians, he was articulate and professional. His experience and calm demeanor were perfect for giving anyone considering a career in law enforcement a look at life on the streets.

The thirty-two-year-old woman with long black hair and slate-blue eyes waiting for him appeared calm and confident, dressed in jeans, athletic shoes, and a cream-colored knit sweater. Hidden beneath the sweater, she wore a T-shirt emblazoned with the image of aircraft carrier *USS Constellation*, upon which her younger husband was a Navy aviation ordnance sailor.

Riggs looked over the ride-along request form and asked about her interest in law enforcement. The woman told him she had already applied to the department and was scheduled to take the entrance exam in two weeks. Her subtle New England accent betrayed her origin as the daughter of a Buzzards Bay lobsterman, a childhood spent on isolated Cuttyhunk Island in the waters off Cape Cod, and high school years growing up in tough Massachusetts fishing ports north of New Bedford. Riggs pushed a release form across the counter. The woman read it over: "I assume the risk of all dangerous conditions or occurrences which may be encountered during said patrol and waive any and all . . ." When she was done, she signed her name at the bottom: Sarah J. Pina-Ruiz.

Per department protocol, Riggs familiarized Pina-Ruiz with the police radio and emergency lights and sirens before leaving the vehicle lot. Inside the patrol unit, she noticed there was no shotgun in the mount at the center of the dashboard. She asked him about it. Riggs shook his head. "They're useless," he said. At 3:30 p.m., Riggs notified dispatch that unit 414-Alpha was on the air with a ride-along on board. They responded to a routine traffic accident and were back in service ten minutes later. The next few hours were uneventful but informative for

Pina-Ruiz as they backed up calls, took victim statements, and made accident reports. And then at 5:52 p.m. came the dispatch for the possible person with a gun on Brooklyn Avenue.

"Is there a unit that can respond to a possible 417," the dispatcher broadcasted over the Southeast frequency. "A male in a maroon sweater is supposed to have a gun."

"Four-fourteen," Riggs radioed, rarely using the "Alpha" at the end of his designator. "I can head that way from 3700 National."

"Four-fourteen-Alpha, 10-4," she acknowledged. "Is there any unit that can clear and cover at 6-1-3-0 Brooklyn on a possible 417?"

"Four-thirteen-Alpha," Donovan Jacobs responded. "Why don't you go ahead and show me in route."

Eight minutes later, at exactly 6:00 p.m., Jacobs arrived first on scene. "Four-thirteen-Alpha, I'm 10-97 on Brooklyn," he radioed.

NOTHING ABOUT THE scene looked threatening to Donovan Jacobs. He exited his vehicle, retrieving his police baton from the bracket on the car door. Like most officers, Jacobs preferred to carry the new PR-24-model baton with a short ninety-degree side handle, allowing for a multitude of additional blocking and striking capabilities. But he had forgotten the key to his equipment locker and had to borrow a SWAT bag and scavenge around the office for a clipboard, ticket book, map book, and other gear. All he could come up with was an old-school hickory-wood beat-cop billy club, which he held in his hand as he approached the young man and the girls.

"Can you help me get my glasses back from these girls?" the frustrated young man asked before Jacobs could address him first.

"I'm not here for a call about sunglasses," Jacobs answered flatly. "I'm here for a call about a man with a gun."

Seventeen-year-old Glenn Edward Jones was the star running back for the Lincoln High football team. He had also been a member of the Lincoln Park Pirus, a local street gang affiliated with the Bloods. But Jones had given up the gang life, at least to the extent that anyone can ever really get away from it. That Sunday afternoon turned out to be an example of just how hard that could be.

Jones had been to the San Diego Sports Arena with his stepfather that day to watch Hulk Hogan and Mr. T team up to beat "Rowdy" Roddy Piper and Mr. Wonderful on the closed-circuit broadcast of WrestleMania I. When it was done, he and his stepfather stopped by their old Encanto neighborhood on the 6100 block of Brooklyn Avenue for a barbecue at his godfather's house. Jones and the two older men were standing on the porch of the house when three teenagers walked by showing the blue colors of the Crips street gang and recognized Jones from his days as a Blood. One of them called him out.

Jones walked out to the street. "What do you wanna do?" he said. The punk pushed him in the chest. Jones slapped him across the face. The kid fell back against a chain-link fence, reached into his waistband, and pulled out a handgun. Jones darted behind the shelter of a broken-down van and then ran back to his godfather's house, losing his sunglasses along the way. The Crip followed him, waiving the gun around. Jones stood in the yard with a neighborhood full of people looking on. "What are you gonna do now," he yelled, "shoot me in front of all these people?" The Crip thought about it and then put the gun back in the waistband of his jeans, pulling his shirt down to conceal the weapon. After a few last promises to kill Jones next time, he joined the other two, and they walked eastbound on Brooklyn.

A neighbor who witnessed the scene called 911. "I've got this guy out here on Brooklyn, and he's flashing a gun, walking around the neighborhood here," Rodrigo Garcia told the 911 operator.

Glenn Jones may have just had a gun pointed at him, but at the moment he was more concerned about his sunglasses. He referred to the girls as "Cripettes," which Jacobs knew to mean they hung out with members of the Crips. "Give him his sunglasses back," Jacobs said. They gave the glasses back to Jones.

Tom Riggs arrived on scene and pulled his patrol unit to the curb behind Jacobs's. "I'd better stay here," Pina-Ruiz said when she saw Jacobs mediating the dispute over the sunglasses. "I know those girls." Pina-Ruiz lived in the neighborhood, and two of the girls, the Graham sisters, had recently been involved in a fight with her fourteen-year-old daughter, Teresa. It ended in a physical fight between Sarah and the girls' mother after the woman barged into her apartment with other family members. Afterward, she reported it to the police.

SDPD agent Thomas Hoenes had taken the dispatch to the apartment at 658 Stork Street, just off Brooklyn Avenue. After taking Sarah's statement, Hoenes hung around and talked with her. She told him she was interested in police work. Hoenes suggested she do a ride-along, and then he set one up for her himself. Two weeks later, she was assigned to Agent Tom Riggs. And here she was now, looking at the Graham sisters all over again.

WHILE PINA-RUIZ REMAINED in the car, Riggs walked to where Jacobs and Jones were talking. As he stood several feet away, listening, one of the older men from the group across the street approached them. "What do you have to do with this?" Riggs asked.

"That's my stepson you're talking to," Craig Mercer said. Mercer was concerned about the way the other officer had approached his stepson. "When he got out of the car, he pulled his nightstick out and was waving it," Mercer said of Jacobs. "It just bothered me." The two spoke calmly as Riggs explained the situation. When Mercer returned to his friends on the other side of the road, he was still uneasy about Jacobs. "That officer there is looking for some trouble," he said.

Jones provided descriptions of the three Crips. He said they were probably on their way to the Encanto Recreation Center a few blocks away on Sixty-Fifth Street, a known hangout for local gangs.

While they were talking, a young man came down the street in their direction. "What's up, Cuz?" he said to Jones as he passed.

Jones glared at him. "What's up, Blood?"

Familiar with the messaging of gang members, Jacobs knew what the exchange meant. The man walking by was a Crip, or "Cuz." Jones claimed Blood. Referring to a Blood as "Cuz" was an insult and invitation to fight. Jones was throwing the insult back by calling the Crip a Blood.

Jacobs ignored the exchange, and the Crip continued down the street with the Graham sisters. "Do you want us to make out a report?" he asked Jones, referring to the gun incident.

"Nah," said Jones. In all his years of getting guns pulled on him in Encanto, he'd learned that talking to the cops about it never got him anywhere but onto a Crip drive-by list.

At 6:07 p.m., Donovan Jacobs radioed dispatch confirming a 417, gang member with a gun. "Uncooperative witness, no report wanted," he added, indicating that Jones declined to make an official report of the incident.

Tom Riggs had already begun to roll east down Brooklyn toward Sixty-Fifth Street searching for their suspect. He slowed to look down cross streets as they passed. Pina-Ruiz kept her eyes open too, but the situation made her nervous. They turned left and began ascending the gradual incline toward the Encanto Recreation Center a block and a half north. Jacobs made the turn onto Sixty-Fifth behind them. On their left was the playground and classrooms of Encanto Elementary School. To their right was a row of small residential houses busy with residents socializing and wrapping up their weekend.

As they continued, a white pickup truck came down Sixty-Fifth Street, headed in the opposite direction. As it passed, Jacobs took note of the young Black men sitting in the back. At 6:08 p.m., Jacobs made a U-turn and radioed to Riggs, "Four-thirteen-Alpha, I have to turn around and stop that pickup truck with a load of Crips."

3

—

AS DUSK DESCENDED OVER ENCANTO, DONOVAN JACOBS
made a left turn to follow the truck into the 6500 block of Brooklyn Avenue. Tom Riggs followed a few moments later. Jacobs activated his overhead lights with the truck halfway up the block. When he did, adults outside their homes, children playing in yards, and a group of women standing in front of the church on the corner, almost all of whom were Black, stopped to watch. It was not unusual to see police pull over a Black driver in Encanto, but there was something particularly ominous about the sight of a pickup truck carrying so many young men being followed by two cop cars up a dead-end street.

Encanto was a neighborhood anchored by hardworking, churchgoing citizens, influential community institutions and leaders, and a strong sense of ethnic and cultural pride. It was this tight-knit social fabric and focus on friends and family life that made a street like Brooklyn Avenue a lively place on a late Sunday afternoon.

But as a low-income area of a large American city, the roads were frequently no more than stretches of cracked asphalt crumbling at the edges with no sidewalks and inadequate drainage. Many of the driveways were unpaved, the front yards mostly patches of dead grass or overgrown with brush and weeds. Paper cups, smashed soda cans, and fast-food wrappers could be found on the side of the road, caught up in shrubbery or clinging to the base of chain-link fences. Perpetually broken-down junker cars sat waiting for repairs that often never came. Low homeownership resulted in undermaintained houses with missing shutters, crumbling front stairs, and sagging roofs. Most dwellings had bars on the windows, a reminder of the high crime rate.

Just five hundred feet long and running west to east with a gentle upslope from Sixty-Fifth Street, the 6500 block of Brooklyn Avenue dead-ended at a wooden barricade that encouraged cars not to plunge down a thirty-foot embankment of scrub brush to the residential street below. The lack of through traffic attracted families with small children and made the block a destination for kids from the surrounding streets. On the south side of the street were a half dozen tidy but modest homes, some with converted garages or additional units in the rear. A two-story rectangular stucco building with eight apartments sat mid-block.

Although it was approaching suppertime, the sound of laughter and shouts of youngsters playing games, roughhousing, throwing balls, and riding bikes could be heard throughout the neighborhood. Kaye Specks had just come back from church services, and she stood in front of her house chatting with her landlord, Oscar Julien. Betty-Sue Paradero was cooking dinner while her husband, Primo, prepared to run to the store, and their daughter Carmen played next door. Margarita Amaral was watching the local Telemundo TV channel with her husband, Daniel Benitez-Lopez.

At the corner of Sixty-Fifth Street was a source of even more activity. The Apostolic Faith Garden of Prayer was a large, pink plaster chapel with a tall spire and an adjoining two-story activity center and fellowship hall. Nestled behind it was the Spring Valley Community Baptist Church, more modest in size and architecture but no less active. On this Palm Sunday, a women's Bible group, Sunday school class, and choir practice were all getting set to begin. Churchgoers stood outside chatting and catching up before filing inside.

Situated at the middle of the block and set back from the street, the adobe-style home of Irma and Carlton Smith was the center of activity for neighborhood children, including six of their own. Sunday school teacher Demetria Shelby visited with Irma, while church organist David Demps sat in a back room with Carlton and a friend named Allen Cepeda. The front yard—a rectangle of hard-packed dirt, dead grass, and several shade trees—teemed with a dozen children practicing their latest dance moves, playing tag, and tossing around a football.

Next door to the Smith home was a ramshackle one-story house that had been divided into a duplex. A wood-and-fiberglass carport had been appended to the front of the house, and two broken-down sedans, one missing its hood and a front fender, were parked in front. The house was set back one hundred feet from the street at the end of a rutted dirt driveway that ran flat and straight between Carlton Smith's home and the Paradero house to the east. Reaching the driveway from the Smith property required stepping up a three-foot-high fieldstone retaining wall.

Anthony Lovett and his girlfriend, Angela McKibben, lived in the left side of the duplex at the end of the long driveway. Twenty-year-old Angie McKibben was a sometimes waitress, sometimes dancer at the notorious Jolar Cinema strip club and one of the few white residents of the neighborhood. When not at his job in the maintenance department at the downtown Wells Fargo Bank, Lovett was sharpening his delivery and songwriting skills through live performances and rehearsals with the Mighty Key Gang.

McKibben was still in her bathrobe while Lovett waited for Junius Holmes and Ricky Clipper to get back from Balboa Park for a Mighty Key practice. Out her bedroom window, she saw a white pickup truck approaching their house. "Do you know this truck coming up our driveway?" she called to Lovett. "Nah," he said, joining her at the window. "Never seen it before." They watched as a police car turned into the driveway behind the truck, its overhead lights on. "Shit," said Lovett.

The truck pulled up and parked in front of the carport, twenty feet short of the house. The first police car, with its overhead lights flashing, stopped a half dozen feet behind the truck, blocking it in. From the back of the truck, Junius Holmes had been watching it all the way. He leaned over the side of the pickup. "The police are here," he said.

Sagon Penn turned off the engine and stepped out of the truck onto the driveway. Bryan Ross and Doria Jones exited the cab on the other side, and those riding in the back began climbing out near the tailgate on the passenger side. Jacobs exited his vehicle while Riggs was still just turning into the driveway. He slipped his baton through the ring on his belt as he walked directly to the driver's side of the truck. "What's up, Blood?" Bryan Ross heard him say as he approached Penn.

"What are you talking about?" Penn said, surprised to see a police officer approaching him and addressing him as a gang member. "What's wrong?"

"What do you claim, Blood or Cuz?" Jacobs said, meeting Penn a few steps outside the driver's side door.

"I don't have nothin' to do with any gangs," Penn said. "If I claim anything, I claim myself."

Jacobs asked to see his driver's license while the others watched from the opposite side of the truck, and Lovett and McKibben looked on from their bedroom window.

Tom Riggs stopped his vehicle twenty feet short of Jacobs's patrol unit. He exited, removed his PR-24 baton from the door bracket, and slipped it into his belt ring. To Sarah Pina-Ruiz, who remained in the car, Riggs did not seem particularly concerned about the situation. He approached the young men standing near the rear of the truck and requested identification. Some of the younger boys didn't have any. Bryan Ross handed Riggs his social security card. "Have I arrested you before?" Riggs asked Ross. No, Ross said. Riggs said something that made Ross and Junius Holmes laugh.

On the other side of the pickup, Penn took a thin nylon wallet out of his pocket and held it out for Jacobs.

"I can't take your wallet," Jacobs told him. "I need to see your license."

Penn continued to offer the wallet to Jacobs. "It's okay, you can take the wallet," he said. "It's inside the wallet."

"I don't want to see everything you got in your wallet," Jacobs told him. "I want to see your license."

"It's okay, you can take the wallet. I got nothing in there to hide."

Jacobs told him again that he needed to remove the license from the wallet.

Penn opened the wallet and held it out so Jacobs could see the license behind the clear plastic window. "That's my license," he said. "All the information's on the front." Junius Holmes thought Penn appeared flustered by Jacobs's refusal to accept the wallet. "Take the license out of the wallet," Jacobs said sharply, appearing increasingly agitated by Penn's failure to follow his request.

To Angie McKibben, Jacobs's terse ultimatum seemed to frustrate

Penn even more. He shoved the wallet into his pocket. "Aw, man!" he said, throwing up his hands and turning away from Jacobs. Jacobs reached out and grabbed him by the right shoulder and pulled him back around to face him. Penn jerked his arm out of Jacobs's grasp. "Don't grab me," he said, backing away. "Why are you messin' with me?"

Tom Riggs looked up to see the situation between Penn and Jacobs escalating. He hurried along the passenger side toward the front of the truck. By the time he got there, Jacobs had drawn his baton. Riggs pulled the portable radio from the holster on his hip. "Four-fourteen, cover now!" he called into it, urgently requesting additional personnel to respond to their location for assistance. Removing his baton, he continued around the truck to assist Jacobs.

"You're making a big mistake," Penn said, as Jacobs advanced on him with the baton. "I didn't do nothin'." When Jacobs swung at him from the side, Penn thrust a forearm out to meet the baton and deflected it away from his body with a sweeping motion. A twenty-six-inch hickory-wood billy club was considerably heavier than a martial arts rattan escrima stick, but Penn had blocked hundreds of strikes coming at him from that same angle in tae kwon do studios and competitions. A backhand swing by Jacobs was also intercepted by Penn and swept to the side. "Why are you doing this?" he said.

As Penn backed away blocking additional blows, he and Jacobs moved toward the area near the front of the truck. The left-handed Riggs came around from the passenger side, approaching Penn from behind, and swung at him with the PR-24, striking him across the left flank of his back. Before Penn could react, the return backhand blow from Riggs caught him in the same area on his right side.

Penn repositioned himself so that he was facing both officers rather than one on each side. He began to back around the front of the truck to the passenger side with his hands up in a defensive position while both officers struck at him with the batons. What he could not block connected painfully with his shoulder and lower abdomen as he attempted to twist away to lessen their impact. "What are you doing?" he asked.

The passengers from truck began to protest. "You don't have to do him like that," Ricky Clipper hollered, growing angry. "Stop hitting him!" Sean Arkward called out, dismayed at the sight of his brother being struck with batons. "Leave him alone!" someone else shouted. The young men followed the confrontation as it edged down the driveway. "Stay back!" Riggs ordered, poking Clipper and Junius Holmes in the stomach with the end of his baton when they moved in too close.

Jacobs continued to come at Penn with a flurry of hard baton swings. Lovett and McKibben were now watching from their open front door. McKibben was stunned by the ferocity of Jacobs's attack. "They're going to kill him," she said to Lovett. A moment later, Jacobs was tumbling backward, his baton coming out of his hand and skipping away as he fell to the ground. Riggs quickly scooped up the loose baton and tucked it under his arm. By the time Jacobs got back to his feet, he was in such a rage he did not even attempt to retrieve it back from Riggs, charging at Penn instead.

In the house next door, Carlton Smith heard the commotion and came outside. When he saw the altercation involving two officers and the young Black man, he shouted to McKibben and Lovett. "Call the police," he said. "And make sure they send some Black ones."

McKibben ran to the front room, where the phone was set on the carpet. The cord from the wall was missing the small plastic clip that attached it to the back of the phone. When she picked up the phone, the cord fell out. She frantically struggled to reattach it.

By now, over thirty people from the neighborhood had approached the driveway and were witnessing the struggle from various distances. Children playing in Carlton Smith's yard ran to the retaining wall bordering the driveway and watched from just feet away. People came out of houses or from the area around the two churches. Kaye Specks and Oscar Julien stopped their conversation and watched from the other side of the street, directly across the driveway. A half dozen more children clustered near them, afraid to get any closer to the violent confrontation moving in their direction. "You don't have to hit him like that!" an alarmed Specks shouted at the officers from halfway across the road.

The group of young men from the truck followed the altercation in the direction of Brooklyn Avenue and moved within several feet at times. "Stay back!" Riggs warned again. Inside the house, Angela McKibben finally reattached the phone cord and called 911 with trembling fingers.

Sarah Pina-Ruiz was watching the altercation as it moved in the direction of Riggs's vehicle, where she sat inside with the windows rolled up. With the car parked slightly off to the side, there was fifteen feet of driveway between the vehicle and the three-foot drop off the retaining wall into Carlton Smith's yard. Allen Cepeda's black Chevrolet Chevelle was parked in front of Smith's house, parallel to the retaining wall with a six-foot space between. As they came closer, Pina-Ruiz could hear the shouts of the crowd through the closed passenger window.

When they reached the driver's side of Riggs's vehicle, Jacobs charged at Penn. Penn turned his body away and put up no defense as Jacobs slammed into him. They fell to the ground with Penn on his back perpendicular to Riggs's vehicle, his feet near the car door and his head in the direction of the drop-off into the Smith yard. Jacobs was on top of him, scrambling to straddle Penn's pelvic area. "You think you're bad? I'm going to beat your ass," Pina-Ruiz heard him say.

Once on the ground, Penn's martial arts skills were of little use to him. When Jacobs grabbed for his arms, Penn jerked them away and began flailing them in front of himself to fend off Jacobs. "Turn over!" Jacobs ordered, attempting to get Penn into a position where he could be handcuffed.

"Please, stop," Penn said. "You got me!"

Standing two feet to the right side of Penn's head, Riggs continued to order those crowded around to stay back. As Penn continued to keep his hands away from Jacobs's grasp, Riggs struck at them with short chopping motions. "Put your hands down," he ordered.

"Why are you doing this?" Penn asked, continuing to resist Jacobs's attempts.

Over the shouts of the crowd, a transmission from dispatch over his portable radio caught Riggs's attention. "Units, it's gonna be 6100 Brooklyn," the dispatcher informed the incoming patrol cars responding to his request for backup. Riggs pulled his radio from the holster on his hip and keyed the talk button. "Four-fourteen. I think we're about 6500 Brooklyn now," he corrected.

"Okay, 6500 Brooklyn for the units," the dispatcher repeated urgently. "Sixty-five hundred Brooklyn on the 'cover now.'"

The forty or more people now witnessing the altercation were mostly Black, reflecting the population of the neighborhood and congregants of the two churches. Some encouraged Penn to do as he was told and turn over to end the confrontation. Others were outraged at the officers. "You don't have to be hittin' him like that," someone shouted. "Why are they doing this to him?" a woman watching from the Smith yard asked loudly. "This ain't justice," Carlton Smith said in disgust. "Is that how y'all got those stripes, beating people like this?" he called out, referring to the agent-rank insignia on their sleeves. "Get back!" Riggs barked at those closest, using short jabbing motions with his baton to discourage them from crowding in.

Jacobs finally succeeded in grabbing one of Penn's hands and reached to retrieve the handcuffs secured in a case on his duty belt. Penn pulled his hand free from Jacobs, who abandoned the attempt at the cuffs, grabbing instead at either Penn's throat or the clothing near his neck with his left hand and punching him several times in the area of his upper body. "Turn over," Jacobs ordered.

"Why are you doing this? You got me," Penn said, waving his arms to block the blows coming from Jacobs.

"You don't have to do that to him," an enraged Ricky Clipper said. Knowing her boyfriend's fiery temper, Doria Jones came down the driveway and grabbed Clipper by the back of his shirt and pulled him away. "Ricky, you get out of there," she snapped. "You get back in that house." Clipper backed away and then reluctantly walked in the direction of the house with her.

Riggs chopped at Penn's hands several more times with the baton. "Knock it off," he said. "Just put your hands down."

"Stop hitting him!" Sean yelled.

"If you get back, we'll stop," Riggs snapped.

In the house next door, Betty Paradero heard voices outside her window. She saw the group of young men in a semicircle around the two police officers. To her, the crowd appeared threatening, as though they might attack the officers at any moment. She called for her husband. Primo came to the window and saw Riggs poking his baton at the men crowded around. He saw Riggs raise his baton up to waist level and swing at what he assumed to be a person on the ground, but the police car was obstructing his view.

At that moment, Irma Smith was trying to get her husband, Carlton, away from the altercation, afraid he was so close he might get himself mixed up in it. As she gathered her small children, she called to him sharply to get in the house. He turned and walked away from the altercation, still incensed. "They're gonna kill you!" he shouted over his shoulder.

AT 6:13 P.M., a San Diego Police Department emergency operator picked up Angela McKibben's incoming 911 call. It had been just under two and a half minutes since the interaction between Donovan Jacobs and Sagon Penn turned violent.

"San Diego Police, emergency seventeen," the operator said.

McKibben told her the reason for the call. The operator seemed to ignore her. "What's the emergency?" she asked. "The emergency is . . . ," McKibben began, but she became flustered and panicky. "Hey, I don't know what to say here," she said, holding the phone out to Doria Jones, who had just come through the front door with Ricky Clipper. Jones hesitated, not knowing what McKibben was talking about. "Doria, hurry!" McKibben snapped, thrusting the phone into her hands.

"Hello?" Jones said, unsure of who was on the other end of the line.

There was a sharp popping noise from somewhere outside the house. "Oh!" Anthony Lovett gasped, looking out the open front door.

"Yes, what's the emergency?" the operator asked.

There were three more popping sounds. "He's shootin' 'em!" Jones cried into the phone, her voice rising sharply. "Hurry up!" There were two more popping sounds, and Jones dropped the phone receiver onto the carpet. Angela McKibben began to scream.

"What's the address there?" the operator asked, but there was no reply, just screaming and shouting in the background.

Sean Arkward came racing through the front door. "He killed my brother, man!" he cried out.

"Oh, no," Jones gasped.

"Hello?" the operator said.

"Fuck, you're kidding!" Ricky Clipper shouted, while McKibben continued wailing in the background.

"He shot and killed 'em," Jones said, looking out the front door in disbelief.

"You're, like, dead, man," Clipper yelled, heading for the door. Lovett blocked his way. "We saw it. We saw it, Ricky."

"Where's Sagon?" Jones asked.

"Where's the gun?" Sean shouted at them. "Where's Sagon?"

Still on the other end of the phone line, the 911 operator could make out the words of two male voices in the background.

"He killed both of them," said the first.

"Sagon killed them."

"Hello?" the operator tried again. "This is the San Diego Police."

A moment later, someone in the house stepped on the phone cord and the line went dead.

SEAN AND BRYAN Ross stepped out the front door, followed by Cedric, Keno, and Junius. The scene outside made no sense to them. Lying motionless on the driveway near the police car was one of the police officers, but the other officer was gone. The woman who had been inside the police car was nowhere to be seen. All the people who had been watching moments before had run away. They looked for Sagon, but he was not there. A moment later, he appeared, stepping up the retaining wall from the neighboring yard, near where the officer lay in the driveway. In his hand was a gun. As he hurried in their direction, he slid the gun, barrel first, into the waistband of his jeans.

Anthony Lovett and Angela McKibben stood in the doorway as Sagon approached. "Get out of here, man," Lovett shouted to him. "We can't help you," McKibben said. Penn stopped when he saw that his pickup truck was blocked by Jacobs's patrol car. He hesitated and then headed toward Jacobs's car instead. "Sagon, throw me the keys to the truck," Ross called to him. Sagon stopped, fished them out of his pocket, and tossed them to him.

Penn hurried to Jacobs's idling police car, got behind the wheel, and placed the gun on the seat beside him. The overhead lights on the car continued to whirl, and the police radio on the dashboard crackled with the transmissions of police units announcing their locations on

Sixty-Fifth Street and the area of the Encanto School. He could hear the wail of the sirens getting closer.

It took Penn three Y-turns to get the car pointed in the direction of Brooklyn Avenue, with Tom Riggs's vehicle angled on the dirt driveway thirty feet in front of him. The route on the passenger side of the car was impeded by tall weeds and uneven terrain gradually sloping upward toward the Paradero house. On the driver's side, there was only one thing obstructing his path, and that was Donovan Jacobs, lying on his back between Riggs's vehicle and the retaining wall.

AT 6:14 P.M., a second 911 call came into the San Diego Police Department from a resident of Brooklyn Avenue. At the first sound of gunfire, Kaye Specks rounded up five young neighborhood children and herded them to the safety of her house. Once inside, she ordered fifteen-year-old Brian Williams to call 911 while Specks went to the front window to search for her own children, who had been playing in the Smith yard.

"Emergency forty-seven," the 911 operator answered.

"Police department, please," Williams said breathlessly.

"What's the problem?"

"A shooting."

"Somebody shooting?" the operator asked. She could hear people talking loudly and excitedly in the background.

"Uh-huh," Williams replied.

"What are they shooting, a gun?"

"Uh-huh."

Horrified at what she was saw on the driveway across the street, Specks called out to the boy. "Tell them it's an emergency. A police officer got shot."

"It's an emergency," he said. "Police officer got shot."

"Are you sure?" the operator asked.

"Yeah."

As the operator hurriedly typed the information into the dispatch system, she heard a woman cry out in the background. "Oh, he got run over!" Specks screamed in horror, as she watched the police car roll over the officer lying in the driveway. "The man, he got run over!"

"Are you sure?" the operator stammered. "Are you sure, or are you just saying that?"

"Positive," Williams said. "Person just got run over."

AS HE LAY in the dirt, Donovan Jacobs knew he had been shot in the neck but was having difficulty processing what had happened. He remembered struggling and then reaching back for his handcuffs and then . . . bam! The sound of a gunshot and he was falling off to the side. When he hit the ground, people were screaming, and he thought to himself, "I've got to get up. I've got to get up." But he could not move. There were more gunshots and more screaming. Staring up at the trees and sky, Jacobs saw the young man he had been struggling with pass through his field of vision and then heard the sound of footsteps walking away. Still, he could not move.

A few seconds later, he heard the sound of an engine revving up the driveway. "He's going to run over me," Jacobs thought. He willed his body to move out of the way. *Get up. Get up.* It did no good. He heard the engine accelerating, the tires crunching the earth beneath them, all of it getting closer. Seconds later, the front bumper flashed by just inches over his face, and then, just for a fleeting moment, Jacobs found himself looking up at the greasy, dark undercarriage of an automobile.

With a ground clearance measured in inches, there was not enough space beneath the 3,500-pound Ford LTD to simply pass over a 165-pound man lying in its path. The undercarriage of the vehicle became a sixteen-and-a-half-foot-long gauntlet of mechanical parts—the differential, axels, oil pan, catalytic converter—that dragged, rolled, burned, and flayed Donovan Jacobs at a speed of eighteen miles per hour. When the rear bumper finally passed over him, he was a dozen feet down the driveway, lying in the dirt, bleeding, and still unable to move.

He heard the car pulling away and the sound of tires transitioning to asphalt, and he saw the red and blue lights from the light bar fading away. His chest felt as though it had been crushed, and there was the sensation of warm blood flowing freely from the gunshot wound in his neck. He could hear the howl of sirens closing in. "Hang on," he told himself, "the cavalry is coming."

4

I N THE COMMUNICATIONS CENTER OF THE SAN DIEGO POLICE Department, veteran dispatcher Don Boughton studied his computer screen for any clue about who had just put out the "cover now." Whoever it was had called out their identifier so fast Boughton was not sure what he heard. It was 6:11 p.m. and, according to the screen, the only patrol unit in the field currently involved in a traffic stop was 421-King with Officers Cassie Goldstein and Richard Schnell. "Four-twenty-one-King is requesting cover now," Boughton radioed. "Units move into his area."

"Where's he at?" Officer Bill Jeffers asked.

"Thirty-five hundred Main. That's the last place I show him, 3500 Main."

Within seconds of Boughton's transmission, frequency one lit up with SDPD units reporting themselves in route to the 3500 block of Main Street, five miles west of Tom Riggs's actual location. Neither he nor Jacobs had notified dispatch that they were executing a traffic stop, so no one on the San Diego Police force knew they were currently up a long private driveway on a dead-end street in Encanto. Eight-year patrol veteran Bill Jeffers was returning an overheating patrol unit to the Southeast substation when he heard the "cover now." At the time, Jeffers was only two and a half minutes away from Tom Riggs's location. Instead, he took a hard left onto Paradise Valley Road and raced toward 3500 Main Street, away from Brooklyn Avenue. Officer Mike Moran was transitioning from the South Bay Freeway onto Interstate 805 north when he heard the "cover now" to 3500 Main. Instead of proceeding northeast to Encanto, he exited at the Forty-Third Street off-ramp and headed west toward San Diego Bay. Both shift sergeants in the field, John Wray and Hal Hiskes, also pointed themselves in the wrong direction as Boughton continued to transmit the location of the only unit shown to be involved in a traffic stop.

In the 421-King unit, Goldstein and Schnell were confused. Did dispatch just put out a "cover now" on . . . *them*? Goldstein grabbed the radio mic. "Four-twenty-one-King, it's not us who put out the cover."

"Did you hear who it was?" Boughton asked urgently.

"Negative," Goldstein said. "I couldn't tell."

"Sounded like 414," another officer radioed.

Boughton checked the screen for Riggs's last known location. It was the Glenn Edward Jones 417 dispatch to the 6100 block of Brooklyn Avenue, but he and 413-Alpha had cleared that call over five minutes earlier. There was nothing to indicate Riggs and Jacobs were almost a half mile away at that point, but Boughton knew one thing: they were nowhere near 3500 Main Street. "Units, it's gonna be 6100 Brooklyn," he radioed, going with the best information he had at the moment.

Tom Riggs heard the transmission while standing over Jacobs and Penn and corrected the error with his last transmission: "Four-fourteen. I think we're about 6500 Brooklyn now."

"Okay," Boughton relayed. "Sixty-five hundred Brooklyn for the units. Sixty-five hundred Brooklyn on the 'cover now.'"

It had taken a minute and a half to identify the correct location. It was an eternity on a "cover now," made worse with the responding units headed away from the location during that time. "Have the closest units roll code," said Sergeant Hal Hiskes, upgrading the responding units to lights and sirens. He needn't have bothered. By that time, every unit on the "cover now" was rolling code.

After traveling almost two miles in the wrong direction on Paradise Valley Road in the 411-John unit, Bill Jeffers executed a sliding U-turn in the middle of a busy intersection and raced back toward Encanto. Having just reached the area of 3500 Main near the waterfront at San Diego Bay, Mike Moran now had four and a half miles to travel over surface streets to reach the scene in Encanto. At the Southeast subdivision on

Skyline Drive, Sergeant Lesli Lord realized Riggs's location was much closer than originally indicated. She rushed to get a patrol unit.

At 6:13 p.m. and seventeen seconds, there was a mic click with no accompanying transmission. "The unit calling?" Boughton asked. There was no response. For the next thirty-one seconds, San Diego Police frequency one remained eerily silent. The transmission that broke the silence let everyone know something terrible had just happened on the 6500 block of Brooklyn Avenue. "We need help. We need help," came the trembling, frightened voice of a woman.

"What is your *exact* location?" Boughton asked.

"I don't know. I'm the ride-along with Riggs," Sarah Pina-Ruiz responded, her voice rising in despair.

"Are you on Brooklyn Avenue? Are you on Brooklyn Avenue?" Boughton asked. He waited six long seconds for a response, but there was none. "The units responding to Brooklyn Avenue, I need your locations and your ETAs," he requested urgently. He began calling out unit identifiers one by one, each crackling back with their location.

"Twenty-four-John, Euclid and Logan."

"Four-eleven, Woodman and Skyline."

"Okay," Boughton transmitted to all units, in case any had not heard. "There was a female on the air just now saying that they needed help. She doesn't know where she's at."

Mike Moran and Bill Jeffers were both on Imperial Avenue now, bearing down on Sixty-Fifth Street at a high rate of speed from opposite directions. Ahead of them, Officer John Halsey reached the intersection of Sixty-Fifth and Brooklyn Avenue thirty seconds after Pina-Ruiz's call for help. "Sixty-five and Brooklyn, I don't see him yet," he radioed. Boughton announced Halsey 10-97, on scene. But when Halsey looked east, he found the 6500 block mostly empty as witnesses and bystanders remained huddled behind whatever they had put between themselves and the gunfire. "Getting a lot of people on the 6400 block of Brooklyn," he radioed, turning westbound on Brooklyn, speeding away in the opposite direction of the scene.

One minute and four seconds after her initial cry for help, Sarah Pina-Ruiz came over the radio again. "Two officers down," she said in a controlled but trembling voice. "I'm the ride-along, and I've been shot. I don't know the location."

"Where have you been hit?" Boughton asked her.

"In the back and in the side. And the officers, I can hear them moaning."

"Okay, stay calm, we've got officers in the area. Are you in the vicinity of Brooklyn Avenue, do you know?"

"We're past the Encanto School," she said.

"Units, she's in the vicinity of the Encanto School. She's in the vicinity of the Encanto School."

"West of the Encanto School," she attempted to clarify, but she was disoriented. Her true location was one block east of the school.

"She's west of the Encanto School," Boughton relayed. "I have two officers down and one ride-along shot."

For those responding to the scene, it was a stunning transmission, worse than any of them could have imagined. It had been Riggs on the cover, so who was the second officer down?

"Put out an 11-99," Hiskes ordered, indicating the radio code police everywhere dread the most.

"Eleven-ninety-nine, officers down, the vicinity of the Encanto School," Boughton transmitted. "Eleven-ninety-nine, the vicinity of the Encanto School on Brooklyn Avenue. Eleven-ninety-nine in the vicinity of the Encanto School."

With the 11-99, every police unit within miles not already responding to the "cover now" raced in the direction of the 6500 block of Brooklyn Avenue. Inside patrol units, hands shot forward and threw switches on dashboards and center consoles as the air throughout Southeast San Diego came alive with the screams of police sirens. Blue-and-red lightbars swirled to life, sweeping over the facades of taquerias, convenience stores, auto-repair shops, gas stations, and storefront churches. Citizens on the sidewalks stopped to watch, covering their ears as the units raced past. Police cars weaved through traffic, darted in and out of oncoming lanes, bailed off nearby freeways onto surface streets without slowing. Motorists got out of their path any way they could. Even in an area familiar with the sound of sirens, this many cops all headed in the same direction was alarming. Four miles away, San Diego Sheriff Department's

ASTREA helicopter lifted off. Within minutes, its rotors were chopping the sky over Encanto, its spotlight sweeping back and forth over streets, hillsides, canyons, and the backyards of the ramshackle houses.

"Please hurry," Pina-Ruiz cried desperately.

MOMENTS AFTER JOHN Halsey had made his turn from Sixty-Fifth onto Brooklyn headed in the wrong direction, Bill Jeffers came through the intersection on Sixty-Fifth headed one block north to the Encanto School, the location indicated on the 11-99. "Four-eleven-John 10-97 at the school," he radioed. He made a visual of the area and quickly determined the incident was not there.

"We have it as 6500 Brooklyn, or thereabouts," Boughton broadcasted. "Somewhere in the vicinity of 6500 Brooklyn."

Jeffers spun a U-turn at the entrance to the school and raced back down the block to Brooklyn. Two additional units reached the area seconds later. "Twelve-John, in the area," Officer Donald Braun radioed, scanning the neighborhood for any activity that would identify where in the hell the three shooting victims were. Mike Moran reached Brooklyn and Sixty-Fifth Street. "Twenty-four in the area," he announced. Moran looked east and saw people waving him in. At 6:17 p.m., Mike Moran became the first unit to radio himself on scene, a full six minutes after Riggs put out the "cover now." "Four-twenty-four-John, it's at 6500 Brooklyn."

"Four-twenty-four-John advising that the incident is at 6500 Brooklyn for units responding on the 11-99," Boughton transmitted.

Moran pulled his patrol unit into Carlton Smith's driveway and leaped from the vehicle. The area was now cloaked in evening darkness, but Moran could see the body of Donovan Jacobs lying on the driveway, ten feet behind an idling patrol unit. Moran rushed to his fellow officer. Jacobs lay gulping air, blood gushing from a wound in the side of his neck. The damage to Jacobs's neck was similar to the type Moran had handled in his four years as a combat medic in the Vietnam War. Jacobs tried to speak but could manage only a whisper. Moran told him to stay calm. As a medic, he was trained to assess a scene and locate all the injured before administering aid. He scanned the area for Riggs and the wounded ride-along.

"There's another one over here," a voice called out to him. Neighborhood resident Daniel Benitez-Lopez was pointing at a spot just below the retaining wall. "Right there." Moran found Tom Riggs face down in the neighboring yard between the retaining wall and the black Chevelle. "Tommy," Moran said sharply, shaking Riggs's body. He pressed two fingers to Riggs's carotid artery and detected a pulse. Moran saw more police units arriving, officers jumping out from their vehicles. "Tom, hang on. We're here."

Moran searched for the final victim. When he jumped back up the retaining wall, he saw movement through the shattered side window of Riggs's patrol unit a dozen feet away. Inside, Sarah Pina-Ruiz was slumped in her seat, bent over at the waist, her knees drawn up to her chest. When he opened the passenger-side door, he did not notice the .38-caliber slug of lead that fell out onto the grass, disfigured from having traveled into one side of the woman's body and out the other. He assured her she was safe and conducted a rapid assessment for life-threatening conditions. He asked her name, whether she was having any trouble breathing, and if she knew where she was. She was pale and frightened but answering his questions.

The areas of blood on her sweater indicated where she had been shot. Moran raised her sweater and shirt to expose the wounds. In his years as a combat medic, he had assessed a number of gunshot victims and knew the difference between entry and exit wounds. On the body of Sarah Pina-Ruiz, he found three of each. The most worrisome was an entry hole the size of a dime punched through the skin directly below the breast. Experienced in handling multi-casualty incidents, Moran sized up the overall situation. "None of these three patients are okay," he thought. "We could lose them all."

Bill Jeffers arrived on scene within seconds of Moran. He exited his patrol unit holding his shotgun, thought better of it, and secured it back in the center mount. He went to where Jacobs lay in the driveway and knelt beside him. "Who shot you?" he asked, putting his ear next to Jacobs's mouth so he could hear the faint reply.

"Black male," Jacobs said, laboring to get a word or two out with each breath. "Driver of the truck."

Jeffers had been an EMT on the department ambulance for three years before moving to patrol. He checked the wound on Jacobs's neck. "What did he shoot you with, a shotgun?"

"My gun," Jacobs gasped.

With no other way to address the uncontrolled bleeding, Jeffers pushed his fingers inside the wound to hold direct pressure on an exposed hemorrhaging blood vessel.

Moran assisted Jeffers, packing the neck wound with gauze from a medical kit while Jeffers pulled out his knife and began cutting off Jacobs's clothing and equipment in preparation for the arrival of EMS personnel. Soon the area around Jacobs was littered with handcuffs, a duty belt, boots, and a portable radio still blasting out the transmissions on frequency one.

Arriving on scene, Halsey and Sergeant Lesli Lord went to the aid of Tom Riggs. With a command of emergency medicine and reputation for composure under stressful conditions, Lord executed her initial assessment with rapid precision. Her first action was to check for a carotid pulse. Unlike Moran moments before, she detected none. They rolled Riggs onto his back and ripped open his uniform shirt. Lord's first thought was "Where is his goddamn bulletproof vest?" Most on the force wore them in the field. Tom Riggs rarely did.

Her attention was drawn to a hole in the center of Riggs's upper abdomen. She knew exactly what was in that anatomical location: the abdominal aortic artery, one of the largest blood vessels in the human body. When she checked his pupils, they were fixed and unresponsive. As they commenced CPR, Lord had no illusions about their chances of saving Tom Riggs. She provided mouth-to-mouth ventilations between each set of Halsey's chest compressions, knowing the whole time that Riggs's decision not to wear his bulletproof vest had cost him his life.

Riding in a patrol unit together, Officers Gerry Kramer and Cherie Curley reached the scene. Kramer ran to where Lord and Halsey were working on Riggs while Curley went to the aid of Sarah Pina-Ruiz. For Kramer, the sight of CPR being performed on one of his closest friends on the force was almost more than he could bear. He jumped down from the retaining wall to assist Halsey and Lord.

The first EMS and fire department units arrived on Brooklyn Avenue at 6:22 p.m., nine minutes after the shootings. Paramedic Wayne

Johnson and firefighter Steve Bowlin were directed by officers to the location of Tom Riggs. Johnson reassessed pulse and respiration and inserted an airway while Bowlin took over chest compressions.

The first of the television news crews arrived at almost the same time as the fire and EMS units. The Channel 39 camera operator began filming the crew working on Riggs. "Hey, can you turn on your light?" Gerry Kramer asked the cameraman as he moved into position to pull Riggs's legs out from under the Chevelle. "Yeah," the cameraman said, instantly flooding the area with light and capturing the grim sight of Riggs's body stripped to the waist, intubated, and heaving beneath the force of the chest compressions. With the camera rolling, Kramer pulled Riggs away from the car. When he did, he spotted a service revolver on the ground beside Riggs's body. "Take Tommy's gun! Take Tommy's gun!" he shouted, handing the weapon up to Sergeant John Wray. Wray checked the chamber of the weapon and saw that it was empty.

A second ambulance arrived less than a minute later. Medic Elizabeth Smith grabbed her first-in bag and ran to Jacobs. A dozen feet away, she caught a foot on the uneven driveway and tumbled face-first onto the dirt, medical supplies spilling out of her bag. Shaken, she scrambled to her feet and continued to Jacobs as officers retrieved her gear. A third ambulance came, dispatched mutual aid from neighboring National City. Medic Dallas Johnson assisted Smith in putting Jacobs on oxygen and inserting IVs of saline in both arms to replace the tremendous amount of blood lost to prevent their patient from slipping into hypovolemic shock.

Medics Rick Jones and David Floyd lifted Sarah Pina-Ruiz out of the patrol unit, laid her down on a patch of grass, and put her on oxygen. She was coherent, answering questions, and maintaining an adequate heart rate and blood pressure. Still, Floyd had no ability to assess the extent of the internal damage and worried that any extensive bleeding could, at any moment, send the woman crashing into shock.

SERGEANT KEN GROTE had been supervising a traffic radar detail at 3100 Euclid when Riggs sent out the "cover now." He arrived moments after Moran and Jeffers and parked his unit in the road halfway down the 6500 block of Brooklyn and announced he would be assuming temporary control of the scene. Grote was a veteran cop with a commanding presence. He quickly assessed the scene. Bystanders were everywhere, the witnesses having come out of their hiding places and the curious wandering over from nearby streets. With no suspects in custody, the scene was rapidly becoming unsafe. "Three-fifty-three-Sam to all frequencies," he radioed. "I want you to raise my traffic. I want every unit, and I want 'em right here, Sixty-Fifth and Brooklyn."

Boughton asked if he wanted the Life Flight medevac helicopter dispatched from UC San Diego Medical Center. "Affirmative," Grote barked without hesitation. "Bring it."

As Grote stepped out of his patrol unit, a man ran toward him. Timothy Beard had been talking with friends outside his apartment when shots rang out. He made it to the street in time to get a clear view of the man driving away. "The guy who shot your officers was wearing a white shirt, and he left in one of your police cars," he told Grote. At 6:19, Grote put out the first information on the suspect. "Three-fifty-three-Sam, give me the air," he demanded. "Go ahead," Boughton responded. "The suspect, according to a witness, left the scene. He is wearing a white shirt and he's driving a police car."

Boughton asked if there was an approximate time the vehicle left the scene.

"The vehicle left just prior to our arrival," Grote responded. "The witnesses say that the officers were going up and down Sixty-Fifth and the suspect drove right on past them."

5

THE TIME STAMP OF 6:14 P.M. AND THIRTY-SEVEN SECONDS on the recording of Kaye Specks's 911 call marked the moment Sagon Penn exited the driveway at 6564 Brooklyn Avenue and officially became a fugitive on the run from the San Diego Police Department. Penn could hear everything over the radio mounted on the dashboard of the police car he was driving. Even if he could not understand the jumble of codes and jargon, the sirens in the background of each transmission told him all he needed to know. The cops were coming after him, and they were coming fast. Sagon knew the only person in the world who could help him now was the man he called "Daddy," his grandfather Yusuf Abdullah.

As he drove down Brooklyn Avenue toward Sixty-Fifth Street, the faces of strangers watched him go. Specks, Timothy Beard, Margarita Amaral, Oscar Julien, fourteen-year-old twins Keith and Kenneth Taylor, and twelve-year-old Charles Alexander were among those who told of peering out windows, peeking over parked cars, or standing outside the Apostolic church as he drove past. They reported the vehicle was traveling at a strangely slow rate of speed before pausing for a moment near the bottom of the road as the driver looked around the interior of the police car, as though searching for something. When he began to drive forward again, he looked over at the women in front of the church, including Cynthia Clantion, who had witnessed much of the incident. "When I was on the church steps, he drove past us real slow and he looked at us eye to eye," she later said. "He looked like he was going to cry."

Penn had every reason to despair as he reached the four-way stop at Brooklyn and Sixty-Fifth Street. The police were already moving into the area. One was bearing down on him from the left at a high rate of speed, coming up Sixty-Fifth Street with its overhead lights on. When it reached Brooklyn, it blew through the stop sign and kept going on its way to the Encanto School. With a second police car turning north-bound onto Sixty-Fifth from Imperial Avenue, Penn accelerated through the intersection, threading his way between the police units driven by Jeffers and Moran, and continuing westbound on Brooklyn. Coming from the opposite direction was Officer John Halsey. After traveling three-quarters of a mile in the wrong direction on Brooklyn, he was returning eastbound when he encountered Penn traveling westbound.

But this was before Sergeant Ken Grote had radioed that the suspect was fleeing the scene in a police car. With multiple units swarming the area, John Halsey never noticed the young Black man in a white shirt behind the wheel of the patrol unit as he drove past it. Right about then, Penn heard the sound of a woman's voice coming from the police radio mounted on the dashboard: "Two officers down. I'm the ride-along, and I've been shot."

He continued west on Brooklyn to Sixtieth Street, passing through the 6100 block where Jacobs and Riggs had responded to the dispatch for a gang member with a gun. Penn turned left on Sixtieth Street and, after two long blocks, made a quick jag to the right and was on Market Street. From there, it would be a straight run westbound on Market for 2.2 miles to his grandfather's house on Fortieth Street. He passed an auto-parts yard, a tire-supply store, and more scruffy-looking stucco and adobe-style houses. The two-lane road cut through an unlit stretch of undeveloped hillsides covered in tall grass, chaparral, and tumble-weeds. Coming from the opposite direction was another police car, its siren wailing as it sped past him on its way to Brooklyn Avenue.

It was moments later that Grote alerted units to be on the lookout for a suspect wearing a white shirt driving a police car. If he was able to understand the police chatter that quickly followed, Penn would have known the San Diego Police Department was rapidly gathering infor-mation on him. "Okay, it's going to be equipment 744," dispatcher Don Boughton radioed just after, relaying the unit number emblazoned on the outside of Jacobs's car. "What's the direction of travel?" someone asked. "Westbound on Brooklyn," another responded. Penn was now on Market Street, but they knew his direction of travel.

"Is there a roof number on that vehicle?" the spotter on the sheriff's ASTREA helicopter asked. The unmistakable sound of helicopter blades chopping in the background let Penn know a police helicopter was up there somewhere looking for him.

Still westbound on Market, Penn came through a mix of residential and commercial buildings, crossing Euclid Avenue one block north of Imperial, the intersection local street gangs called "the four corners of death." Motorists who saw the police car with the overhead lights approaching from behind dutifully pulled over and yielded him the right of way. Information about Penn continued to come over the airwaves. "Four-twenty-four-John," Mike Moran radioed from where he was still assisting EMS personnel with Donovan Jacobs. "Suspect will be armed with the officer's weapon." "Advise units that these are probably going to be Crips," Gerry Kramer radioed, passing along information received from Jacobs. "Let's start the 994 units," he added, referring to the department's street-gangs team.

Cresting over a long rise, the skyscrapers of downtown San Diego appeared, backlit by a sky streaked orange and yellow just above the horizon of the Pacific Ocean. At the intersection of Market and Forty-Seventh Street, he passed the Sunrise Market, where he had intended to hand in the completed job application that was now lying on the floorboard of the pickup truck back in Encanto. Another police car with its lights on came at him from the opposite direction, then became the fifth unit to drive right past him. Even with all the suspect information coming over the radio, it seemed as though no one on the San Diego Police force was looking for Sagon Penn. Turns out, there was at least one.

ORIGINALLY FROM MEMPHIS, Tennessee, Officer Leroy McDowell was a former U.S. Marine who had seen combat in the Vietnam War and went on to become a boot camp drill sergeant at Camp Pendleton. His brand of policing was shot through with the same discipline and intensity he showed as a drill sergeant. By 1985, McDowell had over five years on the force and was one of the few African Americans in the department. On this day, McDowell was on patrol with designator 423-Nora when he heard the "cover now" turn into an 11-99.

Arriving at Brooklyn Avenue within minutes of the first units, McDowell began gathering information from bystanders, which he relayed to units over the radio. When he learned that the person they were looking for left in a cop car westbound on Brooklyn, McDowell hurried to his patrol unit. At 6:19 p.m., Leroy McDowell became the first Southeast patrol officer to shift his focus away from the crime scene and engage in an active search for the suspect.

Following the only information he had, McDowell headed west on Brooklyn, carefully monitoring radio traffic for any additional clue about the location of his suspect. He went the length of Brooklyn and then south toward Market. By then, several of the officers were coming to the painful realization they might have passed the suspect going the opposite direction. "Four-fifty-two-Tom. When I was coming into the scene, I saw a police car going westbound on Market Street. That possibly could be the vehicle we're missing." McDowell pressed the accelerator, hurtling westbound on Market.

"A witness reports the suspect will be rolling code in the unit," came a report from the scene at Brooklyn. "Repeat, he will be rolling code." Now McDowell knew the police car he was looking for would have its overhead lights on. He blew through the intersection at Forty-Seventh Street, passing the Sunrise Market while scanning the roadway ahead of him for flashing roof lights. Somewhere above him, ASTREA heard the location too and banked into the darkening sky in search of San Diego Police unit 744.

"Can anyone give us a further description on the suspect driving the police vehicle?" dispatch requested. "Just a moment, I can," said Lesli Lord, taking information from an eyewitness at the scene. "He's a light-skinned Black male with a short haircut. White shirt. No glasses or hat."

Still westbound, Penn crossed out of the Southeast Division patrol area and into that policed by Central Division units operating out of police headquarters at 801 West Market Street. Units with Central's "7" designator began to come over frequency one. "Seven-thirteen, Imperial and Forty-Seventh." "Seven-twelve-King also." A dispatcher handling

the Central frequency asked for a confirmation of the suspect description. "Let's try to get that as soon as possible in case they dump that
vehicle," she said.

AT 6:25 P.M., Gloria Alvaro looked out the window of her house on
the 800 block of North Fortieth Street and saw the flashing red and
blue overhead lights of a police car parked at an angle in the road. A
narrow, residential street lined with tidy, low-income homes, Fortieth
Street was in the ethnically mixed community of Mount Hope, sand-
wiched between freeways just east of downtown. Police activity in the
area was not uncommon, but what Alvaro saw struck her as unusual,
so she called 911.

"San Diego Police emergency seventy."

"Yes, there's a stolen police car over here," Alvaro reported.

"A stolen police car?"

"I think so because somebody just left it up here and the light is
flashing and flashing and nobody's in it."

"Okay," the operator began.

"And I seen a Black man get out of it," Alvaro added.

The operator's tone became even more serious. "Just a minute. Stay
on the line with me."

Seconds later, the information was radioed to units in the field. "The
units on frequency one, I have info from a citizen that the suspect is
getting out of a police car at that location, 830 Fortieth."

Still speeding westbound on Market, Leroy McDowell called for
clarification. "Did I just hear somebody say he was getting out of a car
at 830 Fortieth?"

"That's affirmative," said dispatch, "8-3-0 Fortieth."

The 800 block of Fortieth Street was two blocks off Market Street,
and at that moment, McDowell was at Market and Forty-First. "Gimme
some cover," he urgently requested. "I'm almost 10-97 at 830 Fortieth."

AT HIS HOME at 841 North Fortieth Street, Yusuf Abdullah was watching a television show when his grandson rushed through the front door.

"I shot three policemen, but it wasn't my fault," he cried. To Abdullah, it looked as though his grandson had been in a fight. There was dirt and grass in his hair, and one white shoe was smeared with blood. A dried rivulet of blood ran down the left side of his face from somewhere above the hairline. A long red mark on his neck looked as though someone might have had their hand on his throat. "What do you mean it wasn't your fault?" he asked.

Sagon was frantic, speaking rapidly as he tried to explain what happened. They got pulled over in the truck, the officer asked if he was a Blood or Crip, asked for his license. He tried to give him his wallet, but the officer wouldn't take it and kept telling him, "Take it out! Take it out!" Then the officer pulled out his billy club. "I told him, don't hit me, don't hit me." The narrative was so disjointed and his grandson so distraught that Abdullah could scarcely make any sense of it. "It wasn't my fault," he repeated, over and over. "It was self-defense. I couldn't help it; I had to do it." He told his grandfather he didn't want to die and begged him to save him. "They're gonna kill me, Daddy. What can I do?"

"If you didn't do anything wrong, then you should turn yourself in," Abdullah, a man of almost unearthly composure, explained calmly.

"Okay," said Sagon, breathing hard. "Okay."

"Then come on, let me take you on down there right now." Abdullah opened the front door and saw the empty police car parked at an abrupt angle in the street, its lightbar whirling. Sagon told him he had driven the car there and asked if he should return it to the police. "Oh, no. We'll go in my car," Abdullah said, referring to the brown Cadillac parked in the driveway. "But you're gonna have to move that police car so we can get out."

Sagon ran to the car and moved it a dozen feet up the street and ran back to the Cadillac. He told his grandfather there was a gun inside. "Do you think I should bring it and turn it in?"

"No, no, no," Abdullah told him, police sirens sounding very close by. "Leave the officer's gun there," he said. He urged Sagon to get into the Cadillac right away. "If you stay here very long, somebody gonna kill you."

AT 6:27 P.M., Leroy McDowell was the first unit to arrive at Market and Fortieth. He saw the police unit parked in the middle of the block.

"Four-twenty-three-Nora, I see the vehicle now. The overheads are still going," he radioed.

"Units responding to Fortieth, the vehicle is still there, the lights are still going," dispatch relayed.

McDowell held his position, waiting for backup. It did not take long before Central and other units arrived. "Seven-thirteen-John, 10-97 Fortieth." "Five-thirty-one-X, 10-97." "Five-thirty-four-Nora, 10-97." "Three-twenty-three-King, also 10-97."

"See if you can get ASTREA over that police car at that Fortieth Street address," Ken Grote requested, adding the chopper to the equipment descending on the scene.

Officer Roger Howes was the first officer to arrive on scene after McDowell. As units flooded into the area, he began directing officers to surround the block. "Okay, we need officers in the east alley of 800 Fortieth, and we need officers in the west alley of 800 Fortieth to seal the area off. We need officers at Hilltop and as far north as Broadway. We need officers as far south as F as in Frank Street."

Within minutes, the 800 block was surrounded by police units on all sides. Officers positioned themselves using their vehicles for cover, service revolvers drawn, shotguns aimed over hoods. McDowell and Howes approached slowly from the Market Street side. Officers trained their weapons on houses and the police vehicle as cover against an attack. Inside the houses, residents took shelter in back bedrooms or crouched low while peering out windows. McDowell and Howes cautiously approached the vehicle from two angles, one with a drawn .38-caliber service revolver, the other with a raised shotgun, racked and chambered. They reached the car and saw over the sights of their weapons that there was no one inside.

GLORIA ALVARO WAS still on the phone explaining what she had seen to the 911 operator. "He jumped in a car with an old man. They went toward Market, like going back downtown."

"This Black man jumped into a car?" the operator asked.

"Yeah."

"With an old man?"

"Yeah."

Alvaro gave a description of the car and the young man. "He's tall and skinny and has a white shirt on. Not real black. Like a light-skinned brown. Like a Mexican brown."

"Okay," the operator told her. "We have some police officers shot and somebody had stolen the car."

"Oh my God," gasped Alvaro.

AT 6:35 P.M., about the same time Leroy McDowell and Roger Howes were peering over the barrel of their weapons into an empty vehicle, dispatch came over the radio with information from Alvaro and another 911 caller. "All units, all frequencies. The suspect left the police vehicle, went into a two-story white house with a chimney, then got into an eighty-five brown Cadillac with his father."

McDowell lowered his shotgun and walked back to his patrol unit. Considering his route into the crime scene and the time of his arrival on Fortieth Street, it was possible the suspect he had been pursuing for the last fifteen minutes had driven past him . . . twice.

At 6:39 p.m., just four minutes after the report that their suspect fled in a brown Cadillac, the Central Division dispatcher put out a transmission over the Southeast channel: "Frequency four to frequency one, the unit in command of the command post?"

"Four-forty-Sam, go," replied Lesli Lord, who was in the process of establishing a command post at the Encanto School.

"Per the division lieutenant, the suspect is in custody at Central," the dispatcher reported.

At 6:42 p.m., the order to stand down went out over all radio frequencies used by the San Diego Police Department: "All units, cancel code ten."

The search for Sagon Penn was over.

AT 6:31 P.M., the Life Flight emergency medical helicopter set down at a temporary landing zone established on the playground of the Encanto School, blasting the area with dirt and debris kicked up by the rotors.

Dressed in blue flight suits with gold trim, Dr. David Guss and nurse Michael Epperson were led to the crime scene a block away. Tall and bearded, Guss was head of the emergency department at the prestigious UCSD Medical Center and had been the first surgeon assigned to the Life Flight program when it was launched five years earlier. Guss went to the most seriously injured patient while Epperson checked with personnel attending to Donovan Jacobs and Sarah Pina-Ruiz.

By the time Guss got to him, Tom Riggs had been unresponsive and without vitals for over fifteen minutes. Guss ordered CPR to be discontinued and palpated the carotid artery but found no pulse. He checked pupils; they were mid-position and not responsive to light. He pressed his stethoscope to Riggs's chest, but there was only silence. ECG pads detected zero electrical activity from his heart. "We're going to have to call this one," he told the EMS team, ordering them to cease all patient care or transport. Firefighter Steve Bowlin, who had been performing chest compressions, sat back in the dirt and hung his head.

As he turned to check on the other two patients, Guss paused beside Officer Gerry Kramer standing at the edge of the retaining wall. "I'm sorry," the surgeon said, briefly placing a hand on Kramer's shoulder as he passed. Kramer turned away from the sight of his dead friend and began to sob. Sergeant John Wray put an arm around Kramer as a nearby news team recorded the scene.

Guss checked on Jacobs. Officers Mike Moran and Bill Jeffers had secured an anti-shock suit on Jacobs's lower extremities to decrease the amount of blood flowing away from the vital organs in the upper part of his body. Bilateral IVs of saline fought to replace the substantial amount of blood lost from the gunshot wound to the neck. With Jacobs's shirt cut off, Guss could see abrasions and contusions on his torso and a large burn on his right bicep from where it had contacted the scorching-hot undercarriage of the vehicle as it ran him over. As medics continued to package Jacobs for immediate airlift, Guss questioned him about the event and his injuries, leaning his ear in close to hear Jacobs's raspy replies through the non-rebreather oxygen mask secured over his mouth and nose.

Beside Riggs's patrol unit, Sarah Pina-Ruiz was put on oxygen and lifted onto a stretcher. She told Officer Cherie Curley that her children were with a babysitter at the apartment just down the street and gave her the address and phone number. David Guss was briefed on her condition, did a quick evaluation, and agreed with the decision to airlift her to nearby Mercy Hospital aboard Life Flight along with Jacobs.

At 6:52 p.m., Life Flight lifted off from the playground of the Encanto School. Pilot Dave Patrick radioed ahead to Mercy Hospital that they were inbound with two critically injured gunshot patients. At Mercy, trauma teams scrambled to their positions and waited. As the chopper disappeared into the night sky, Sergeant Margaret Schaufelberger and Officer Bobby Wight solemnly stood guard over the body of the one patient left behind. Thomas Riggs would be receiving no additional medical attention from anyone other than the county coroner.

6

S CHUNTAY SPECKS JUST WANTED TO GO HOME, BUT SHE couldn't get anyone's attention. All around her in the Smith house, children were crying, adults were screaming, everyone talking at once. Like the other children playing in the Smith yard, fourteen-year-old Schuntay watched the struggle between the two officers from several feet away and then fled into the house at the sound of the first gunshot. She didn't know who got shot or who did the shooting. By the time she looked out the front window, the police car with the swirling lights on top was driving away.

She saw Carmen Padgett standing nearby looking frightened. "Do you want to go home, Carmen?" she asked the ten-year-old daughter of Betty and Primo Paradero. It was scary thinking about going outside, but Schuntay knew Carmen's parents would be worried. She opened the front door and peered into the dusk. She could not see anyone, and there were no more swirling police lights, just sirens in the distance, voices coming over a radio, and some movement down the street. She eyed Carmen's house up a small rise on the other side of the driveway where the men had been fighting. There was still a police car on the driveway, but she had no idea what else they might find along the way. She took Carmen's hand. "Walk fast, but don't run," she said.

They hurried past the black car parked in the Smiths' yard and reached the short retaining wall leading to the neighboring driveway. Schuntay saw the police officer lying face down between the car and the wall no more than three feet away. "Don't look, Carmen," she said. She scurried up the retaining wall onto the dirt driveway, reached down, and helped the little girl up. She turned and found herself looking through the shattered side window of the police car with a woman slumped over in the front seat. She gripped Carmen's hand and kept walking toward the rear of the car, where they came upon another police officer lying in the dirt covered in blood. "Just keep going," she said to Carmen. "Don't stop."

When they reached the edge of the Paradero property, they ran the last twenty feet to the door, where Betty stood waiting for her daughter. After turning Carmen over safely to her parents, Schuntay heard her mother call to her from across the street, and ran as fast as she could to reach her.

INSIDE THE SMITH house, Sunday school teacher Demetria Shelby and choir director Cynthia Clantion were wondering if anyone was still alive. Almost two minutes had elapsed, and the police still had not come up the street. "We should go see," twenty-eight-year-old Shelby said. Both women had watched the altercation from the Smith yard and ran when they saw "a ball of fire" along with the crack of a gunshot. They knew the officers had been shot, but they did not know how. The two cautiously walked toward Allen Cepeda's car parked at the base of the retaining wall. Near the front of the car, Shelby spotted the police officer lying on the neighboring driveway covered in blood. She let out a scream of pure terror so loud that Clantion ran the other direction, back to her apartment across the street. Shelby fled back into the Smith house.

Inside, Irma Smith was trying to calm eleven crying children who had just witnessed something no child should ever see. When she took a head count of her own six children, she could account for only five. "Where's Krystal?" she asked, but no one heard her above the cacophony of shouting and screaming. "Find Krystal!" she shouted loud enough for the others to hear. After a frantic search of the house, Irma found her ten-year-old daughter trembling in a back closet. "Are we all gonna die?" Krystal asked her.

"THIS IS AWFUL," Kaye Specks said as she watched medical personnel working to save the lives of the wounded. It was 6:30 p.m. and Specks was still on the 911 call she had initiated sixteen minutes earlier. Now the area was swarming with police, EMS, and media, and Specks was fielding rapid-fire questions from an emergency operator while trying to control a house swirling with the frantic children she had herded inside when the shooting started. She held the receiver away from her mouth. "Tell those kids to stay in the house!" she yelled at one of the older children. "Danielle!" she hollered when she saw her nine-year-old daughter being led to the house by fourteen-year-old Tracie Alexander. "Hold on, let me get my daughter," she told the operator.

"I want you to stay on the line with me, okay?" the operator pleaded. "You've been very helpful, and we appreciate this."

Specks promised not to hang up before setting down the phone to fetch Danielle. "Tracie, you get home now!" she could be heard shouting. "Tracie, you get home!"

"I just came in from church, you know," she said when she got back on the phone. "And, and I just never seen anything like this before. I just, I just had this feeling to come home from church. I started to stay at church, and I said, I better go home."

The operator said they were sending one of the officers to her house. At 6:33 p.m., Officer Scott Wilkinson rapped on the open front door and stepped inside. "Are you okay?" he asked her.

"I'm fine," Specks said, beads of sweat on her forehead, the phone still held to her ear.

"Did you see anything?"

Specks looked at the man. "I saw the whole thing."

SERGEANT LESLI LORD scanned the scene around her. Patrol units continued to stream into the dead-end block of Brooklyn Avenue. Scores of neighborhood residents were emerging from houses, from the two churches, and from behind cars, bushes, a dumpster, or wherever they had sought cover when the shooting started. She needed to bring order to the site before the crime scene was overrun or eyewitnesses disappeared.

She conferred with Sergeant John Wray. He would take control of the crime scene while Sergeant Ken Grote continued directing incoming personnel from his location across from the Apostolic church. Lord radioed dispatch that she was setting up command at the Encanto

School: "Four-forty-Sam, have the vehicles start up there, that's where the command post is going to be."

The Encanto School had the signature layout of Southern California public schools—one-story detached rectangular buildings, each with a single row of classrooms facing an outdoor covered walkway. Lord assigned roles to available personnel, established a press room, and designated the school library as the central processing point for witnesses. As eyewitnesses arrived, they would be spread out one to a table and told not to talk to each other about the incident until a detective could take their statement. A custodian opened school classrooms and the main administration building. The Encanto Recreation Center across the street was cleared for witness overflow and other police activities.

As additional patrol units arrived on Brooklyn Avenue, Grote instructed officers to start identifying eyewitnesses and processing them up to the command center. It did not take long for the lights and commotion to attract an even-larger crowd from the surrounding area. They gathered at the intersection of Sixty-Fifth and Brooklyn, outside the perimeter of the crime scene being monitored by SDPD officers.

Among the officers, grumbling had already begun about the neighborhood residents. They swapped stories of uncooperative witnesses, hostile citizens, and unhelpful bystanders who played dumb when arriving units asked where the scene of the shooting was. "When we got here, there wasn't a single person out there helping the wounded," one agitated officer told another.

On the other side of the crime scene tape, word was spreading among the mostly minority crowd that the guy involved didn't attack the cops; they had been beating the hell out of him with batons. Same old shit, they said—white cops giving a young Black man a hard time for no reason. The atmosphere soon grew tense, a whiff of menace in the air. At 6:50 p.m., a supervisor radioed a request for additional police personnel for crowd control. For some in the neighborhood, "crowd control" was starting to look a lot like a police lockdown. "Would you be doing all this if this was a white part of town?" Carlton Smith asked a group of officers. An on-air CBS reporter told viewers that "confused residents found themselves in an armed camp."

Some in the neighborhood resented how they were being treated by police. One eyewitness asked if she could leave to pick up her child before giving her statement at the command post and was told she could not. When an officer overheard Patricia Ann-Lowe Smith telling a television reporter that police had been beating Penn, she was ordered by officers to go to the church. "Stay inside and don't talk to anyone else," one said. When Rita Gotell asked where they had taken her two children, she found herself detained as a witness even though she had been inside her house the whole time. "I ain't seen nothing and I don't know why you're holding me," she protested.

SIXTEEN OF THE eyewitnesses were age fourteen or younger, some of whom had just watched the violent altercation take place from several feet away. "I mean, they were right there!" a distraught Kaye Specks told the 911 operator in reference to her own children. Standard procedure in law enforcement was to isolate eyewitnesses prior to taking a statement to prevent their memory of the event becoming "contaminated" by the recollections of other eyewitnesses. But the sight of mostly white police officers taking mostly Black children away in police cars to interview them out of the presence of their parents only added to the tension between the two sides.

Parents protested, but it did little good. The two Graham sisters were not released to their mother until after 10:00 p.m. It was almost 11:00 p.m. by the time nine-year-old Danielle Harris was returned to Kaye Specks. Shirley Taylor did not see her young twins, Keith and Kenneth, for three hours, the whole time wondering what emotional impact the experience might be having on them. Christine Williams saw her fourteen-year-old son Dwayne being led away to a patrol unit for transport to the Encanto School and told the officer she wanted to stay with her son and be in the room when he was interviewed. She explained that her son was very susceptible to suggestion and could unintentionally provide inaccurate information. She was told that she could not ride in the car with her son but could walk up to the school if she wished. Once there, she was not allowed to speak with her son or be present while he was interviewed.

ANTHONY LOVETT, ANGELA McKibben, Ricky Clipper, and Doria Jones were still inside the house at 6564 Brooklyn Avenue when Officer

George Hoffman banged on the door at 6:25 p.m. Lovett had been trying to keep things calm since the shooting, preventing an angry Clipper from charging outside, quieting a hysterical McKibben, and calling 911 again, this time to request help for the wounded officers outside. Doria Jones appeared stunned, staring at the television to see if the news crews outside their door would go live with their reports.

Hoffman told them they would be transported to the Encanto School to have their statement taken. "Just grab a few things you need," he told them, "because you are not coming back here tonight." "Where the hell are we supposed to go?" asked Lovett, who worked in the morning. "I don't know," Hoffman said, "but you're not coming back to a house in the middle of a crime scene." As they were escorted down the driveway, Lovett could sense this thing was not going to end with a simple interview at an elementary school.

"WE'RE GONNA GET blamed for this," Junius Holmes said to his brother DeWayne as they listened to the sound of sirens closing in just after Sagon Penn drove away. "Or killed," Keno said. The backyard of their house was directly behind Lovett's house. "Let's get out of here" he said. Cedric Gregory, Bryan Ross, and Sean Arkward followed Junius and DeWayne over a low chain-link fence. Angry, upset, and amped up, the five boys walked down Wunderlin Avenue amid the howls of sirens and flashing lights. Looking over the tall weeds of a vacant lot directly behind Carlton Smith's house, they watched the activity on Brooklyn, one street over, as police swarmed over it. "We ain't going back there right now," Cedric said.

None of them were as shaken and angry as Sagon's brother, Sean. He told the others he needed to call his mother, so they walked to a nearby house where a friend of Cedric's named Manny Ford lived. Manny's mother, Elizabeth, turned on the television and told the boys to stay right there while she walked a block over to Brooklyn to see what was going on. She returned a half hour later. "They have Bryan's identification," she said, referring to the social security card Bryan Ross had handed to Tom Riggs moments before the altercation broke out. "They think he did it." The boys asked her what they should do. "Don't go over there," she said, "they'll kill you."

———————

IT WAS JUST after 7:00 p.m. when Officer John Halsey was directed by a patrol sergeant to contact the people inside the house at 6562 Brooklyn Avenue and begin transporting them up to the command center. Halsey knocked on the door and told Carlton Smith that everyone needed to go. Smith shook his head. It was too late for the younger children. "They're exhausted and upset at what they just saw," he told the officer. If they wanted to interview his family, they could do it at his house and in his presence.

Having performed chest compressions on Tom Riggs less than an hour before, Halsey was in no mood to be told how to conduct witness interviews. Unable to persuade Smith, he was determined to at least preserve the integrity of the eyewitnesses in the house until detectives arrived. He radioed for additional officers, none of whom were sympathetic to Smith's position. One turned off the television and began to separate the children from the adults. "Why are the police in the house?" one of the youngest of the Smith children asked. "What did we do?"

"Is this legal?" a furious Carlton Smith asked. "Can y'all just come in my house and do this?"

"A police officer has been killed," one of the cops growled. "We can do what we want."

AT 9:00 P.M., Homicide Lieutenant Paul Ybarrondo called together Sergeant John Kennedy and his Homicide Team II for a special assignment. "There's a residence west of where the shooting took place with ten witnesses who are hostile and don't want to talk to us," the lieutenant told them. "Go down there and get their statements."

At 9:20 p.m., Kennedy approached the house with Detectives Dickey Thwing and Fred Dreis. All three were veteran investigators with years of homicide work. They were a physically imposing trio. Kennedy, a big, round-shouldered man with a quick smile, was eyeing retirement. Dreis was lean, serious, and efficient. At six foot five inches tall, 250 pounds, and never far from a lit cigarette, Dickey Thwing still maintained the powerful build of the star football player he had been in high school. Kennedy wasted little time on an introduction before stepping through the front door. "We need to talk to you," he said to Smith. Before Smith could voice an objection, Dreis and Thwing followed Kennedy into the living room. "Oh, I didn't know you could just come over and tell a man what to do in his own house!" Smith snapped at Kennedy.

Kennedy suggested he and Smith speak in another room while Thwing and Dreis interviewed Allen Cepeda and Demetria Shelby. "Look," Kennedy said once they were in the next room, "we either talk to the children now, or the DA will subpoena them later. We're going to talk to the people in the house and then leave."

"Then do it and get out," Smith said, disgusted.

AT 10:45 P.M., the last interview was completed at the Encanto School. In all, over forty eyewitnesses and a handful more from the Fortieth Street location provided statements. The detectives took handwritten notes, from which they would type up their formal investigation reports. None of the statements were audio recorded.

On the 11:00 p.m. news, an on-air reporter stationed outside the emergency room entrance at Mercy Hospital updated viewers on the scene. Sarah Pina-Ruiz's daughter was shown arriving, as was a steady stream of San Diego Police officers and a young woman described as the fiancée of Donovan Jacobs. As the doors to the ER slid open, the camera caught one officer sobbing and a second leaning against a wall looking stricken. The *News 8* reporter ended her segment by telling viewers the incident had "left one officer dead and a second clinging to life."

An indication of the severity of Donovan Jacobs's injuries was discovered a short time later. At 11:05 p.m., patrol unit 744 was towed from where it had been abandoned on Fortieth Street to the department vehicle garage at 801 West Market for further inspection. When the vehicle that ran over Donovan Jacobs was raised on a hydraulic lift and the undercarriage inspected, an evidence technician made the grisly discovery of "what appears to be hair hanging off the oil pan." The inspection report went on to note that "additional traces of what appeared to be hair and a red substance consistent with blood is found adhering to various undercarriage parts."

7

A T 6:54 P.M., THE UCSD LIFE FLIGHT HELICOPTER SET DOWN on a rooftop helipad at Mercy Hospital. The moment the rotors ceased turning, the Stokes basket containing Donovan Jacobs was placed on a gurney and wheeled down a ramp to the hospital entrance, into an elevator, and down to the emergency department. Another team brought Sarah Pina-Ruiz in the same way moments later. Two trauma teams awaited their arrival, gowned up and ready to act.

Trauma surgeon Joseph Devin listened to the briefing from Dr. David Guss as his team quietly transferred Jacobs onto the examination table. With over twenty years practicing general and thoracic surgery in civilian and military environments, Devin had seen just about every sort of injury inflicted upon the human body. What he encountered with Donovan Jacobs would rank among the worst.

Devin addressed Jacobs. The wounded officer was clearly in pain and struggling to speak but was otherwise alert and oriented. Devin asked Jacobs if he remembered losing consciousness at any time. He had not. In addition to the gunshot wound in his neck, Jacobs had cuts to the base and bridge of the nose severe enough to require stitches. Additional lacerations, bruising, and abrasions covered other areas of his face. The three-inch-long laceration at the back of Jacobs's head was so deep it went all the way to the skull.

Devin wanted to clarify something important while Jacobs was still conscious. "Were you struck by a car or run over by a car?"

"Run over," Jacobs said.

Devin had rarely seen anyone run over by a car and survive. "Are you sure?"

Jacobs was positive. "Run over."

Devin did a quick sensory and motor check of Jacobs's extremities—*Can you feel this? Can you move it?* Jacobs could neither feel nor move his left arm. When Devin lifted it a few inches, it was flaccid and fell limply back onto the table. Nerve damage somewhere in that neck wound, he noted.

With his rapid cranial and neurological assessment complete, Devin shifted his attention to the area of greatest concern, the massive gunshot wound to the left side of Jacobs's neck. Approximately four pints of blood had drained from Jacobs's neck into the dirt on Brooklyn Avenue. Currently, the blood flow from the wound was continuous but moderate. Moran and Jeffers had done as good a job as possible controlling the bleeding. Perhaps too good. By stanching the flow exiting the body, blood had begun backing up inside the neck, resulting in an expanded hematoma.

"During the hour of resuscitation," Devin noted, referring to the time prior to Jacobs's arrival at the ER, "the left side of the neck increased considerably in size." What worried Devin most about the grotesquely distorted mass was that "it was getting larger as we watched it." So large, in fact, that Jacobs was in danger of being strangled to death by the pressure from it.

Jacobs was rushed into a surgical room, intubated, and put under general anesthesia. His vitals continued to look dismal, his blood pressure dropping and his heart rate increasing, the signature indicators of a body going into shock. Jacobs's heart was beating faster and faster in a life-and-death race to make up for the increasing hypovolemia due to blood loss. But like a man frantically bailing out a leaking boat, it was a battle Jacobs's heart would inevitably lose. Eventually his body would slip into the decompensation process, a death spiral from which not even a skilled trauma surgeon like Joseph Devin could bring him back. And if that half-gallon balloon of blood in his neck were to suddenly explode, it was game over. Devin's assessment of the situation was that Donovan Jacobs could die on the table at any moment.

Devin ordered additional units of blood brought to the operating room, anticipating that once he got into that expanding hematoma, it was going to bleed like hell. He was right. With the direct pressure released, the hematoma let loose. Over the next ten minutes, Jacobs lost ten pints of blood as Devin furiously tried to locate and close the source of the hemorrhaging. With the additional four pints spilled on scene, Jacobs had now lost nearly two gallons, approximately 60 percent of his entire circulatory supply. The only thing saving Jacobs was the fourteen units of blood that Devin's trauma team managed to fast-track into his veins.

Devin located the problem: the three-quarter-inch-diameter vein responsible for taking 50 percent of the blood supply away from the brain and back to the heart had been cut in half. Donovan Jacobs's circulatory system was no longer a closed loop. While the carotid and vertebral arteries were dutifully carrying out their mission of delivering oxygenated blood to his brain tissue, the left jugular vein was simply dumping it out the side of his neck.

Devin determined the distal and proximal ends of the severed vessel were too far apart to reattach. Instead, he clamped and sutured each of them shut to stop the blood loss. Donovan Jacobs's left jugular vein was now permanently closed for business. If he survived, his right jugular would be the sole route for returning all the blood from his brain back to his heart.

Even after closing the vein, Devin was distressed to find blood still pulsing from somewhere else within the neck. Further exploration revealed the issue. After missing the trachea by less than an inch and tearing the jugular vein in half, the bullet slammed into Jacobs's spinal column, shattering a section of vertebrae and bisecting a vertebral artery, one of the four major vessels supplying blood to the brain. While the artery was smaller in diameter than the severed jugular, the blood was under greater pressure and flowed out from both the proximal and distal ends of the transected vessel. Being entirely encased within the bony canal of the vertebrae, it was extremely difficult to address. By the time Devin managed to connect the artery using an over-sew technique, Jacobs had lost even more blood.

With the artery reattached and blood suctioned away from the area of the shattered vertebrae, Devin discovered more problems. "Also in that area are the nerves to the arm," he said. "We could identify some of them as being destroyed by the bullet injury." Unable to definitively identify the affected nerves under the current conditions, Devin could not address the issue at that time without the possibility of causing additional damage. The impact of the bullet slamming into the vertebrae was the cause of Jacobs's temporary inability to move at all before being run over.

The bullet itself was discovered just under the skin at the back of his neck. Its failure to punch through that final layer of tissue probably saved Jacobs's life. The unbroken skin served as a tamponade, contributing positive pressure to the wounded area. An exit wound would have created an avenue for additional blood loss, which Jacobs would not have survived. The mangled slug would have to stay put for now. Devin could remove it later through an incision in the back of the neck, completing the .38-caliber hollow-point bullet's destructive journey in one side of Jacobs's neck and out the other.

Devin decided the neck area had taken enough trauma for the time being. "Because of the inability to absolutely clean the wound 100 percent," Devin said, "we elected to leave the wound open and return at a subsequent date to close." For the time being, the left side of Donovan Jacobs's neck would be an open, five-inch vertical incision with the skin butterflied out to create a gaping wound three inches wide and four inches deep, revealing tendons, muscle, fat, and sutured blood vessels.

While Devin had been working on Jacobs's neck, a member of the surgical team inserted a tube into the abdominal cavity. When fluid was injected, drawn out, and examined, it was found to contain blood, necessitating exploratory surgery to identify the source. The doctor opened the entire length of Jacobs's abdomen with an incision from the breastbone to the pubic area, snaking around the belly button on its route. Inside, he identified an evulsion of blood vessels on the left colon. To keep the affected region of bowel under observation, that intact segment of the colon was looped outside the body, where it would remain exposed for several days. The main abdominal incision was then sutured closed.

In comparison to the abdomen and neck, the rest of the work on Jacobs amounted to cleanup. Abrasions and lacerations to his body were cleaned and sutured where necessary. The patch of skin on his bicep that had been roasted on the scalding undercarriage of the car was dressed in sterile gauze. There was nothing to do about the fractured ribs, which the X-rays showed to be held in place by the intercostal muscle. When blood was found collecting in the right chest cavity, a drain was placed to give it someplace else to go. The bone-deep laceration on the back of his head was sutured and a drain placed to prevent the accumulation of blood and fluid in what the surgeon referred to as a "dead area" of flesh. Most importantly, a CT scan revealed no sign of cranial fractures, brain bleeds, subdural hematoma, or other life-threatening head injuries.

After three hours on the operating table, Jacobs was transferred to the surgical ICU in critical condition, his survival still far from assured. His mother, Mary, had been sorting through her children's old high school papers when a report came on the television news of police officers shot in Encanto. She rushed to Mercy Hospital and was given the status of her son's condition. "Before you go in to see him," they said, "we have a question we need to ask you: Have you and your son ever discussed organ donation?"

SARAH PINA-RUIZ WAS brought into the emergency room looking frightened and pale with a tangle of IV and oxygen tubes and heart-monitor wires traversing the stretcher. Life Flight nurse Michael Epperson briefed trauma surgeon Robert Jacobs on her condition. Vitals were steady and strong, mental status was alert and oriented, everything they were monitoring looked okay. All of that was great news for Dr. Jacobs, but there was still the issue of the six holes in the woman's body. As the doctor urgently began assessing the wounds, his worry soon turned to wonder. One bullet appeared to have caused four of the holes by passing completely through the triceps of her left arm before reentering her body below the left shoulder blade. From there, it tunneled beneath the flesh for five inches and exited just short of her spinal column. The other bullet took an even more remarkable journey. It struck her beneath the left breast, traveled on a diagonal path across her abdominal area, and exited on her right side just above the waistline.

Two .38-caliber bullets, three entrance wounds, three exit wounds, and not an organ, nerve, bone, or major blood vessel appeared to be damaged. The chest cavity, abdominal cavity, spinal column, and brachial artery in her left arm had all been skirted by centimeters. The bullet that entered under the left breast and exited her lower right abdomen failed to penetrate the peritoneal membrane encasing vital abdominal organs. Unlike the bullet that seemed to find every vital area of Donovan Jacobs's neck, those passing through the body of Sarah Pina-Ruiz had limited their damage to soft tissue, avoiding even muscle. The worst physical trauma Sarah Pina-Ruiz suffered that night was the abdominal incision made by Dr. Jacobs during the exploratory surgery, which turned out negative. Physically speaking, she was an extremely lucky woman. The psychological impact of what she had experienced that night remained to be seen.

The abdominal procedure took just over an hour, ending shortly after 9:00 p.m. At 10:50 p.m., Detective Dave Ayers from Homicide Team IV took a bedside statement from Pina-Ruiz. Despite her condition, she was lucid and detailed in her description of what she had witnessed, including the shootings themselves. When it came to how she had been shot, Pina-Ruiz had a harrowing story to relate. She said the moment the first shot went off, she began looking for something with which to defend herself. She glanced at the shotgun mount at the center of the dashboard, but there was nothing in it. "They are useless," she remembered Riggs telling her just three hours before. She saw the police radio, but an instant later she was looking down the barrel of a gun aimed at her from outside the driver's window. She raised her left arm to shield her face and twisted her body away from the gun. When she did, the first shot shattered the window. There was a dull thump like being hit by a hammer on the left side of her chest followed by the sickening burning sensation of a foreign object traveling through her body.

The second shot came half a second after the first. With the window already blown out and no glass between her and the barrel of a Smith & Wesson .38-caliber revolver eight feet away, it was an especially terrifying explosion. This time, the hammer blow was to her back, just below the shoulder blade. Her upper arm also burned with pain. She was sure she had only heard five shots so far—three outside the car and two aimed at her. She waited for the next bullet to tear into her body, but there were none, just an odd click, click, clicking noise and then nothing but the sound of footsteps on dirt. She slumped down in the seat and played dead until she heard the car pass her on the way out the driveway. Only then did she reach for the radio microphone and make her first transmission: "We need help. We need help."

Detective Sue Payne from Southeast Division was assigned to assist Sarah and her family in the aftermath of the shooting. Payne arranged to bring Sarah's children, Joshua and Teresa, to the hospital and then began the process of locating her husband, Rocky, on board an aircraft carrier somewhere off the coast of the Philippines. Payne spoke with Pina-Ruiz after the exploratory surgery. She told Payne she remembered Penn looking through the car window and making eye contact. "I knew I was dead by the look in his eye," she said. "I turned to my right, and he fired."

SAN DIEGO POLICE chief William Kolender was at a local restaurant when notified of the shooting in Encanto. Kolender joined the force in 1956 and worked his way up to chief by age forty. But even Kolender's engaging smile could not entirely hide the perpetual look of concern from a decade leading the police force of a major American city.

Kolender was aware he had lost an officer by the time he reached the crime scene on Brooklyn Avenue. He took a briefing from his Homicide lieutenant, Paul Ybarrondo. When he was told the dead officer was Tom Riggs, the anguish was even more acute. Kolender had come up through the ranks with Riggs's father, Charlie, who had retired as a sergeant just three years earlier.

News 8 reporter Lena Nozizwe said the chief was "visibly shaken and close to tears as he visited the scene of the shooting." When he was done, Kolender asked two officers to accompany him to notify Riggs's wife. Cassie Goldstein and Mike Moran volunteered. Goldstein and her fiancé, Gerry Kramer, were close friends of Tom and Coleen, often joining them for one of Tom's twenty-five-dollar date nights, in which one of the young couples was challenged with providing a night of entertainment within that budget. It made for a lot of evenings involving sunsets on the beach, board games, and cheap bottles of wine. Mike Moran and his fiancée were also friendly with Coleen and Tom. Together, Kolender, Moran, and Goldstein set off on the fifteen-minute drive to El Cajon.

Inside the little starter home by the freeway, Coleen Riggs had been getting baby Adam fed and bathed when Tom's sister Kathy called. Something had gone wrong in Encanto, but she was not sure what. She was on her way over, she said. Coleen turned on the television, but there was no news. She left it on in case the network broke in with a report. Within minutes, the phone rang again. It was Judy Woods, a young officer on maternity leave. Tom had been Judy's training officer, and she looked up to him like a big brother. Judy had troubling news. The cop shot in Encanto was one of the three agents who worked the second watch. She did not know which one or how bad.

With her odds now down to one in three, Coleen hung up the phone and went to her room. She changed into more presentable clothes, checked on the baby, and then sat down to wait. Kathy arrived, followed by another of Tom's sisters, Nancy. They waited some more. There was no news from the police, and even Tom's father could not get an answer. A short while later, three people walked past Coleen's picture window on the way to her front door. One was Kolender. Coleen knew then that her husband was gone. She opened the door and looked at Kolender. "Is he dead?" she asked, eyes searching the chief's face. "Yes," said Kolender. She looked at Cassie Goldstein. "Is he dead?" she repeated. Goldstein nodded. Coleen looked at Moran. "Is he dead?" Overcome with sadness, Moran could barely answer. Yes, Tommy was dead.

BEHIND THE INFORMATION desk at the civilian entrance to the sprawling Spanish-style headquarters of the San Diego Police Department, a young officer named Ray Beattie was chatting with his fiancée, Linda Kissel, while eating a sandwich she had brought him. Beattie could hear the radio traffic and was aware of the incident in Encanto. At 6:35 p.m., just minutes after Life Flight touched down at Sixty-Fifth and Brooklyn, an elderly Black man opened the door and approached the desk with a young man just behind him. Beattie spotted what looked like blood on the young man's shirt, shoes, and face, and he saw dirt and grass in his hair. Beattie was not alarmed; people walked into the station to report fights and crimes all the time. "Can I help you?" he asked.

"My grandson would like to turn himself in," the older man said in a deep, soft-spoken voice. "He told me he shot some police officers."

"It wasn't my fault," the younger man blurted. "They were harassing me, man. It wasn't my fault."

"Who was harassing you?" a surprised Beattie asked.

"The police. They were asking for identification, they kept wanting to know my name." Sagon Penn reached in his back pocket, took out his wallet, and opened it up to show Beattie the license. "I opened up my wallet and told him, 'See, there is nothing else there, you can have it.'" He set the wallet onto the counter. Beattie removed the handcuffs from his belt and came around the counter while Penn continued speaking excitedly and without pause. "They were hitting me with their sticks, and I was just defending myself like this," Penn said, raising both hands in a defensive position. "I told them to stop hitting me, but they didn't. And I warned them they better stop because I felt something coming up inside me. They didn't stop and that's when everyone started getting shot." Penn dropped his arms and allowed Beattie to cuff them behind his back.

Sergeant Joe Molinoski was in the process of a shift briefing when he was called to the front desk to take custody of a walk-in prisoner. "What did he do?" Molinoski asked. "He said he shot some officers," Beattie said. There was no break in the young man's monologue as Beattie transferred the prisoner to Molinoski. "They didn't have to hit me," Penn said. Molinoski radioed for a patrol unit from his squad to return to the station. At Molinoski's instruction, Officers Richard Lundy and Sylvester Wade took Penn into the watch commander's office located just steps from the front desk. A few minutes later, Lundy stepped into the hallway and flagged down Molinoski. "Hey, this guy's talking," he said.

Inside the office, Penn sat in front of the commander's desk, one arm handcuffed to his chair. "Are the officers okay?" he asked Wade, seated on the other side of the desk. "I don't know," Wade answered flatly. Penn's eyes darted around the room nervously, his body trembling. Wade could see he was scared. "Is it okay if I read my book?" Penn asked politely, indicating the pocket-edition Buddhist sutra book Molinoski had allowed him to keep. "Sure," Wade said. Penn opened the book with his one free hand and began to chant softly. The trembling subsided somewhat.

Molinoski retrieved a portable cassette tape recorder and blank tape and gave it to Lundy. He told the officer not to read Penn his Miranda rights or ask him any questions. Just let him talk. So long as Penn was talking on his own without prompting, his comments could qualify as "spontaneous utterances," potentially admissible at trial. "Testing, one, two, three . . . ," Lundy said into the machine. Satisfied it was working properly, he rewound it, set it on the table, pushed record, and promptly introduced the recording as though he were about to do exactly what Molinoski told him not to. "March 31, 18:59 hours, interview with Sagon Aahmes Penn," Lundy said, stumbling over the pronunciation of the middle name several times until Sagon helped him out with it.

Penn then recited his name and address and immediately launched into a formal narrative of the events of that night, awkwardly referring to himself in the third person. "Um, a confrontation occurred in Encanto and Sagon was stopped by a police car," he began. "He got out and he asked the officer what was going on because he hadn't been speeding, he had just pulled up into a, uh, a driveway, and uh, to drop some neighbors off at their house." Penn began anxiously bouncing the heel of one foot. He soon abandoned the third person, but his speech was rapid and stammering, as though desperate to explain himself. Lundy and Wade listened silently as Penn continued "babbling off," as Lundy called it. Sagon looked about the room as he spoke, studying the walls, desktop, and bookshelves, but rarely at the two uniformed officers.

Penn told his version of the story from start to finish in an unbroken monologue, ending at the point he left the scene to drive to his grandfather's house. His voice trailed off then, and he seemed to turn inward. He sat with his hands folded in his lap, speaking very softly. He chanted, "Nam myoho renge kyo," and explained it was to help the wounded officers: "my life force chanting to their life force and it's going to make things be better for them." His voice became even softer, and then he spoke to himself in a barely audible whisper before finally becoming overwhelmed by the circumstances in which he found himself. "Why? Why? Why? Why?" he cried. "What'd I do wrong? I didn't do anything wrong."

AROUND 9:00 P.M., Detectives Alfonso Salvatierra and Bob Lopez from the street-gangs detail took custody of Penn from Lundy and Wade. Penn was taken to the gang unit and handcuffed to a chair to wait for the Homicide Team IV detectives to finish up at the crime scene and interview Penn. They did not read him his Miranda rights or question him. Again, a tape recorder was placed on the table to capture anything he said on his own. Penn spoke almost nonstop, this time in a monologue replete with non sequiturs and wild tangents. But when it came to the incident itself, Penn again became focused and coherent, telling his version of events in even greater detail than before.

It was 11:30 p.m. when Homicide Team IV detectives Larry Lindstrom and Gary Murphy went to the street-gangs unit to pick up their suspect. Salvatierra turned over the cassette tapes containing Penn's statements made while in custody. Penn was taken downstairs to an office in the Homicide department, where Lindstrom read him his Miranda rights. Murphy's first impression was that Penn was far from a hardened criminal or streetwise gangbanger. He seemed like a polite, naive, and very frightened young man. He was also clearly going to be a talker.

After asking a few questions, Penn said he understood his Miranda rights. "I'm willing to talk to both of you," he said. "I'm willing to tell you guys everything that happened." Five and a half hours after the incident, Penn still believed that all he had to do was explain what had happened and the whole thing would be cleared up.

By the time the interview with Lindstrom and Murphy was concluded near 12:30 a.m., investigators had over two and a half hours of audio recordings in which Sagon Penn had given his version of events three different times, all of which had the potential to be used in a court of law to send him to the gas chamber.

After the interview was done, the official processing of murder suspect Sagon Aahmes Penn began. He sat handcuffed to another chair as information was taken, including name, address, family members, height, weight, and blood type. When asked to produce identification, he told them he had not seen his wallet since he tossed it on the front counter when he walked in. A search of the station by personnel came up empty.

Evidence technicians swabbed his hands for gunpowder residue, took fingerprints, and collected visible evidence from his clothing and body. At 2:45 a.m., he stood against a plain white wall and was photographed from several angles to document appearance and injuries. He was dressed in a white jumpsuit and foot coverings to preserve any additional evidence.

At 3:30 a.m., Penn was led from the building to an unmarked police car by Lindstrom and Murphy, his hands cuffed behind him. When he caught sight of the multiple news cameras aimed at him, his eyes widened. He appeared equal parts surprised and dismayed, his eyes darting about, trying to take it all in. As Lindstrom guided him toward the vehicle, Penn was so fixated on the commotion around him that he bumped into the vehicle before being guided by Lindstrom into the caged back seat. With Murphy behind the wheel and Lindstrom beside him, the car pulled away to take Penn to the hospital for evaluation. In the back, Penn leaned forward, turning his head left and right to see out the windows at the scene outside, a look of utter disbelief on his face.

At 4:20 a.m., Penn was examined by nurse Elaine Hilliard and Dr. Barbara Groves in the emergency department of Physicians and Surgeons Hospital. After a physical inspection and X-rays of Penn's chest and right hand, Groves determined his condition satisfactory enough to be released back to police for transfer downtown to the county jail. At 5:15 a.m., Penn was booked into the San Diego County Jail, a facility operated and guarded by the San Diego Sheriff's Department. There, he was stripped, searched, and issued an inmate's blue jumpsuit and rubber sandals.

At 6:00 a.m.—twelve hours after driving his pickup truck up a dirt driveway in Encanto to drop off some of his little brother's friends after a day in the park—Sagon Penn was assigned a cell in the fourth-floor isolation unit reserved for dangerous prisoners. At the bottom of the intake form, a sergeant noted the reason for the assignment along with instructions for handling of the new inmate:

> *Penn was arrested for the murder of a police officer and the attempted murder of another police officer and a female civilian. He has claimed to be a martial arts expert and reportedly was able to overpower two officers using batons. Penn should be considered an extremely high security risk and should be treated with the utmost caution. He should always have both waist and leg chains on whenever he is outside his cell and should be accompanied by at least two deputies.*

PART 2

8

ON APRIL 2, 1977, OFFICER DENIS ALLEN AND HIS PARTNER convinced an emotionally disturbed man to drop the butcher knife he was holding. When Allen went to handcuff him, the suspect drew a gun and shot him in the chest. Just after 1:00 a.m. on November 4, 1978, Officer Archie Buggs, one of the few Black officers on the San Diego Police force, pulled over two teenagers for a minor traffic violation. While he spoke with the driver, the passenger fired a .38-caliber handgun, hitting Buggs five times. While Buggs lay bleeding in the gutter, the gunman stepped out of the vehicle and shot him in the head. In March 1979, Officer Mike Anaya confronted a twenty-four-year-old man who had just attacked several family members with a knife. The man attacked Anaya, got the officer's gun, and fatally shot him in the neck before turning the gun on himself. Officer Dennis Gonzales was struck by a vehicle on Interstate 8 in June the following year. The impact was so hard that Gonzales was pulled out of his boots. The driver of the vehicle fled the scene, leaving Gonzales to die.

On June 6, 1981, there was a dispute between two neighbors over the location of a rosebush along the property line. As Officers Ron Ebeltoft and Keith Tiffany stood on the driveway of the man who had punched his female neighbor, a gun barrel poked out from between the planks of a wood fence. "There he is!" another neighbor shouted as the officers were hit by multiple rounds. The two bled to death before other officers could reach them. On February 20, 1983, a sixteen-year-old put on his stepfather's San Diego County Sheriff's uniform, took his gun and patrol car, and drove to Marian Bear Park near the campus of UC San Diego. When SDPD officer Kirk Johnson pulled up for a friendly conversation with his counterpart, the "deputy" standing beside the vehicle shot him multiple times in the head with a .357 Magnum service revolver.

Just past 11:00 p.m. on Friday, September 14, 1984, San Diego Police officer Timothy Ruopp spotted a parked car with four shadowy figures inside in the Grape Street area of Balboa Park. Ruopp radioed for backup and approached the vehicle. Inside the convertible were two men in their early twenties drinking whiskey and 7UP with two underage girls. "Isn't it a little late for these young ladies to be out this evening?" asked Ruopp, an ordained minister described as unfailingly polite. Rookie Kimberly Tonahill arrived on scene to assist. As Ruopp wrote the men a citation for contributing to the delinquency of a minor, Tonahill conducted a routine pat-down search of one, a twenty-five-year-old Encanto man. Suddenly pushing Tonahill away, the man pulled a handgun and shot her point-blank from a crouching position. Tonahill collapsed to the pavement as a 9mm bullet entered her side just above the protection of her ballistic vest, piercing her heart. He then fired on Ruopp, hitting him in the leg. Ruopp fell to the ground. As he struggled to unholster his sidearm, the gunman approached and shot him in the head.

Over three thousand people attended Ruopp's memorial four days later. Among the pallbearers was yet another cop from his wife's side of the family, his brother-in-law, Agent Thomas Riggs. Unable to locate the coat to his dress uniform in time for the service, Riggs borrowed one from another agent at the Southeast Division named Donovan Jacobs.

On April 3, 1985, San Diego Police chief William Kolender found himself speaking to much the same crowd of mourners sitting in the front pews of First United Methodist Church in Mission Valley. "Six months ago, in this church, I promised the family of Tom Riggs, as we gathered to honor the memory of his brother-in-law, Tim Ruopp, that they would never have to face a greater pain in their lives than the pain they were feeling at Tim's loss," he said. "But that turned out to be a promise that could not be kept, and today we mourn the death of Tom."

Kolender may have been "simply disgusted and upset" by the death of another of his officers, but he certainly could not have been surprised. With the death of Tom Riggs, the San Diego Police Department surpassed Memphis, Tennessee, for the highest officer mortality rate of any major city in the country. In the decade under Kolender, ten officers had been killed in the line of duty, all but one shot to death by a civilian.

IN A STATEMENT the day after Tom Riggs's death, San Diego Police Officers Association president Ty Reid noted that a San Diego cop was 6.7 times as likely to be shot on the job as their NYPD counterparts, who policed what was then a nightmarishly violent city. The five years dating back to 1980 had been particularly deadly for the department, with 4.6 deaths for every one thousand officers, far more than the next highest on the list and fifteen times higher than Los Angeles, their big brother just up the freeway. Reid also linked the line-of-duty death rate to the comparatively small size of the force—one cop for every 714 citizens versus ratios of 1:237 in Philadelphia, 1:270 in Chicago, 1:272 in New York City, and 1:437 in Los Angeles. Reid was not afraid to point a finger at the citizens and city government of San Diego for their refusal to face a new reality. "It's time to look at the fact that we are a big city with big-city problems," he declared. The message from the cops to the city of San Diego was clear: Time to grow up.

WITH DONOVAN JACOBS's survival still in doubt, the department was facing the prospect of a third incident in less than four years in which two officers were killed, prompting one officer to say, "We have so many cops killed because in San Diego they kill us in pairs." Chief Kolender blamed the killing on a general decline in the value of human life. "In the past, people were shot for the wrong reason," he said two days after Riggs's death. "Now they are shot for no reason."

Patrol officers agreed with Kolender's assessment that things were getting increasingly vicious out on the streets. "People don't try to get away from us anymore. They just attack you."

Others blamed a host of progressive policing policies instituted throughout Kolender's administration limiting use of force and options for reacting to violent confrontations. "I don't know what these guys were thinking," a veteran officer said, referring to Jacobs and Riggs, "but

I can tell you that fifteen years ago, I wouldn't have grabbed a suspect like [Penn] on his arm, I would have knocked him on his ass." One reporter termed the high line-of-duty death toll "the curse that haunts the San Diego Police Department." No one was more cursed than the members of the Riggs family.

It was a week before Coleen Riggs spoke to a television reporter about her husband's death. Seated on a sofa in the little home in El Cajon, she exhibited the same strength and composure she had at Tom's service five days earlier. She responded to questions thoughtfully, her answers, in the words of the reporter, "almost philosophical." "You can't let your husband walk out the door every day and panic," she said. "What kind of life would you have then?" She commented on her strong faith and belief that things happen when they are supposed to. "If he was meant to go, he was meant to go."

At the funeral service, three widows of slain officers offered their help and support to the newest among their ranks. Eileen Gonzales was several years younger than Coleen when her husband was killed. "The things you had to take care of when you're twenty-three years old—picking a coffin, picking a grave site—are not things you can call up your girlfriends and talk about." She said despite all the support Coleen Riggs had, an inevitable loneliness would follow. "Everyone gets to go on with their lives, and you have to go home alone."

THE CUMULATIVE EFFECT of the death rate under his administration was taking a heavy emotional toll on Chief Bill Kolender. When Deputy Chief Norm Stamper entered his office the morning after the incident, he found Kolender looking drained and defeated. "Normy, I cannot knock on another door," he said, referring to the family-member notifications he always insisted on doing himself. "I don't ever want to do it again."

Bill Kolender had not been seeking a career in law enforcement in 1956 when he went looking for a job to support his young family after leaving the military, but he took to the occupation fast. After five years as a beat-patrol officer, he became one of the youngest sergeants in department history. At age thirty, he was a lieutenant and president of the San Diego Police Officers Association, the de facto police union, skillfully navigating the tricky relationship between the city council and the rank-and-file cops he represented. In 1967, he became the department's community-relations officer. It was an era of tremendous social upheaval and a particularly challenging time to be managing the relationship between the public and the police. But Kolender's calm demeanor, patience, honesty, and quick wit helped establish a respectful and productive dialogue between the two.

In 1975, Bill Kolender fulfilled the expectations of most everyone around him by becoming chief of the San Diego Police Department. Kolender was unique among the chiefs that had come before him. He was Jewish, the first religious or ethnic minority member to hold the rank, and the first to have a college degree. From the start, he was heralded as one of the new breed of progressive police chiefs, part of the next generation of law enforcement leadership set to bring the institution of American policing kicking and screaming into the modern age. He was certainly a stark contrast to the man he replaced. Ray Hoobler, who had taken over in 1971, was referred to as a "macho-cowboy blood-and-guts police chief" with an "in-your-face management style." He was a strong leader, was intolerant of misconduct on the part of his officers, and worked to rid the department of much of its old-school police corruption. But he never entirely broke with the law enforcement attitudes of the era from which he came. When a subordinate once suggested that he run for mayor, Hoobler reportedly snapped, "Can't do it. I don't like the niggers, and the Mexicans don't like me."

On his first day as chief, Bill Kolender called his command staff together and let them know that sort of thing was going to change. "I am aware of the racial and ethnic slurs and the sexist jokes that go on around here," Kolender told them in a speech that would become legendary in the department. "I am also aware of how certain people are treated differently than others. I am telling you right now that if any of you do it from here on out, the first time you will be reprimanded, and the next time you will be fired." When it came to epithets and slurs directed at individuals or groups of any kind, he warned them that "these walls have heard the last of that sort of talk." Bob Burgreen, who would become Kolender's assistant chief, was at the meeting. "That was the day the SDPD went from being just another law enforcement agency into something special," he remembered.

"I'm here to tell you there's racism in the department, just like anywhere else in our society," Kolender told a reporter. "But, damn it, we're trying to do something about it." Kolender knew it took much more than talk to change a culture as notoriously entrenched as that of law enforcement. When three patrol-officer trainees abruptly quit the force in the spring of 1976 over things they had witnessed in the field, Kolender took note. All three, two white and one Latino, were undergoing field training in the Southeast Division and became disgusted by the conduct of the officers. Less than one year into the job, the chief decided it was time to find out what the hell was going on.

To spearhead the effort to reform the San Diego Police Department, Kolender chose a thirty-year-old captain named Norm Stamper. Like Tom Riggs, Stamper grew up in National City and attended ethnically diverse Sweetwater High. With a head of bright-red hair, pale skin, narrow shoulders, glasses, and a love of jazz music, Stamper did not fit the typical profile of a San Diego Police recruit. But he was brash, creative, and undeniably brilliant.

The "Southeast Investigation," as Stamper's study came to be called, was a sweeping fact-finding mission to assess the degree and severity of racism and misconduct among patrol officers and their supervisors. Stamper began by interviewing twenty-seven patrol officers, three sergeants, and one lieutenant from the Southeast Division. He laid out the simple ground rules at the start of each interview: complete honesty in return for complete confidentiality.

What he learned was startling, even for a man expecting the worst. Thirty of the thirty-one interviewed said they had used racial or ethnic slurs. Most said they used the epithets among themselves and only in public to diffuse a situation or when they were "really pissed." Racial slurs were used over the radio with impunity. The problem went beyond racist attitudes to include unlawful stops, searches, and arrests. Over 70 percent of the officers said they had used or seen the use of excessive force. One interviewee estimated that "25 percent of the officers do it on a regular basis; 50 percent do it on 'special occasions.'"

Stamper presented his findings and recommendations from the

"Southeast Investigation" in a 114-page report. He said the SDPD was "the only police department in the country that has undertaken such an exhaustive process of self-examination in the field of race relations."

Kolender gave Stamper the green light to implement aggressive reforms. Stamper modified officer-recruitment and academy-training standards, instituted performance reviews to evaluate officer fitness to work in minority neighborhoods, and began rigorous investigations of accusations of racism and excessive force to identify bad actors within the department. From then on, the stated department policy called for "the discharge of employees who used racial slurs or who otherwise demonstrated contempt for the rule of law in policing ethnic minority communities."

By 1985, the leadership of the San Diego Police Department—Chief William Kolender, Assistant Chief Bob Burgreen, and Deputy Chief Norm Stamper—was widely considered the most progressive and effective in the country. Vernon Sukumu of the Urban League said "Kolender was someone we could work with." Kolender was at the top of his profession, wildly popular locally, well-liked by his officers, recognized nationally, and on the short list for a major law enforcement position in the Reagan administration. And then came the Sagon Penn incident.

ON THE AFTERNOON of Wednesday, April 3, three hours after Tom Riggs's memorial service, Sagon Penn was arraigned on one count of murder and two counts of attempted murder. Security was tight at the San Diego Superior Court. All those entering the courtroom—including Yusuf Abdullah; Sagon's father, Thomas Penn; and leaders from the Black community—were scanned by metal detectors and subject to search by bailiffs. Penn entered via a side door dressed in a blue jumpsuit with his hands cuffed behind his back. He stood beside his attorney Robert Slatten throughout the proceedings with the straight-up posture of a soldier at attention. The article in *The San Diego Union* newspaper noted that "he did not appear to have any marks or bruises on his face in connection with the melee."

"It's too early to tell if we are going to ask for special circumstances," said Deputy District Attorney Michael Carpenter in reference to conditions by which the prosecution could argue for the death sentence. Slatten told Judge J. Richard Haden that his client was pleading not guilty to all charges. Carpenter asked for $500,000 bail. The judge set it at $250,000. Penn left the courtroom without acknowledging family or friends. Yusuf Abdullah, who suffered from high blood pressure, was so shaken by the proceedings that he had to be helped from the courtroom by family members.

In the hallway outside, Robert Slatten told reporters in his measured, soft-spoken voice that Penn should have been released without bail. "He's never been in trouble before," he explained. "The entire family is highly respected in the community, as is Sagon." When asked if he thought race would become a factor in the trial, Slatten shrugged. "I hope not."

FAMILY, FRIENDS, AND the Black community rallied behind Sagon Penn with testimonials to his fine character and gentle personality. His sister, Subrena, who, along with several others, had visited him at the county jail by then, described her brother as quiet and shy. "I've never seen him lose his temper with anybody." Sean Arkward called his brother a "calm and generous person" who neither drank, smoked cigarettes, nor cursed. "That boy has never been in trouble, ever," his great-aunt Betty McDonald said. A local barber told the press, "Sagon is a real nice boy."

His former tae kwon do instructor, Master James Wilson, said Penn was "totally committed to the mental and physical discipline demanded of the martial arts" and knew never to use his skills outside the studio unless his life was in danger.

Reverend Robert Ard of the San Diego Black Leadership Council said, "He's seen as a good kid, law abiding with good values." Vernon Sukumu had known the Penn family for years and called Sagon "the kind of young man whom every father would want to have take his daughter to the prom." A police spokesman said a records search of their files turned up no previous contact between law enforcement and Sagon Penn, confirming the assertion of family and friends that Sagon had never been in trouble with the law before.

Although emotions were running high with police and Penn supporters having conflicting views of the situation, the message from both sides four days after the incident was one of continued restraint, patience, and even constructive cooperation. Homicide lieutenant Paul Ybarrondo said police felt that Penn was responsible for the incident, but he was otherwise reserved in his comments to the media. "It was just one of those things that escalated," he said, softening the stronger statements made by some officers and police officials. Kolender declined to make any premature statements about the incident, saying he would prefer to wait until he knew more facts. Reverend Ard said, "I'm not ready to put it into a white/Black situation, because I don't have all the information in at this point." Kathy Rollins, executive director of the Black Federation, told a reporter, "I want to express my condolences to the chief. The loss of the officer is a great loss to the community."

Whatever patience and restraint may have existed on April 4 would be gone by the end of the following day.

9

JUST AFTER 9:00 AT NIGHT ON AUGUST 16, 1983, A TWENTY-four-year-old pool cleaner named Edward Prosinski parked his car in the lot of the Wells Fargo Bank on Balboa Avenue in the Clairemont Mesa area of San Diego. Moments after making a forty-dollar withdrawal from the twenty-four-hour ATM outside the bank, Prosinski heard someone approach from behind. Looking over his shoulder, he caught a glimpse of a young man before a two-inch blue-steel revolver was pressed into his back. "Give me the fucking money," the assailant said. Prosinski handed the two twenty-dollar bills over his shoulder. The robber demanded more. Prosinski withdrew another sixty dollars from the machine and handed over his wallet along with the money.

When the suspect fled, Prosinski did exactly what police advise a victim never to do—he ran after him. Prosinski saw the thief run to a Chevrolet Monte Carlo parked on the street behind the bank. When Prosinski got close, the man lifted the gun and pointed it at his pursuer. "You better stop or I'm gonna blow you away," he said. Prosinski ducked behind a tree, and the robber ran away. This time, Prosinski let him go.

As Prosinski approached the Monte Carlo, twenty-three-year-old Johnny Bradford opened the driver's door and stepped out of the car. "I witnessed the whole thing, man," Bradford said. "I was just sitting here in my car waiting for my girlfriend." Prosinski knew it was bullshit. He asked Bradford to come with him to a nearby pay phone to call the police. Bradford took off.

The first SDPD officer on scene intercepted Bradford walking south through the Wells Fargo lot. A second officer responding to the scene saw a man fitting Prosinski's description of the man who robbed him exiting an alley behind an apartment building a half block away. Twenty-two-year-old Andre Smith told the officer he was a professional boxer out for his nightly exercise walk. But his story fell apart under questioning, and Smith was put under arrest.

The officers checked the alley behind the apartment building and heard something moving. Crouched beside a juniper bush between the front of the pickup and the wall of the apartment building was a third suspect. Beside the young man was a pile of clothing matching those described by Prosinski. Underneath the pile of clothes, police found an H&R .22-caliber blue-steel revolver with a two-inch barrel, cocked but not loaded. A foot away was Prosinski's wallet. In the pocket of the suspect's jacket were five twenty-dollar bills.

According to police, suspect three, a Black male in his early twenties, was discovered kneeling in the bushes beneath an apartment window, chanting softly while working a string of Buddhist prayer beads between his fingers. When questioned, he was noncommunicative, refusing or unable to provide police with even his name. Prosinski was brought down for a curbside ID but could not positively identify him as the robber.

Police transported all three suspects to the Northern Division substation for processing. Suspect three was booked under the name of John Doe. In their report, the arresting officers wrote they suspected John Doe was noncommunicative because he "was suffering emotional shock" and in a state of "extreme fear."

Smith and Bradford were transported to a cell in the county jail. Suspect Doe was transferred to a psychiatric facility and held for seventy-two hours before being released. Three weeks later, the DA's office notified police of their decision not to prosecute any of the three for the robbery of Edward Prosinski. "It is quite likely that one or two or three of the [suspects] were involved," a prosecutor from the DA's office wrote. However, "Even circumstantially, we can't prove which one did it." No one was ever charged.

Although suspect three did not answer police questions regarding the incident, somewhere during his seventy-two-hour psychiatric detainment, authorities learned the young man's real name. All records and documents related to suspect three were updated and subsequently filed by the San Diego Police Department under the name as it appeared on those materials: First name: Penn. Last name: Sagon.

IT TOOK THE San Diego Police Department four days to discover the administrative mistake. On Friday, April 5, news of the previous arrest was featured in all three local papers and television newscasts, one day after police spokesman Bill Robinson had announced Penn had no previous contact with the department. Assistant DA Richard Huffman would not comment on why his office declined to prosecute the case. "It would be highly unethical for this office to release past criminal history records on anyone, including Sagon Penn."

It was left to Edward Prosinski to lay out the details of the incident in a *Los Angeles Times* article titled "Victim 'Almost Sure' Penn Was Robber." In it, Prosinski lamented that Penn had not been prosecuted. "They just said there was a lack of evidence, but I think there was plenty of evidence. Maybe if they hadn't of dropped the charges, that cop wouldn't be dead."

Edward Prosinski was not the only one who felt that way. On April 10, *San Diego Union* editorial page editor Ed Fike gave full voice to that sentiment in an opinion piece titled "More Should Be Said About San Diego Police Killings." The sixty-five-year-old Fike was a former Navy lieutenant, seasoned newspaper man, and unabashed conservative with an affinity for western bolo ties. He was a heavyweight in the San Diego press community and had been a journalist and editor on papers throughout the country going on forty years, the last fifteen for *The San Diego Union*. He was opinionated, plainspoken, and did not pull punches in his editorials.

Dripping with sarcasm and disgust in the 1,437-word opinion piece, he began by calling out "friends and family" who "vowed that Penn had never before been involved with the police." He sneered at Vernon Sukumu's characterization of Penn as the type of kid you'd want to take your daughter to the prom. "Penn, this 'real nice boy' was described by those who know him as a clean-living athlete . . . The truth has belatedly come out, casting the suspect in an entirely different light. No choir boy he."

Summarizing Penn's 1983 arrest, he concluded that "the known evidence certainly warranted prosecution and San Diegans are left to wonder why Penn was not brought to trial. Otherwise, a splendid young officer might still be alive."

Fike addressed allegations of excessive force on the part of officers. "Criminals and friends of criminals blame the police first and last," he wrote. "Say what the criminals will," Fike assured his readers, "police officers do not go around beating citizens; they are careful about using force only when it is necessary to subdue a wrongdoer." He rejected the idea that any police force would tolerate an abusive officer among its ranks: "The bad cop is soon exposed and cashiered." "The fault lies not with our police officers," he concluded, "but with the punk elements that inhabit this fair place."

Even for an editorial piece, Fike's reporting was sloppy, containing mostly inaccurate details and conjecture about Penn's motivations presented as fact. "The horror of that recent Sunday evening began with the accused killer's arrogance for authority," he wrote. Jacobs was warranted in using whatever force necessary because Penn "is an athlete who has already communicated his prowess in the black belt arts and made threats that he better not be 'provoked.'" He went on to note that "Penn showed no signs of being beaten in the photographs taken of him the very next day." His comments almost perfectly echoed the position among investigators within the police department, where Fike had many friends.

He dismissed assertions the incident had anything to do with race. "Because Penn is black and the officers white, racist overtones have unfortunately arisen. The San Diego chapter of the National Association for the Advancement of Colored People is exacerbating the racial aspect of the tragedy by raising money for Penn's legal defense. This is widely being seen as a perversion of that organization's traditionally noble purposes."

Among the younger journalists on the paper, Ed Fike was considered an excellent writer but one who often wrote his editorials from the gut rather than with full knowledge or details of the issues. Most felt he had overreached in the Penn piece, without verifying information and lumping in unrelated cases as evidence of Penn's guilt. As the elder statesman among San Diego newsmen, few in the media were inclined to publicly take Ed Fike to task over it. But the one who did wasted no time doing so.

ONE WOULD HAVE been hard-pressed to find anyone in the news business more different from Ed Fike than Michael Tuck. Born and raised in Houston, Texas, Tuck earned a degree in journalism from Trinity College. At the age of just twenty-four, he landed a major-market television news anchor position at independent Channel KTVU in Oakland, California. The station paired the handsome, photogenic, and fiercely intelligent Tuck with a more senior reporter and built their nightly 10:00 p.m. news program around the "Tuck & Fortner Report." Tuck quickly drew the attention of the major networks and was picked up by the CBS affiliate WCAU in Philadelphia and became the centerpiece of the anchor team there. In 1979, he received a call from sportscaster Ted Leitner, who had recently jumped ship to CBS's San Diego affiliate KFMB. The news division was looking for a fresh new anchor, Leitner said. "How would you like to come out to paradise?"

Tuck took Leitner up on the offer and joined him on air as part of the *News 8* team in what was at the time a lucrative yet rather complacent and unimaginative television news market. In addition to anchoring both the evening and late-night news, Tuck investigated stories from the field and gained a reputation as a talented writer. With his youthful energy, compelling personality, and flawless delivery, Tuck propelled CBS past ABC to claim the top ratings spot among local newscasts. He was so effective, in fact, that *ABC News 10* hired him away from CBS in 1984. By 1985, having just turned forty, Michael Tuck was the dominant news personality in the San Diego market.

The media outlets Tuck and Fike represented were as different as the two men themselves. Both *The San Diego Union* and *Evening Tribune* had been under ownership by Copley Press since 1928. Except for a few years in the 1940s, a Copley family member had headed up the news conglomerate ever since, the current being Helen Copley. Copley papers historically skewed heavily conservative in their coverage and editorial positions, almost always endorsing Republican candidates and frequently accused of underreporting on the Democrats running against them.

The paper had been taking pragmatic steps to adapt to the changing, less conservative San Diego demographic by adding younger and more diverse reporters and an ombudsman to give voice to underrepresented communities. But top management remained dominated by old-guard newsmen. Jerry Warren, former White House press secretary for the Nixon and Ford administrations, had been managing editor since 1975, while another former Nixon aide, Peter Kaye, held the influential senior political reporter role. The third member of the leadership group was their senior editorial writer, Ed Fike.

At *News 10*, Michael Tuck was doing his best to transform the station's image to that of a more contemporary, adventurous news organization. While anchoring two early evening newscasts, he was writing and presenting a commentary segment entitled "Michael Tuck's Perspective" at the end of the late-night broadcast. Doffing the suit jacket, loosening the tie, and rolling up his shirt sleeves for the segments, Tuck's first few outings were, by his own account, "pretty soft and boring" and made little impact. "But then I read something in the paper one day and I got really mad," he later said. "I delivered it mad, and the phones started ringing." What Tuck had read was Ed Fike's April 10 editorial piece on Sagon Penn. In his "Perspective" that same evening, Tuck took aim at Fike and *The San Diego Union*.

"Give editorial writer Edward Fike a rope and a tree limb and he'd be dangerous," Tuck said in what the *Los Angeles Times* later described as "a voice that seems to emanate, in tone and intent, from behind a burning bush." Tuck continued: "Sagon Penn would be just a memory" if Fike had his way. "Why waste taxpayer's money? Ed Fike is your man." Whatever thoughts Ed Fike had on the scathing commentary, he chose not to share them with his readers. But *The San Diego Union* itself termed it a "venomous attack" on the paper that had "also dealt harshly with the author."

It was not just the *News 10* phones that were ringing off the hook after the segment aired. While Fike's position still had substantial support among readers, *The San Diego Union* was being flooded with calls and letters criticizing his column as grossly unfair and even downright racist.

Reverend Ard of the San Diego Black Leadership Council weighed in, saying, "We will not allow *The San Diego Union* to convict Sagon Penn in its editorial pages." When the onslaught continued into the following week, the paper's levelheaded and diplomatic ombudsman, Cliff Smith, felt compelled to respond.

In an April 22 op-ed column titled "It Was Less Than Evenhanded," Smith pointedly addressed the Fike piece. "One of journalism's inviolable tenets is to never try and convict a criminal suspect by newspaper," the column began. "Some readers have said they believe *The San Diego Union* failed to keep that trust." He tersely countered Fike's assertion that "the known evidence certainly warranted prosecution" of Penn in the 1983 incident. "Apparently, the known evidence did not warrant prosecution."

IN JUST TWO weeks, the Sagon Penn incident laid bare a social division that had been developing in San Diego since the dramatic increase in real estate development in 1970s. The resulting influx of a young, educated, and socially liberal demographic began to challenge the existing older, conservative, career-military, and overwhelmingly white establishment. As the feud between the two newsmen commenced on April 10, it did so among the public in letters to the editor and talk-radio chatter. So long as the accepted view of Sagon Penn was that of a young Black man with a clean record, Fike's devoted readers were willing to suspend judgment, or at least keep it to themselves. But with the revelation of the armed-robbery arrest and Fike's permission to presume the worst, all reservations vanished. "It was like throwing a match into a pile of dried leaves," *Union* journalist Tony Perry said of the impact of Fike's commentary. When Tuck fired back, his loyal viewers, who were less trusting of the police, staked out their territory as well.

Fractures were beginning to show in another relationship of great importance to the city. Many people on both sides had worked hard over the previous decade to improve the uneasy relationship between the San Diego Police Department and the Black community. But with the Sagon Penn story refusing to leave the headlines, tensions continued to grow. A leader in the Black community termed the relationship "strained to the breaking point." Republican mayor Roger Hedgecock warned of "a growing unrest in Southeast San Diego." Irma Castro of the Chicano Federation called the Southeast a "volcano ready to blow." Reverend Ard spoke of a "great rage that exists in our communities." He warned that "it could be a long, hot summer in this city unless the police can reconcile differences with the Black community."

THE MATCH IN the pile of dried leaves created by the Ed Fike editorial continued to smolder for a month before bursting into flames during the preliminary hearing for Penn. The four-day hearing concluded as expected, with Judge J. Richard Haden ruling there was sufficient evidence for Penn to stand trial on the charges brought by the district attorney. For many, the testimony of a frail and weakened Donovan Jacobs delivered from Grossmont Hospital offered the most dramatic moments in the proceedings. But for the San Diego Black community, something else of even greater significance had occurred the day before that.

"Racial Slurs Told in Police Slaying Case," read the May 9 headline on page one of the San Diego edition of the *Los Angeles Times*. On the stand the previous day, Junius Holmes testified that Donovan Jacobs straddled Penn, shouting, "You think you're bad, boy? We're gonna beat your Black ass," as he repeatedly punched Penn in the face. DeWayne Holmes and Anthony Lovett testified to hearing something similar. Sean Arkward accused Jacobs of ordering Penn to "turn over on your back, nigger" and Riggs of shouting, "Turn over on your back, Black bastard."

Much of Arkward's testimony was shot through with factual inaccuracies and inconsistencies. Nevertheless, when video of Sagon Penn's soft-spoken younger brother on the stand leveling the accusations was broadcast unedited on the evening news, the impact was incendiary. "A lot of people in the community are comparing this situation to [Apartheid] South Africa," activist Makeda Cheatom told a reporter in the hallway outside the courtroom.

Reverend Thomas McPhatter said the Sagon Penn incident was just the most visible in a long history of abuse. "There have been scores of young Black men, including my own son, who are regularly mistreated and harassed by police in this community for no other reason than they are Black." "Black people are sick and tired of police who make racist remarks and do nothing but demonstrate hostility to this community," Southeast resident Willie Johnson told a reporter. "That's what Sagon Penn has come to represent to us, our disgust and contempt for the system."

TO MANY OFFICERS policing the Southeast beat, the reaction of the community to the Penn incident was symbolic of a simmering resentment of their own.

"The Blacks have rallied around Penn like he is some kind of hero, and to us cops that shows no respect for law and order," an officer told *Union* reporter Terry Colvin. "It says all cops are potential targets for death."

"We'll never go back to business as usual, because too many cops have died in this city in the last few years," a high-ranking department official said. "It is our blood that is being spilled and our lives that are endangered."

There were moments in the preliminary hearing that outraged police and their supporters. "The officers said they are haunted by the testimony of one witness," Colvin wrote in a May 24 article. The reference was to witness and truck passenger Doria Jones. When asked by prosecutor Mike Carpenter if she had gone outside to help the wounded officers after Penn left, she said, "I stayed in and started watching TV."

"While those police officers were out there on the ground?" Carpenter asked with undisguised contempt.

In his ruling on the hearing, Judge J. Richard Haden commented on the exchange. "I must also note briefly the testimony of Doria Jones, who watched television," he said. "I have seldom seen a more callous disregard for human life than the testimony of that witness."

But Jones—who sometimes worked as an exotic dancer at the Jolar Cinema along with Angie McKibben—had not adequately explained her actions. She turned on the television only after TV news teams arrived on scene to see if they were going live with their reports. Nevertheless, she instantly became the poster child for what some saw as a general disregard for the lives of police officers among citizens of the Southeast. "That says police officers are less than human beings to some of these people," said a police official.

A WEEK LATER, Reverend Ard, Urban League president Rudy Johnson, and members of the Interdenominational Ministerial Alliance of Southeast San Diego announced a town meeting to be held at Lincoln High School the evening of May 30. The event was intended to provide the public with a forum to address their concerns over what the organizers called an increase in violent confrontations and complaints of misconduct on the part of police. "The moral indignation of Southeast San Diego residents can no longer be ignored," said Ard.

Bill Kolender said he was "flabbergasted" when he heard of the barrage of accusations aimed at him and the department by clergy and community representatives at the May 24 press conference. "I can't understand what these people are saying," he told reporters. "I meet regularly with Black leaders. Nothing about police misconduct has ever been said to me by any of these people." He challenged the claim by Rudy Johnson that complaints to his Urban League office were up tenfold in recent weeks. "Rudy never mentioned any complaints about police misconduct in Southeast San Diego and I am puzzled by what he has said publicly." He rejected the notion that there was a "great rage" building in the Southeast. "As far as we can see there is no real problem existing between the Black community and the police department."

In announcing the May 30 meeting, Reverend Ard said no formal invitation had been extended to Kolender, but he added he hoped the chief would consider the open invitation to the public to include his department. Kolender was not about to have his department go unrepresented. He had worked too hard over the last decade improving the relationship between his department and the Black community to stand by and watch it fall apart over a single incident. Although he could not be there himself, Kolender knew the best person to send in his place.

Norm Stamper arrived at Lincoln High with two other top police officials, including Assistant Chief Bob Burgreen. He found the 900-capacity gymnasium filled with restless, agitated citizens, none presumably there to heap praise upon the department. Several dozen protesters, mostly white, ringing the perimeter held handwritten signs, one of which read, PUT THE PIGS ON TRIAL! with a drawing of a pig wearing a policeman's hat. Another wore a shirt with the slogan FREE SAGON PENN, TRY JACOBS! inked across it. Others wore the FREE SAGON PENN shirts made up by Thomas Penn and sold to raise funds for his son's defense. Bumper stickers reading FREE SAGON, JAIL DON were passed out.

There only to listen, Stamper and the others, all dressed in brown suits, were perched on folding chairs on the gymnasium stage alongside organizers, awkwardly holding their notebooks in their laps. For two and a half hours they sat looking stiff and uncomfortable while a parade of mostly minority citizens told of being beaten, threatened, insulted, and treated disrespectfully by officers in the two months since the Penn incident. Others expressed pent-up feelings of animosity toward a department they felt had victimized the community for years.

"This is the only community where you have to call the police to stop the police from beating you," said Roberto Martinez. "San Diego is the finest racist city in the country," a man shouted into the microphone, making a play on the city's slogan. Another offered his opinion for why the SDPD had the highest mortality rate in the country: "They have lost respect and support all over, not only in Southeast." There were calls for Kolender's resignation, the formation of a police oversight committee, and other actions to reign in the police. The only Black official to show up, City Councilman William Jones, was loudly booed when he said he did not want the rest of the city to think the Southeast was anti-police. "We *are* anti-police!" some in the audience shouted.

Afterward, Burgreen said he was "impressed with the large turnout and sincerity of the comments." He conceded that "relations aren't as good in this community as I thought."

A second town meeting held three weeks later drew an equally large and even more volatile crowd to a muggy Lincoln High School auditorium. The chief made a point to attend. This time, members of the audience held up signs that read SDPD IS OUT OF CONTROL and referred to SDPD STORM TROOPERS. At times, the meeting seemed ready to spin out of control as residents took turns berating the department and

Chief Kolender, who sat listening without expression or comment. At one point, members of the audience began chanting, "Review boards won't stop racist killer cops."

When it was over, Norm Stamper defended his officers while acknowledging the message from the crowd was loud and clear. "People are asking our officers to treat them with dignity and respect, and I don't think that is unreasonable." Sitting in a patrol unit across the street from Lincoln High, Officers Ron Featherly and Richard Massman had a different take on the event. They did not understand why people were angry at the police department over the Penn incident. "How come one of our officers gets killed and people are mad at us?" asked Featherly. "The problem is not how we do business," added Massman. "I think they are just tired of being put in jail."

10

D ETECTIVE SERGEANT BOB MANIS WAS FINISHING UP DIN-
ner at a restaurant with his wife and some friends on the evening
of March 31, 1985, when the pager on his hip began to vibrate and
buzz. He excused himself from the table and used the house phone to
call the communications center. He was given a summary of the nature
of the incident and wrote down the crime scene location on Brooklyn
Avenue. When he got back to the table, his wife, Susan, already knew the
meal was over. If Bob's pager went off on a weekend, somebody was dead.
"What is it?" she asked as they walked to the car. "Another cop," he said.

It was eight days before Donovan Jacobs was conscious and strong
enough to be interviewed by Manis, the head of the San Diego Police Homicide Team IV and the man leading the investigation. In his early fifties,
solidly built, with a broad forehead, thinning hair, and dry sense of humor, Bob Manis was a seasoned investigator with a decisive manner and
no-nonsense approach to casework. As he entered Mercy Hospital on the
morning of April 8, Manis had with him Detective Larry Lindstrom, a
whole bunch of questions, and a piece of paper that he was not at all happy
about. The document was called a Reverse Garrity Warning, and agreeing
to it was the price he had been forced to pay if he wanted to talk to Donovan
Jacobs. The Reverse Garrity Warning flipped the conditions of the Miranda
warning given to a suspect in a criminal case. Instead, Donovan Jacobs was
voluntarily giving up his right to remain silent in exchange for a guarantee
that *nothing* he said could be used against him in a criminal proceeding.

"Don, I'm gonna start out by telling you you're not a suspect in anything, okay?" Manis said, addressing the document while standing at the foot of Jacobs's hospital bed. "I don't know if you trust me or not, but I'm telling you that."

The person responsible for the document was seated in the hospital room alongside his client. Two days after the incident, attorney James Gattey received a call from Ty Reid, president of the San Diego Police Officers Association. Gattey was one of a handful of attorneys used by local law enforcement organizations to represent officers, usually in Internal Affairs investigations. He had represented cops involved in shooting incidents before, but they had always been the ones doing the shooting, not the ones who had been shot. When some eyewitnesses began referring to the confrontation with Sagon Penn as a "beating" on the part of the officers, Reid figured it was time to get Donovan Jacobs a lawyer. "Whatever he needs, you provide it," Reid told Gattey. "We are behind him all the way on this."

Gattey's request for a Reverse Garrity surprised Manis. He had never seen the warning implemented by an officer outside of an internal investigation of alleged misconduct. They did not even keep a copy of the document in Homicide, so Manis had to walk over to Internal Affairs to obtain one. Gattey assured Manis that he insisted on a Reverse Garrity for all his clients. Manis didn't care and told Gattey he thought the whole thing was a bunch of horseshit.

Over the course of the previous week, Donovan Jacobs had had his neck sown up, the bullet removed from a cervical vertebra, his intestine returned to the inside of his abdomen, and the breathing tube extracted from his trachea. When Manis and Lindstrom entered the hospital room, Jacobs remained bedridden, IV lines, oxygen tubing, and wires running from his body to an array of medical devices. His voice was a raspy whisper from the intubation, which had lasted almost four days. He was very weak, and the pain was at times almost unbearable despite the high doses of Demerol that kept him drowsy around the clock.

Manis asked Jacobs how he was feeling and then took out the text of the Reverse Garrity. "I want you to know that this normally is not read to an officer," he said. "The only reason I am doing it is at your attorney's request." Only Gattey brought a cassette tape recorder, which he turned on at that time. Manis read the Reverse Garrity. "Okay," he said, setting the paper aside. "I now order you to answer the following questions."

Manis had Jacobs begin by recounting the dispatch to the 6100 block of Brooklyn for the report of a possible man with a gun. He strained to answer in his barely audible voice, limited to two or three words at a breath, each sounding as though someone was swiping sandpaper over wood. It was exhausting and slow going, but his recall of the incident down to the fine details appeared to be excellent, seemingly undiminished by the traumatic experience or his current condition. He described responding to the dispatch for a possible gang member with a gun and his interaction with Glenn Jones and others on scene.

He said he first saw the white pickup truck after turning left onto Sixty-Fifth Street. "I think it was a Chevy pickup truck, it looked like. It was parked at the east curb of [Sixty-Fifth]," he said, placing the truck pointing uphill, *away* from Brooklyn Avenue. Jacobs remembered there being about three people in the bed of the truck, the driver and possibly a passenger in the cab. He took specific notice of the left rear passenger in the bed of the truck, a Black male, age seventeen or eighteen, wearing a black hat and shirt, which he believed signaled membership in the Crips street gang.

"As Tom passed them, they began to pull from the curb to make a U-turn in front of me, so I started to slow down and stopped." He said he allowed the truck to complete the U-turn and then watched as it headed south on Sixty-Fifth and turned left onto Brooklyn Avenue without signaling.

"Why were you going to stop the truck?" Manis asked.

"Because of the traffic violations and because they were possible gangbangers."

"What violations?" asked Manis.

"Failure to signal a left turn, violation of right of way."

"Violation of right of way?"

"When he made the U-turn in front of me."

Manis asked if anyone in the truck matched the description of the suspects they had been looking for at the time. Jacobs said he wrote the description in Riggs's notebook and would have to look.

Manis asked Jacobs about the initial exchange with Penn.

"He wouldn't take the license out of the wallet. He just kept trying to hand me the wallet. I declined the wallet. I asked him a couple more times for his license . . . and [he] turned around and he started to walk back toward the house." After a few steps, Jacobs said, Penn turned back to him and snapped, "Don't you touch me!" in a loud, angry voice.

"Had you touched him?" Manis asked.

"No," answered Jacobs. "Tom Riggs walked up on the left [driver's] side, I believe. I went up around the right side of the truck to cut him off," he continued, indicating the passenger side. "I could see Tom lift his baton up in front of his face to protect it. When I came around the front of the pickup truck, I could see Tom was backing up and looked like he was fending off blows from the driver." Jacobs paused to catch his breath. "I took out my baton and I started to hit the driver in the back and shoulders as he was driving Tom back. I hit him three or four times with my baton, and it didn't look like it was fazing him."

Jacobs said he thought the driver must have been "whacked out or something" on "PCP or some other strong drug."

"I hit him a couple times, he started toward me. I jumped on him and wrestled him to the ground," Jacobs said. "The next thing I remember is we're on the ground and I'm straddling him, and I don't have my baton."

Jacobs called the scene "mass confusion." "I'm looking up and I can see about six people, not cops, staring down at me, yelling at me." He said he was holding both Penn's hands, but "he keeps fighting with me, trying to get his hands loose and kicking his feet. I keep telling him, knock it off, knock it off, to roll over, to get on his stomach. At one point, he breaks loose of my hands, and he grabs at my gun. I reach back and there's Tom's baton, the knob, hanging over my gun butt." He thought Riggs must have been protecting his gun with the baton. "We keep struggling and I hit him a couple times in the chest with my fist." Jacobs said it seemed as though Penn relaxed and was about to turn over. "And then the next thing, boom, I'm down on the ground. I can't move . . . Then it's just commotion all over the place. Yelling, screaming. And then I try to get up but my body's not working. I don't know why. And then I get run over."

"Don, during the fight with him, at any time while you're sitting on him, or standing, or whatever, did you hit him in the face with your fist?" Manis asked.

"I may have," Jacobs replied.

"Okay. Do you remember if you did or not?"

"No," Jacobs said this time. "Because I don't hit people in the face."

Jacobs had a question of his own. "I'm only five foot nine and a half, 165 pounds. How big is this guy?"

"Five eleven, 170," Manis said.

It was unclear how Jacobs felt about learning he and his adversary had been evenly matched, physically.

A nurse entered the room and asked Jacobs if he was in pain. Jacobs said yes and requested additional pain medication. Manis decided that was a good indication to terminate the questioning. "If we decide at a later date we need to talk to him some more, you want me to notify you when I'm going to be here?" he asked Gattey.

"That's up to you if you don't want me here," Gattey said to Jacobs.

"I want you here every time we talk, okay?" Jacobs replied.

"I gotta tell you," Manis said to Jacobs, "I know you want him here, but believe me, you don't need him. I don't mind him being here, but you're not in any fucking trouble, and anyone who tells you you are is full of shit. You are a witness and victim." He and Lindstrom gathered their papers. "Okay, we're gonna let you get some rest," Manis said. "I'm sure we'll need to talk to you again."

AFTER THE DETECTIVES departed, Mary Jacobs returned to sit at her son's bedside, as she had every day since the shooting. Of Native American and French extraction, she had been born on a Sioux reservation. She married an Air Force pilot in the Strategic Air Command and settled in Biloxi, Mississippi. When they had twin boys in the summer of 1956, she and her husband flipped a coin to see which would be named after the babies' uncle. It was Donovan. When Donovan was eight, his namesake died when his plane struck a powerline while crop-dusting a bean field outside of Texarkana. A year later, his own father died of cancer.

Mary raised her twin boys and an older sister alone in Spring Valley, what was then the far-eastern edge of where the San Diego sprawl was gobbling up canyon lands in the insatiable quest for affordable housing. As a child, Donovan and his brother, Michael, rode dirt bikes, explored the canyons and hillsides with friends catching snakes and lizards, or searched out backyard swimming pools in which to keep cool. Michael was the athletic one. Donovan was smaller and frequently among the last to be selected for pickup sports games according to one friend. With shoulder-length blond hair, he looked like a typical San Diego surfer kid.

During his time growing up on Del Rio Road, Donovan became friends with a neighborhood kid his age named James Stevens, a good-looking athletic young man with interests similar to Jacobs's. James's father, Ed Stevens, a lieutenant with the San Diego Police Department, became the closest thing to the father figure Donovan was missing. Mary referred to the elder Stevens as Donovan's "hero figure." With the most important adult male in his life being a cop, and his best friend determined to follow in his father's footsteps, Donovan Jacobs's career trajectory was virtually preordained. "[He] used to tell me war stories about police work," Jacobs recalled, "and it interested me."

It was not long after high school that Donovan left the scrawny physique of his childhood behind, replacing it with an extremely fit five-foot-nine-inch frame and 165 pounds of mostly muscle. He lifted weights, ran, hiked, climbed, repelled rock faces, and participated in quasi-military adventure weekends out in the desert with friends. He had blue eyes, a mustache, and enough sandy-blond hair to cover the area that was beginning to thin on top. His sculpted jawline, sharp nose, high cheekbones, and steady gaze communicated an inner intensity and caught the attention of more than a few young women.

Although he had seen his share of danger, hardship, and death during six years on the force, half of it in the Southeast Division, it was something that happened at the very beginning of his law enforcement career that had the biggest impact on Jacobs. At 9:01 a.m. on September 25, 1978, hundreds of San Diegans heard a sharp noise and looked up to the sky to see a Boeing 727 passenger jet descending sharply, its starboard engine and wing engulfed in flames. Moments after colliding with a Cessna light aircraft upon approach to Lindbergh Field, Pacific Southwest Airlines Flight 182 slammed into the densely populated residential neighborhood of North Park. All 135 passengers on the PSA plane, two in the Cessna, and seven people on the ground were killed.

Short on personnel to manage a catastrophe of that magnitude, the San Diego Police Department enlisted recruits from its training academy to assist. Just weeks into his initial training, twenty-two-year-old Donovan Jacobs spent seventeen hours at the scene of the worst air disaster in California history walking a search grid, marking the location of body parts scattered across several neighborhood blocks, dangling from tree limbs, and resting on rooftops. "It will never be as bad as this again," he told his mother afterward.

WHEN DETECTIVES MANIS and Lindstrom returned to Mercy Hospital a week later, Donovan Jacobs was still in a hospital bed, but his condition had markedly improved, especially his ability to speak in full sentences. One thing that had not changed was the presence of James Gattey and the Reverse Garrity.

"At this point we'd like to go over your statement that you gave us on Monday the eighth," Manis began. He asked Jacobs to describe again his first encounter with the white truck. Jacobs repeated that he had spotted the truck parked against the curb mid-block, facing northbound. "Is there a chance that there could have been another truck similar to that that perhaps got involved in this incident that was, in fact, not the truck parked at the curb?"

"No," Jacobs said.

Manis produced a diagram of the neighborhood and asked Jacobs to point to specific locations where the truck had been. Jacobs indicated just north of the corner of Sixty-Fifth Street.

"So, it's not up by Encanto Elementary?" Manis asked.

"Okay, this . . . I'm telling you what I remember," Jacobs said.

It was the first time in either interview Jacobs had expressed doubt about his memory, but now he began to punctuate his recollections with qualifiers: "So, I don't know if my memory is screwed up or, or what, okay?"; "It's just all not that clear"; "I don't know if my brain cells got scrambled or what"; "I'm just telling you straight out what I remember."

Manis moved to the initial interaction with Penn. "When he walked away from you, is it possible that you could have gone up and stopped him and taken him by the arm and turned him around and that Officer Riggs then joined you at that point?"

"No. What I recall is, I never laid a hand on him," Jacobs said. "It looked like this guy could go off at any second and I didn't think I needed to escalate it by grabbing him at that point."

"Is there any chance at all?" Manis asked again.

"I never recall ever touching him prior to that point."

Before wrapping up the interview, Manis gave Jacobs one last opportunity to clarify or change any details. "Don, is there anything you would like to add to your statement at this time?"

"I'm telling you everything that my memory cells can, can give them to you, you know. So, you know, if I'm totally messed up on the truck being where it's at or whatever it was, it's not because I'm lying or something like that, or conscious of lying, it's because that is what my memory is telling me."

WHEN MANIS AND Lindstrom met with Jacobs and Gattey at 6:40 p.m. the following evening, it was in room 154 of the physical-rehabilitation center at Grossmont Hospital, where Jacobs had been transferred that morning to begin the long process of returning function to his left arm and leg. This time, the detectives brought a cassette tape recorder of their own.

"We'll try to make this as quick as possible, then," Manis said, pushing down the record button. He read the Reverse Garrity again. What he did next was throw Donovan Jacobs the world's longest lifeline. "Okay, Don, I'm going to give you some information about this incident that you may or may not have received in the past, okay? My hope is . . . that when I give you this information, perhaps you can assist us or it will jog your memory or make your recollection different, and if so [or] if not, tell me why." The message from Manis could not have been clearer: *We've got some problems with your previous statements, and this is your last chance to get it straight.*

Manis began with the issue of the U-turn. "We have, since talking to you, interviewed five of those people a second time, to clarify that particular point about the U-turn," he said, referring to passengers in Penn's truck. "Without any of them having any knowledge of your statement, we asked them to retrace the route they took in the truck. They all five gave us exactly the same account of the route they took home from

Balboa Park to the incident which resulted in your injuries. All five of those people interviewed do not mention any U-turn, they were never stopped, or parked at a curb anywhere."

"One other bit of information for you, before I ask you the question," Manis continued. "We measured that street [and] we have been able to obtain the wheelbase and the turning radius on that truck. That truck could not have made a U-turn in that street without running up on the curb or without stopping and backing up." Manis's tone was formal and businesslike, neither accusatory nor friendly. "My only question is, is there any chance that you were mistaken about this U-turn, or do you have any explanation for the difference in the witnesses' statements and in yours?"

"What I was going on, on my previous statements," Jacobs answered, "was what my mind, my memory was telling me as to what I saw before I stopped the truck. That's what I remember. If it's incorrect, and it could be possible, it may be because of my injuries or the incident itself. If they say that's what happened, I guess it could be possible I made a mistake, but it's not that I made an intentional mistake or changed my memory, but that's what my memory was telling me . . . I don't have any reason to lie about that, you know."

"Okay," Manis said somberly. He moved on to the subject of the initial contact with Penn. "Believe me, there are about somewhere in the neighborhood of forty to fifty witnesses to this incident," he informed Jacobs. "In almost every case, the witnesses indicate that you walked after him and that you catch up with him and that you take him by the arm, not violently, but you take him by the arm, and you turn him back around to face you . . . and that at that point is when Penn makes the statement about 'Do not touch me!'"

He continued on to Jacobs's assertion that the initial confrontation had been between Riggs and Penn. "There is not *one* witness available who says, as you do, that you walked around the truck on the other [passenger] side. When Penn turns and walks away from you, [witnesses] indicate that Riggs sees this, and he then comes around and joins you." Manis's questioning was so methodical and precise it sounded as though he were reading from a script so that there would be zero misunderstanding. "Is there any possibility, again, or any explanation for the variance in the witnesses' statements and yours that maybe we don't understand?"

Jacobs was emphatic that he never grabbed Penn and that the initial physical confrontation was between Riggs and Penn but conceded he was just going by what his memory was telling him. "It's like a videotape and I'm trying to replay it through my mind what happened."

"Don, is there anything you'd like to add to the tape now before we stop?" Manis asked after a few more questions.

"I'm just telling you what my memories are telling me," Jacobs said. "I don't want, you know, to change the truth or change what's happening. I just replay in my mind again what my memory tells me and that's what I'm telling you, what my memory tells me."

"Okay, Don," Manis said, reaching for the cassette tape recorder. "That'll be the end of this tape, and the time is 1857 hours."

HOMICIDE LIEUTENANT PAUL Ybarrondo joined the San Diego Police Department in 1959 and worked patrol for five years before being assigned to investigations as a burglary detective. He became a Homicide detective in 1967, leading Homicide Team III through much of the 1970s. In 1982, Ybarrondo was put in charge of a Homicide division that had grown to four teams, each consisting of three detectives supervised by a detective sergeant.

When Ybarrondo learned of the Reverse Garrity and inconsistencies in Jacobs's statements, he decided to do some asking around. Opinions about Jacobs were mixed among his fellow officers. "Based on the comments of others, he was cocky, aggressive, and hardheaded," Ybarrondo said. Along with a reputation for effective policing and high arrest numbers was one for quickly escalating situations if he felt someone was not being cooperative or honest with him. Several said they did not like backing him up on calls. One patrol officer referred to Jacobs as a "shit magnet," the name for cops who always seem to attract trouble on the street.

Ybarrondo asked his old Homicide boss Lieutenant Ed Stevens about Jacobs after learning Stevens had known him as a neighborhood kid and his son's best friend since childhood. Ybarrondo told him of Jacobs's reputation among many in the department. Stevens agreed with that assessment.

It soon got back to Jacobs that Ybarrondo had been checking on his reputation within the department. "He became very uncooperative with us and the investigation after stories about his prior statements and aggressive personality surfaced," the Homicide lieutenant later said. However, it did not change Ybarrondo and his investigators' overall assessment of the case against Sagon Penn. "As far as I am concerned, the murder of Riggs and the shooting of Jacobs and Pina-Ruiz met all the elements of murder and two counts of attempted murder."

But his appraisal of the initial interaction that triggered the violent confrontation was not so simple. "Probably, both Jacobs's and Penn's personalities and attitudes helped to escalate the situation," Ybarrondo concluded. "You have the case of a hardhead [Jacobs] and a possibly mentally unstable man [Penn] clashing."

11

YUSUF ABDULLAH HAD BEEN WORRIED ABOUT HIS GRAND-son for a while. The sweet, polite young man who called him "Daddy" had begun to have episodes of erratic behavior over the previous year and a half. He became increasingly irritated when corrected or when his suggestions were rejected. And then just as quickly he would be back to the cooperative, helpful young man most knew him to be.

There had been increasingly troubling incidents. When Sagon went to the downtown Federal Building to get a patent application for an instant-bean-pie-mix idea, he became suspicious that there might be listening devices in the air conditioning ducts throughout the building that would allow the government to steal his idea. "You can hear it when you go inside the building 'cause it affects the equilibrium in the ear," he said. So he fled the building. While working as a security guard at an industrial facility in Los Angeles, Penn demonstrated the same sort of paranoia. At one point, he reported to his boss that Russians were in the parking lot using binoculars to spy on the place. He was soon let go.

After bringing Sagon to the police station the night of the incident, Abdullah waited for several hours before speaking with Detectives Lindstrom and Murphy. He told them that one month before the confrontation with police on Brooklyn Avenue, there was an incident at Yusuf's restaurant that was particularly concerning. When Sagon came in to help with the dinner rush, he was in a frenetic state, speaking animatedly about how his Buddhist faith had changed his life and how it could do the same for Yusuf. His grandfather reminded Sagon that he was a Muslim and not interested in exploring a new faith. "I didn't want to hear it," Abdullah told Lindstrom and Murphy. "I wanted him to work." But Sagon would not stop, following his grandfather around the restaurant, insisting he come to the temple with him. "I tried to get him to leave. He wouldn't leave."

Yusuf became concerned that his grandson might be in some sort of psychological crisis. He called the police. Sagon was cooperative and respectful with the two officers and left the restaurant after they spoke with him. "After he left, one of the officers sort of told me, 'Looks like to me that he needs some mental treatment there,'" Abdullah told the detectives. When Yusuf got home later, Sagon was back to his polite, soft-spoken self.

Police investigators suspected almost immediately after taking him into custody the night of March 31 that Penn might have mental health issues. During the two hours Detectives Salvatierra and Lopez guarded Penn, the young man's rambling monologue was so disjointed and bizarre they felt compelled to mention it when transferring the suspect to Lindstrom and Murphy. When he was not addressing the incident, they said, he spun off on wild and incomprehensible tangents on a host of subjects including numerology, photosynthesis, genetic sequencing, Buddhism, and boxing. A breathless description of cheerleader pom-poms went on for over a minute.

Linda Kissel, the fiancée of the front-desk officer who was present when Penn surrendered, reported that Yusuf Abdullah said Sagon "was a good kid [but] had some mental condition and tonight just set him off." Lindstrom and Murphy spoke with Abdullah, just before interviewing Penn. "Is your grandson under any kind of doctor's care for anything at present?" Lindstrom asked.

"No, no," Abdullah said, "he's not under no kind of care."

"You know if Sagon ever had any problems with the police in the past?"

"I mean, seemed like to me they had him down there one time maybe a year ago or something like that," Abdullah began in his halting manner of speech. "They supposed to have 'em down there for something about a robbery or something or other like that. But they never did do nothing about it, you know, they just kept him down there a few days and they had to turn him loose."

"As far as you know, no charges were filed, or he didn't go to court or anything?" Lindstrom asked.

"Right. Yeah. He said something about they told him that if he'd sign a statement, they'd turn him loose. But he said he hadn't done nothing, so he wasn't going to sign. He wouldn't sign no kind of plea bargain or statement. He wouldn't sign nothing, so then they went on and turned him loose." The older man paused. "But he said they put him in a room down there, I guess they call it a rubber room, you know, where they put people, um, [when there is] mentally something wrong with them or something."

WHEN BOB MANIS arrived at police headquarters the night of the incident, he was informed that the suspect's father, Thomas Penn, was at the station. At about 11:00 p.m., he interviewed the elder Penn in a private room and asked when he had last seen his son. He said Sagon had visited him at his job as a security officer at a housing development a little over a week before. "We talked about a lot of things, but mainly he is involved in a new Buddhist religion, and he talked about that a lot. He's been involved with about ten different religions over the last few years." Manis asked if Sagon had ever been in any trouble. "No problems. He was a real good student, I don't think he's ever been involved in any gangs, and to my knowledge he doesn't use alcohol or drugs." Penn shook his head. "I can't imagine what would have caused him to do this." But Thomas Penn had grown worried about his son. "The last couple times he's been with me, his attitude has been a little weird. He told me a week ago Friday that his grandfather had taken him to Los Angeles to see a psychiatrist. He said they put some things on his head and took some tests. He wouldn't answer me when I asked him what the outcome was. He just laughed."

At the 12:30 a.m. critique following the incident, Bob Manis informed investigators from the district attorney's office of the possibility Penn had psychological issues. The DA investigators immediately placed a phone call to the office of psychiatrist Dr. Wait Griswold to request an evaluation be conducted at the county jail first thing in the morning.

At approximately 9:30 a.m. on the morning of April 1, an exhausted

Sagon Penn was led into a small interview room at the county jail. Seated at the table was a woman in her sixties. Abigail Dickson had a PhD in psychology with "violent, premeditated death" her stated "center of interest." She worked under Griswold, who had an agreement with the district attorney's office to conduct psychological evaluations of prisoners.

Dr. Dickson introduced herself to Penn. "Won't you be seated," she offered. Penn declined, saying his back hurt. "Why does your back hurt?" she asked.

"I was beaten with billy clubs," he said. "I didn't want to get hit in the face, so I turned, and my back was hit."

"Show me where it hurts," she said.

He turned and lifted his shirt. Dickson noted the bruises on each side of his back. He said his head also hurt, on top, toward the back. Penn sat in the chair across from her. She studied the young man. He was handsome but looked sad and very frightened. There were scratches on his face, a bruise on his neck. "How do you feel?" she asked.

He shrugged. "What difference does it make?" He said he had not slept.

"How do you feel emotionally?"

Penn said he was worried about what was going to happen to him. He hoped the officers would get better and that he felt bad one policeman was dead. "I wish they wouldn't have been so evil," he said, "like telling me, 'Shut up! Shut up!'"

"Who said that?" Dickson asked.

"The one with the blond hair. He was on top of me throwing punches. And the one with the black hair, he was hitting me with the billy club." He recalled the look in the blond officer's eyes. "It was frightening." Dickson scribbled her notes in the margins of the Patient's Record form. "They didn't even act human," Penn suddenly blurted out with what she described as a profound display of emotion. She wrote the quote on the page and circled it.

Dickson noted that throughout the interview, Penn's body would visibly tremble in waves. She had seen it in other newly arrested prisoners, almost always in incidents in which a life had been lost. "They don't know what is going to happen to them," she said. "It is like you see when an animal is cornered."

Dickson queried Penn about his personal and family history. He told her about his parents' divorce at age two, the stepfathers that came after, being shuffled around to different homes and families, what he believed to be the unfair and harsh treatment he often received there, and ultimately landing with his grandparents whom he loved very much. Dickson asked if there was any history of psychological problems in his family. Sagon said there was. In her report, Dickson wrote, "There does appear to be a history of neuropsychiatric disorder in that he reports that his mother was hospitalized in a 'psycho ward' and that at another time she had a 'nervous breakdown.'" He said his mother's hospitalization had lasted about a month.

Penn was cooperative throughout the personal-history portion of the evaluation, but it had been painfully slow going. He took forever to answer questions, some of which she had to repeat multiple times to get a response. When he did provide an answer, it was often so hard to hear or understand that Dickson had to ask him to repeat it several times. Other times he swayed his body as though keeping time to music.

Dickson went on to administer several standardized psychological tests used to evaluate intelligence, reveal hidden emotions and internal conflicts, and identify evidence of psychological disorders, particularly schizophrenia. The evaluation came to an abrupt stop when an attorney sent by the Public Defender's Office to represent Penn ordered the session be halted immediately.

Within hours of the termination of Abigail Dickson's jailhouse evaluation, San Diego District Attorney Ed Miller decided which of his prosecutors would handle what he knew would be one of the biggest cases to cross his desk during his long tenure in the position. The attorney assigned the case turned out to be the person in his office who wanted it the least.

DEPUTY DISTRICT ATTORNEY Michael Carpenter took advantage of a momentary lull in his caseload to head out to Yuma, Arizona, on the last weekend in March to watch the defending National League–champion San Diego Padres wrap up their spring training schedule before the start of the 1985 baseball season. It was not until Monday morning while returning to the office that he first heard about the incident on the car radio.

Carpenter was not, by temperament, a limelight kind of guy, and this already looked like it was going to attract major media attention. There were plenty of prosecutors in the department who would love the sort of visibility the case promised, so he hoped his superiors would let one of them have it. That way, he could go on doing what he loved most about being a prosecutor—quietly putting bad guys in prison. When Carpenter arrived at his office an hour later, he was informed he had been assigned case number CR-74094: *The People of the State of California v. Sagon Penn.*

Carpenter was a Midwesterner and became interested in the law through his early love of Perry Mason mystery books. After taking two military deferments to complete his education, Carpenter promptly went down to the local Marine Corps recruiting station and volunteered at the height of the Vietnam War. He went through officer-candidate school at Quantico, served as a lawyer for the Marine JAG Corps, did a tour with the First Marine Division in Da Nang, and was discharged at the rank of captain in 1972.

Like tens of thousands of young men and women, Carpenter's introduction to San Diego was a training stop on the way to one military conflict or another in the Pacific theater. And like so many, when he was shipped back home through San Diego, he stepped off the transport and never left. Carpenter rented a house in La Jolla, bought himself a Corvette, and joined the DA's office. After initially prosecuting misdemeanors and minor felonies ranging from small-time marijuana busts, shopliftings, and chicken-coop violations, his workmanlike approach soon had him trying serious felony cases. Carpenter put together an impressive string of guilty verdicts.

By the time he was assigned the Penn case, Carpenter was forty-two years old with over a dozen years of prosecution experience. His light complexion, blond hair, and mustache earned him a nickname he knew would be better off avoided during the Penn case: "Whitey." His sensibilities, skills, and temperament were uniquely suited for prosecution work and, by his own admission, not at all for what he saw as the creative "smoke screen" approach required of defense work.

Carpenter had an immense respect for the jury system and saw the role of the prosecutor as essential to the American institution of justice. "The public needs prosecutors," he told *Union* journalist George Flynn after his appointment to the case. "It is one way to impact the system in a very positive way, to see that justice is done and to make certain that the guilty go to prison. It is a large responsibility." He saw the trial process as a search for the truth, in which it was his job to present the facts to a jury and respect their verdicts.

Carpenter's respect for institutions and ideals about right and wrong left him with no uncertainty as to who was responsible for the incident on Brooklyn Avenue. "The uniform demands a certain amount of cooperation," he said. "It was noncooperation on the part of Penn that precipitated the event. All he had to do was take out his license."

For Carpenter, the observable actions of the participants alone told anyone all they needed to know about who was to blame. When the officer asked for his license, Penn refused. He was considered "detained" at the time but walked away. When restrained, he broke free. When they attempted to place him under arrest, he resisted. When ordered to turn over, Sagon Penn took the officer's gun and shot three people. As for allegations of excessive use of force, Carpenter agreed with a statement made by Paul Ybarrondo: "People who judge what is excessive and what is not have never had to roll around on the ground with a resisting, uncooperative subject who is failing to comply with a lawful order."

Mike Carpenter was made aware of Penn's apparent psychiatric problems but initially dismissed their relevance to the incident or his case until a man who said he worked at a local Safeway supermarket contacted the DA's office within days of the incident. The man said Sagon Penn used to work at another Safeway in the area, and he encouraged them to talk to the manager over there.

On April 12, DA investigator Oscar Tron met with Safeway store manager Ed Kramer. In his late twenties, Kramer had been Sagon Penn's direct supervisor for the fourteen months Penn bagged groceries, stocked shelves, and collected shopping carts. Kramer said Penn was a good employee most of the time but became increasingly insubordinate in his final months at the store. If he did not think something needed to be done, he simply would not do it. His behavior became inexplicably erratic, and he often had volatile reactions when corrected or reprimanded. He began to push his religion on other employees, first Jesus, then Buddhism, sometimes chanting on the job. Penn was counseled, but it had little effect.

In the week leading up to his termination, Penn left carts uncollected in the lot and stopped bagging groceries, even when asked. When Kramer observed Penn talking on the phone while on the clock and lingering with friends in the parking lot, he called him inside to speak with him about it. Penn became angry and aggressive as they walked to the office. "What's your problem?" he snapped as they ascended the stairs.

Kramer was concerned enough about the display of hostility to leave the office door open during the meeting. He told Penn he was suspended and to punch out on his timecard and then leave. "Why don't you punch me out?" Kramer reported Penn saying. "You're a big man, go ahead and punch me out." After he refused to clock out as ordered, Penn went into the locker room and began laughing. After that, he went downstairs and hung around in the market until Kramer ordered him to leave. On April 15, 1984, Penn was terminated. On two occasions soon after, Penn showed up at the store causing such disruption that Kramer called the police to have him removed. And then, just a week before the Brooklyn Avenue incident, Penn walked up to Kramer in the parking lot, shook his hand, and talked with him as though none of it had ever happened.

Tron spoke with other employees at the store who offered mixed reviews about Penn. "He seemed to get along with everyone," one said. But most felt that Penn was subject to erratic, abrupt mood swings. "Hot and cold," one termed it. "Sagon had two personalities," said a cashier. "One was nice. Other times he would do angry things for no reason." Another employee concurred: "He was schizophrenic almost."

When Oscar Tron's Safeway reports were forwarded to psychologist Abigail Dickson for consideration in her evaluation, she took note of manager Ed Kramer's comment that Penn had angrily snapped, "What's your problem?" when reprimanded. Another incident recounted by employee Karlene Hull also caught her attention. "Sagon did not like to be touched," Hull told Tron. "One day I was going up the steps behind Sagon and touched him and he turned around and said, 'Don't you ever touch me. I don't let people touch me unless I say they can.'"

Junius Holmes, Cedric Gregory, and Jacobs himself reported Penn saying, "Don't touch me!" or "Don't grab me!" Others including Sean Arkward recounted him also saying, "What's the problem?" when grabbed by Jacobs. In her report, Dickson noted: "Of possible further significance is the threat of 'Don't touch me!' and 'What's the problem?' noted in his verbalizations at his former employment which were repeated at the inception of the conflict with police officers." Her conclusion was that Penn's aversion to being touched may have resulted in an explosive reaction when grabbed by Donovan Jacobs, triggering the violent physical altercation that followed.

When Abigail Dickson's final evaluation landed on his desk on May 24, Carpenter skipped over the body of the report to the summary of findings. Factoring in her observations of Penn, his patient history, and her interpretation of her testing at the jail, Dickson drew several conclusions. "This individual is best placed in the category of a Passive Aggressive Personality Disorder with Authority Figure Conflict and Sociopathic Features with the possibility of an underlying Latent Schizophrenia." However, it was Dickson's assessment that "there is nothing to suggest that he was suffering from any major psychiatric disorder at the time." She also concluded Penn was "legally sane . . . at the time of the commission of the alleged offense."

The Safeway interviews, Dickson's conclusions, and the 1983 arrest convinced Mike Carpenter that Penn's issues with authority figures, refusals to comply with requests, and hyper-aversion to being touched explained what he saw as Penn's volatile and ultimately violent reaction to Donovan Jacobs's lawful requests. When he conferred with Paul Ybarrondo on the issue, he found the Homicide lieutenant had come to much the same conclusion. "Penn's actions and past hostility toward authority—problems with his boss at the Safeway store, etc.—were the main contributors to this case," Ybarrondo said. However, both men knew that barring a major slipup by the defense attorney, none of the psychiatric assessments, Safeway interviews, or incidents of emotional instability reported by family would ever be allowed inside the courtroom.

Nevertheless, after considering all the evidence and conferring with police investigators and his superiors all the way up to District Attorney Ed Miller, Carpenter had no reservations about charging Sagon Penn with first-degree murder and attempted murder. "We all felt there was sufficient evidence to prosecute and convict, and therefore our duty to file charges."

MIKE CARPENTER HAD had one last decision regarding charges on the case, and it would prove to strain his relationship with the San Diego Police Department.

Carpenter waited until the last possible moment before announcing that decision. "We thought that because [the shootings] grew out of a volatile situation between officers and the defendant that this is just not the type of case where we would seek the death penalty or life without parole," he told reporters.

The cops were quick to express their unhappiness. Bill Kolender referred to Penn as "a cop killer" and said he should be sent to the gas chamber if convicted. "He killed an officer, wounded another one permanently, and attempted to murder a woman civilian ride-along," he said. "I think that the decision for the death penalty should have been left up to the judge and the jury, not made in the district attorney's office." Assistant Chief Bob Burgreen assured reporters it was not just the brass that felt that way. "The men and women of the department are not happy with the decision." Patrol officers expressed their displeasure to reporters in more explicit terms. When asked, Kolender said he had no plans to complain directly to his longtime counterpart Ed Miller. "He's going to read the newspaper, isn't he?"

Carpenter defended his decision. "Sagon Penn is not a Robert Harris," he said, referring to the cold-blooded murderer who abducted two teenagers from a fast-food restaurant in 1978, shot them to death in a canyon, and then ate one victim's cheeseburger afterward. "He's never been convicted of anything before. He didn't lie in wait for a police officer."

Despite his confidence in the decision, Carpenter was stung by the scope of the criticism coming from all levels of the police department. In his dozen years prosecuting cases for the DA, he had never been second-guessed or pressured by the police. Then again, Mike Carpenter had never been involved in the trial of an alleged cop killer. But he wasn't alone; the defense attorney in the case had never been involved in one either.

ROBERT E. SLATTEN was a sole practitioner in his early forties with fifteen years of experience in defense work and as an attorney for the court of appeals. His reputation was as an experienced, proficient, and thorough attorney, well versed in procedure. If your case was straightforward and mostly routine, Robert Slatten could be counted on to provide a competent defense or cut a satisfactory plea deal. But Slatten had never distinguished himself in the courtroom, where he spoke in a monotone and often appeared stiff and lacking in charisma. He was considered just an average litigator, competent but not especially creative in his defense tactics.

Slatten came to the attention of the Penn family by way of attorney and accountant Rick LeVine, who happened to have an appointment the morning after the incident with his client, Sagon's grandmother Monie Barnes. "They arrested my baby," the woman cried. "You got to help my baby."

Slatten met with Sagon's father, Thomas Penn, who would soon become a constant presence in the media. He was impressed by Slatten and asked him to represent his son. By the morning of April 2, Robert Slatten became the attorney of record in the defense of Sagon Penn.

Throughout the summer, Slatten and his team set about building a defense for his client. They collected evidence, interviewed witnesses, and filed requests for discovery, including a Pitchess motion to access the police personnel files of Donovan Jacobs and Thomas Riggs in search of instances or complaints of excessive use of force or racial bias.

On October 28, 1985, a confident and well-prepared Robert Slatten strode into the San Diego Superior Courthouse on the opening day of the Sagon Penn murder trial. "I'm ready to go," he told reporters outside the courtroom. "I could have tried this case two months ago." He would never get the chance. The trial of Sagon Penn was about to come to a screeching halt due to the work of four men—a jailhouse guard, a triple murderer, a famous television news anchor, and a man they called "The Walkman."

12

O N APRIL 5, 1985, ADMINISTRATORS AT THE COUNTY JAIL decided the fourth-floor isolation unit was not secure enough to hold Sagon Penn. "Penn is to be rehoused in 5-A, maximum security," the transfer order read. The reasons given for the move were "adverse media coverage and publicity" and that he "poses a threat to jail staff." The order reiterated that "Penn is to be moved with chains and rovers at all times."

In the sparsely populated unit, Penn became familiar with one of the few Black guards at the downtown facility. The man was no fan of accused cop killers, but he believed that everyone deserved a fair trial and doubted the young man in his unit was going to get one. Penn needed a miracle worker on his side, and it wasn't Bob Slatten. You better get a new lawyer, the guard told him when no one else was around. He told Penn the name of the only attorney in town known for pulling off miracles. That's the guy you want.

PENN RECEIVED ANOTHER unsolicited attorney recommendation from an unlikely source. Ronaldo Ayala and his brother Hector were pending trial for shooting three men in the head, execution-style, in an attempted heroin theft. Both were career criminals, members of the Mexican Mafia prison gang, and extremely dangerous. The two brothers were housed separately. Unit 5-A got Ronaldo.

At first, Penn kept his distance, but he soon found out the best friend he had in the place was Ronaldo Ayala. Ayala took a liking to Penn. Other prisoners noticed and word got out: Fuck with Sagon Penn, and you're fucking with Ronaldo Ayala.

Like the guard in 5-A, Ayala thought Penn was going to get railroaded if he stuck with Slatten. He asked his own highly regarded defense attorney, Bob Boyce, to recommend the best lawyer in San Diego. Boyce did so without hesitation. Ayala passed the name along to Penn.

CHANNEL 10 ANCHORMAN Michael Tuck's "Perspective" commentaries about the Penn case were starting to get on some people's nerves. A fellow reporter at the station who held more conservative views threw a computer monitor across the newsroom after listening to one of Tuck's monologues. The chief of the San Diego Police Department was no fan either. "My problem with him is he plays on emotion more than facts," Bill Kolender told a *Los Angeles Times* reporter. "He makes personal opinions. He knows nothing about facts."

But there were some things Michael Tuck knew that the police did not. Tuck's first "Perspective" on the Penn incident had cautioned viewers not to automatically accept that the officers had engaged in excessive force, as accused by some. But within days, a former lieutenant at the San Diego Police Department began anonymously passing along to Tuck unflattering information about Donovan Jacobs. Tuck then learned that a day or two after the incident, Channel 10 reporter Larry Roberts had secured an off-the-record interview with Jacobs's childhood friend and fellow Southeast officer James Stevens at Stevens's home. According to Roberts, Stevens showed him hundreds of Polaroid instant photographs of alleged gang members taken by Stevens and Jacobs for their own personal file kept at Stevens's home. Roberts told colleagues that all the alleged gang members in the photographs he saw were Black or Hispanic. Tuck's view of Jacobs and statements coming from the San Diego Police Department soon darkened.

Right about the same time, another Channel 10 field reporter named Ted Dracos locked onto the Penn case and did not like what he saw. He told Tuck the cops were out to get Penn at any cost. He urged the popular anchorman to use his influence and connections to find the young man a top lawyer.

Like the jailhouse guard and triple murderer, Tuck knew who that attorney was. When he next crossed paths with Penn family members, he asked off-air how they felt about their current attorney. What he got back was expressions of uncertainty and lack of enthusiasm. They said that it was Thomas Penn who had asserted control over the situation and insisted they use Slatten. Tuck took a deep breath. "Well," he began, aware he was about to violate a sacred rule of journalistic ethics. "You didn't hear it from me, but the attorney you want is . . ."

While the anchorman joined the jailhouse guard and triple murderer in offering their suggestions to Sagon and the Penn family, the mysterious and charismatic figure known as "The Walkman" was cutting out the middleman and going straight to the attorney himself.

ON THE MORNING of August 5, 1985, Robert Slatten filed a short-notice request with the superior court to allow two men to meet with Sagon Penn inside the county jail. He stated the two "have lent substantial psychological and financial support to the defendant and his legal representation." Judge Barbara Tuttle Gamer granted the request in a directive that read in part, "The Sheriff of the County of San Diego is hereby ordered to admit to the San Diego County Jail Mr. Muhammad Ali and Mr. Abuwi Mahdi for the purpose of visiting with defendant, Sagon Penn."

Ali had been invited by leading members of Yusuf Abdullah's mosque, Masjid Muhammed No. 8, to attend two fundraisers for Penn's defense. He had fought his last professional fight in 1981 but remained one of the most recognizable people in the world. There had been only periodic developments for the media to report in the months following the May preliminary hearing, but news of the Ali visit pushed the Penn case back onto page one of local newspapers, and onto the national stage.

Before attending an event titled "Human Rights, from South Africa to Southeast San Diego" at the Radisson Hotel that evening, "The Champ" stopped by the La Jolla home of newspaper publisher and former mayoral candidate Si Casady for an intimate afternoon fundraising event. Ali did not comment on the fundraiser, but he did play "Chopsticks" on the piano, joke around with children, eat some ice cream, and admire the motorhome parked in Casady's driveway.

Seated in an upholstered chair at the event was a Black man in his early forties with dreadlocks neatly pulled back from a receding hairline, an expressive face, and eyes that searched the room around him, missing nothing. Even as he sat in a white linen jacket nibbling on appetizers, Edward Lawson radiated a restless sort of energy. When he leaned forward and spoke to reporters, it was with the smoldering intensity and razor-sharp intellect that others found riveting.

Unlike Ali, Lawson had a lot to say about the Sagon Penn situation. "One, I am participating in and facilitating fundraising," he said with crisp and precise enunciation. "Two, I am facilitating public relations in terms of seeing that a story that has been told over and over again in Black America is taken to the national audience." The third point, which Ed Lawson was not yet prepared to tell reporters, was his intention to find Sagon Penn a new attorney.

Ed Lawson was an enigma, and he liked it that way. "Who is Lawson exactly?" a *Los Angeles Times* reporter wrote. "That is a tough one. He is apparently almost as pure as he portrays himself, a vegetarian who won't take so much as an aspirin, and a man who says he has neither a significant other nor personal life. He is mysterious, even secretive. He doesn't reveal his age or his address or exactly how he makes a living." In a rare autobiographical statement, Lawson referred to himself as "a police magnet." As far as the cops were concerned, he said, "I'm an unidentified flying object."

Lawson's preferred mode of transportation was by foot. "He liked to walk whenever possible," *Hastings Constitutional Law Quarterly* succinctly noted, "especially in white neighborhoods late at night." He also liked to walk through vacant industrial parks, closed business districts, or long stretches of empty roadways. Sometimes he danced along rather than walked. He was usually dressed in tennis shoes, slacks, and a collared shirt, with his long dreadlocks bouncing up and down on the shoulders of his sports coat as he strode. The press dubbed him "The Walkman."

During an eighteen-month period from 1975 to early 1977, he was stopped and detained fifteen times by San Diego Police officers, twice resulting in arrest for failure to produce identification.

The officers' stated reasons why Lawson met the state vagrancy statute's "reasonable cause" to initiate a "stop and identify" contact with him usually included the color of his skin. One stopped Lawson because he found it "exceptional for a Black person to be crossing the neighborhood at that time of the evening." Another said, "He was walking in an area uncommon for Blacks to be walking at that hour."

Ed Lawson challenged the constitutionality of the vagrancy statute through the California court system, preparing and arguing the cases himself. San Diego law enforcement agencies challenged his string of court victories all the way to the United States Supreme Court in a case labeled *Kolender v. Lawson*. On May 2, 1983, the court ruled in Lawson's favor, declaring that major "stop and identify" elements of California's long-standing vagrancy law violated an individual's Fourth Amendment protection from unreasonable search and seizure.

"Sagon Penn was stopped and asked for identification, and the end result was tragedy," Lawson told reporters at the Si Casady fundraiser. "Had the San Diego Police abided by the Supreme Court ruling in my case, Thomas Riggs would be alive today."

Lawson was intent on getting Penn a new attorney. He remained plugged in to the San Diego legal community and began by informing the Penn family of the name of the attorney they needed if Sagon was ever going to walk the streets of San Diego a free man again. He also began campaigning the attorney himself, regularly dropping by the law office throughout the summer to persuade the man to take the case. "I can't just 'take' a case from another lawyer," the attorney told him. "Penn has to ask the judge for permission to fire his current attorney and hire me."

Ed Lawson turned his efforts back to members of the Penn family to get Sagon to request the new attorney. Lawson could be a very persuasive man, but they were running out of time. On the first day of the trial, it was still Robert Slatten seated beside Sagon Penn at the defense table as jury selection commenced. Judge Earl J. Maas began screening jurors, dismissing the first five for a variety of reasons before recessing for the day. At 9:10 a.m. the following morning, a court clerk located

Judge Maas in chambers and handed him an envelope. Inside was a two-page handwritten letter dated the previous day. The cursive writing was gracefully loopy with a confident slant. Maas was stunned by the content of the note.

> *Dear Judge Moss [sic]*
>
> *I am the mother of Sagon Penn. For several months Sagon has made efforts to get rid of Mr. Slatten for his attorney because he does not have full confidence in him.*
>
> *This morning [the previous day] Sagon tried to hand a letter to the bailiff, to be handed to you stating that he did not want Mr. Slatten for his lawyer. I found out that Mr. Slatten got ahold of this letter and called in my former husband Thomas Penn to the cell where Sagon was. Tremendous pressure was put on Sagon not to do this. I believe Mr. Slatten was with Thomas when this happened but I don't know for sure.*
>
> *Sagon gave the letter to Thomas Penn and said quote: "I don't care what happens to me." I have known for several months that Sagon did not want Mr. Slatten for his lawyer. Sagon did not hire Mr. Slatten. This was done by Thomas Penn.*
>
> *Thomas Penn did not raise Sagon. I have raised him for twenty years. I know Sagon asked Mr. Slatten to contact Mr. Silverman for him and Mr. Slatten said Mr. Silverman did not do criminal work.*
>
> *I love my son and I just want the very best for him. I request that you find out from Sagon why he doesn't want Mr. Slatten whereas everybody is pressuring him. And would like to request that Mr. Silverman be appointed. My understanding is Mr. Silverman is willing to do this if you say it's all right.*
>
> > *Respectfully*
> > *Yours*
> > *Peggy Barnes*

The judge set the letter down and summoned a bailiff into chambers. Somebody find Milt Silverman and get him down here . . . now.

———————

MILTON SILVERMAN JR. was born in Denver, Colorado, in 1944, the son of a brilliant naval officer and a strikingly beautiful yet chronically ill mother. During Silverman's childhood, his father was usually away at sea, while his mother was hospitalized so frequently that he scarcely knew the woman. Like Penn, Silverman was raised by a loving grandparent. He credited his grandmother Hilma with saving his childhood from one of loneliness and sorrow. When he was ten years old, his mother died, and Milt was taken away from Hilma to the Clairemont area of San Diego to live with his father. He never saw his grandmother again.

Milt attended a private military school followed by public high school. He was scrawny, had few friends, ran track, played drums in the school band, and was an average student with poor study habits. With an emotionally distant father and stepmother who disliked him from the start, he escaped into the world of mystery books, quickly consuming the entire Sherlock Holmes and Hardy Boys catalogs. In the last quarter of his senior year, he discovered the Greek philosophers and a switch clicked on in his brain. He found it was the world of ideas, not science, that most appealed to his intellect. He dove into the subject, reading everything he could find by the great thinkers. From that point on, what he learned from legendary detectives and philosophers would inform his approach to most everything in life.

He studied political science and philosophy at San Diego State University and attended law school at UCLA. Along the way, he was influenced by several brilliant, free-thinking fellow students and professors. Admitted to the California State Bar in January 1970, Silverman entered the legal profession with long hair, a distrust of authority, an intolerance of injustice of all kinds, and a determination to stop it whenever he could.

Accepting a prestigious Reginald Heber Smith fellowship dedicated to legal reform and advocacy of impoverished and underserved communities, he was given a one-year assignment to rural, poor Pueblo County, Colorado. He defied all odds by successfully suing the Pueblo public school system over misuse of federal funds intended for a free-lunch program for poor children. The ruling forced the school system to reinstate the program.

In 1972, he was back in San Diego handling Navy court-martial cases and defending draft dodgers. He was so broke he slept on the floor of his office and showered in the locker room at San Diego State. He won his first murder case defending a Black Marine charged with murder and attempted murder of two military police officers in Vietnam. Shortly thereafter, he was retained by the NAACP to assist in the defense of twenty-three Black sailors charged with rioting against white sailors aboard the aircraft carrier *Kitty Hawk*. Silverman coordinated an undercover sting operation using a private investigator who moved into the apartment building of the key prosecution witness, befriended the man, and recorded him admitting he lied in the *Kitty Hawk* trials out of racial hatred. Silverman received the NAACP Freedom Award for his work on the case.

The case that brought Silverman his first widespread attention came in 1974. Freda Adkins attempted to hire a hit man to kill her husband when she found out he had been molesting their teenage daughter. The hit man turned out to be an undercover San Diego Police officer, and Freda was caught red-handed after making a down payment on the murder.

Silverman uncovered an astonishing conspiracy on the part of Adkins's financial adviser to coerce the woman into having her husband killed and then cheat her out of the life insurance money. At the trial, Silverman told the jury that Freda Adkins never made the conscious decision to kill her husband; it was made for her through posthypnotic suggestion by the financial adviser, who routinely hypnotized Freda and her daughter. His defense case was essentially, Yes, my client committed the crime, but she is not guilty. The jury agreed with Silverman, and Freda Adkins was free to go.

Milt Silverman was of medium height and build, with the easy stride of a former athlete who kept himself in shape as much as his heavy legal caseload would allow. His dark-brown hair was slightly thinning above a broad forehead and was offset by a neatly trimmed sandy-brown mustache. He bore a passing resemblance in look and swagger to high-profile entrepreneur and sportsman Ted Turner. His subtly expressive mouth could change the entire tone of his demeanor with an almost imperceptive curl of his thin upper lip. His most compelling feature was pale blue eyes that radiated attentiveness and a sharp intellect.

He carried himself with confidence both in and out of the court-room. While not short on ego, his sly sense of humor, willingness to make fun of himself, and general likability prevented his confidence from being interpreted as arrogance. In the courthouse, he wore con-servative, well-tailored suits, with cufflinks, a tiepin, and a pocket hand-kerchief. When he unbuttoned his suitcoat, one could catch a glimpse of the brightly colored suspenders he preferred over belts.

Reporters and fellow attorneys variously termed his approach to law as tenacious, flamboyant, creative, clever, and crafty, but most recognized that he won trials by being better at the fundamentals of trial law. His case preparation and work ethic were legendary. If a case involved technical or complex subjects, he would immerse himself until he became fluent in the matter. It was not uncommon for Silverman to confound an expert witness with his knowledge of terminology and complex concepts.

In Silverman's view, law schools taught too much about law and not enough about investigation. "They study Oliver Wendell Holmes when they should be studying Sherlock Holmes," he said. He became a su-perb crime scene investigator with a sharp eye for evidence the cops missed. He kept a pair of mechanic's overalls, gloves, and a flashlight in the trunk of his car for climbing around crawl spaces and attics, under cars, and through thick brush.

After the Freda Adkins case, a string of startling courtroom vic-tories brought Silverman a measure of local celebrity. In 1977, young mother and PhD candidate Susan Driscoll killed her husband and two small children with a .357 Magnum while they slept. When Silverman scoured the crime scene after police were through, he discovered a sui-cide note in an outside trash can and three live .357-caliber rounds next to an open Bible. Silverman used the additional evidence and his in-terpretation of the Bible passage to convince the jury his client was not guilty by reason of insanity.

In 1979, college student Clifford Lee Stone walked up an isolated canyon with an older female student, where he was accused of raping her and bashing her head in with a rock. Silverman successfully argued it was the woman who had raped his homosexual client, who had only been defending himself when he hit her with the rock. Twice.

In 1982, a prominent local attorney named Robert Neville shot his wife ten times with an assault rifle. Silverman corroborated a key detail in his client's story by returning to the crime scene and digging three .223-caliber slugs out of a floorboard joist that police had overlooked. Tried for first-degree murder, Neville was instead convicted only of manslaughter and sentenced to eight years. Silverman had a simple explanation for his success. "The best trial lawyers are those who are comfortable with themselves, honest, straightforward, and hardworking," he said. "God made me to be a trial lawyer."

ON THE MORNING of Tuesday, October 29, Milt Silverman was conducting a deposition at a downtown law office not far from the superior court building when he received word that Judge Earl Maas was requesting his immediate presence in the courtroom.

With coverage of the story heating up again as the trial approached, every seat in the courtroom was filled by members of the media, supporters of the victims and the accused, and the public, even for the usually uneventful jury-selection process. Notified of a delay in the start of the morning session, reporters from all the local outlets chatted with journalists from the *San Jose Mercury News* and *The New York Times* while waiting in the corridor outside the courtroom. Sitting around doing nothing was a big part of covering any trial, so they had no reason to think anything unusual might be going on. Thomas Penn, Yusuf Abdullah, and other family members and supporters sat on benches, many wearing T-shirts with JUSTICE ON TRIAL or FREE SAGON PENN written above a large photo of Sagon. Outnumbered by the Penn supporters, Coleen Riggs and one of Tom's sisters stood down the hallway speaking quietly to each other. Inside, Bob Slatten, Mike Carpenter, and their teams used the time to prepare for the second day of jury selection, unaware of the reason for the delay.

A local reporter was the first to spot the lone figure striding purposefully down the long corridor. Conversations tapered off and all eyes became riveted on the man as he approached. "You got to be fucking kidding me," one of them said. When Milt Silverman reached the courtroom door, those gathered in front silently stepped aside. "It was like the Red Sea parting," one remembered. Silverman swung the door open and disappeared as a bailiff closed it behind him. So dumbfounded was the press corps outside the courtroom, no one had thought to ask Silverman the most obvious question: What the hell was he doing there?

Mike Carpenter knew what it meant the moment he saw Silverman walking down the aisle. He let out a long breath and glanced at his second chair, Bob Phillips. Phillips shook his head. Bob Slatten knew what it meant too: he was about to be kicked off the biggest trial in San Diego history.

Just after 10:00 a.m., Slatten, Silverman, and Sagon Penn convened in Maas's chambers. The judge read the letter from Peggy Barnes and asked Penn if it was true that he wanted to dismiss his current attorney, Robert Slatten, and replace him with Milton Silverman. "Yes, sir," Penn answered. He asked Silverman if he was willing to act as Penn's attorney. Silverman acknowledged he would.

Maas reconvened the open court at 11:17 a.m. With the spectator gallery filled, he summoned Mike Carpenter to the bench and handed him the Peggy Barnes letter. Carpenter read the letter and handed it back, shaking his head. "Out of an abundance of caution, I am inclined to grant the motion," Maas announced to the courtroom.

Carpenter could barely disguise his dismay at the development. "If you can change attorneys now after the trial has started, what's to prevent you to change attorneys and get a new trial during jury deliberations?" he told Maas.

"Do you want to try this over again if it's reversed on appeal?" Maas shot back.

"I think it would be upheld," Carpenter countered.

"I think it would not," said the judge.

After granting the change, Maas cleared up one last technicality by saying Silverman would have to be assigned to the case by the Office of the Public Defender. The attorney who had recently won a $32 million civil suit against the Hare Krishnas would receive sixty dollars an hour, the going rate for a public defender. Maas gave Silverman two and a half months to prepare and set the start date of the new trial for January 13. He then promptly announced he would be stepping down from the case due to his impending retirement.

Standing at the defense table, Slatten told the judge he would turn over all materials and work product to Silverman as soon as possible and cooperate with the new attorney in any way he could. He then turned and shook Milt Silverman's hand and wished him luck. "Thanks very much," Silverman said. "You have been a real gentleman."

When Maas recessed the court, Mike Carpenter quickly gathered up his papers and left wearing a sarcastic smile and shaking his head in amazement. He and Bob Phillips passed Silverman in an aisleway without so much as an acknowledgment. They did the same to the swarm of reporters in the hallway desperate for some sort of comment.

Bob Slatten spoke briefly with the reporters. "We had a good, bold, viable defense," he said. "I am really disappointed I will not get the opportunity to present it."

"I was just helping him [Sagon] out," Peggy Barnes said of her letter to the judge. "He is the one in jail. He can choose anyone he wants."

Thomas Penn told reporters he suspected something had been going on behind the scenes. "There's been outside influences at work," he commented cryptically. Pausing in an empty corridor to speak with *Channel 10 News* field reporter Bob Donley, Penn accused his fellow Channel 10 reporters Michael Tuck and Ted Dracos of "exercising improper influence on the case."

The tanned and handsome Donley was waiting for Milt Silverman when he exited the courtroom, but Silverman walked past him without a word. "What about the comments that are being alleged that Channel 10 interfered with the selection of the attorney?" Donley asked, catching up to the new defense attorney while his cameraman filmed the interaction.

Silverman looked the man directly in the eye as he continued to walk down the hallway. "I don't have any comment," he said. Donley asked again. "Do you know what that means?" Silverman responded. "It means that I have no comment."

Donley, who occupied the opposite side of the ideological spectrum as Michael Tuck, had no intention of sparing the Channel 10 anchor from a courthouse scandal. "Did you meet with Mike Tuck on this?" he asked, tilting the microphone toward Silverman.

This time Silverman stopped to face the reporter. "I have no comment," he said.

"Did you discuss with him any of this?" Donley said, now in a hallway standoff with the attorney.

Silverman shoved his hands deep inside the pockets of his crisp blue suit and fixed Donley with a piercing stare. "Do you understand the English language?"

"What about Ted Dracos, did you discuss any of this with him?" Donley pressed.

Silverman paused, leaned back, and gave Donley a bemused look. "I have no comment."

ON DECEMBER 29, *San Diego Union* writer George Flynn profiled the two attorneys in the trial in an article titled "Penn Case Pits Pair of Worthy Foes—Opposing Lawyers Are an Ex-Marine, a Legal Magician." Flynn went on to handicap the matchup of Milt Silverman and Michael Carpenter as though it were an upcoming heavyweight boxing title bout: "Deputy District Attorney Michael Carpenter is a trial warrior combining Marine Corps roots with the equally disciplined intensity of a triathlete and thirteen years of prosecution experience." By contrast, Flynn wrote, "Silverman's sometimes flamboyant, seemingly cavalier courtroom style belies a no-nonsense core: exhaustive preparation, a keen eye for hidden facts, and the ability to ram home those points to jurors."

Flynn let his readers know that although Milt Silverman had stolen the spotlight with his eleventh-hour entrance into the case, Michael Carpenter was not to be underestimated. He stopped short of laying odds on the outcome of the trial, but the consensus around the courthouse was close to unanimous: despite his history of longshot victories in the courtroom, Milt Silverman didn't stand much of a chance of winning this one.

PART 3

13

I N EARLY APRIL 1985, DEFENSE INVESTIGATOR BOB MCDANIEL sat in the law offices of Robert Slatten reading through a stack of over forty eyewitness statements taken the evening of the Sagon Penn incident less than a week before. McDaniel was a fifty-one-year-old former San Diego Police lieutenant who retired after twenty years to launch an independent private investigation firm. He was short and solid in stature with thick white hair, a broad forehead, and a handsomely lined face from spending most of his time outdoors. Like most longtime police detectives, he was even-tempered, methodical, and careful not to jump to conclusions. But he was having a hard time believing there was anything that could justify taking a police officer's gun and using it to shoot two cops and an innocent woman.

McDaniel also knew his way around an eyewitness statement. He had written hundreds of reports himself and reviewed even more in his years leading criminal investigations. By the time he had come to the end of those related to the Penn case, Bob McDaniel had the feeling something was very wrong.

SEVEN MONTHS LATER, Milt Silverman read through those same eyewitness-statement reports for the first time. "Fuuuuuck me!" he said, tossing the last of the reports onto a stack over an inch thick. While there were descriptions of two cops striking baton blows at his client and other details favorable to the defense, the overall impression was that

Penn had failed to comply with requests for his license, tried to walk away, and then engaged in a full-blown fight with the officers, hitting them at least as much as they were hitting him. One said Penn threw his arm out when grabbed, striking Riggs. Another termed the confrontation "quite fierce," and two others were quoted as referring to it as "a real knockdown, drag-out type of fight." There were reports of Penn throwing a "punch" or "kicks." One witness allegedly said that both officers were on the ground at the same time after being hit by Penn.

Silverman was seated at the large desk in his wood-paneled corner office in the Quartermass-Wilde House, a stately Victorian mansion in the Golden Hill area east of downtown he bought and had restored. He leaned back in his leather chair, thinking through the implications the reports would have on his case. He was wary of police reports of any kind, and even more so those in which victims included police officers. But the words and reports of police always carried a lot of weight with a jury. They were considered honest and accurate until proven otherwise, which was never easy for a defense attorney.

Silverman grabbed his car keys and located his law clerk, Carl Lewis. "Come on, we're going out to Encanto," he said. Only recently hired, the thirty-three-year-old Lewis, in his last year of law school, learned quickly that Milt Silverman did not like to be kept waiting. Fifteen minutes later they were at the 6500 block of Brooklyn Avenue, stopping residents on the street, poking their heads inside the churches, and knocking on doors. After interviewing a dozen eyewitnesses, they began to see the disparity between the police reports and their current version of events. When he read through Bob McDaniel's reports of his own earlier eyewitness interviews and spoke with the investigator, it only strengthened his belief that the reports did not accurately reflect the statements made to detectives.

Carl Lewis took the analysis a step further by crafting a standard list of questions to ask every eyewitness, focusing on the most critical moments within the incident. The questions included "Who was the first to start the fight?" "Did you see when the first shot was fired?" and "When Sagon drove away, did he stop or slow down?" Question twenty-one on the list addressed a subject that had not appeared on any police eyewitness-statement reports but had been brought up by a few of the eyewitness: "Did you hear the police say, 'nigger,' 'Black bastard,' 'motherfucker,' 'boy,' or any such language?" The answers allowed them to tabulate and compare the witness accounts for detail and consistency.

THE TRIP TO Brooklyn Avenue with Carl Lewis was not the first for Silverman since taking the case. Investigating a crime scene was always at the top of his list after taking a case, even if it was already seven months old. Silverman knew just the man he wanted there with him.

Jim Gripp's introduction to the Penn case came in a phone call from Bob Slatten's office on the morning of April 2, 1985. Slatten wanted to know if Gripp could go to the county jail with a camera as soon as possible and document Penn's injuries. The young man Gripp met in a small interview room that afternoon was polite, quiet, and cooperative. While handcuffed, Penn pulled down his prison jumpsuit and stood in his underwear while Gripp photographed each injury, including a raised abrasion on his scalp the size of a quarter, which had previously been overlooked. During the process, the two engaged in brief conversation. Penn said he had an acting tryout that coming weekend. "Do you think I'll be able to make it?" he asked, as though the whole thing was just a misunderstanding that would get all straightened out in a matter of days. "My god," thought Gripp, "this kid has no idea how much deep shit he's in right now."

Gripp's main business was as a "forensic artist," revolutionizing the field of "litigation graphics" with his eye-popping courtroom displays, illustrations, photographs, video presentations, and diagrams. Gripp had a youthful appearance and energy, creative mind, and quick sense of humor. By the time he was on the Penn case, he had over eleven years of experience working civil and criminal cases and was operating under his company name, Legal Arts.

The day after Silverman took over the case, Gripp met him at 6564 Brooklyn Avenue. "Here, hold this," Silverman said, taking the half-smoked cigar out from between his teeth. "And don't drop it; it's a Cuban." Gripp winced and held the fuming, spit-soaked cigar at arm's length as Silverman, wearing the mechanic's coveralls he kept in the trunk of his Toyota Supra, lowered himself down and lay on his back in the dirt. "Here?" he asked.

Gripp looked down at the curious spectacle of the defense attorney lying in the dirt but was not surprised; he had worked with Silverman before. He directed Silverman to change his position, pointing out the spot where the evidence and eyewitness accounts indicated Penn and Jacobs had struggled while on the ground. Silverman scooted around in the dirt until Gripp had him in Penn's position perpendicular to his car, which was standing in for Riggs's. Silverman stood up, took his cigar back, and surveyed the spot in relation to the car.

They roamed the crime scene, tracing the route of the altercation while playing the roles of Penn, Jacobs, and Riggs in reenactments, backing down the driveway, one with his hands held up defensively and the other slashing an imaginary baton. Neighborhood residents wandered over to watch, some offering their own information. After a few hours, Silverman seemed satisfied, but Gripp knew it would not be the last time he would find himself crawling around in the dirt, simulating Riggs's fall over the retaining wall, or jumping up to fire an imaginary gun at the driver's side window of the car.

Gripp already knew the crime scene inside and out; he had created more-accurate measurements, diagrams, and timelines than the police investigators had. But, on January 7, 1986, he suggested the added step of a professional land survey of the driveway and surrounding area. He hired an experienced surveyor named Al Arnson, who plotted the location of every structure and object of permanence, or "monuments," including retaining walls, fire hydrants, telephone poles, bushes, and trees. His survey of the land itself determined elevations, distances, boundaries, grades, and other features. Combined with Gripp's own diagrams of evidence locations, there was little the defense did not know about the crime scene as it existed on March 31, 1985.

THE HISTORIC QUARTERMASS-WILDE House was perched on a raised corner lot, with tall stained-glass windows, a soaring turret, and a grand staircase that curved majestically to the second floor. In addition to Milt Silverman's office, it also housed a modern crime lab located in the basement operated by the premier criminalist in the city of San Diego. In his early forties with hair worn slightly long, Richard Whalley had a bright and energetic personality and intensely curious nature. He worked for the San Diego Police Department for three years before moving into the private sector and had been in the thick of some of San Diego's most notorious criminal cases. He had become an indispensable team member for Milt Silverman on his own cases.

Whalley was focused on the shooting itself. He pored over the autopsy report, medical records, photos of wounds, and ballistics tests. He inspected evidence, including the gun and clothing worn by all three victims. He spent hours at the crime scene with copies of Jim Gripp's detailed diagrams and measurements. At the SDPD vehicle yard, he sketched, measured, and photographed the shattered side window and interior of Riggs's vehicle, determining timing, angles, distance, and trajectories he hoped would tell the real story of the shooting of three people.

Bob McDaniel and Milt Silverman had not worked together before and were initially wary of doing so on the Penn case. But during the process of transitioning the case, each was impressed with the other's thoroughness, candor, and investigative skills. The unexpected discovery of a mutual interest in Christianity was the real breakthrough in the relationship. When Silverman asked the former police lieutenant to stay on as defense investigator, he had a team whose members had been working on the case for seven months. Silverman now had two and a half months until the trial to catch up.

SILVERMAN BEGAN AN exhaustive campaign of motions and pretrial hearings over access and right to use evidence and information, especially concerning Donovan Jacobs's history at the SDPD. In an earlier meeting, Bob McDaniel asked Silverman if he also wanted to look into the background of Tom Riggs. "Bob," Silverman said to his investigator, "there's only room for one villain in this trial."

In hearings beginning December 18, 1985, before Judge Kenneth Johns, Silverman made it clear who he felt that villain was. He pursued a tip linking Jacobs to white supremacy groups and his participation in paramilitary training exercises, as well as an accusation that Jacobs walked into the Northern substation wearing a T-shirt with an emblem on the breast of a Nazi eagle clutching a swastika. All the accusations had come from the same former SDPD lieutenant who had been providing information to Michael Tuck. Silverman refused to name him in the requests for discovery, citing the danger of possible attempts to silence him before the trial. It was clear that he felt the biggest threat to his source was members of the San Diego Police Department.

After numerous witnesses and days of arguments, Judge Johns made no attempt to hide his irritation. "I can't see anything but a cloud of smoke," he said, shutting down Silverman's quest. "I'm tired of hearing all the damn things that have nothing to do with this case." Silverman's attempts to access Jacobs's protected employment files through a request called a Pitchess motion yielded an in-camera private viewing of the files by a judge, who concluded that it contained nothing of relevance to the trial or Jacobs's racial views or complaints of excessive use of force. Silverman would continue to fight for access to the files throughout the trial.

As the trial approached, the phone threats and hate mail arriving at the Quartermass-Wilde office increased. Many came with a threat: "A number of us are watching you and black Penn . . . There are long sharp blades and shotguns with your names on them . . ." Someone else went to great effort to modify a handbill announcing a Penn support rally to read RALLY TO HANG SAGON PENN, with a racist slur scrawled below the photo of a younger Sagon. Silverman was not surprised to receive that sort of material from the public, but he was not prepared for what a judge not involved in the case said to him in the superior court building during pretrial hearings: "If it were up to me, your client would be in a little green room sucking gas out of the end of a pipe." The little green room was the gas chamber at San Quentin.

With emotions running high, Silverman was determined not to have the trial become a referendum on the entire police department and its popular chief and disavowed attempts by some to cast Penn as a symbol of their social cause. "Hey, I cut my distance from that stuff," he said emphatically when asked about endorsements from controversial politicians and lightning rod activists such as Congresswoman Maxine Waters, Vernon Bellecourt of the American Indian Movement, and Angela Davis. "They are doing it without my blessing or Sagon Penn's blessing." He told Penn's friends and family members to tone down displays of support that carried political overtones, such as the FREE SAGON PENN T-shirts many wore in the courtroom stretched over their dress shirts and ties. He told Thomas Penn never to wear anything like that near the courthouse again.

MONTHS EARLIER, PSYCHOLOGIST Oscar Kaplan, PhD, had conducted a public-opinion survey of three hundred jury-eligible San Diegans to help Slatten determine whether he should request a change of venue. Silverman had no interest in such a change but was eager to hear what the people of San Diego thought about the case. After reviewing the findings, Silverman had a question for Kaplan: What were his chances of winning? "Close to none," Kaplan said flatly. However, the psychologist said he had developed a profile of the ideal juror for the defense. His findings showed the most important determining factor was not race but age. When they were finished reviewing the demographic breakdowns, Silverman had scribbled a few simple conclusions in the margins of the Kaplan report:

> *Avoid 55 years and above*
> *Best group 18–24*
> *Women, better*
> *More educated, better off—College or better is best*
> *Ethnics good*
> *Whites bad*

At the top of one of the pages, Silverman summarized even more succinctly:

> *Best: Young, Educated, Ethnics*
> *Worst: Old, Stupid, Whites*

Silverman's approach to jury selection, or voir dire, was a rigorous combination of the scientific and unorthodox. Besides Kaplan, Javad Emami, who held a PhD in clinical psychology, helped design his list of juror questions and sat beside Silverman evaluating jurors throughout the selection process.

Graphological investigator Linda Larson analyzed jurors' handwriting to identify personality traits and offered recommendations: "Easily forgives." "Does not like to fight." "A good listener." "Get to the point quickly." "Would be better off without him."

The final member of Milt Silverman's voir dire team was also the most important person in his life. While having lunch one afternoon years before at a downtown eatery frequented by attorneys and courthouse staff, Milt struck up a pleasant conversation with the hostess. Beautiful, elegant, and curvy, she had a wide smile revealing what seemed to be an impossible number of teeth. "I want to ask you out," Milt said to her. The bartender polishing glasses nearby overheard him, threw up his hands, and hollered, "Doesn't everyone!"

Maria Garcia was a hardworking single mother of two young children who had immigrated from Mexico several years earlier. Milt fell hard for her, and they were married a few years later. She attended all of Milt's trials, and he came to depend on her intuition in evaluating prospective jurors. Maria sat in the spectator gallery behind her husband, signaling or whispering her thoughts on each jury candidate after questioning.

Jury selection for the murder trial of Sagon Penn began on February 24, 1986, presided over by Judge Ben W. Hamrick. Hamrick was a sixty-one-year-old former World War II tail gunner with sweeping silver hair, a calm disposition, and the sort of noble facial features found on paper currency. His former law partner called Hamrick "square and honest. He can handle this one and anything else that comes along." Hamrick also knew when to put his foot down. "He can be cantankerous if he thinks he's being pushed," another attorney offered.

Roughly forty-five prospective jurors who passed the questionnaire screening were then evaluated by Hamrick in open court. At times, questioning revealed an obviously unqualified prospective juror who had somehow squeaked through the initial screening process. "What concerns me is the grandfather is a Black Muslim," one offered. "Minorities use their color or race for excuses," another said. Another flew for the Nazi Luftwaffe in World War II. "We may have seen each other over the skies of Europe," Hamrick joked in reference to his days aboard B-17 bombers. "I may have even shot at you."

Silverman's method of voir dire questioning was deeply rooted in behavioral psychology akin to the advanced qualitative market research conducted by major consumer products companies such as Procter & Gamble and Coca-Cola. He was likely to ask what bumper stickers the prospective juror had on their car, if they have ever had a near-death experience, or which section of the paper they read first. His open-ended questions elicited revealing narrative responses.

The one question he asked every jury candidate was "Which do you value more, loyalty or truth?" Silverman knew the premium police officers placed on unwavering loyalty to their fellow cops and did not want jurors who would admire or somehow accept it as an excuse for anything less than the whole truth.

Mike Carpenter had also used jury consultants and understood juror psychology. But his approach to voir dire was more straightforward; he ran through a list of questions, some of which elicited less useful one-word answers. Was the juror a member of the American Civil Liberties Union? Would they avoid communications with reporters? Carpenter was concerned that Silverman would sway juror opinions with his famously dynamic courtroom performances. "Do you feel that the verdict in the case should be based on the evidence and not the brilliance and showmanship of a particular attorney for either side?" he asked. Silverman flashed a knowing smile the first time his opponent asked the question.

As he would be throughout the trial, Carpenter commented on the issue of race and the precarious position in which it placed him. "That is a particularly difficult area for a prosecutor," he said of jury selection. "As soon as you kick off a Black juror, you're labeled a racist."

The inevitable clash between the two attorneys over race came on the last day of jury selection. Silverman fought to keep a young Black sailor on the jury despite the risk that he could be ordered out to sea at a moment's notice. Carpenter flared at the effort, accusing Silverman of a double standard. "Had he been white, he would have been gone ten days ago," he complained to Hamrick. Silverman bristled at the suggestion he was executing a strategy to place minorities on the jury because they would favor the defense, calling it "an insult to Black people." Hamrick upheld Carpenter's peremptory challenge, excluding the sailor for practical reasons.

Mike Carpenter told reporters that it might take an entire month to select a jury, but after only three days they had selected twelve jurors and four alternates willing to interrupt their lives for an estimated three months in return for ten dollars a day. The panel was made up of six men and six women. Four were in their twenties, five in their thirties, three in their forties. The youngest was twenty-one, the oldest forty-six. Eight were white, two Black, one Filipino, and one originally from Guam. Their level of education ranged from some junior college to master's degrees. Of the four alternates, two were Black, one Hispanic. After the selection of alternates on March 6, Judge Ben Hamrick addressed the two attorneys from the bench. "Gentlemen," he said, "we have a jury."

WITH THE JURY in place and opening statements in the Sagon Penn murder trial set for March 11, 1986, a week away, Milt Silverman met with his client in a tiny interview room in the San Diego County Jail. There were no more questions to ask and nothing more to be said between them about the incident one year before. Silverman only wanted to prepare the young man for what was to come. Sagon had attended all the pretrial hearings and procedures, so he was familiar with the unusual routine of moving prisoners from the county jail on one side of the sprawling building to the opposite end, where the court facilities were located. In a building designed specifically to include both the county jail and courtrooms, no one had thought to provide a secure passageway for moving between the two, so prisoners traveled the same corridors as the general public. To many, the sight of a modern-day chain gang of shackled prisoners in jail-house jumpsuits being led down a hallway was alarming. When Penn was among them, he was protected by a bulletproof vest beneath his uniform.

Silverman provided some new instructions: Sagon was to arrive at the courthouse immaculately groomed. In the holding-cell area, he would change into a blue suit before entering the courtroom from a side door. Once inside, he was to sit up straight, display no facial expressions or emotions, and not react to anything that occurred inside the courtroom. "I do not want you to do anything that can be interpreted by a juror one way or another," Silverman told him. For all intents and purposes, he wanted his client to disappear in plain sight.

Milt Silverman then asked if there was anything else Sagon wanted to know. Penn shook his head. Silverman suggested they pray, as they had the first time they met in the jail months before. Sagon said he would like them to pray for the family of Officer Riggs.

14

COLEEN RIGGS WAS ABOUT AS READY AS SHE WAS EVER going to be. No matter how painful, or how much she would grow to dread the media, protesters, and crowds, she was determined to be at the courtroom every day to represent her husband. Somebody had to. After the memorial services were over, the interviews with family were played on the evening news, and all the profiles of her husband were written, Tommy seemed to disappear from the story. All that was left was a name dispassionately mentioned in the brief, perfunctory description of the incident included in every article. She knew she could have no participation in the proceedings, but at least her presence would be a constant reminder of what had been lost on March 31, 1985.

Riggs felt the coverage had been one-sided for Penn, which prompted her self-imposed silence. She was particularly unhappy about the media constantly providing Milt Silverman with a platform from which to dominate the narrative. "He has things in the paper almost every day and he knows that if he puts out enough suggestions or accuses the officers of prejudice or any kind of wrongdoing, the more people will believe it. It's like 'the big lie'; if you say it often enough, people will believe it." She rejected the allegations that race played a role in the incident. "I wasn't there with my husband, I don't know exactly what happened, but race was not an issue with my husband, and I don't think it was with Officer Jacobs. I think it was just an arrest."

———————

INSIDE HIS RESTAURANT on Imperial Avenue, Yusuf Abdullah was readying the place for closing. The big mixing bowls used to prepare bean pies were washed out and set to dry. The cast-iron frying pans for cooking breaded fish were scrubbed clean. The aluminum sheets for the baked chicken were put away, the commercial ovens wiped down, the gas lines to the burners twisted shut, the refrigerators emptied, the floors mopped. Yusuf walked to the front of the restaurant. Beside the large poster in the storefront window proclaiming WORLD FAMOUS DELICIOUS BEAN PIE MADE AND SOLD HERE, he hung a second sign which read CLOSED. With the trial set to begin the following week, the closed sign meant not just for the night, but for the foreseeable future; maybe for good.

"People come in, asking why Yusuf's is closed, asking why they can't get their bean pie," said the woman who owned the beauty-supply store next door. "I tell 'em Yusuf's too busy down at the courthouse."

SOMETHING BIG WAS going on at the downtown superior court building on the morning of March 11, 1986. Television news vans were parked along the curb in front of the old granite building, while mounted officers patrolled the area around Union and C Streets. On the sidewalk outside the main entrance, people lined up early to claim one of the few seats in the spectator gallery made available to the public. When the doors opened at 8:00 a.m., those familiar with the combination courthouse and jail had the advantage of knowing where to go, while those who were not wandered about a bewildering network of corridors that seemed to go on forever.

Outside the fourth-floor courtroom, Coleen Riggs spoke softly with Tom Riggs's sisters, Nancy and Kathy. Thomas Penn wore a three-piece suit, and Sagon's mother, Peggy Barnes, stood nearby, the two back on speaking terms. Yusuf Abdullah looked emotionally drained and shaky from ill health related to a heart condition. At the end of the hallway, "The Walkman," Ed Lawson, stood in front of television news cameras and proclaimed that the Penn case would determine whether a Black man could receive a fair trial in San Diego, California. Members of Sagon's Buddhist temple, Black community leaders, and the Sagon Penn Defense Committee were there, dressed in everything from business suits to colorful West African garments. Women from Yusuf Abdullah's mosque wore traditional hijabs, while men in taqiyah skullcaps knelt upon prayer rugs in the corridors, bowing to the east at the required times.

An additional six to eight seats were set aside for news media, a photographer, and a *News 10* cameraman providing a video feed made available to all television news outlets. Members of the public hoping for one of the remaining ten to twelve seats held their positions in line on wooden benches outside the courtroom door; as many as twenty-five to forty turned away most days watched a closed-circuit video feed on a small monitor that had been set up in the hallway.

The courtroom itself had more in common with a well-maintained overcrowded business office than a marble-floored hall of justice. The floors were carpeted, walls paneled in light wood with floor-to-ceiling built-in shelves stocked with legal references taking up much of one wall. Tables that would become increasingly cluttered with displays, paperwork, and boxes of physical evidence were set up in front of Judge Ben Hamrick's bench. Maps, aerial photographs, and diagrams leaned against a wall waiting to be displayed, and a television monitor on a rolling cart was set off to one side. The air conditioning in the old, obsolete building was temperamental, rarely delivering sufficient cold air through the vents.

The display that would come to dominate the courtroom throughout the trial was a full-color, to-scale diagram of the 6500 block of Brooklyn Avenue detailed down to the exact location of the shrubbery lining the driveway where the incident took place. In what was only a slight exaggeration, *Union* reporter George Flynn described the display as "as big as a roadside billboard." Measuring seventy square feet, it reached almost to the ceiling of the courtroom and required Silverman to climb a stepstool to mark the upper area. Sheets of clear acetates could be layered over the diagram, upon which witnesses could indicate the location of people, objects, and events. As the trial progressed, the prosecution came to rely on the diagram too. Sheepishly referring to his own as "paltry little diagrams," Carpenter frequently asked permission to use the defense's monster exhibit. "I hate to ask, but can I refer to your diagram?" he said at one point. Silverman motioned generously to the expansive display. "Absolutely. Joint property."

Carpenter; his second chair and appeals and motions expert, Bob Phillips; and DA investigator Oscar Tron occupied the prosecution table surrounded by boxes of documents and evidence. When not examining witnesses, Milt Silverman leaned back in his chair, one leg crossed over the other, left arm draped over the back of Sagon Penn's chair, his eyes lowered, contemplatively stroking his mustache. Investigator Bob McDaniel sat at a smaller table to Silverman's right, file boxes of tapes and evidence and indexed documents arrayed around him for instant access. Maria Silverman sat in the front row, carefully studying witnesses and the reactions of jurors to testimony and evidence and consulting with her husband during breaks. Court clerk LaRue Slaugh tagged and managed exhibits and evidence and wrote up the daily minutes. Bailiff Mike Rodelo ran the courtroom, escorted witnesses to and from the stand, scolded spectators when needed, made sure the jury was left alone during breaks, and generally kept the peace.

"YOUR HONOR, COUNSEL, ladies and gentlemen of the jury," prosecutor Michael Carpenter said, beginning his opening statement at 9:25 a.m. "If you will recall during voir dire, we asked you all if you were prepared to deal with all the publicity attendant to this. One of the things we didn't ask ourselves, were we ready to deal with it?" He glanced in the direction of the area of the spectator gallery packed tightly with reporters. "I am not sure I am ready for that." He took a deep breath and smiled. "In any event, it is time to proceed. March 31, 1985, was a Sunday. It was a cloudless day, a warm day, a sunny day."

That was as close to narrative adornment as Carpenter would get. Maintaining his position behind the podium facing the jury box, he spoke in his measured, precise manner, keeping his narrative linear, simple, and spare. For him, and he hoped the jury, this was not a complicated story: "All he had to do was give him the license."

Yet Carpenter unexpectedly conceded that Penn held his wallet open and displayed the license to Jacobs through the clear plastic window. He did not assign evil intent to Penn's actions during the initial interaction with Jacobs, saying he "got extremely upset" and appeared to turn away out of frustration because "he didn't think he had done anything wrong." When Jacobs grabbed Penn's arm, "Sagon Penn pulled away and refused to let Agent Jacobs contact him, and backed up and said, 'I didn't do anything. Don't do this.'" Carpenter pointed out that in each case, Donovan Jacobs made a lawful request to which Penn failed to comply.

He said the altercation ensued when Penn physically resisted a lawful attempt by Jacobs to place him under arrest. Penn used his skills in tae kwon do to "fight" the two officers. "The struggle was a violent one. At one point in time during the struggle, Agent Jacobs was knocked down as a result of a blow from Sagon Penn."

Carpenter then revealed what even the jury at this early stage recognized as the single most critical series of actions in the entire trial: How Donovan Jacobs's service revolver ended up in the hand of Sagon Penn and how it came to be the three people were shot in a matter of seconds. His description of the retrieval of the revolver and shootings of Jacobs, Riggs, and Sarah Pina-Ruiz was so spare it barely exceeded the length of the event itself. "Assume that Agent Jacobs is on top of Mr. Penn during that period of time when Mr. Penn is on the ground and is continually trying to get Mr. Penn to turn over, to roll over so he can handcuff him. And Mr. Penn continually resists any attempt to have him roll over. Eventually, Mr. Penn gets Agent Jacobs's firearm and uses it. He shoots Agent Jacobs in the neck, and turns and shoots Agent Riggs three times, and gets up and shoots into the car carrying Sarah Pina-Ruiz, twice. Penn had fired six rounds from a six-shot revolver. All six found their mark and all six required no more than six seconds."

Carpenter continued with the events immediately following the shooting. Penn jumped down the retaining wall to where Riggs lay motionless, threw down Jacobs's empty gun, and retrieved Riggs's loaded revolver from his holster. He hurried to his truck and, finding it blocked, fled in Jacobs's patrol unit instead, running over the helpless, wounded officer on the way out.

Carpenter's description of the incident from start to finish lasted less than ten minutes. He had not raised his voice, inserted dramatic pauses, gestured expansively, or embellished anything. He declined to include any seriously contested facts or details. There was almost nothing in his presentation that the defense would have disagreed with, at least on the surface. It said volumes about the way Mike Carpenter saw not only the case but also the world: the whole thing was just that simple. The prosecutor had, in effect, quietly and calmly shifted the burden of proof over to Milt Silverman to explain how in the world this could add up to anything other than murder and attempted murder on the part of his client.

BEFORE SAYING A word, Milt Silverman moved the podium from which Carpenter had not strayed off to the side and out of his way. "The well," as the floor area in front of the jury box, judge, and witness stand is called, was now all his. It was the first indication to the jury that they were about to see a very different type of attorney.

"Sagon Penn woke up on March 31, happy," he began, pacing the floor. "His half brother Sean Arkward had some friends in town. They planned that day on going to Balboa Park and just spending the day at the park. Nobody took any drugs, nobody drank any alcohol, nobody did anything illegal. Nobody did anything except have a good day at the park." He added that "Sagon didn't know any of Sean Arkward's friends except one, Bryan Ross." There was no reason for Donovan Jacobs to have initiated any contact with the truck. "Nobody in that truck matches the description of the assailants down the street. Nobody in that truck was a member of a gang. Nobody in that truck is showing or wearing [gang] colors."

Silverman described a calm and professional Tom Riggs "approaching [the truck] in a low-key, polite, nonaggressive, nonhostile way and then addressing Junius Holmes and Bryan Ross. 'Hi. Any of you guys got any identification?'" An instant later, Silverman's whole aspect darkened. "Jacobs is a Doberman pinscher," he snarled, prowling back and forth in front of the jury box. "Jacobs approaches Penn and says, 'What's up, Blood? You claim? You claim?' Penn doesn't know what's up. He's just come back from the park. He doesn't know why he's stopped."

Silverman switched to the role of a polite Penn. "What seems to be the trouble, officer?"

"You claim Blood or Cuz?" he growled, as Jacobs.

"What are you talking about? If I claim anything, I claim myself."

Silverman acted out the exchange over the driver's license as one in which Sagon Penn is attempting to comply but becomes more frustrated and confused as Jacobs's demands turn increasingly aggressive before culminating in a threat. "Listen, boy, I'm going to tell you one more time or you're going to get hurt."

"Penn takes his hands and puts them up like this," he said, throwing his hands up as one would in frustration. "Jacobs grabs him by the left shoulder and pulls him hard, like this." Silverman jerked at an imaginary Penn with his left hand, while arcing a vicious punch with his right fist. "And hits him in the side of the face, right here," he said, placing his fist against his own face to show the location of the punch.

Silverman was a whirlwind of activity, viciously cutting at the air with a pretend police baton, which he referred to as a "club." "[Jacobs is] coming at his head, slashing this way, this way, this way." He explained that Riggs only "pulls his club out" when he saw "that his partner is thrashing away on Penn." He mimicked Penn backing up, twisting to avoid the baton strikes. Silverman had taken martial arts for several years and drew on his experience to demonstrate the tae kwon do blocking motions used by Penn. "Jacobs is relentlessly attacking, slashing with his club," he said, narrating the demonstration with his version of events.

Silverman stood in front of the giant crime scene diagram and pointed out locations using a wooden pointer. "You have got witnesses coming from everywhere. There's a lady across the street who is out of her house. There's Oscar Julien, who is here at the end of the driveway. There's a whole bunch of witnesses clustered here. Mr. Smith is standing here. Allen Cepeda standing here. Right here is a church. There's a total of over thirty people that are actually at some point seeing what's going on there."

"Sarah Pina-Ruiz is, of course, sitting in that car," he indicated before describing how Penn and Jacobs fell to the ground beside Riggs's vehicle. The defense attorney dropped to his knees on the courtroom carpet to simulate Jacobs straddling Penn. "He said, 'You think you are bad, nigger? I am going to beat your Black ass,'" Silverman shouted in a threatening voice. He cocked an arm back and punched down at the carpet twice. "Boom! Boom! 'Turn over, nigger. Turn over.'" Some in the room winced as he shouted the racial slurs.

A moment later, Silverman was lying on his back, assuming the role of his client. "Penn, of course, is on his back and can't turn over because Jacobs is on top of him. Penn has his hands up in front of his face, saying, 'Please, please, you have got me. Please stop, please stop.' In the meantime, Riggs is up by the top of his head and is coming down over his head with a club and striking down toward the face."

With all the imaginary characters in place, Milt Silverman demonstrated for the jury how his client ended up with Donovan Jacobs's gun and used it to shoot two police officers and an unarmed woman, and why none of it was his fault. Like Carpenter, he used a clear, unadorned narrative, but one that contained critical details not found in the prosecutor's version. When he was finished, he thanked the jury, wiped the sweat from his brow, and returned to his seat beside his client. Penn poured a glass of water for his attorney. Silverman drank.

15

"**A**FTER YOU PASSED THE POLICE VEHICLES, DID YOU OB-
serve what they did?" Mike Carpenter asked.

"Turned around at the Encanto School and came behind us."

"Did you feel they were coming over to follow you?"

"Yes, sir."

Junius Airfield Holmes was twenty-two years old when he took the stand as the first witness in the trial of Sagon Penn. Junius was employed as a hotel manager, taking some college courses, and concentrating on his rapping. At the preliminary hearing, he entered the courtroom dressed as though about to take the stage at the local Purple Rain hip-hop club, with his Jheri curled hair pulled back on the sides, parachute pants, crimson-and-black vinyl jacket with flared shoulders, and dark sunglasses the judge asked that he remove before taking the stand. Junius toned down his look this time around and was hesitant and soft-spoken on the stand, answering questions with "yes, sir" and "no, sir," and referring to "Mr. Riggs" and "Mr. Jacobs" or, simply, "the officers."

Under questioning from Carpenter, Holmes told how he, Ricky Clipper, and Doria Jones were picked up by Penn outside of Balboa Park. They had never met Sagon Penn before. He said the truck pulled up the dirt driveway to drop everyone off.

When Jacobs approached, "Sagon said, 'What is the problem?' and he [Jacobs] said, 'Can I see your license.'" Penn offered his wallet instead and Jacobs wouldn't take it.

"Did you observe what happened then?" Carpenter asked.

"Sagon walked away, and Mr. Jacobs walked behind him and grabbed him by the arm. Sagon told him to get back because he didn't know what he was doing. And then he [Jacobs] took his stick out and started swinging at him."

Asked to characterize the altercation after Riggs joined in, Holmes said, "They was just fighting it out" but that Penn was "just blocking the hits." He saw Jacobs get knocked to the ground but said the blow from Penn was open-handed, "Like a hard push." "When he got back up, his stick was still on the ground, and he just started using his hands. Jacobs was swinging and the other officer had picked Jacobs's stick up, so he had one under his arm, and he was swinging the other one."

Penn "slipped" and fell to the ground with Jacobs on top of him. "[Jacobs] had his hand on his neck and he was hitting him in his face." Riggs was "standing above him hitting him with a stick." Riggs hit Penn twice in the area of the head and shoulders, Holmes said. He recalled Jacobs ordering Penn to turn over and that he and others in the crowd were encouraging Penn to comply. "But he couldn't because Jacobs was sitting on his chest."

"Did you hear anything that Jacobs said other than 'turn over'?" Carpenter asked.

"Yeah," Holmes replied. "He said, 'I'm going to beat your Black ass.'"

Carpenter knew his own eyewitnesses would offer some details favorable to the defense. But the jury needed to know the basics of what happened in the altercation, and the only way to do that was to call the people who saw it. "Sometimes you just have to go with what you got," Carpenter said of his list of imperfect witnesses.

"What did you observe happen then?" he said, moving on.

"Sagon reached and got the gun."

Junius Holmes provided the first eyewitness account of how Donovan Jacobs's gun ended up in the hand of Sagon Penn. While lying on his back, Penn reached his right arm across his body to the holster on Jacobs's right hip and pulled out the gun. "Did you observe what he did with it then?" Carpenter asked.

"He put it to his [Jacobs's] neck."

"Did you observe what happened then?"

"Then Officer Riggs, he kicked him [Penn] in his shoulder or arm, and the gun went off."

"What happened then?" Carpenter asked.

"Everyone started running."

The racial slur and Riggs's kicking of the gun most certainly did not fit into the prosecution's version of events, but the young man had something else that Carpenter felt was worth the trade-off.

Holmes said he ran at the sound of gunfire, going fifty feet up the driveway to the front step of Anthony Lovett's house. During that time, he heard three shots. When he turned around, Tom Riggs was no longer there and Sagon Penn was standing beside the patrol unit with Sarah Pina-Ruiz inside. He was holding the gun.

"Did you observe Sagon Penn shoot into the vehicle?" Carpenter asked.

"Yes, sir."

"Did you hear what he said when he shot into the vehicle?"

"He told her she was a witness."

AS HE DID with all eyewitnesses on cross-examination, Silverman went back to the start and revisited the whole event in significantly more detail. He fashioned a rectangular piece of cardboard cut from the back of a yellow pad to act as Penn's wallet in the exchange with Jacobs and acted out the scenario with Holmes standing in the position of Jacobs. When Junius began to describe the first baton swings, Silverman handed him Jacobs's baton. "Demonstrate," he said, "but don't really hit me." Holmes slashed at the air with the baton while Silverman played the role of Penn, backing away with his arms held up in a defensive posture. With Holmes describing the actions of Penn and Jacobs on the ground, Silverman lay on the carpet or knelt in a straddling position throwing punches down at an imaginary Penn. "Like this?" "Harder." "This?" "Yeah." As he would throughout the trial, Silverman repeated the alleged insults and racial slurs in a gruff, snarling voice. "'I'm gonna kick your Black ass!' Did he say it like that?" When they came to the critical point of Holmes's testimony about how the first shot went off, Silverman made sure the jury understood exactly what the young man was saying about the gun discharging as the result of a kick by Riggs.

"Penn grabs the gun and pulls it out. Holds it up to his neck?" Silverman asked.

"Yes, sir."

"Then Riggs kicks his arm?"

"Yes, sir."

"Was it at that instant the gun went off?"

"Yes, sir."

"So, the minute that the kick connects, the gun went off?"

"Yes, sir."

Silverman raised his foot and stomped it in a downward motion, clapping his hands to simulate a gunshot. "Just like I did it just then?"

"Yes, sir."

Although Holmes recounted the same sequence of events as he had with Mike Carpenter, the additional details and the vivid demonstrations with Silverman transformed Junius's story into something very different. Instead of a belligerent, defiant Penn refusing to comply with a simple request, he now appeared to be a flustered young man trying to comply with the demands of an aggressive cop. Instead of "fighting" with the officers, Penn was beaten and taunted by them.

Junius Holmes's assertion that Penn shouted "You're a witness!" before shooting Sarah Pina-Ruiz was potentially devastating. If the jury were to conclude that Sagon Penn announced his intent to murder an unarmed civilian for the purposes of eliminating a witness, he would most certainly spend most of his adult life in prison for first-degree attempted murder.

But Silverman was sure Holmes was confused about the detail, as evidenced by the young man's conflicting previous statements on the subject.

According to Detective Bob Manis's report of his initial statement the day after the incident, Holmes said Penn walked over to the vehicle, "Then he looked at her and said, 'You're an eyewitness!'" before firing. However, at the preliminary hearing on May 8, he denied telling Manis or hearing Penn say it. When Silverman spoke with Holmes before the trial, he assured him he never heard Penn say those words. And now Holmes was changing his story again. Silverman read from his preliminary testimony:

QUESTION: *What did he do then?*
ANSWER: *Walked to the car and shot the lady.*
QUESTION: *Did you hear any words said between the lady and Mr. Penn when he shot her?*
ANSWER: *No, sir.*

He asked Holmes to explain the discrepancy. "Because I couldn't understand the big words he [Carpenter] was using."

Silverman was not confrontational or accusatory with the personable and stylish young man, but he did point out where Junius's recollection of events following the first gunshot abruptly veered into the improbable, contradicted physical evidence, and in one instance defied the laws of time and space by requiring him to have been in two places at the same time. The point at which the accuracy of Holmes's recollection abruptly changed was critical for Silverman. Holmes's assertion that the gun fired as the result of a kick by Tom Riggs occurred during the clear and coherent part of his testimony. If Penn shouted, "You're a witness!" it was after the first gunshot, during the period of time when Holmes's memory was clearly playing tricks on him. Silverman asked Holmes a few simple questions that might have explained his confusion.

"Were you scared?"

"Yes, sir."

"Had you ever seen anything like this type of thing before?"

"No, sir."

"Could you feel your heart beating?"

"Yes, sir."

"And all of that bedlam that was going on, you were right there in the middle of that?"

"Yes, sir."

But Holmes stuck to his testimony that he heard Penn say it. "When Mr. Penn shot into that vehicle where Sarah Pina-Ruiz was, did you hear what he said just before he fired those shots?" Carpenter asked him on redirect examination after Silverman was done.

"Yes, sir."

"And what was it you heard him say?"

"'You're a witness.'"

"There is no doubt in your mind about this?"

"No, sir."

DRESSED IN BLACK sneakers and jacket, the now-fifteen-year-old Dwayne Williams could have passed as a preteen with his slight frame and baby face. As he entered the courtroom, he appeared nervous and disoriented. Williams had been playing in the street with neighborhood kids when the pickup truck followed by two police cars drove past them. He said he watched the altercation from Carlton Smith's yard and fled into the house the moment the shooting started, but turned back to see Penn fire the final two shots.

"What did you observe happened then?" Carpenter asked about that moment.

"Then he [Penn] just got up and went to the other police car."

"What did he do at the other police car?"

"He shot in."

"Did he say anything before he shot in?"

"Not that I remember," said Williams.

Carpenter stopped and looked at the boy in disbelief. Detective Dave Johnson's report of Williams's statement the night of the incident read, "Williams heard the subject tell the female, 'You're a witness; I'm going to kill you, too.'" Testifying at the preliminary hearing a month later, Williams repeated the allegation. Carpenter had no reason to think Williams was going to say anything different this time.

Carpenter stalked over to the prosecution table and retrieved a copy of Williams's preliminary-hearing testimony and read from the transcript.

"'Did you hear what he said before he shot her?'" he read. "And your answer was: 'I think he says, "Since you are a witness, I am going to kill you, too."'" Carpenter lowered the transcript. "Do you recall testifying to that?"

"I said: *I think*," Williams responded.

Carpenter asked why his preliminary testimony differed from his testimony today. "I didn't understand what you were saying," Williams replied.

It was Carpenter's habit during witness examinations to speak in the stiff vernacular more commonly associated with police reports. People were "individuals" who "contacted" each other, engaged in "altercations," and "indicated" rather than spoke. He used words like "penultimate" and "alighted," asked witnesses if they were "oriented to the diagram." Some of the younger witnesses, and an occasional adult, admitted difficulty following what he was saying. Now the prosecutor had two consecutive witnesses claiming their previous testimony was inaccurate for the same reason: they couldn't understand what he was asking them.

Carpenter pushed on, frequently having the teenager read silently to himself from the transcript to refresh his memory. With each inquiry from Carpenter, Williams looked more and more confused, visibly withering until answering every question with "I don't remember." He finally gave in and conceded that he might have heard Penn say it.

Mike Carpenter should not have been surprised at the obvious confusion of the fifteen-year-old boy on the witness stand. One person had been telling everyone involved in the case right from the start that Dwayne Williams was not a reliable witness. That person was his mother.

Christine Williams asked police on the night of the incident not to speak with Dwayne without her present, explaining that he was immature and highly impressionable. "He might become confused and give you inaccurate details if you don't ask him questions the right way." They ignored her and kept her separated from her son for three and a half hours. When Dwayne told her what he had seen, it was obvious to her he was mixing in details he heard from other children or were suggested to him by police. She begged the DA's office not to subpoena her son because his statement was undoubtedly inaccurate. "I believe he may have been led to say what he did, if not by direct words in his mouth, by inference." The prosecution subpoenaed Dwayne anyhow.

"HI, DWAYNE," MILT Silverman said pleasantly as he approached the young man for cross-examination. "Are you a little nervous?"

"No," Williams said, bravely denying what was obvious to everyone in the courtroom.

Silverman and Carl Lewis had visited the Williams home during one of their trips to Brooklyn Avenue and spoke to Dwayne with his mother present. He told them he never heard Penn say those words. Speaking privately to Silverman and Lewis afterward, Christine explained why her son may have testified to hearing Penn say it. "I have raised my son to believe police officers are his friend, and to do what is right," she said. "He is a little slow and would be very susceptible to suggestions from them. He would feel if he did what they felt was helpful, he would be doing the right thing." So sure was she of the inaccuracy of his statement, Christine offered to take the stand and impeach the testimony of her own son, if necessary. "I would be willing to testify that he has told me several different things about what he saw and heard."

Now Silverman was faced with the delicate task of showing the jury why Dwayne was an unreliable witness. He asked Dwayne if he understood the roles of the various people in the courtroom. He did not. It was clear the young man was in an alien world, little of which made any sense to him. "Now these folks right here," Silverman said, walking to the jury box. "Do you know who they are?"

"No."

"Okay. That's the jury. Do you know what the jury does?"

"No."

"The jury has to figure out what happened, that's their job. And they are listening real close to what you're saying. Now, it is real important that you tell them the truth, okay?"

"Okay," Dwayne said.

Silverman rested his hand on the witness stand. "Now since you promise to tell the truth, can you tell these folks here how you do in school?"

Dwayne paused. "I do bad," he said softly.

"You do bad?"

"Yes."

"You're not proud of that?" Silverman asked sympathetically.

"No," Dwayne said, looking down.

"What sort of grades do you get, Ds and Fs and that sort of thing?"

"Yes."

"All right," Silverman said, moving on to Williams's ability to understand Carpenter's courtroom terminology. "He asked you, 'Did you see the original *contact* between Sagon Penn and the first officer?' What did that question mean to you?"

"It meant did I see them fighting."

By then, everyone in the courtroom understood that Carpenter used the word *contact* to refer to interaction, not physical contact. "So, when you answered, 'No, I just saw some dust flying,' what you were trying to say is that you didn't see the actual fighting at first."

"Yes," Dwayne said.

He used photographs and the to-scale diagram of the scene to patiently show Dwayne that according to his own recollection, he would have been over fifty feet away and inside the Smith house at the time Penn shot into the car. "Okay," Silverman asked when he was done. "Did you hear those words?"

"I am not sure," Williams said.

"Dwayne, I'm sorry, but I'm going to have to ask you a few more questions, okay?" Silverman said, resting a forearm on the witness stand. "You know I wouldn't ask you anything to embarrass you. Or to hurt your feelings. I wouldn't do that, would I?"

"No," the teen answered warily.

"Now, Dwayne, you have been asked several times here today to read things, right?"

"Yes."

"And you can't read that good, can you?"

Williams lowered his head. "No."

"In fact, you can hardly read it all, can you?"

"Yes," Williams agreed.

"So, let's take part of this that you were asked to read by Mr. Carpenter when you were sitting here looking at it and everybody was staring at you." Silverman said, opening the preliminary trial transcript. "You really didn't know what you were reading, did you?"

"Some of it," Williams said with obvious humiliation.

"Okay," said Silverman. "Let's start, say, on page 166, line twenty-five. Would you read that to me, just out loud."

Williams looked at the page and began haltingly, one or two words at a time, with frequent long pauses. "And then he was . . . hitting . . . on him . . . telling . . . him to turn . . ." He stopped. "Wait," he said, silently reading over the line again. He looked up at Silverman with pleading eyes. "What is that?" he asked, pointing at a word.

"*Subject.*"

"Then was—"

"There was."

"There was . . ." He pointed at the page. "I don't know that one."

"*Female.*"

"I will object to anything further," Mike Carpenter said, protesting the painful demonstration. Hamrick indicated he was not inclined to have Silverman continue much longer.

After Williams stumbled through a few more sentences, Silverman took back the report. "Okay," he said softly.

Williams slumped in his seat, his upper lip quivering. "Are you doing okay?" Silverman asked. "Yes," the teenager answered unconvincingly.

"Thank you, Dwayne," Silverman said, bringing Williams's grueling and painful ordeal to a close. "That's all."

Williams slid off the witness chair, putting on his bravest face as he left the courtroom, avoiding eye contact with the jury or spectators. Once in the outside corridor, he spotted his neighbor Kaye Specks awaiting her turn to testify. The tiny teenager ran to her and buried his face in the big woman's arms, sobbing tears of humiliation.

PHYSICALLY FIT WITH fashion-model good looks, twenty-three-year-old Ricky Clipper had an upbeat personality and warm smile to match. Clipper was standing near the tailgate of the truck while he observed the interaction between Penn and Jacobs on the other side of the truck. Like many, he did not know exactly what caused the altercation to turn physical. "It must have been some type of fight or something. I remember them pulling out some sticks and swinging at Sagon. He was like blocking the sticks."

"Did you ever see Mr. Penn hit either of the police officers?" Carpenter asked.

"He just hit one of the officers and he fell somewhere."

"Was it with his open hand, closed hand?"

"As I recall, it was [his] closed hand."

Under cross-examination by Silverman, Clipper further described it as "a jab" to the face. Silverman did not challenge Clipper's characterization, but the image of his client dropping a police officer with a punch to the face was not what he wanted in the minds of the jurors.

ANTHONY LOVETT CAME straight to the courthouse after an overnight shift in the maintenance department at Wells Fargo Bank. The rapper with a talent for projecting his voice onstage spoke so softly at times that even Silverman became frustrated. "Mr. Lovett, would you try not to have a personal conversation up there and raise your voice."

Lovett, who shared the duplex at the top of the driveway at 6564 Brooklyn with Angie McKibben, was at the bedroom window when he saw Penn appear to become frustrated with Jacobs. "He turned away, like kind of threw his hands up. Like he was disgusted." He said Penn seemed surprised at having been grabbed. "He kind of . . . pulled away and backed up. That's when it started. He pulled out his baton and started swinging at Penn." Lovett shook his head. "It happened so fast, you know."

Carpenter challenged Lovett over the discrepancies between his current testimony and Detective Bob Aceves's report of Lovett's original statement made the night of the incident, in which he indicated Jacobs was knocked down by Penn. "Did you observe Mr. Penn hit the police officers at all?" Carpenter asked.

"I can't really say whether he hit them or not because he could have tripped over bricks," he said of Jacobs falling to the ground.

"Superman could have hit him too," Carpenter snapped sarcastically.

He claimed to have heard one officer say, "You think you're bad, don't you, boy?" while they were on the ground. He said Carlton Smith shouted at the other young men to get back. "He was seriously yelling," Lovett said. "He said, 'You guys get away from there. They will kill you too.'"

"What happened after the shots were fired?" Carpenter asked.

"When the shots went off, Angela started screaming," Lovett remembered. "So, I drug her away from the door, because bullets don't have no name."

"WHY IS EVERYONE staring at me?" twenty-year-old Angela McKibben said as she came down the center aisle on her way to the witness stand.

One of the few white eyewitnesses to take the stand, Angie was from a mixed-race working-class neighborhood of East San Diego. Her slender frame and sometimes shy manner belied an inner toughness.

"He was sort of frustrated," she said of Penn's reaction to Jacobs. "Like, 'Oh, man, leave me alone.' That sort of thing. He was just trying to get away from the situation." She said Penn took one step before Jacobs grabbed his arm and yanked him around hard, "Like you would open a big, heavy door." She saw Penn back away with his arms held up in a defensive posture. "Next thing you know," she said, "I see the officer pulling out his club." She was "just amazed the way he was blocking most of the blows." She said after Riggs joined in, Penn was "kind of like pushing back to keep them away from him." She saw Jacobs fall from a hard push. When he got to his feet, he no longer had his baton, and his face was red with rage. "Oh, he was so mad."

With her rough-around-the-edges manner, blunt way of speaking, and unguarded nature, McKibben's testimony was not without its amusing moments. She referred to the baton as a "billy stick, or whatever." Carpenter asked if the car was accelerating as Penn drove out the driveway. "You have to accelerate to go, don't you?" she replied. While trying to get her perspective on the degree of martial arts skill Penn exhibited, Carpenter asked, "If two officers tried to hit you with the batons, would you have been able to do that [block the blows]?" "No. Look at me," she said, motioning to her slender frame. Silverman asked her to role-play the part of Donovan Jacobs in a demonstration. "Gawd!" she exclaimed with distaste. When he asked her if Jacobs was swinging the baton "soft or hard," she gave him a puzzled look. "He's swinging hard," she said. "Why would he swing soft?"

But the brief moments of levity did not diminish the fact that McKibben was a young woman who had witnessed a terrifying event unfold in front of her without warning. She alternately referred to herself as "panicky," "petrified," and "hysterical." "I didn't know how to handle the situation. I had never been involved in anything like this before." She recounted the moment she realized Penn was going to drive over Donovan Jacobs. "I said, 'No, he's not going to do that!'" Asked how she could not have seen Sarah Pina-Ruiz inside the car, she answered, "I was scared. I didn't want to see anything."

But whatever Angela McKibben had to say on the witness stand could never carry as much weight as what she said to the emergency operator during the 911 call she placed as the altercation between the young Black man and two officers was taking place outside her front door. The jury sat transfixed as the recording of McKibben's 911 call filled the courtroom.

OPERATOR: *San Diego Police, emergency seventeen.*
MCKIBBEN: *Yes, I'd like to report some police brutality right in front of my house.*
DISPATCHER: *What's the emergency?*
MCKIBBEN: *The emergency is, they were . . . I, I . . . Hey, I don't know what to say here. Doria, hurry!*
JONES: *Hello?*
LOVETT: *Ohhh! (in background)*
DISPATCHER: *Yes, what's the emergency?*
JONES: *He's shootin' 'em! Hurry up!*
DISPATCHER: *Pardon me?*
MCKIBBEN: *Nooooo! (in background)*

What followed was forty-five seconds of incomprehensible screaming and shouting in the background. But it was McKibben's initial unambiguous statement to the operator spoken in a clear, confident voice, with a slight edge of anger to it, that seemed to hang in the courtroom air even after the tape was over: "Yes, I'd like to report some police brutality right in front of my house."

THREE OTHERS RIDING in the truck were called by Carpenter to give their version of events. While the quality of their recollections varied, Cedric Gregory, DeWayne Holmes, and Doria Jones confirmed the basic details of the altercation leading to Jacobs and Penn falling to the ground. None of them remembered seeing the gun, why the first shot went off, or even who had done the shooting. Jones was closest to the altercation when it suddenly turned physical, but her answer as to how it started was typical. "Just everything started happening so fast. That's when they started hitting him with the club."

In his report of their statements, Detective Dave Ayers paraphrased both Cedric and DeWayne Holmes as calling it "a real knockdown, drag-out type fight." Carpenter asked Cedric about the characterization. "A knockdown drag-out?" Cedric said, puzzled over a phrase he had never used in his life. "No, because it was really a defensive fight." When Carpenter told Holmes that the term "knockdown, drag-out fight" had been attributed to him by Ayers, Keno knit his brow and mouthed, "What?"

"THE FIRST THING that I saw was the policeman lying on the ground . . . and there was a boy, a colored boy, he was standing up," thirty-two-year-old Margarita Amaral said, testifying through a Spanish-language interpreter. She was watching television with her husband in the house directly across the street when she heard gunshots and rushed outside to find her children. Instead, Amaral saw a young man standing over the motionless body of Tom Riggs at the base of the retaining wall in the yard across the street. "And then with his foot, he lifted up the policeman's body a little bit. Then he bent down and he picked up something that at that time I thought was a gun."

Carpenter asked Amaral to step down from the stand to demonstrate how Penn had moved Riggs's body with his foot. "The policeman was lying on the ground and the boy did this with his foot," she said, bending her knee and lifting her foot off the ground. "And then when he had his foot like this, he bent over and picked up the gun. And then he let the body fall back. And it fell back in a heavy manner." When Carpenter sought to show her a photograph of Riggs's position, she waved him off emphatically. "I don't want to see the policeman's body again." In the spectator gallery, Coleen Riggs tightened her jaw and looked up at the ceiling as she listened to yet another heartbreaking detail of her husband's death.

KAYE SPECKS SAID she became so alarmed at the beating Penn was receiving while on the ground that she walked halfway across the road and shouted, "You shouldn't be hitting him like that."

Carpenter questioned Specks about Penn running Jacobs over with the car as he exited the driveway. "In your opinion, could Mr. Penn have driven out this way, to the right [passenger] side of [Riggs's] vehicle, between that vehicle and the tree?" he said, indicating the opposite side of where Jacobs had been.

"It couldn't have, because of the tree," Specks said.

"Okay, are you aware that a car *does* fit between there? The fact that a car actually *was* driven between there?" he said in reference to a test by crime scene investigators the following morning.

"No, I am not," Specks said defiantly. "I didn't see anybody do it."

"Was there anybody around there who was preventing Mr. Penn from, let's say, stopping the car, getting out, going to the front of the car, pulling the officer out of the way, and *then* driving away?"

"No," Specks conceded.

Carpenter pursued what had become a familiar line of questioning for the prosecutor. "How long was it until police officers came?" he asked Specks.

"After he [Penn] left? I would say about twenty minutes," Specks said.

"During those twenty minutes, what was happening with the people who had been shot out there?"

"They were just lying there."

"Was anybody helping them?"

"No."

"Was anybody out there at all?"

"There were people out there," Specks said, "but they weren't helping the officers."

Silverman was irritated at what he saw as Carpenter's attempt to discredit the mostly Black eyewitnesses in the neighborhood as having so much preexisting hostility toward police that they would simply leave them to die. Silverman showed Specks that police arrived on scene two and a half minutes after Penn left, not twenty. He asked her if she knew how many people in the neighborhood, in addition to herself, had called 911 during that time. "I thought I was the only one that called."

Silverman used a long pointer to identify specific houses on an aerial photograph of the neighborhood. "I think it will turn out these folks called," he said, indicating both the Lovett and Paradero houses. "And

Margarita Amaral called, and you called, and basically everyone that had a phone along there was calling." He paused. "You know, the thing I guess I am getting at is, your little street here, it is a nice little street? A nice little neighborhood?" She agreed. "Is there some reason to feel that the people in your block are coldhearted, and cold-blooded, and just wanted to have the officers bleed to death on the street or something?"

"No," Specks said, taken aback at the suggestion.

"Do you feel better now that I have told you that this house called, and Margarita Amaral called for the ambulance right away?"

"Yes," she said, looking relieved.

THERE WAS ONE exchange between Carpenter and a prosecution witness that illustrated how life for some in the Southeast Black community was very different from elsewhere in the city. The former star running back of the Lincoln High School football team, Glenn Edward Jones, took the stand to tell about the Crip who pulled the gun on him, resulting in Jacobs and Riggs responding to the 6100 block of Brooklyn Avenue. Carpenter asked Jones if he called the police after having the gun pulled on him.

"No, I didn't," said Jones.

Carpenter seemed genuinely surprised at the response. "How many times have you had a gun pulled on you?"

"Quite a few times," Jones said without hesitation.

"Have you *ever* called the police as a result of having a gun pulled on you?"

"No, I haven't."

"I think the next question is obvious," Carpenter said. "I think the jury would like to know, why not?"

"Why would you call the police?" Jones answered, looking puzzled that Carpenter even needed it explained to him. "I'm not dead or anything. What are they going to do, come out and take a police report? There is nothing going to be done about it, so what is the use in calling the police? Ever since the seventh grade, guys have been chasing me home, shooting guns at me. That's part of life, I guess," he said with a shrug. "Once you are brought up in that area, you can't get out."

16

MIKE CARPENTER LIFTED AN ITEM OUT OF ONE OF THE two dozen paper grocery bags on the table before him, each containing physical evidence. "May I have marked as people's exhibit forty for identification what appears to be a brown paper bag, which contains a pair of bloody undershorts." Carpenter used the monotonous process of admitting numerous items of physical evidence into the trial to illustrate, one object at a time, the horror of what occurred on the driveway of 6564 Brooklyn Avenue. He held up the mangled slugs of lead that tore through victims' bodies, Tom Riggs's duty boot with a ragged bullet hole through the sole and top, and crime scene photos of police equipment and medical waste strewn about the bloodstained dirt.

He called to the stand a procession of patrol officers and emergency medical personnel to describe their shock at discovering the horrific scene of the three gunned-down victims. Over Silverman's strenuous objections, Carpenter played the video taken by a television news crew showing a bloody Donovan Jacobs straining to speak through an oxygen mask, a dazed and frightened Sarah Pina-Ruiz loaded onto a stretcher, and CPR being conducted on a lifeless Tom Riggs. Holding back tears in the spectator gallery, Coleen Riggs watched the images of her husband's legs being dragged out from under a car, a paramedic hopelessly pumping his bare chest, trauma flight surgeon David Guss pronouncing him dead, and their friend Officer Gerry Kramer sobbing at the news.

Donovan Jacobs's uniform told a gruesome tale. The shirt showed markings of grease from the undercarriage of an automobile. His solid-metal police badge, found torn from his shirt and bent almost in half, communicated the force exerted upon his body by the patrol unit that ran over him. Displaying the uniform pants cut off Jacobs, Carpenter indicated to coroner's pathologist David Katsuyama an area just above the right knee. "There appears to be some numerals and letters printed in there," Katsuyama said, studying the marks closely. "It looks like possibly grayish lettering on the side of a tire." The markings were the letters *s-t-o-n-e*, of *Firestone*, the brand of tire. The SDPD reverse-mounted tires on their patrol vehicles so the raised brand name faced the inside. Jacobs had come within inches of having the entire length of his right leg, or even more, mangled by the tire of a Ford LTD.

HAVING WORKED FOR years in the temperamental old superior court building, Judge Ben Hamrick learned to keep an eye on the streamers tied to the HVAC vent that fluttered and danced when the air conditioning system was working and hung flaccidly when it was not. When they stopped dancing, Hamrick knew they were in for a long day. On one particularly stifling session, jurors cooled themselves with colorful paper fans bailiff Mike Rodelo purchased from a nearby Pier 1 Imports store. Hamrick frequently checked in with pregnant juror Vernell Hardy. "You let us know if you are not feeling comfortable, okay?" he told the woman, now just six weeks short of her due date.

Carpenter called several witnesses to support his contention that Jacobs and Riggs acted in accordance with department policy and used an acceptable level of force to meet the escalating conditions.

Officer Bill Jeffers made an impression as he entered the courtroom in patrol uniform, antiballistic vest beneath his shirt, and a loaded .38 on his hip. An eight-year veteran, Jeffers was brash and burley, with rounded shoulders, a thick neck, and a square head. He recounted arriving first on scene along with Officer Mike Moran and finding Donovan Jacobs on the ground with a gunshot wound to his neck. "There was so much damage, I thought he had taken it in the face with a shotgun. Every time his heart beat, blood was pouring from his neck." Jeffers used a Buck knife to cut off Jacobs's equipment and clothing.

Jeffers was also a field training officer, responsible for teaching academy graduates how to work on the streets. Jeffers confirmed that officers are trained never to handle a subject's wallet and that Penn's refusal to remove the license was neither common nor acceptable.

Silverman asked Jeffers if he were making the Penn stop, would he have notified dispatch before contacting the people in the vehicle. "I probably would," Jeffers said. Silverman asked why. "Safety. Because other officers would hear what you were doing, and if they weren't busy, they would start heading that way to cover you, whether it was dangerous or not at that point."

Silverman asked about his decision to leave his shotgun in his vehicle when he arrived on scene. "I guess the idea you put it back was because you didn't want to shoot somebody?"

"I didn't mind shooting somebody," Jeffers said matter-of-factly. "I didn't want to shoot the wrong person."

Jeffers was unapologetic when it came to the use of physical force required of an officer to control a resisting subject. Silverman asked if he had ever used the baton in the field. "I, personally, punch somebody before I use the baton," he said. Silverman later asked his method for getting individuals to comply with orders. Jeffers gave him a sly smile. "Want me to give you an example?" "Sure," Silverman said. Jeffers launched into a favorite recitation of his. "In the past, I've told them that I shall strike them with such force and dexterity to render them helpless, with each succeeding blow more deadly than its predecessor, indubitably so." He paused. "If they don't understand that, I tell them I'm going to knock them on their ass."

Jeffers explained the "use-of-force continuum" and the "graduated-levels-of-force" policies of the San Diego Police Department. "You first talk to the person." Then, "any type of restraint method with physical hands," including "grabbing ahold of someone physically." "The next step would be the baton." Jacobs had used that same order of graduated level of force. The continuum did not address the degree of force, leaving that to the judgment of the officer. However, Jeffers said, the officer better be able to justify the degree of force used.

"Let's say you were arresting me, and I'm on my back," Silverman said, kneeling on the floor to simulate Donovan Jacobs's position. "Have you ever in your experience, Officer Jeffers, been on top of a subject with your knees like this, holding him on the throat and hitting him in the face and saying, 'You think you're bad? I'm going to beat your Black ass?'"

"I haven't had that opportunity," Jeffers answered flatly.

Silverman assumed the role of a supine Sagon Penn. "Why don't you get right on top of me," he said to Jeffers. "Sit on you now?" Jeffers asked, equal parts surprised and amused. The courtroom was soon treated to the sight of the brawny Jeffers in full uniform, antiballistic vest, and gun belt straddling a man in a dress shirt, tie, and red suspenders. "I would like you to basically arrest me, okay?" Silverman requested. Jeffers lifted his weight off Silverman, rolled him onto his stomach, and had him fully cuffed in a matter of seconds. Silverman got to his feet with the help of Jeffers and continued his questioning with his hands still cuffed behind his back. After a while, he turned and offered his cuffed hands to Jeffers. "All right," he said, "you better get this off." Carpenter suggested Jeffers lose the key.

ON CROSS, SILVERMAN asked Officer Gerry Kramer how he would have approached the stop of a potentially armed "truckload of Crips." Kramer replied, "You probably would run the license plate and advise communications [dispatch] where you were making the stop just in case something should happen like happened in this situation where an officer needed coverage. They have to know where you are." Kramer, who assisted in CPR efforts on his close friend Tom Riggs, was well aware of the deadly consequences of the agents' failure to do that. Asked what he would do to control a suspect on the ground resisting efforts to be handcuffed, he said, "I would probably end up punching him." "Where would you punch me?" Silverman asked. "Probably in the face."

"I AM THE lead arrest and control instructor for the San Diego Police Academy and the San Diego County Sheriff's Academy," Lieutenant Larry Smith said when he took the stand after Kramer and Jeffers. "I just finished a course in pressure point control and Filipino knife fighting," he offered after reciting his long list of martial arts experience. Smith's familiarity with department rules and regulations regarding use of force was encyclopedic, and his adherence to them strictly by the book. "What is the ultimate objective in the use of any of those items of force?" Carpenter asked. "If anyone resists in making a lawful arrest, the objective is to control that individual," Smith answered. He defined *control* as "once that person is submitted to custody, and that's usually when they are in handcuffs." A "verbal submission"—such as Penn allegedly calling out, "I give up"—did not constitute having a subject under control. "The person might be lying to you," he said.

When Carpenter was through with direct questioning, Judge Hamrick called for a fifteen-minute recess. "It will give you a chance to limber up for your acrobatics," he told Silverman. "I better take my watch off," Silverman said. "You better take your coat off," Hamrick added, "you may be in for a long session." Over the course of two hours of cross-examination, the two engaged in martial arts striking and blocking techniques, wrist restraints, baton strikes, take-down moves, and handcuffing demonstrations.

Smith was reluctant to second-guess the actions of the two officers but said he personally would not have escalated to the baton as quickly as Silverman alleged Jacobs had when Penn pulled away. "You wouldn't hit me under these circumstances?" Silverman asked. "Not at that point."

Silverman held up the jet-black PR-24 used by Riggs. "This club, the PR-24, is capable of killing someone?"

"It is capable of killing someone," Smith confirmed. Silverman held aloft a thick, bound manual. "This is the police department instructions from the chief of police to all sworn personnel regarding the use of force." The lieutenant was intimately familiar with the text. One section indicated numerous places on the human body that were to be avoided by officers because forceful strikes to them with a police baton could result in death. Silverman made sure Smith demonstrated every one of them, including a blow to the kidney area, just below the spot where the visible baton bruises could be seen on Penn's back. "If you hit me pretty good there with that stick, you could kill me?" Silverman asked. "Probably," Smith said.

To close out his cross-examination, Silverman read from another section of the manual. "Under number six here in the departmental rules and regulations it says that 'Members shall be courteous to the public. Members should be tactful in the performance of their duties, shall control their tempers, and exercise the utmost patience and discretion, and shall not engage in argumentative discussions even in the face of extreme provocation in the performance of their duties. Members shall not use coarse, violent, profane, or insolent language or gestures, and shall not make derogatory comments about, or express any prejudice concerning—'" Silverman paused and motioned toward the page. "And then there is a whole bunch of lists there, but the number one item says, 'Race.'"

Smith said he agreed with the rules of conduct listed. By then, everyone in the courtroom was aware of Milt Silverman's contention that on March 31, 1985, Donovan Jacobs had violated every one of them.

17

A T 3:50 A.M. ON THE MORNING OF APRIL 1, 1985, AN UN-
marked police sedan pulled up to the emergency room entrance of
Physicians and Surgeons Hospital in the Grant Hill area just east
of downtown San Diego. Detectives Larry Lindstrom and Gary Murphy
got out and opened the back door of the car to assist their prisoner out of
the vehicle. Sagon Penn emerged looking as wide-eyed and dazed as he
had when he left police headquarters ten minutes earlier under the glare
of lights from the television news crews.

Dressed in a white paper jumpsuit to prevent evidence contamina-
tion, Penn was escorted into the ER with his arms handcuffed behind
his back. As they came through the sliding doors, patients and visitors
stepped clear and stared as they passed, but personnel in the busy ER
paid little notice to the handsome, shackled young man flanked by the
two big detectives in sports coats. The same scene was repeated multiple times a night at the hospital, which was under contract with the
San Diego Police Department to perform what were termed "special examinations" of suspects to determine their fitness for transport to the
county jail.

As they waited in an examination room, there was none of the earlier chatter from Penn, who was by this time emotionally and physically
exhausted. Nurse Elaine Hilliard entered the room with a clipboard and
examination form on which to record her findings. Hilliard had a stiff
bearing and went about her business with a clipped efficiency that left
little room for displays of comfort or compassion for these particular

patients. In her almost two decades working the Physicians and Surgeons emergency room, the parade of drunks, junkies, gang members, rapists, murderers, and whatever else the SDPD deposited in her examination room for evaluation had shown little interest in treating her any more warmly than she had come to treat them.

Just after 4:00 a.m., Dr. Barbara Groves slid back the curtain and joined Nurse Hilliard in the examination room. Groves was a Texan who earned her medical degree at the University of Texas and had her first placement at Mercy Hospital. Like most who came to San Diego for any extended period, she never left. By 1985, she had been practicing at San Diego–area hospitals for eleven years. At Physicians and Surgeons, she received forty dollars for each of the one hundred or so special examinations she conducted each year for the San Diego Police Department.

Groves was informed that her patient was the suspect in the shooting of the police officers in Encanto. After concluding her physical examination of Penn, she dictated her findings into a tape recorder, which were later transcribed by hospital records personnel. X-rays taken of Penn's chest and wrist came back. "My ribs are broken, huh?" Penn said, lying face down and handcuffed on the examination table. Groves did not think so and approved Penn to be released for transport to the county jail.

MIKE CARPENTER WAS confident that the extent and nature of the injuries found on Penn following the altercation did not support Milt Silverman's contention that his client had received a vicious beating at the hands of the two officers. Now, he was counting on the two medical professionals from Physicians and Surgeons to explain why.

Almost a year to the day since she initially examined Sagon Penn, nurse Elaine Hilliard took the witness stand with a copy of the medical file from that night.

Hilliard said she believed her assessment report accurately reflected the injuries shown in photographs of Penn's body taken by police the night of the incident.

"Did it appear to you as though Mr. Penn had been the victim of a beating?" Carpenter asked.

Silverman immediately saw Carpenter was positioning the nurse as an expert witness on the subject of "beatings." "I object, Your Honor," he called out. "I don't think this witness is qualified to give an answer." Hilliard was clearly offended by the objection.

At Hamrick's instruction, Carpenter set out to establish her qualifications for offering an opinion. "Have you seen, in your eighteen years, numerous persons who had been the victims of beatings?"

"I have seen many, many cases of assaults and beating."

"And do you feel that you can give an informed opinion as to whether the person has been the victim of a beating or not?"

"Oh, yes, without question," Hilliard responded.

"Did it appear to you that Mr. Penn had been the victim of a beating when you examined him?"

"It appeared to me from the nature of his injuries that he had been in a scuffle of some kind, he was not severely beaten or injured."

ON CROSS, MILT Silverman had some hard questions for nurse Elaine Hilliard, beginning with a standard hospital form titled "Medical Report—Suspected Sexual Assault," upon which she had recorded her findings. The form had the telltale faded ink and tilted orientation of a document that has survived generations of photocopies. For a facility that examined hundreds of police suspects a year, they inexplicably still shoehorned the information into a form designed for assessing rape victims. Hilliard had adapted the form for use on a standard trauma patient by slashing a line across the sections containing checkboxes for "Acts Committed—coitus, fellatio, cunnilingus, sodomy"; "Ejaculations— vaginal, oral, anal, other"; and the crude anatomical drawings of a penis and vagina.

In addition to noting the shoddiness of the form, Silverman asked Hilliard about three fields reserved for recording basic medical information obtained on any patient being evaluated—"Impression," "Accident Trauma Details," "Chief Complaint." Instead of containing medical information, each had some variation of the term *Special Exam Suspect* written in it, the terminology to indicate a patient in police custody.

"And what 'Accident Trauma Details' does 'Special Exam Suspect' provide?" he asked. "I mean, is this a medical classification of some kind?"

"It tells me he is there for a suspect exam," she said, ignoring Silverman's point that she failed to record a fundamental piece of medical information.

"Under 'Chief Complaint,' what does it say?"

She rolled her eyes at the question. "It says that the patient—" She paused after looking down at the form. "It says, 'Special Exam.'"

"Wait a minute," Silverman said with mock surprise. "That *is* what it says! It says, 'Special Exam.' Now is that a medical complaint?"

Silverman's questioning about the examination conducted on Penn was exhaustive and so minutely detailed it seemed intended to try the nurse's patience. "Who was present for this examination?"

"The doctor, myself, and one of the police detectives."

"Was Penn dressed or undressed?"

"He was undressed and put in a patient gown."

"Okay. How long did that take?"

"How long does it take you to take your clothes off?" she snapped, annoyed.

"Depends on why I'm taking them off," Silverman fired back.

Hilliard was one of the few people in the courtroom who did not laugh.

He lingered on the findings of the examination of Penn's face and head, which included minor cuts and abrasions, but also bruising under one eye and in several other locations. Silverman asked if she had checked Penn's pupil reaction when exposed to light. "I didn't do a complete neurological exam," she said. "Well, you didn't do *any* if you didn't look in his eyes, right?" Silverman responded.

Carpenter's objected to the relentless testing of the nurse's medical knowledge. "You mean this *beating expert* here?" Silverman said sarcastically.

Silverman asked about the paucity of standard information in the report. "I normally do not ask a lot of questions of homicide suspects, because the less I know, the less frequently I get subpoenaed to court," Hilliard replied.

"During this twenty minutes that you were in Mr. Penn's presence, was Mr. Penn ever asked what happened, where it happened, and how it happened?"

"I am not aware," she said.

"In fact," Silverman said, holding up the medical file on Penn's examination, "we can look through this report, and there is not a single word relating to Mr. Penn making any kind of statement as to how these bruises and ecchymosis areas happened to appear on his body?"

"That is correct."

"Because he wasn't asked?"

"He wasn't asked by me."

"And I take it you didn't ask him these standard questions of when the event happened, how it happened, and so on . . . because you would rather not be subpoenaed to court to testify?"

"That's correct."

"How many beating victims have you seen?"

"Too numerous to recall."

"About fifty thousand perhaps?" he said, throwing out an obviously ridiculous number.

"That's a good ballpark figure."

Silverman repeated the absurd number and the term *beating expert* with obvious sarcasm throughout his subsequent questioning. She conceded that *beating* was not a medical term.

Silverman read the dictionary definition of the word: "To strike repeatedly." "And Mr. Penn, in your expert opinion, was not struck repeatedly?" he asked.

"I don't believe he was," she said. "I don't believe he was severely beaten so as to cause injuries to his body."

"What in your opinion *as an expert* caused those injuries?"

"Based on this history I received from the police, he was probably beaten with a stick."

Silverman was dumbfounded. The woman had spent an hour on the stand claiming not to have known or asked about the mechanism by which Penn sustained the injuries and denying he was beaten. "The police told you he was *beaten with a stick*?"

Hilliard did not answer.

"Didn't you just tell us that he was probably *beaten with a stick*? Isn't that the sentence that you used?"

"Yes," she said.

Hilliard stood by her assessment that the injuries found on Penn did not indicate a beating. As a result of the contentious exchange between the two, Silverman afterward referred to her in private as Nurse Ratched, the coldhearted, malevolent head nurse of the psych ward in the movie *One Flew Over the Cuckoo's Nest*.

SLENDER AND PRIM, Dr. Barbara Groves entered the courtroom with the stiff and proper bearing of a librarian and a prickly and defensive attitude from the start. "No, I did not note any injuries that would be consistent with that," she answered when asked if it appeared Penn had "been struck repeatedly by police batons in the head, neck and shoulder, or collarbone or pummeled repeatedly with the fists of a person sitting on him." She said there was no sign of bruising to indicate Penn used his forearms to block those types of blows. She conceded that the marks on Penn's back and lower abdomen were consistent with being caused by a police baton but termed them "superficial abrasions."

"Did Mr. Penn tell you or did you ask Mr. Penn [how] he had received any of the injuries that you have noted for the jury?" Mike Carpenter asked, heading off what he knew would be a focus of Silverman's questioning.

"I did not ask, and he did not volunteer," she answered. "It is felt how these injuries are received is not within the medical realm, that's in the legal realm."

"Gosh, we have covered so much, it's hard to know where to start," Milt Silverman said facetiously as he approached Groves carrying Penn's medical file. Groves's examination report was more extensive than Hilliard's but lacked much of the standard information routinely asked of trauma patients and neglected to note many of the lesser injuries visible in the photographs. She conceded she had not done the extensive neurological exam one would with a head-injury patient. In reference to the bruises on Penn's back, Silverman read her preliminary-hearing

The driveway at 6564 Brooklyn Avenue, looking west. Penn truck and Riggs police vehicle visible. Jacobs's vehicle positioned between the two. Carlton Smith house at top. *(San Diego Police Department)*

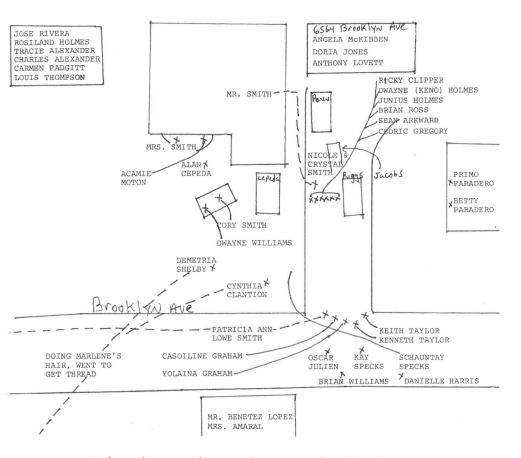

Defense diagram of reported eyewitness locations during incident. Not to scale. *(Milton Silverman)*

"To this day, there is no doubt in my mind that I did exactly what I was supposed to do," Agent Donovan Jacobs said of his actions leading to the altercation with Penn.
(San Diego U-T via ZUMA Press)

Agent Thomas Riggs was a rising star in the San Diego Police Department.
(San Diego U-T via ZUMA Press)

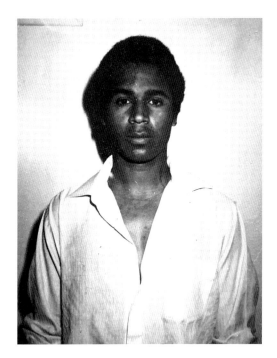

Sagon Penn in police photograph the night of the incident.
(San Diego Police Department)

Ride-along Sarah Pina-Ruiz denied hearing officers use racial slurs.
"I was married to a black man, and I have two black children," she said
in court. "I would have remembered that, I am sure."
(Tony Doubek/San Diego U-T via ZUMA Press)

Popular television news anchorman
Michael Tuck angered police and
conservative viewers with his on-air
editorial pieces supporting Penn.
(Courtesy of Jill Tuck)

Judge J. Morgan Lester accused police
witnesses of perjury and misconduct. "I've
been in the legal business twenty-one years,
and I have never seen a case where this type
of thing was going on." *(Los Angeles Times)*

A journalist described prosecutor Michael Carpenter as "a trial warrior combining Marine Corps roots with the equally disciplined intensity of a triathlete." *(Tony Doubek/San Diego U-T via ZUMA Press)*

The press called defense attorney Milton Silverman "a legal magician" whose "flamboyant, seemingly cavalier courtroom style belies a no-nonsense core." *(Tony Doubek/ San Diego U-T via ZUMA Press)*

Former SDPD Lieutenant Doyle Wheeler accused fellow officers of leaving a dead rat on the hood of his truck flowing his testimony.
(Tony Doubek/San Diego U-T via ZUMA Press)

Officer Nathanial Jordon was asked if he feared for his life after testifying that Donovan Jacobs once called him a racial slur in a station house altercation. "Absolutely. I know how police officers feel about snitches."
(Joel Zwink/San Diego U-T via ZUMA Press)

"I don't think we ever got the truth out of Jacobs," one juror said of Donovan Jacobs's grueling days of trial testimony.
(Tony Doubek/San Diego U-T via ZUMA Press)

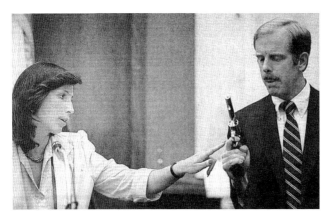

"We had eye contact," Sarah Pina-Ruiz said of the moment she was shot by Sagon Penn. "Then the next thing I looked at was the barrel of the gun, and I knew he was going to shoot me in the face."
(Tony Doubek/San Diego U-T via ZUMA Press)

Coleen Riggs felt her husband's death was forgotten by a media who found a better story in the controversies surrounding the incident. *(Tony Doubek/San Diego U-T via ZUMA Press)*

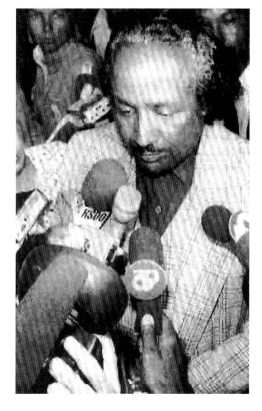

Thomas Penn attended every day of his son's trial. *(H. Ramirez/San Diego U-T via ZUMA Press)*

Sagon Penn in the custody of Detective Larry Lindstrom the night of the incident. *(San Diego U-T via ZUMA Press)*

Reenactment of defense version of shootings created at scene by Jim Gripp, standing in the role of Tom Riggs. *(All images on this page copyright © Legal Arts, Inc.®)*

Shot 1:
Jacobs

Shots 2–4:
Riggs

Shots 5–6:
Pina-Ruiz

"We charted the heavens and moved the earth." Defense window-glare photo.

Milt Silverman presents closing argument amid tables of physical evidence while Judge Ben Hamrick looks on. *(Tony Doubek/San Diego U-T via ZUMA Press)*

Silverman striking Penn's tae kwon do instructor, Master James Wilson, with police baton in hallway demonstration. *(Tony Doubek/San Diego U-T via ZUMA Press)*

Sagon Penn and Milt Silverman, as verdicts were read. *(Joel Zwink/San Diego U-T via ZUMA Press)*

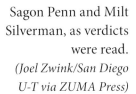

REAP THE WHIRLWIND   183

testimony that she "would have serious doubts if they were caused by an actual direct blow to the skin." He then asked, "And your opinion is the same today, or is it changed?"

"I would say that my opinion is still the same," she asserted.

As expected, Silverman went after Groves over the failure of anyone to ask Penn how he received his injuries, noting that "mechanism of injury" is one of the first questions asked any trauma patient. "You are familiar, I guess, with recordkeeping?" he said, holding up her examination report. "And one of the things you learn in medical school is how to keep records and to write narrative summaries. You put in chief complaints, history, etc. [There] is no 'chief complaint' noted in your report anywhere, is there?" he said, referring to information provided by patients when asked what is bothering, hurting, or concerning them most.

"Yes," Groves confirmed.

"So, you were not following the standard protocol that you learned in medical school in filling out these types of reports?"

"I guess you would say that," she said.

"Because it's true, right?"

"Right."

Silverman questioned whether Sagon Penn received the level of care afforded other patients and had been properly evaluated as to the severity of his injuries. Groves defiantly stuck to her opinion that her examination and documentation were appropriate for the circumstances under which Penn had been admitted.

He pressed her on her conclusion that Penn lacked injuries to his forearms consistent with having blocked a police baton swung at him with any significant force. "In my opinion, if one of these batons had been swung 'full blast,' as you describe it, at Mr. Penn's body, I would have expected to have seen [a] much more extensive size of injury."

He explained to the doctor that Penn was experienced in the use of tae kwon do blocking techniques, which cause the baton to skip down the side of the arm and away from the body rather than connecting directly. He played a video his team had created the previous weekend showing Penn's former tae kwon do instructor, Master James Wilson, demonstrating the blocking technique. He told her to assume Penn "had the proficiency to block blows with the skill demonstrated on that videotape." He asked her if knowing that changed her opinion about the degree of injury she would expect to find on Penn's forearms.

"I would say, no," she answered curtly. "Based on this film, I am not quite sure that contact was made with the stick and the arm, especially on the slow motion."

Shortly thereafter, Dr. Barbara Groves left the witness stand unaware that by expressing her doubts over the authenticity of the video, she had triggered an event that would go down in San Diego legal lore.

"FOR THE RECORD, we are now in the north end of the courthouse on the fourth floor by the elevator bank," Judge Ben Hamrick announced for the benefit of the court reporter. Those who exited the elevators over the following thirty minutes were startled to discover what was going on in the hallway outside.

A fifty-foot segment of the corridor had been roped off with yellow caution tape at each side, a growing crowd of spectators gathering behind it to watch. Also surrounded by caution tape were designated areas containing journalists, photographers, and television news crews, their cameras raised in anticipation. The jurors were positioned separately so they would not be captured by the news cameras. Employees with offices along the corridor stood in open doorways. Lined up against one wall was a white-haired judge in black robes, a court reporter sitting on a chair punching away at the keys, and a smattering of attorneys and their investigators. An ample security detail guarded the entire area while bailiff Mike Rodelo stood beside a young man in handcuffs who was by now recognizable to most everyone in San Diego.

In the center of it all, Milt Silverman doffed his suit coat, revealing a white dress shirt and red suspenders. He was holding a police baton, tapping it softly in the palm of the other hand. Facing him and bouncing back and forth on the balls of his feet like a fighter was Master James Wilson, wearing a white martial arts uniform with black belt and trim to signify his advanced rank and TAEKWONDO KOREA emblazoned on the back.

"Mr. Silverman, you are going to take a few whacks at him, as I understand?" Hamrick said. Indeed he was, Silverman answered. "From what angle are you going to be hitting him?" the judge asked. "I don't want you swinging in this direction." "We have four alternate jurors," Silverman joked. "But you don't have an alternate judge," Hamrick responded.

With a nod from the judge and acknowledgment of readiness from Wilson, Silverman pulled the baton back so far overhead that it nearly touched his shoulder blade and then tomahawked it down hard toward Wilson's head. Wilson let out a frighteningly loud "Hiyaaap, ha, hoooo!" as he stepped forward to intercept the baton with his forearm, deflecting it down the length of his arm and harmlessly away from his body. Wilson followed through with a ferocious flurry of hand strikes that whooshed within inches of Silverman's face and struck his shoulder area hard enough to drive the defense attorney back.

Wilson retreated to his original position, bouncing back and forth on the balls of his feet the entire time. Silverman shrugged off the counterattack, walked up to his position, stepped forward, and repeated the overhead blow a second time. Again, Wilson let out a sharp martial arts yell and deflected the baton away. This time, his counterattack was even more forceful, driving the retreating Silverman against the hallway wall ten feet behind him. The display was repeated two additional times with the baton strikes thrown from a side angle at Wilson's torso, which the tae kwon do master dispensed with similar forearm-blocking motions and counterattacks.

Silverman then asked Wilson to perform a traditional *kata*. There was total silence in the corridor as Wilson gorgeously executed a sequence of flowing tae kwon do forms punctuated with hand strikes, kicks, sweeps, and blocks, each accompanied by the traditional "Ki-hup!" yell. When he was done, the hallway erupted in applause. Wilson bent forward at the waist in traditional reciprocation of respect.

"Very impressive, Mr. Silverman," the judge quietly remarked.

"I think that is all for the day, Your Honor," Silverman announced.

When Master James Wilson returned to the courtroom the following Monday for the purpose of having his arms inspected for bruises, none were found.

18

FROM THE FIFTH-FLOOR MAXIMUM-SECURITY UNIT OF THE San Diego County Jail, Sagon Penn could look through a thick sheet of reenforced plexiglass at the streets and high-rises of downtown San Diego. He was only a mile from the spot where he had picked up three additional passengers as he left Balboa Park exactly one year before, but staring out at a blanket of ocean mist settling between the steel-and-glass buildings, it seemed as though it was all light-years ago.

His dreary jailhouse routine included weekly visiting hours with family, friends, or an occasional supporter. Yusuf Abdullah came when he felt his heart could take it. His sister Subrena, who bore a striking resemblance to her brother, came frequently. A woman named Geraldine Moses from the local NSA temple visited occasionally to lead him in Buddhist prayer. Reiko Obata, who had been working so hard and effectively on his behalf while heading up the Sagon Penn Defense Committee, wrote him letters of encouragement. The rest of the time he spent reading magazines or books made available to prisoners from the jail library, exercised when allowed, ate his meals in his cell, and did what he was told.

While in the courtroom, Penn strictly followed the instructions given to him by Milt Silverman on the eve of the trial. Other than an occasional drink of water during breaks, Penn sat rigid and stone-faced, occasionally observing the activity of the witnesses and attorneys but just as often staring straight ahead as though unaware of his surroundings. There were rumors that he was sedated, on lithium, suffering from a psychiatric meltdown. Was it indifference? Fear? Arrogance? It was impossible to know because Penn betrayed nothing while seated at the defense table.

But once out of view of the jurors, spectators, and media, it became apparent how affected he could be by what he experienced inside the courtroom. Day after day, the events of March 31, 1985, were replayed in the form of bloody clothing, graphic photographs, demonstrations of slashing police batons, courtroom reenactments, the detailed descriptions of eyewitnesses, and the sound of a terrified woman pleading for help over a police radio. Sometimes his eyes filled with tears as he entered the holding cell, or he fell into quiet prayer or simply receded into deep and troubled thoughts. His constant companion was the feeling of confusion and utter bewilderment as to how things had ever come to this.

THREE WEEKS INTO the trial, Milt Silverman recognized an unexpected opportunity to humanize for the jury the otherwise unreadable young man. The moment came when Mike Carpenter called to the stand Detective Guy Johnson, who had executed the search warrant at Yusuf Abdullah's house at North Fortieth Street where Penn lived. They had been looking for evidence of gang involvement, weapons, or anything to indicate Sagon Penn was capable of murder. What they got was a three-foot-tall tae kwon do trophy, boxing gloves, martial arts clothing, boxing trunks, and some athletic equipment inside a gym bag. Carpenter's only objective in introducing the items through the testimony of Johnson was to show Penn's expertise in several forms of fighting.

On cross, Silverman read from the extensive list of items to be seized as specified in the warrant written by Johnson in the early morning hours of April 1, 1985. "You were given a warrant that allowed you to look for firearms?" Silverman asked. "Yes, sir." "Did you find any?" "No, sir." "You were given a warrant that allowed you to look for ammunition?" "Yes, sir." "Did you find any?" "No, sir." "Did you find any drugs in the house at all?" "No, sir." When Silverman had exhausted the list, receiving a "No, sir" response from Johnson in all cases, he lowered the document. "In both the truck and house, you found absolutely nothing of that ilk?"

"That is correct," Johnson answered.

"There was nothing at all in that house to suggest to you that the people that were occupying that house had anything at all to do with gangs, was there?"

"That is correct."

"Okay, let's move then to the items here in the bag," he said, peering inside Penn's gym bag at the remaining contents that had not been displayed by Johnson.

"This is one set of gloves," he said, pulling out a pair of bright-red boxing gloves tied together by the laces. He read the inscription written in felt-tip pen across one: "To Sagon Penn. Pernell Whitaker, '84 Olympic Team." Silverman asked, "Were you aware that Mr. Penn had volunteered his time to work with the United States Olympic team in 1984, and that these were a gift to him by the United States Olympic team?"

"No, sir," Johnson said.

"Two photos of a young lady," he said, displaying a yearbook-type photo of a girlfriend a boy might carry in his wallet. "Now let's look at this one," he went on, successively removing items that any young man might carry in a gym bag. "Something from Yves Saint Laurent. A [audio] tape of some kind. A letter. Looks like a tie. Here's a belt. Something from the Selective Service people?" Silverman said, displaying a document confirming Penn had registered for the military draft. He held up an official-looking laminated identification card with Penn's photo on it. "Something from Chief Kolender?"

"It's a solicitor's identification," Johnson said. "It's issued by the police department for persons going door-to-door for solicitation of sales." Penn had obtained the identification so he could sell his grandfather's bean pies.

Silverman turned the card so the jury could see it better. "It looks like a somewhat more youthful Mr. Penn in the photograph," he noted. "At least smiling." He held the card up for several more seconds, as if to say to the jury, look, this is the real Sagon Penn. "So, it appears that the person who got this was complying with the rule about getting a license to go door-to-door?"

"That is correct," Johnson affirmed.

"A little pin here," Silverman said, squinting to read it. "It says, 'Southern California Police Athletic League Amateur Boxer.'" He set the pin on the table. "Wasn't there something in here relating to Mr. Penn having applied for or gotten some sort of license as a community service operator?" he asked Johnson. "Do you know what that is, sort of being a police officer?" Johnson did not recall the document but knew what the position was. Even without the document, Silverman had made the jury aware that his client had been trying to enter the field of law enforcement.

Silverman had done more than show the absence of incriminating evidence. He had given Sagon Penn a personality that contrasted sharply with the prosecution's version of an arrogant, defiant young man, resisting arrest. Silverman's Sagon Penn was a handsome, smiling young man, perhaps with a very sweet-looking girlfriend, accomplished in his athletic pursuits, who made his bed, dutifully registered for the draft, conscientiously obtained all the credentials required to sell door-to-door, and was interested in a career in law enforcement. And the police? They had rummaged through all his stuff, found nothing, and even broke his tae kwon do trophy, which now lay in pieces on a table among other evidence.

ON THE EVENING of March 31, 1986, a blanket of low clouds hung over San Diego, the air damp with a persistent mist and occasional drizzle. By six o'clock in the evening, nearly 150 Sagon Penn supporters stood on the sidewalk across from the county jail to mark the one-year anniversary of the incident on Brooklyn Avenue. For a few fleeting minutes, the setting sun shone brightly as it passed though the thin space between the cloud cover and Pacific Ocean before sinking below the horizon at 6:09 p.m. Minutes later, the multiracial crowd gathered behind a long banner that read FREE SAGON PENN. Some held candles that flickered in the dusk as the crowd fell into silent observance of the moment Sagon Penn first encountered Donovan Jacobs. Inside the tiers of jail cells facing the street, inmates could be heard whistling, whooping, and applauding the protesters. And then from the cell block came the persistent chant of "Free Sagon Penn! Free Sagon Penn!"

Two and a half miles away from the county jail, a crowd of almost 250 gathered at the War Memorial Building in Balboa Park to mark the one-year anniversary of the death of Officer Tom Riggs. Dressed in white, Coleen Riggs was among the assemblage of family, officers, police officials, and law enforcement supporters seated on folding chairs set out on the long, manicured front lawn stretching up to the gracious and unassuming building. Now three and a half years old, Adam Riggs held a stuffed chick he had gotten for Easter the day before. Coleen said she helped organized the event rather than stay home alone on the anniversary. "The more active I am today, the better I am." By the 7:00 p.m. start of the ceremony, a slow drizzle had begun to fall. Chief Bill Kolender came to the podium to make a few brief remarks. Standing off to the side, a middle-aged Black man dressed in a suit and tie shouted at Kolender, "Who is responsible for protecting the people in the neighborhood?" An officer in the crowd led the man away as he continued to heckle the chief. To close out the ceremony, local musician Steve Vaus played a song called "My Daddy," which he penned the day after the Riggs shooting, in which a heartbroken child struggles to understand that his murdered police officer father is never coming home again.

Coleen Riggs had her own thoughts about the trial. She said it was hard listening to the details of her husband's death. But overall, "I think it is going rather well," she said. "You never know until it is over, and it is really hard to know how some things are going to end. But the DA is a fine man and handling it very well." However, there was one specific aspect of the trial that she felt was not going well. "It's not Penn who is on trial, it's the officers, and I feel sad that it's going that way," she said.

AFTER NEARLY THREE months of rigorous physical therapy at Grossmont Hospital, Donovan Jacobs had finally been released on June 25, 1985. A welcome-home party was thrown for him by his childhood friend James Stevens. It was attended by friends, fellow officers, and their spouses. One especially notable guest was Sarah Pina-Ruiz, brought to the party by Agent Thomas Hoenes, the officer responsible for arranging the ride-along that had ended in her being shot.

Six weeks later, Jacobs broke his public silence in a long interview in *The San Diego Union*. He expressed bitterness over accusations he and Riggs used excessive force and were responsible for the altercation. "Makes me wonder if everyday citizens are buying this," he said. "If so, then you wonder, as a policeman, what we're out there busting our butts for." He said most cops in the Southeast "are miserable down there" and that the work was often dangerous. "Yeah, I've been scared down there. There is quite a bit more violence in the Southeast." He ended the interview on an introspective note: "A lot of cops feel unappreciated for what they do. And they feel, if the citizens don't care, why should they?"

Jacobs's first interview was followed two weeks later by another article related to the wounded officer. "Women Are Out in Force to Get a Peek at Thirteen of San Diego's Finest Beefcake," read the playful headline in the August 23, 1985, edition of *The San Diego Union*. "Police officers sure can draw a crowd," the article began. "At least they did Wednesday as thirteen officers who posed for 'San Diego's Finest: SDPD Off Duty,' a 1986 Beefcake calendar, held an autograph session at a downtown restaurant. 'I feel like a kid in a candy store,' said Linda Kamman as she thumbed through her calendar and then peered at the officers. 'They can arrest me anytime they want.'"

Chief Bill Kolender stopped by the party, calling the event "excellent" and the calendar "in good taste." On the cover, a very off-duty officer emerges from a tropical grotto, water running off his tanned and sculpted body. Inside, a dozen handsome dudes sporting blow-dried hair, mustaches, and finely toned bods pose in testosterone-fueled settings holding fishing rods or guns, straddling a motorcycle, or stretched out before a fireplace.

The article went on to reveal that the person behind the calendar was Donovan Jacobs, who conceived the concept long before the Penn incident and bankrolled it with $18,000 of his own money. After twenty-two officers posed for test photos, Jacobs had the female employees at two banks rate the photographs. "I knew their selections would be different than mine would be," Jacobs said. If any of the original twenty-two had been Black officers, they apparently did not meet the approval of the bank women.

Profits from the calendars were to be donated to the Thomas Riggs Memorial Fund. Dedicated to "All the San Diego police officers who have lost their lives in the line of duty," the back of the calendar included a list of twenty-six names dating back to 1913. Centered at the top in bold was the name Thomas Riggs, with the inscription, "Friend, Father, & Hero. He will remain in my heart and mind forever—D.J."

19

ON THE MORNING OF APRIL 8, 1986, DONOVAN JACOBS ENtered the courtroom from a side door to avoid the overflow crush of spectators and media there for the most anticipated day in the trial of Sagon Penn. Jacobs looked like a man still in the process of recovering from a serious traumatic injury. Reduced nerve-impulse activity caused him to walk with a slight limp, and he wore a sling on his left arm due to partial paralysis, which would take more rehabilitation to improve. He was underweight and wore a serious, almost pained expression as he took the stand dressed in a blue suit with dark-blue elbow patches and a striped tie to match.

"I recall the truck was parked on the east side of Sixty-Fifth Street facing northbound," Jacobs said of the moment he first laid eyes on Sagon Penn's pickup.

"Did you see what it did?" Mike Carpenter asked.

"It made a U-turn and started heading southbound on Sixty-Fifth Street."

"Now are you sure it was parked there and that it made a U-turn?"

"I know there is a point of contention over what happened, and I repeat in my mind everything from that day, and I keep coming up with the same thing: that it made a U-turn in front of me."

"After the initial interview, they [Manis and Lindstrom] came back and were talking to you about the fact that that truck couldn't have made a U-turn in the street there. So, you were aware of that controversy, is that right?"

"Yes," Jacobs replied. "That is just what my memory tells me. It is possible it did not do that."

"Did you notice anything about anybody in the bed of the truck?"

"My attention focused on one individual in the bed of the truck. He had a black golf-type hat on and a black shirt. Those are colors, and type of hat, gang-type hat, and the colors indicate Crip." Carpenter asked what he did as a result. "I made a U-turn, and got on the air real quick, and said I had a truckload of Crips and I wanted Tom to follow me."

Jacobs was confident enough in the accuracy of his memory to provide a detailed depiction of his interaction with Penn over the license. But at the point Penn turned and walked away, his recollections became "real vague." He said his first reaction was "I'm going to have to intercept him and keep him from going up toward the house," but then described taking an inexplicably circuitous route around the back and up the passenger side of the truck. When he got near the front, "I remember seeing Tom with his baton, he had the PR-24, the one with the handle. He had a baton in front of his face deflecting blows from the driver."

"When you remember seeing that, what did you do?" Carpenter asked.

"I came up behind Penn and I hit him about four or five times with my baton across the back and the shoulders."

"And with what force did you hit him?"

"Hard." Carpenter asked what affect the blows had on Penn. "None at all. I remember thinking this guy is on something. You know, hitting him that hard with my baton that many times and I didn't do anything."

"What was going through your mind of the possible things he could be on?" Carpenter asked.

"PCP," Jacobs said. He was referring to "angel dust," the street drug that at the time was attracting major media attention for highly publicized incidences of users in extremely violent confrontations while exhibiting almost superhuman strength and ability to withstand pain. The jurors knew Penn had tested negative for drugs and alcohol, but if Jacobs truly believed he was engaged in a violent confrontation with a PCP user, it would justify him using an increased level of force to control the individual.

"After you hit him and didn't appear to have any effect on him, what happened?" Carpenter asked.

"I remember he turned to me, and then the next thing I remember I am on top of him, and he is below me on the ground."

"Do you recall being hit by Mr. Penn?" Carpenter asked.

"No, I do not."

"Do you recall falling to the ground as a result of being hit by Mr. Penn?"

"No, I do not."

Jacobs's failure to recount anything that occurred between initially striking Penn with the baton and being on the ground represented the third significant gap or period of inaccuracy in his recollection of the incident, each separated by periods of detail and clarity. When describing what occurred while on the ground, Jacobs's memory was clear. "I remember at one point that a crowd had moved within inches of my face, and I remember thinking that I was going to get my face kicked in by somebody in the crowd." He recounted feeling a tug at his holster. "I thought, 'This guy is going to try to go for my gun. He is going to try to shoot me.' I said, 'Enough is enough.' Then I started to hit him with my fist."

"Did you ever call Mr. Penn a 'nigger'?"

"No, I did not," Jacobs said emphatically.

"Is that a word that is in your vocabulary?"

"It is not. I do not use racial slurs."

At one point in the struggle he detected that Penn might be attempting to turn over on his stomach, so he reached back to retrieve the handcuffs from the holder on the back of his duty belt. "What happened then?" Carpenter asked.

"I got shot," Jacobs said. "I remember seeing his face, and a gun, and a flash. I remember I rolled off onto the ground, and I remember thinking, 'I have got to get back up. I have got to get back up.'"

"Were you able to?" Carpenter asked.

Jacobs cleared his throat and began to answer, but then paused for a moment. His jaw tightened and released. He swallowed and his eyes glistened for an instant. But the display of emotion vanished as fast as it had appeared. "No," he answered in a clear voice.

He knew he had been shot, but he felt no pain. "I just recall the shots and people screaming," he said.

"Did you recall actually seeing [Penn] do anything to either Miss Pina-Ruiz or Agent Riggs or anything like that?" Carpenter asked.

"No," Jacobs said. "I remember hearing an engine, car engine revving. I thought that I was going to be run over."

"What happened then?"

"I got run over," Jacobs answered in a soft voice.

"OFFICER JACOBS, I wonder if you could tell the jury here some of the things that you are confused about, about that day," Milt Silverman said to open his cross-examination.

"The events leading up to the stop, the stop itself," Jacobs said. "The whole events of that night are confusing."

Silverman asked about his memory of the U-turn. "Do you have any idea why that particular thing might be an area of confusion?"

"I don't know," Jacobs said. "I was in pretty bad shape. Being shot and run over, I don't know what my mind was doing."

"Did it have anything at all to do with the fact that you felt you needed a reason for stopping that truck, and that seemed as good a reason as any?"

"No. I had what I thought was a gang member in the truck. I felt that was good enough to stop it."

Silverman turned his attention to the stop itself. "Now, the fellow that you were worried about as being a gang member, the fellow in black, where was he?"

"He was initially in the bed of the truck. I don't remember what happened to him afterward. My contact was with the driver, I was trying to keep him in focus. But there were so many people moving I wasn't able to do a very good job."

"Well, did you think about maybe focusing on the fellow that you maybe thought was the Crip?"

"I don't remember why I didn't focus on him or if I was focused on him."

"Did you think that it was possible that there was a gun in that truck and that somebody had it on them?"

"It was possible."

"Okay, and you look at the driver and he's wearing a white shirt and some dark pants, and you don't pay any attention at all to the fellow wearing, quote, 'classic Crip garb'?"

"I was looking all over the place. There was a lot of people in the truck getting out. I couldn't narrow my attention to one. I would have liked to, but there was too many things going on."

"Now, in this conversation that you had with the driver when the driver got out of the car, did it look to you like he was upset with you?"

"No. In fact, I remember thinking nothing keyed me as to what was going to happen."

"Would it be unusual for you to approach a, quote, 'truckload of Crips,' and go up to the driver and say, 'You claim Blood or Cuz?'"

"That wouldn't be unusual, I don't think," Jacobs replied.

"Well," Silverman said, "what we have here is a possibility . . . that you may have approached the driver and asked him, 'Do you claim Blood or Cuz?'"

"I don't remember saying that," Jacobs answered.

When Jacobs described his reaction to Penn walking away from him, Silverman could barely disguise his incredulity. "When Penn said in a loud voice, angry voice, 'Don't touch me!' over his shoulder, your response to that was to turn around and begin walking in the opposite direction?"

"I remember thinking I went along the passenger side of the truck. That is what my memory tells me."

"When Mr. Penn turned and started to walk away, you didn't grab him and spin him around and hit him?"

"I don't remember if I did or not."

"And you didn't then pull out your stick and begin swinging at his head?"

"I don't remember doing that. But I would never use the head as a target anyway as far as that goes." He reiterated that he struck Penn hard across the back four or five times.

Silverman asked him to step down and demonstrate how he swung the baton at Penn. He handed Jacobs the PR-24 and turned his back to him. "Slow motion, if you would," he said. "Just try to place the club where the club came across his back." Jacobs demonstrated a forehand arm swing, resting the baton against the flank of Silverman's back at a forty-five-degree angle. "Probably right across like that," he said. Jacobs demonstrated a backhand swing, connecting on the opposite flank of the back at a similarly expected angle. Together, the rod-shaped areas of contact created a V shape on a subject's back.

"And you hit him as hard as you could?"

"I hit him hard. Not as hard as I could, but I did hit him hard."

"What was your objective in hitting him?"

"To cause him to cease the attack on Tom. To install pain where it became counterproductive for him to continue the attack."

"You are right-handed?" Silverman asked.

"Yes."

"And Riggs is left-handed?"

"Yes."

"Isn't it true that you were at the front of the truck, and that it was Tom Riggs who came around the other side of the truck with his baton and struck Mr. Penn on the back?"

"I remember coming around the side of the truck. That is what I remember."

Silverman retrieved a large blowup of a photograph and placed it on an easel. "Officer Jacobs . . . this is a photograph of Mr. Penn's back, and to my somewhat-feeble mind, it looks like the person that inflicted the blows across the back was left-handed and was striking in this fashion." Holding the PR-24 in his left hand, he simulated the same forehand and backhand swings Jacobs had moments before. The resulting contact points matched the angles of the bruises seen on Penn's back. He switched the baton to his right hand and repeated the motion from that side. "If you had struck Mr. Penn across the shoulders in this fashion, I would have expected that we see a somewhat different pattern of injuries on the back." He looked at Jacobs. "Wouldn't you agree with me?"

"I agree," Jacobs answered without hesitation.

"Does the photograph at all help refresh your recollection as to whether it was Thomas Riggs or you who came around the truck and began striking Mr. Penn in the back?"

"No," Jacobs said.

"The absolute next event that you can recall is that you are on top of him on the ground?"

"That is what I remember, yes."

Silverman moved to the giant diagram of the scene. "We have some physical evidence, Officer Jacobs . . . and some testimony that you and Mr. Penn wound up down here in this area by Agent Riggs's patrol car. You can see that coming from this location, we have got twenty, forty, you know, maybe fifty feet or so as this thing is going down the driveway." He lowered the pointer and turned back to Jacobs. "Can you help us at all in telling us what might have happened between this point and this point?"

"I just remember what I said. The next thing I remember I was on top of him."

With his cross-examination resuming following day, Silverman questioned Jacobs about his role on the PCP street unit and expertise in recognizing signs of drug use. He went through the list of all indicators of PCP use. Jacobs had not recognized any on Penn other than the absence of a reaction to the initial baton strikes. The clear implication from Silverman was that Jacobs knew damn well he was not engaged in a fight with someone on PCP.

He questioned Jacobs about the need for the Reverse Garrity immunity and his insistence that his attorney James Gattey be present at all interviews with Manis. Jacobs said it was Gattey, not he, who insisted on both. "And does Mr. Gattey represent you in a $5 million lawsuit that you have filed against Mr. Penn?" he asked, holding a copy of the seven-page document Gattey filed one week earlier.

"Yes," Jacobs confirmed.

Silverman located a section in the document. "Officer Jacobs, in this paragraph you indicate that the plaintiff—that is you—was attempting to arrest the defendant—that is Mr. Penn—and that he willfully and unlawfully committed a battery upon you by striking you and then removing your service revolver and shooting you." Silverman lowered the document. "Now, I had understood from your testimony yesterday that you did not recall Mr. Penn ever striking you. And I am wondering if this document which was filed by your attorney refreshes your recollection as to whether Mr. Penn in fact struck you?"

"This document was prepared by my attorney independently. I didn't assist in the preparation of it. I stand by what I said yesterday; I do not recall Mr. Penn hitting me."

Silverman asked why he chose to punch Penn when he thought

Penn might be grabbing for his gun. "Why not grab your gun and make sure you have got it in your holster or secured, or step back off of him and pull the gun out and say, 'Don't move'?"

"I can't argue with that," Jacobs conceded.

"Did you hit Mr. Penn in the face?"

"I may have," Jacobs said.

Silverman moved on. "You mentioned yesterday, Officer Jacobs, that you never used racial slurs."

"That is correct."

"Never in your police work have you ever used racial slurs?"

"That is correct."

"You wouldn't be confused about that at all, would you?"

"Not a doubt."

"There either are, or will be, witnesses that have, or will, state that they heard you say while you were on top of Mr. Penn striking him with your fists, 'You think you're bad, boy? I am going to beat your Black ass.' Or 'You think you are bad, nigger? I am going to beat your Black ass.' Words to that effect. Those aren't words that you would say?"

"No, they are not," Jacobs said.

"Are you sure you didn't say them?" Silverman pressed.

"I am positive I did not say them. I know myself real well."

Silverman switched to the transcript of the second Mercy Hospital interview with Bob Manis, and he read a quote from Jacobs about the apparent inaccuracies in his first statement to the detective: "So, you know, I mean, I don't have any reason to lie about that, you know."

Silverman looked up from transcript. "Is it true that you didn't have a reason to lie about why you stopped that truck?"

"That's correct," said Jacobs.

"If you knew in your own mind somewhere deep inside that you didn't have a reason for stopping that truck, you wouldn't lie about why you stopped it?"

"No, I had a reason to stop the truck," Jacobs said.

"You wouldn't have any reason, would you Officer Jacobs, to lie about whether it was you or Tom Riggs that became involved in that initial confrontation and physical altercation with Sagon Penn?"

"No reason at all."

"You wouldn't have a reason even if, in fact, assuming Mr. Penn turned around in frustration, you grabbed him and turned him around and hit him and then drew your club and began swinging at his head with your baton?"

"I didn't do that," Jacobs responded.

"But if you had and you knew you had, you wouldn't make up a lie that it was Riggs that was involved in this initial altercation, would you?"

"I would not lie," Jacob said. "I would not put something on somebody else."

"Isn't it true that what you have done, Officer Jacobs, is that you sat in that [hospital] room and you realized that you had done something wrong at the side of the truck with Mr. Penn, beginning an attack and an assault on him, and that you made this up about going around this side of the truck to cut Mr. Penn off because you knew there were witnesses there that saw an altercation and you wanted that altercation to be between Tom Riggs and not with you?"

"I didn't make anything up and I didn't attack Mr. Penn."

"And there is no confusion in your mind on that at all, is there?"

"In my mind I have no doubt that I did not do what you said, that I lied," Jacobs replied.

"And you are sure of that?"

"I know myself pretty well," Jacob said. "I did not attack Mr. Penn."

"No matter how many witnesses might have seen it another way?"

"They can tell you what they saw. They can view it as an attack. What I did was what I was trained to do, and that is it. I did not go into excess."

FOLLOWING HIS TESTIMONY, Jacobs had an exclusive television interview with reporter Doug Curlee, himself an ex-cop who had been shot in the line of duty. Seated in the now-empty courtroom, Jacobs expressed his own opinion about his two days on the stand. "I think it went really well," he said. "I'm really tired, you know, from just sitting up there and the emotional strain." He offered his thoughts on Milt Silverman's strategy: "From day one it's been Donovan Jacobs who is on trial. People have this perception that I'm some kind of animal or something, a Doberman pinscher I think was the term. I'm not, I'm just a hardworking cop."

20

MIKE CARPENTER SAVED WHO HE BELIEVED TO BE HIS strongest eyewitness for last. Sarah Pina-Ruiz was the only person to provide a detailed description of how Sagon Penn retrieved Donovan Jacobs's gun and then shot three people, including her. It was not good news for Carpenter that six weeks before, the one person he felt most likely to absolve Donovan Jacobs of responsibility for the incident had filed a lawsuit blaming him for it.

The civil suit filed on February 26, 1986, on behalf of Sarah Pina-Ruiz alleged the San Diego Police Department endangered her safety and was responsible for almost getting her killed. The "Personal Injury Complaint" asserted that "Officer Riggs introduced a civilian 'ride-along' into an obviously dangerous situation, one involving a suspected armed gang member." She claimed to have asked Riggs to drop her off if he thought the search for the gang member with a gun could be dangerous. He purportedly declined. The complaint also alleged, "Officer Jacobs conducted his detention in such a manner as to result in a violent reaction which he was unable to control."

Sarah Pina-Ruiz took the witness stand immediately following Donovan Jacobs. She appeared composed and confident in a pink blazer with wide shoulders over a white linen blouse, her dark hair parted on the left and feathered back from her face. All of Pina-Ruiz's observations had been made while in the passenger seat of Riggs's vehicle with the windows rolled up. The patrol unit was positioned forty to fifty feet away from Penn's pickup, with a partially obscured view, so the initial interaction and physical confrontation unfolded for her like a silent movie. Her descriptions of those events were mostly consistent with what others had seen. Like most, she could not say exactly what caused it to erupt into a physical confrontation.

She had a clear view of the altercation once it began moving down the driveway in her direction. "They were just like scuffling and they scuffled and scuffled," she said, never referring to it as a "fight." Jacobs, and to a lesser extent Riggs, swung at Penn with their batons, she said, but Penn blocked almost all of them with what looked like some type of martial arts. She said Riggs struck Penn once hard across the back with his PR-24 baton, to which Penn had no reaction whatsoever: "Not a flinch, not a surprised look, nothing." She described Penn also hitting back "several times," mostly at Jacobs. "They just landed where he could hit him at," she said of the blows.

She thought Jacobs and Penn fell to the ground due to a slip or tangling of feet and that Jacobs ended up on top by "fate or accident." She drew a stick figure on a diagram to represent the position of Penn on the ground just outside the driver's side door of Riggs's vehicle. It showed Penn with his feet close to the car door and his body at a forty-five-degree angle pointing up the driveway. "When he was on the ground and Agent [Jacobs] was on top of him, was there anything obstructing your view of him?" Carpenter asked.

"No. There is a little piece in the middle of the police car that I scooted myself up on," she said, referring to the center console.

From that vantage point, Pina-Ruiz reported seeing Penn flailing his arms while Riggs and Jacobs tried to control him. Through the closed window she could hear Jacobs ordering Penn to turn over. But then the situation seemed to calm down, as though things were getting under control. "I was sitting in the car, and I felt this calm," she said. "I was more relaxed. I could tell the crowd is more relaxed. And I believe that the driver and Officer Jacobs [were] even more relaxed. They're talking. Officer Jacobs was trying to tell him to put his hands behind his back and cooperate, that type of thing. And the driver kept saying, 'Why are you doing this? Why are you doing this?' Then I noticed the driver looking at Officer Jacobs's pistol." She remembered thinking, "He's not going to grab that gun."

"What happened next?" Carpenter asked.

"Then he went after the gun," she said.

"Officer Jacobs had the driver around the neck with his clothing," she continued, "and the driver had the pistol pointed up between his arms." She said Penn moved the gun "several times upward" until he held it to the left side of Jacobs's neck. "I saw the trigger going back, and then my eyes went right to the hammer, and I saw the hammer going back."

"Did you see the hammer actually go back as a result of the pulling of the trigger?" Carpenter asked, holding Jacobs's .38-caliber Smith & Wesson revolver. "Yes," she said. "I saw blood splatter back."

Carpenter pulled the trigger. The hammer went back and then snapped forward with a sharp click. He extended an arm and pointed accusingly in the direction of Sagon Penn. "It was his hand that pulled the trigger that shot Agent Jacobs?"

"Yes, it was."

Carpenter moved on to the shooting of Tom Riggs. Pina-Ruiz described how Riggs turned his body away from the noise of the crowd while speaking on his portable radio. "When the shot went out, he turned around and he was just, what I would say, dumbfounded."

"At that time was the PR-24 still in Agent Riggs's left hand and the radio in his right hand?" Carpenter asked.

"Yes, it was."

"What is the next thing you saw or heard?"

Penn was still lying on his back, she said. "I saw the driver lean back and pull the gun up, and shoot."

"Did you ever see Riggs go for his gun?"

"No. Because I know both his hands were full. He would have had to drop something, and he still had both items in his hands."

"At the time he was shot?"

"At the time," she affirmed.

She said after the first gunshot at Riggs, "I was searching in the car for anything that might protect me in some way." But Penn suddenly appeared outside the driver's side window. "We had eye contact. Then the next thing I looked at was the barrel of the gun, and I knew he was going to shoot me in the face."

"Did you feel fear then?" Carpenter asked.

"Yes."

"What was that fear of?"

"Being dead."

Pina-Ruiz described twisting her body away from the gun barrel and lifting an arm to shield her face. Two gunshots went off in rapid succession, and she knew she had been hit. She thought the gunman still had a sixth bullet, and she waited for him to fire the last round. It never came. She slumped down in the seat and played dead until she heard Penn drive away. When she heard the car tires leave the dirt driveway, she radioed for help. Carpenter played the police radio traffic of Pina-Ruiz calling for help, as the eyes of some jurors welled up with tears.

Carpenter abruptly changed subjects. "I want to talk a little bit about the word *nigger*." he said. Pina-Ruiz stared back at him flatly. "You have heard the word before, is that right?"

"Heard it, yes," she said.

"Are you sensitive to that word?"

"Yes, I am."

"Why?" he asked.

"I was married to a Black man, and I have two Black children."

"You heard an awful lot of things that were said by the crowd, by Mr. Penn, by Agent Jacobs, but you didn't hear the word *nigger*, is that right?"

"No. I would have remembered that, I am sure."

MILT SILVERMAN BEGAN his cross-examination by focusing on inconsistencies between Pina-Ruiz's testimony and the report of her original statement made to Detective Dave Ayers at Mercy Hospital the night of the shooting. "As the Black subject attempted to walk off from Officer Jacobs, Jacobs grabbed him from behind and tried to stop him from going toward the residence," he read from the Ayers report. "Now, that is what Detective Ayers wrote down that you told him on the thirty-first. But that is not the way you remember it?"

"No," she said firmly. "I don't remember saying anything about grabbing, because I didn't see him grab."

"Do you know where Officer Ayers might have got the idea to write that into the report?" he asked.

"I don't believe that I told Detective Ayers that. I think that he just theorized that is the way that actually happened."

She consistently downplayed the severity of the physical altercation between Penn and the officers as they progressed down the driveway. "It wasn't to me like a real fight-fight," she said. "Was more of a scuffle situation."

Silverman proposed that Pina-Ruiz show the position of Penn relative to Riggs's vehicle by way of a reenactment. "What I'm going to do is take this door and I'm going to put it right over here," he said, hauling the actual driver's door of Tom Riggs's patrol unit across the room and leaning it against the jury box. "I'll lay here, where Penn is lying," he said, settling into position on his back. "Where would his head be?" he asked Pina-Ruiz.

"Down that way," she instructed.

"Further down this way?"

"Yes.

"Tell me where."

"Tilt this way."

"Are my feet in the right place?"

For the jury, the sight of the defense attorney in shirtsleeves and suspenders scooting himself this way and that across the courtroom floor no longer registered as the slightest bit unusual.

After adjusting Silverman's position several times, Pina-Ruiz studied the scene. "Like, I would have to be . . ." she paused, shaking her head. "I can only approximate because I would have to be in the car, actually."

THOSE ENTERING THE county parking garage across the street from the superior courthouse the next morning had every reason to believe they had come upon a crime scene. Yellow caution tape wrapped around and between concrete pillars marked off a large area inside which a San Diego Police patrol unit was parked at an awkward angle between rows of parking spaces. Armed sheriff's personnel milled about in their dark-green uniforms while what appeared to be Homicide detectives with grim expressions surveyed the vehicle and surrounding area from different angles. On the concrete floor outside the driver's door of the police vehicle, a man in a jumpsuit lay on his back, motionless. Only the presence of a court reporter clicking away at the keys of his stenograph gave away that it might be something other than a murder.

The man flat on his back in the parking garage was investigator and courtroom-exhibit whiz kid Jim Gripp in the role of Sagon Penn. DA investigator Oscar Tron stood one foot to the right of Gripp's shoulder, representing the position of Tom Riggs. Milt Silverman approached the two wearing dark coveralls. He could have passed for just another repair-shop grease monkey were it not for the black oxford shoes and a police duty belt holstering a .38-caliber revolver cinched around his hips. In his role as Donovan Jacobs, Silverman straddled Gripp, settling in firmly enough that his young investigator gave off a small "oof."

Mike Carpenter led Sarah Pina-Ruiz to the passenger door of San Diego Police patrol unit 785. Grouped together near the rear of the vehicle were the jurors. Dressed in a blue suit and muted blue-and-gray tie, Sagon Penn stood in front of the concrete wall beside investigator Bob McDaniel.

When Judge Hamrick gave the signal, Pina-Ruiz lifted herself up with a forearm on the center console and leaned toward the driver's side to look down at the scene outside the window. Silverman asked Pina-Ruiz if she wanted to adjust Gripp's position, and she instructed Gripp to scoot his upper body to the left, toward the front of the car. Silverman sat again; Pina-Ruiz looked and then had Gripp scoot a little farther. Each time, Silverman and Tron resumed their positions to allow her to reevaluate. A little more. A little more. Yeah, about there.

When she was done, Jim Gripp lay almost parallel to the driver's side door with his head pointing in the direction of the front of the vehicle. Only then did she have a view of Penn's upper body and face that would have allowed her to see what she had testified to.

Back in the courtroom, Silverman went to the large diagram where she had earlier drawn her stick figure of Penn lying beside the car. "A number of other witnesses remember the position being something like this, with the feet pointed directly at the car," he said, drawing his own figure at a perpendicular angle to Riggs's vehicle. "In other words, the car would be in a 'T' position to it." He stepped back. "Are you sure that they were not positioned in that way?"

"Positive," she stated defiantly.

"And there is no doubt about that in your mind?"

"None."

"Okay, have you told me everything that you can remember the officers saying while Penn is on the ground?"

"When Officer Jacobs started to punch him, he said, 'Put your hands behind your back or I'm going to kick your ass,'" she said, making back-and-forth punching motions. "Something like that."

Silverman paused. "That is the first time you ever testified to that."

"That is because, I just . . . I mean, I am recalling it in my mind," she explained. "That is what I heard."

"Did you just remember that just now?"

"Just when you were doing it, I was recalling it. I have been thinking about what he was saying."

He asked her about the force of the punches thrown by Jacobs. He picked up his leather briefcase. "The force would be, what, like this?" he asked, punching it with a resounding thump.

"Approximately," Pina-Ruiz said.

"Could I enlist you into service?" Silverman asked Mike Carpenter as he took an exemplar .38-caliber revolver off the evidence table. "Could you be Donovan Jacobs?"

"Sure," Carpenter said.

Silverman lay on the floor as Penn, with Carpenter straddling him. He held the gun to Carpenter's chest. "He's sitting on him," he said. "Penn has the gun like this." Pina-Ruiz directed Carpenter to lean his torso forward into the gun and grab Silverman's clothing as she said Jacobs had with Penn. "Something in the neck area?" Carpenter asked. "Yeah," she said. "He was grabbing and holding it tight." Carpenter did as she instructed. Even for a trial in which strange spectacles had become commonplace, the sight of the defense attorney holding a gun to the chest of the prosecuting attorney while being strangled with his own clothing was exceptional.

Pina-Ruiz instructed Silverman to tilt the gun up higher so she could see it as clearly as she had during the incident. "Like that," she said. "Then he moved it up."

Silverman moved the gun up until it was pointed at Carpenter's neck. "And does Officer Jacobs do anything?"

"He holds fast, and he was telling him, 'Put the gun down. Don't be stupid.'" She said Penn responded by shouting back, "Get off me!"

"Thanks, Mike," Silverman said, as the two attorneys got to their feet. Silverman stood beside the witness stand, formed a gun shape with his hand, and repeated her version of the exchange in a raised voice. "Jacobs: 'Don't be stupid! Put the gun down!' Penn: 'Get off me!'" he said. "Just like that?"

"Yes," she said.

"Loud?"

"Yes."

"And, 'Boom!'?" he said, indicating the first shot.

"That was it."

"Okay," Silverman said, pausing for a moment. "When Jacobs yelled, 'Don't be stupid. Put the gun down!' did Riggs turn around?" he asked, springing a trap on his witness.

"Riggs was on the radio," she said.

"I know, but didn't he turn around?"

"I don't even think that he even comprehended that he said that. My belief was that he was in the process of getting backup."

Silverman read from the Ayers report. "The next sentence you have is, 'Then the subject shot Officer Jacobs. As the gunshot went off, Officer Riggs reached for his gun.'"

"I never said that," she declared forcefully. "His hands were full. He had a radio in one and a baton in the other. There would be no way I would say that."

"So, Detective Ayers must have heard you wrong?"

"I don't know what he heard, but I know I didn't say that."

Silverman asked about her actions after the first shot at Riggs. "That is when I started looking for protection. I started looking for a gun, or cover, or something."

"If there had been a shotgun in that rack, you knew how to break it out?" Silverman asked, referring to the mount and mechanism for releasing the weapon.

"I felt I would be able to protect myself."

"And you would not have hesitated in an instant, had there been a shotgun in that rack, to pull it out, and pump it, and fire it out the window at Mr. Penn?"

"Maybe not out the window. I probably would have gotten out of the car. But I wouldn't have hesitated, no."

"You wouldn't have hesitated to shoot Mr. Penn?"

"No," Pina-Ruiz said firmly.

21

MIKE CARPENTER RESTED THE PROSECUTION CASE IN chief on the morning of April 15, 1986, confident he had made a solid case for the conviction of Sagon Penn for murder and attempted murder. While Silverman and Carpenter continued their cordial and professional interactions inside the courtroom, emotions were flaring up outside the presence of the jury. Nothing seemed to trigger it more than the testimony of Sarah Pina-Ruiz.

Returning from lunch recess during her testimony, Silverman told Judge Hamrick he had something he wanted to address about Carpenter's intention to call Chief Bill Kolender to the stand next. "I want to say on the record, when I asked Mr. Carpenter a couple weeks ago why he was calling Chief Kolender, he smiled and said, 'Cop killer.'"

"What?" Carpenter, said, springing out of his chair. He pointed a finger at Silverman. "I did not say that. I dispute that. That is an incorrect statement. I *never* said that to you."

"Well," Silverman said in a calm voice. "I will raise my right hand and—"

"'Cop killer'? I said that?" an angry Carpenter interrupted.

"Yes, sir, you did."

Carpenter turned to the judge. "That is not true. That is a lie. An out-and-out lie."

"Well, no it's not," Silverman said. "And I will swear it under penalty of perjury."

"I will swear that I didn't say that, and he is not telling the truth."

Whether Carpenter said it or not, the reference was to the earlier statement made by Kolender that he considered Penn "a cop killer" who should be eligible for the death penalty.

By that time, Hamrick was irritated at having such issues brought up in his courtroom. "Well, I don't know if that has any relevance to what I understand Chief Kolender is being called for by Mr. Carpenter," he said to Silverman.

There would be another clash between the two attorneys during the testimony of Detective Alfonso Salvatierra, in his capacity as a member of the department's gangs unit. It was understood by both sides the purpose of his testimony was to confirm there was no evidence Sagon Penn had ever been affiliated with a street gang. "What was the result of your investigation?" Silverman asked Salvatierra in front of the jury. "None of the individuals in the truck, including Mr. Penn, were identified as gang members," he replied.

The trouble began on cross-examination. "Could I ask you to come down here and take a look at Mr. Penn's hands, please," Carpenter requested. Penn held out his hand, displaying a crude, monochrome blue image the circumference of a pencil eraser on the webbing between his thumb and the index finger. Salvatierra looked and returned to the stand. "Did you see a tattoo on the web of his left hand?" Carpenter asked.

"Yes, I did," answered Salvatierra. "The Playboy Bunny."

"What possible significance does that have, that you are aware of?" Carpenter asked.

"There is a gang in town that uses that particular insignia." Salvatierra said the name of the gang was Playboy Bunny. The name of the defunct and rather tame gang was actually the Emerald Hills Bunny Boys.

"What possible other significance does the tattoo on the web of his left hand have?" Carpenter asked. Salvatierra said it could just be someone who thinks of himself as a "playboy" with the women. "Can you tell, based on what you have seen of Mr. Penn's tattoo on the left hand, as to what category that falls into?" Carpenter asked.

"No," said Salvatierra.

Carpenter returned to the prosecution table. "I have no further questions."

Judge Hamrick was not happy about what he had just seen. "Anything further?" he asked Silverman, with a scowl.

Silverman leaned forward in his chair and fixed Salvatierra with a stare for a long moment before speaking. "Did you know about this before you came in here?" he said.

"I had seen it, yes," Salvatierra said.

"Why didn't you mention it to me?"

"You didn't ask me."

"Well," Silverman said, clearly fuming inside. "I asked you if you had any information at all that Mr. Penn was in any gang."

"I didn't say he was in any gang."

Silverman came to his feet and motioned to the jury box. "Well, what are you telling them? Is he, or isn't he?"

"To my knowledge, he is not," Salvatierra relented.

"Thank you. That is all," Silverman snapped. He turned away from Salvatierra. "There will be a motion," he said to the judge as he returned to his seat.

Outside the presence of the jury, Silverman was livid. "I asked Salvatierra outside directly if there was anything from left field. I was assured there was no 'Sunday punch.' Although I am perhaps, as events have proved, naive, I am not stupid. I have never in sixteen years [as an attorney] stated that I felt something a lawyer did to me was misconduct, but I am saying it now."

"He's the one that put Salvatierra on the stand," Carpenter fired back. "It was a rather daring and rather stupid thing to do. If he is upset with anybody, he should look in the mirror because he has only himself to be upset with."

Judge Ben Hamrick was just as irritated, raising his voice for the first time in the trial, this time at Carpenter. "What possible relevance is there of Mr. Penn having a tattoo of a bunny on his hand? Donovan Jacobs didn't ever look at his hand. He didn't even stop him because he had a tattoo on his hand." The tattoo, he added, might as well represent "a gang of musicians, or girl watchers, or whatever."

Carpenter did not back down. "Am I required to tell him everything I am going to do and everything I am thinking? I don't think criminal law has reached that point. I'm not required to sit here and be beaten around the head and shoulders and say, 'Okay, you can have your verdict.'"

"Up until now, you have tried to get in the evidence in such a way that he [Penn] could say he has had a fair trial," the judge scolded Carpenter. "But this is a cheap shot."

Hamrick backed off the "cheap shot" comment later in the day. "I don't think Carpenter should be tagged with that," he said to the media and spectators while the jury was out. "I've known him too long and he is a reputable, hardworking prosecutor." However, Hamrick instructed the jury to "disregard totally" Salvatierra's testimony related to the tattoo.

A MORE CONSEQUENTIAL rift between the two attorneys developed over the first six weeks of witness testimony. Mike Carpenter often found himself having to refute the testimony of his own eyewitnesses over inconsistencies between their current version of events and their original statements as represented in the reports of the detectives who interviewed them. Whenever Carpenter pulled out an investigator's report to address a conflicting statement, his message to the jury was clear that it was the police they should believe.

Milt Silverman was making it just as clear that it was the San Diego Police Department that could not be trusted. "As I have found in this case as it goes along, the police are not impartial," he said to Judge Ben Hamrick during an argument to obtain the detectives' original handwritten interview notes from which detectives had typed up their final reports. Silverman wanted to compare the two versions for inconsistencies of their own. "Raw notes, the Supreme Court has said, are highly probative," he told Hamrick, noting that SDPD had recently instituted a policy requiring the preservation of original interview notes.

Hamrick agreed. Throughout the prosecution case, as investigators took the stand to vouch for the accuracy of their final reports, Silverman queried them about the fate of their handwritten interview notes. "You destroyed your notes?" he abruptly asked Detective Dave Ayers, who interviewed Sarah Pina-Ruiz, DeWayne Holmes, and Cedric Gregory. "That is correct," Ayers said. "Why?" Silverman asked. "Because there is no reason to keep them." "Do you have your original notes?" he asked Detective Bob Manis. "I destroyed them as soon as I got the typed report and proofread it." "How long has it been your practice to destroy your notes?" he queried Detective Fred Dreis, who interviewed Allen Cepeda and Krystal Smith. "Almost twenty-five years," Dreis said. A half dozen detectives conceded they destroyed their handwritten notes, while a similar number had preserved theirs. Silverman asked Hamrick to instruct the jurors that failure to preserve the notes constituted destruction of evidence on the part of the San Diego Police Department. Hamrick declined.

Silverman took after some of the detectives for the brevity of their reports, lack of detail, habit of paraphrasing witness responses in their own words, and failure to ask follow-up questions. "I write down what she said or perceived she saw," Dreis said of his interview of Krystal Smith. "I was not questioning her or grilling her about the activities that had occurred." "Do you ordinarily interview witnesses as thoroughly as you did this witness?" Silverman asked Detective Dickey Thwing about the one-paragraph report of his interview of a major eyewitness, Demetria Shelby. "Yes," Thwing answered flatly in response to Silverman's obviously sarcastic question.

"Did you record the interview?" Silverman asked several of the detectives. The answer in all cases was no. At the time, portable cassette tape recorders were inexpensive and abundant throughout the police department. Silverman's implication was that the police do not tape-record witness statements for the same reason they destroy their handwritten notes—so they can write whatever they want in their final report, leaving any disagreements over the content purely a matter of their word against that of the witness, exactly what had been occurring over and over in the current trial.

Only two eyewitnesses had their statements recorded, each on three occasions. Bob Manis had not anticipated his first interview with Donovan Jacobs to be taped, but Jacobs's attorney, James Gattey, brought a cassette recorder to make sure of it. Gattey had not been retained to defend his client against Milt Silverman; he was there to protect him from the San Diego Police Department. He told Silverman he believed the reason police do not record interviews is so they have some "flexibility" over what to put in their reports.

Sagon Penn was the other eyewitness who had all of his statements recorded. Under the often-complex rules of hearsay, only the prosecution could admit into evidence legally obtained prior statements made by a defendant. The defense could, but in most cases only by putting their client on the stand, opening him up to cross-examination. In pretrial motions, Milt Silverman had vigorously argued that Penn's statements had not been legally obtained due to violations of his client's Miranda rights and were therefore inadmissible.

Pretrial arguments over the issue of the prosecution's right to admit "the Penn tapes," as they came to be known, dragged on before Carpenter abruptly put an end to it. "So what we are talking about here, in the subject of the motion that we have spent two days on, is my ability to use these tapes in my case in chief?" he said during one of Silverman's arguments. "Is that what I glean it to be?"

"That's right," Silverman said.

"I am not going to use these tapes in my case in chief," Carpenter declared flatly. "I have never even considered it."

It ended weeks of argument, but unknown to Carpenter, it was the last thing Milt Silverman had wanted to hear.

Silverman was stunned when he first listened to the tapes after taking over the trial. After the last tape was over, he thought to himself, "My God, if the jury hears these tapes, we win." But he wanted them to hear the tapes without being compelled to put Sagon Penn on the stand, who he believed would not hold up well under cross-examination. Silverman would later say his whole pretrial effort to exclude the tapes had been a ruse, an exercise in reverse psychology: If Carpenter thought Silverman was so desperate to keep the tapes from being played, it might convince him he should play them for the jury himself. It didn't work.

But Carpenter had not relinquished his right to play them during his case in chief, so all Silverman could do was wait. When the prosecutor rested his case without playing the tapes, Silverman immediately reversed his position and made a motion to allow the defense to admit into evidence the first of Penn's three statements. "Mr. Silverman is trying to get a statement in without having Mr. Penn take the stand and be available for cross-examination," Carpenter argued. He called Penn's statement self-serving. "He is attempting to justify his actions to everybody he comes in contact with. That is completely untrustworthy."

On April 22, Hamrick ruled in favor of the prosecution saying that Penn's statement fell short of meeting the definition of a spontaneous declaration. If Silverman wanted the jury to hear Sagon Penn's version of events, he would have to put his client on the stand. As the trial entered into the defense phase, it was Mike Carpenter's turn to wait and see if Milt Silverman would do it.

22

MILT SILVERMAN LAUNCHED HIS DEFENSE OF SAGON PENN by calling as his first eyewitnesses three young women associated with the two churches located at the corner of Brooklyn and Sixty-Fifth Street. Following the dictates of their faith, the three "promised" rather than "swore" to tell the truth, referred to fellow members as "Brother" or "Sister," and would not utter curse words, verbally spelling them out instead.

Cynthia Clantion was the choir director at Spring Valley Baptist, the small chapel tucked behind the larger Apostolic Faith Garden of Prayer. Clantion was in her twenties, heavyset with a round face, and lived in the two-story apartment building across the street. She mistook Penn's white pickup truck for that of a friend and began to approach before realizing she did not recognize the driver. She watched the altercation from the middle of the Smith yard.

Twenty-eight-year-old Demetria Shelby was the softspoken Sunday school teacher at Spring Valley Baptist. Sister Demetria had come to the Carlton Smith home to collect the younger Smith children for her 6:30 p.m. class. Alerted by Irma Smith that there was trouble outside, Shelby ran to locate her own teenage son, Rasheed. She watched the altercation from twenty feet away, standing near Smith's front door, looking over Allen Cepeda's black Chevelle parked against the retaining wall.

Patricia Ann-Lowe Smith—no relation to the Carlton Smith family—was nineteen years old and attended service at the Apostolic church seven days a week. She was driving up Sixty-Fifth Street when she saw Penn's truck turn onto Brooklyn followed by two police cars. She watched at least some part of the violent altercation that followed standing sixty feet away on the opposite side of the street.

All three women told of witnessing Sagon Penn receive a brutal beating at the hands of Jacobs and Riggs while bystanders screamed at the police to stop. "You know, they weren't playing around. They were meaning to do some damage," Smith said. They all told of Jacobs straddling Penn, ordering him to turn over while pummeling him with both fists. "When he told him to turn over, he just kept hitting him with both fists," Clantion said. They said Riggs alternated between keeping the crowd back and striking at Penn with both his own and Jacobs's batons, sometimes at his raised hands, other times at his body and head. All three reported witnessing Riggs kick Penn.

Mike Carpenter pointed out considerable inconsistencies between their testimony and original statements as represented by detectives in the interview reports. Parts of Clantion's testimony differed so sharply from that of other eyewitnesses that Carpenter openly speculated if she had seen anything at all. He pointed out that from where she stood in the Smith yard, three trees would have been blocking her view. "If you would go in the neighborhood, you would see that the trees was cut down," she said. "I have been there," Carpenter replied tersely, noting the photo of the trees was taken after the incident.

She testified she repeatedly screamed at the officers, "Stop! Stop! You are going to kill him!" while she watched them ruthlessly beating Penn.

"You honestly thought that the officers were going to kill Mr. Penn right in front of fifty people?" Carpenter asked incredulously.

"Yes. The way they were beating him, that wasn't even called for."

"When you say that wasn't called for, you don't really know what preceded that?" Carpenter said.

"I mean, a guy walking back, and an officer comes and straddles him, and just beating him," she said. "Is that the way they protect and serve?"

MIKE CARPENTER'S FINAL witness, Allen Cepeda, had been the first to accuse Jacobs of using one particular racial slur. "I remember him saying, 'You think you're bad, nigger? I'm going to beat your ass.'" Deme-tria Shelby said that Jacobs was "punching him in the face and cursing," while using the same racial slur. Clantion claimed to have heard both Jacobs and Riggs use the word while exclaiming, "You think you bad?"

Carpenter was openly disdainful of the idea that both officers would have used the exact same terminology. "They both did!" Clantion in-sisted. Sitting in the spectator gallery, Coleen Riggs was outraged to hear such remarks attributed to her husband. She had never heard him use the word or express racist views, nor would she have tolerated it if he had.

Carpenter challenged Clantion over the idea that she could have heard *anything* Penn, Riggs, or Jacobs said. He asked her how many times she shouted, "Stop! Stop! You're going to kill him!" "I was scream-ing it from the time they was hitting him" at "full voice" continuously until the first shot went off, she said. She added that twenty or so other bystanders were also screaming "at the top of their lungs" the entire time.

"And during that yelling and screaming you are telling us that you could hear Officer Riggs call Mr. Penn a 'nigger'? Could you explain how you are doing that if you are screaming at the same time?"

"I mean, I could hear," she said.

AS THE CONTENTIOUS exchanges between Carpenter and defense eyewitnesses continued, tensions rose among the spectators. Ham-rick admonished Penn supporters in the courtroom to cease whispers, groans, and facial expressions in reaction to questions by Carpenter, or chuckles of approval at retorts by the witnesses. During a recess, a white spectator was heard to comment, "Those churchgoers pretending they don't swear; those people all swear." Nearby, an elderly woman with a fur-collared coat proclaimed loudly, "They should just hang him and save us all some money."

WITH HIS RECEDING hairline, neatly trimmed beard, and three-piece suit, Carlton Smith looked professorial on the witness stand. Smith spent the first thirty-five years of his life in East Texas and Louisiana. Growing up Black in the Deep South, he had experienced or witnessed all the injustices and hardships those two conditions implied. On the stand, he recounted a scene in which the officers viciously beat Penn even though Jacobs would have had "no trouble" handcuffing Penn, who he said was attempting to comply. Instead, Jacobs shouted, "Didn't I tell you to shut up, boy?" and began punching Penn in the face, hard.

Much of Mike Carpenter's contentious cross-examination of Smith was focused on whether his testimony was influenced by a preexisting anti-police bias. The issue had been brought out during the testimony of Patricia Ann-Lowe Smith, who said, "It is known for a fact, in a Black neighborhood, that a white officer will try to harass, if it is a Black person they are involved with, will try to harass them, intimidate them." Carpenter questioned Carlton Smith about whether that same sentiment was influencing his account. "Before or at the time that this happened, what was your feeling about police?"

"Police in general?" Smith said. "Well, some of them seem to be harrasive [sic], and then some are nice."

"Is that the reason you went outside, because you were convinced that the police officer was going to hassle somebody back there?"

"I went out to see what was happening," Smith said firmly.

Carpenter asked what Smith thought when he first saw the struggle going on down the driveway. "The only thing I could think was that these officers didn't have any respect for the law," Smith said.

"You thought that at that point in time, and you didn't know what happened before that, did you?"

"I saw two officers beating a man down that was trying to give himself up," Smith said.

Carpenter challenged Smith over his claim, and that of other eyewitnesses, that he shouted something to the effect of "They're gonna kill you!" during the altercation. "Did you think he was going to be killed there in front of all those people?"

"The officers looked awful vicious at the time," Smith said. "They didn't even care whether we were looking or not. They had no concern about us standing there looking."

"Were the officers pulling out their guns?"

"No, they were doing a pretty good job with those two sticks and the fists."

"If I told you that you may have been responsible for encouraging Mr. Penn to resist and fight back, would you agree with that?" Carpenter asked, triggering a contentious exchange between the two.

"No, because I didn't," Smith responded sharply.

"You were questioning their authority, weren't you?"

"Do they have authority to beat people?"

"Do you think what you did encouraged Mr. Penn to resist and fight back?"

"Mr. Penn wasn't fighting back when I was there."

"Did you think that you encouraged him not to obey the police officers' instructions?"

"I don't think I encouraged Mr. Penn at all."

"You don't think that by questioning the authority of the police that there was a possibility that he [Penn] heard that and he felt he had the people on his side?"

"I don't think Mr. Penn could hear anything that I was saying at this time. Officer Riggs was busy beating him upside the head with that stick."

"Did the police come to your house?" Carpenter inquired of the attempts to interview Smith and his family.

"They came in full force," Smith said.

"Was that a bad experience for you?"

"For me *and* my kids . . . because they just come in and took over the house, cut the television off, and wouldn't let us talk to each other. I got small kids; they were frightened. It was a terrible experience for them. I was protective of my family."

"Isn't it true, Mr. Smith, that you refused to make a statement until you had about a half-hour conversation with Sergeant Kennedy?"

"They wanted to take us out [at] ten o'clock, eleven o'clock at night to a school. I got small kids, they were asleep. I didn't know why they couldn't take our statements at home."

"Was that a yes or no answer?" Carpenter asked.

"No, I didn't refuse to give a statement," Smith snapped. "They got a statement. They got statements from everybody."

———

KRYSTAL SMITH SAT on the long wooden bench calmly sucking on a lollypop and waiting to be called into the courtroom. The eleven-year-old daughter of Carlton Smith looked angelic in a white lace dress with a pink ribbon tied around her waist. After she promised to tell the truth, Judge Hamrick motioned to the witness stand. "Right up here, young lady," he said. She climbed into the chair and knitted her brow when she realized she was not tall enough to see over the railing in front of her. Throughout her testimony, she often had to raise herself up and lean forward to see the exhibits.

"Were you there at your house when something strange happened on the thirty-first?" Silverman began.

She looked at him disapprovingly. "What do you mean? When this incident happened?" she said, annoyed with being talked to like she was a little kid.

She had watched the incident from the area near her front door, about twenty-five feet away. "Sagon was defending himself and that's when he tripped and fell," she said. She slid off the witness chair and drew a stick figure of Penn on the ground perpendicular to the car, with his head in the direction of the retaining wall. When asked what the officers were doing, she said Riggs had a baton in each hand "and he was just brutally beating him with both of them." He also kicked Penn, she said. Silverman asked if Riggs had been saying anything at the time. "He was calling him Black racial names."

"Jacobs was sitting on his stomach and beating him with his fists," she said. "He said, 'You think you bad? You think you bad?' He called him 'nigger' and he told him, 'I will beat your . . .'" She paused for a moment, thinking. "'*M-o-t-h-e-r f-u-c-k-e-r f-u-c-k-i-n-g a-s-s*,'" she spelled.

"Did you know that Penn had pulled a gun out?" Silverman asked. "No," she said. He asked what she saw after that. "Nothing," she said, "because I ran in the house."

MIKE CARPENTER SUSPECTED Krystal Smith's memory included a tremendous amount of information absorbed from other sources but understood the need to be very careful impeaching the testimony of an adorable twelve-year-old. "You have indicated you know the officer's names now, is that right?" he said. "How did you learn their names?"

"My mother got a collection of all the newspapers that came in on it," Smith said.

"Have you read them?" he asked.

"Yes, I have," she answered proudly. "They [were] always talking about it," she added.

"Who was?" Carpenter asked.

"Everybody who saw it."

Her long and detailed explanation of how she witnessed Penn release the safety-retention strap on Jacobs's holster before removing the gun seemed particularly dubious to Carpenter. "You actually saw him take his hand and unsnap the holster?" he asked.

"I saw it," Smith declared. "And from what I know is can't nobody practically unsnap the holster like a policeman do because it takes a little bit of time."

"How do you know that?" Carpenter asked.

"Because my dad, he knew a little bit about guns. And before the incident happened, we sort of talked about it."

"Your dad told you that?" Carpenter asked doubtfully. "And that was before the shootings occurred?"

"Yeah," she said.

FOURTEEN-YEAR-OLD SCHUNTAY SPECKS was in the Smith front yard teaching dance moves to some neighborhood children when she saw the pickup truck drive up the street. She joined several of the Smith children near the retaining wall when the police cars pulled behind it. She was asked if she had seen the gun go off. "No, not really. I believe I was talking to Krystal." She made no mention of hearing racial slurs.

Schuntay recounted walking ten-year-old Carmen Padgett home to her parents, Primo and Betty Paradero, immediately following the shooting. "I went past the officer that was on the ground, the one that fell off the wall," she said, referring to Tom Riggs.

"Was he moving at all?" Mike Carpenter asked.

"I didn't really look closely," she said. "I just wanted to get her to her house."

"IT SEEMED LIKE he had a rough day, you know, like he was in anger," Sagon Penn's "godbrother" and best friend, Bryan Ross, said of the first encounter with Donovan Jacobs. "Are you guys in any gangs? Cuz or Blood?" he recalled Jacobs asking them. According to Ross, the initial exchange between Jacobs and Penn ended with Jacobs saying, "I am going to ask you one more time, boy, for your driver's license." When Penn pulled out of Jacobs's grasp, the officer immediately drew his baton and began hitting Penn.

Ross positioned Penn on the ground parallel to Riggs's vehicle, as Sarah Pina-Ruiz had. He said Jacobs grabbed Penn by the shirt, punching him while Riggs struck him with the baton. "Everybody was asking Officer Riggs that he shouldn't be hitting him like that, you're going to kill him hitting him in his head like that." Silverman asked if the officers were saying anything to Penn at the time. "Officer Jacobs and Officer Riggs quoted, 'Turn over on your side, you Black bastard.' Officer Jacobs quoted, 'Turn over on your side, you Black nigger.' And then Officer Jacobs quoted again, 'Turn on your side, you asshole.'"

Mike Carpenter began his cross-examination by establishing that Ross had run from the scene and waited four days before giving a statement to police. Carpenter also made it clear that Ross's close relationship with Penn should cast doubt on his reliability as a witness. "I know what I seen," Ross answered when Carpenter challenged his statements. "I'm sure you do," Carpenter retorted sarcastically.

An ongoing irritation to Carpenter was defense eyewitnesses volunteering that Penn could not have turned over because Jacobs was sitting on top of him. The difference between Penn *refusing* to turn over and being *unable* to turn over had enormous consequences. If Penn was able to turn over, it represented an alternative to pulling Jacobs's gun. The eagerness with which Anthony Lovett, Cepeda, Clantion, Shelby, and Patricia Smith offered their unsolicited opinions made Carpenter suspect they knew how important it was too. By the time he came to the subject with Bryan Ross, Carpenter's contempt over the unified response was obvious. "I'm going to say, 'Did he turn over?' And you are going to say, 'He couldn't.' Right?"

"He couldn't because Officer Jacobs was on top of him," Ross answered.

"Right. Okay," an exasperated Carpenter responded.

When Ross said he never saw Penn retrieve the gun from Jacobs's holster, Carpenter confronted him again. "You were watching the two officers and Mr. Penn the whole time? How could he have gotten the gun without you seeing it?"

"At the time, so much was going on," Ross protested. "Everybody was screaming and shouting, and I was trying to control the crowd. I didn't see him with the gun. I didn't even know he had the gun."

The prosecutor's patience with the defense eyewitnesses was clearly running out by the time Hamrick recessed for the day. "It's getting late," the judge said, nodding in the direction of the clock on the wall.

"I know," Carpenter said wearily. "It's been late for me all day."

23

WITH THE PYROTECHNICS OF EYEWITNESS TESTIMONY over for the moment, Silverman moved on to his list of less volatile, but no less important, expert witnesses. The crown jewel of them was the legendary forensic pathologist Dr. Werner Spitz. For the previous dozen years, Spitz served as chief medical examiner of Wayne County, Michigan, which included the city of Detroit, consistently labeled the most dangerous city in America. "I have either performed or supervised, I would say, approximately fifty thousand autopsies," he said. His list of credentials was dizzying, including being a member of the Rockefeller Commission that investigated the assassination of John F. Kennedy.

In his late fifties, Werner Spitz had a precise manner and guttural Germanic accent. He was a masterful communicator of even the most sophisticated medical concepts. Silverman asked Spitz about Dr. Barbara Groves's conclusions related to the linear bruises on Penn's back. "Do you recall her opinion that this is a grazing-type motion? Or that it could have been caused by somebody being on his back?"

"No, neither is correct," Spitz said sharply. "This was caused by this kind of blow," he said, simulating a baton strike by lifting his arm and sweeping it down across his body. Silverman mimicked the move with the PR-24 he was holding. "Like zat!" the doctor confirmed with Teutonic flare. He said that Groves should have easily recognized the source of the bruise. "I don't know where Dr. Groves works, but in any major city emergency room of a big institution, I'm sure that injuries like this are observed." He identified in the photographs bruising on Penn's body from six hard baton blows, adding that those on Penn's back "could cause the tear of an organ." Silverman pointed to a bruise on the lower right abdomen. "Is a blow like that capable of killing somebody if it hits him in a vital spot?" "Yes," Spitz said. In his opinion, the bruise under Penn's left eye was "most consistent with a fist blow." He was shown the video of Master James Wilson deflecting baton strikes and agreed that no bruising would likely result from that type of glancing contact with a high-speed object.

"I am not impressed by some other people in the emergency room as to accuracy," he said in assessing Nurse Hilliard and Dr. Groves. "They should stick to that assessment and not venture opinions beyond their specialty [and] passing themselves off as experts."

On cross-examination, Carpenter failed to shake Spitz's assessment of Penn's injuries. "How much are you getting paid for coming out here and testifying?" he abruptly asked at the conclusion of his questioning. Werner Spitz had been on too many witness stands to fall for that trick. "I am going to submit a bill to the public defender when I'm done," he answered.

WHEN FORENSIC PSYCHIATRIST Haig Koshkarian took the stand for the defense, he brought such terms such as "retrograde amnesia," "antegrade amnesia," "confabulation of memory," and "falsification of memory" along with him. On direct, Silverman went through the transcript of Jacobs's original April 8, 1985, Mercy Hospital statement noting that Jacobs's version of events alternated between detailed and accurate to vague, inaccurate, or nonexistent. Koshkarian called it "selective falsification of memory."

"So, in your opinion, the two possibilities for Donovan Jacobs's misremembering these two facts is either the result of deliberate, purposeful lying, or essentially deceiving himself?" Silverman asked.

"Yes," Koshkarian affirmed. "If I were asked what is more likely, I would say it is more likely conscious falsification."

"You think it is more likely that he is lying to the jury when he testified?"

"Yes," Koshkarian responded flatly.

FAUSTO POZA WAS a senior research engineer in the field of forensic audio at Stanford Research Institute, one of the most advanced technology research labs located in what was becoming known as Silicon Valley. Poza's private consulting practice specialized in forensic acoustics, analyzing audio recordings to identify and interpret voices and background noises. Milt Silverman sent Poza the recording of the 911 call placed by Angela McKibben on the evening of March 31, 1985, and asked him if he could identify the sound of gunshots and interpret the cacophony of voices heard in the background among all the screaming and shouting.

"Did you bring down with you some of the instruments that you have at your disposal to analyze a tape like the one I asked you to analyze?" Silverman asked the scientist.

"Yes," Poza answered brightly. "I brought down probably all the equipment that is crucial to the type of analysis you want."

"And is that it sitting here in front of the jury?"

Poza smiled proudly. "It is!" He indicated the audio cables running across the floor and over the rail to the jury box. "They are individual earphones for each juror, the defense, the prosecution, the Court, and myself."

When all had their headsets on, Poza gazed intently into the screen of his first-generation Apple Macintosh computer, his long face and gray beard bathed in pale light as he launched the first of his digital audio files, a new concept in 1986.

Poza played a version of the 911 recording in which he had inserted a high-pitched beep at the moment of each gunshot's "impulsive sound," which were otherwise so faint as to be virtually undetectable by the naked ear. With the time-coded transcript on the overhead projector; the voices of McKibben, Doria Jones, and the emergency operator in the foreground; and the soft intonation of the gunshot beeps interspersed within, Poza's recording revealed the full story of those horrible few moments. The transcript noted the elapsed seconds in parentheses and the moments of the "impulsive sounds" indicating gunshots and the individual shot:

DISPATCHER: *(0.00) "San Diego Police emergency seventeen."*
(1.00)
MCKIBBEN: *"Yes, I'd like to (2.00) report some police bru-(3.00)-tality right in front of my (4.00) house."*
DISPATCHER: *"What's the emergency?" (6.00)*

MCKIBBEN: *"The emergency is (7.00), they were— (8.00), I,
I— Hey, I don't know what to (9.00) say here.
Doria, hurry!" (10.00)*

IMPULSIVE SOUND 1 (JACOBS—10.12)

JONES: *"Hello?"*

LOVETT: *"Ohhh!" (in background)*

DISPATCHER: *"Yes, what's the—"*

IMPULSIVE SOUND 2 (RIGGS—11.68) *"Emergen—"*

IMPULSIVE SOUND 3 (RIGGS—12.24) *"—cy?"*

IMPULSIVE SOUND 4 (RIGGS—12.70)

JONES: *"He's shootin' 'em! Hurry up!"*

IMPULSIVE SOUND 5 (PINA-RUIZ—15.36)

IMPULSIVE SOUND 6 (PINA-RUIZ—15.88)

DISPATCHER: *"Pardon me?" (16.00)*

SCREAMING FEMALE: *"Nooooo!" (17.00)*

When the tape was over, the courtroom fell silent. Silverman held his hand up in the shape of a gun, looked at the timeline created by Poza, and counted out the fractions of seconds between shots. "Bang! 1.7, bang! 0.5, bang! 0.6, bang! 2.7, bang! 0.5, bang!"

"Exactly," Poza confirmed, although Silverman's rounding had at times gone in the wrong direction by fractions of seconds. "That's the sequence."

All six shots had been fired in a span of 5.76 seconds.

According to Mike Carpenter, Sagon Penn pulled the trigger of a gun six times with the intent to kill. Milt Silverman had a very different version of those short and terrible few moments, and it all had to do with three things: a boot, a radio, and a sunset.

24

MILT SILVERMAN WAS LYING ON HIS BACK AGAIN. "NOW, if the guy grabs and pulls like this," he said, reaching across his body with his right arm to the holstered gun on the right hip of Mike Carpenter, who was straddling him, "he is not going to get it unless that's unsnapped, is that right?" He tugged on the gun, but it would not come out of the holster.

"That's the way it's supposed to work," said Officer Bill Jeffers, explaining the firearm-retention strap designed to keep the weapon from falling out accidentally or being pulled out by an aggressor. At stake was the question of whether Sagon Penn could have successfully removed Donovan Jacobs's .38 revolver from his holster with an impulsive grab in a moment of terror, or whether it would have required "a moment of calm," as Sarah Pina-Ruiz termed it, to methodically and premeditatively work open the strap.

Jeffers did nothing to hide his low opinion of the breakfront-style holster worn by Jacobs. "You would get [the gun] out very easy. That's why I switched to this holster," he said, indicating the one on his hip. "A lot of times they will just kind of unsnap themselves without you even knowing it." Jeffers said he, like many cops, unsnapped it himself "anytime I feel there's a dangerous situation." A firearms examiner for the San Diego Police Department agreed. "It has particularly severe safety problems in terms of weapon retention. One can very easily be taken out of this holster from the rear without the snap being unsnapped." The consensus was that Penn could have retrieved the gun without regard for the retention mechanism.

The subject of the holster design marked the beginning of Milt Silverman's formidable and painstaking task of explaining to the jury exactly how each of the three victims had been shot and why his client should not be blamed for any of them. Step one was his contention that the first shot had gone off accidentally. "Sagon reached and got the gun. He put it to his [Jacobs's] neck. Then Officer Riggs, he kicked him [Penn] in his shoulder or arm, and the gun went off." Junius Holmes and Bryan Ross were the eyewitnesses who linked the discharge of the weapon to a kick by Riggs. Holmes was very direct in saying he observed the gun discharge as a result of the kick. Ross said he saw Riggs kick Penn twice, "And the second time I seen Riggs kick him, that is when I heard the shot."

The first question the assertion raised was under what conditions would a gun accidently discharge as a result of a kick to the weapon or the arm of the person holding it.

A series of experienced criminalists and firearms experts, some with the SDPD, testified to the specific trigger and hammer configurations under which a .38 caliber Smith & Wesson revolver might accidentally discharge.

Sharon Lynch, a criminalist with the police department, explained that the short metal "hammer" mechanism at the rear of the gun moves back and springs forward to strike the primer at the rear of the bullet cartridge, causing it to discharge. She demonstrated the two hammer positions from which a revolver can be positioned and fired: single action and double action. "When the gun is fired double action, only the trigger is pulled." She pulled the trigger to show the hammer move back and strike forward. It was the movement Sarah Pina-Ruiz described in her testimony.

"When a gun is fired single action, the hammer is pulled back," she said, using her thumb to pull it back, locking it into the rear "cocked" position. "Then the trigger is pulled." The critical difference between the two hammer positions was the amount of force on the trigger required to discharge the gun. "Almost four pounds in the single action and almost eleven pounds on the double action," she said. Neither was a lot of pressure, but four pounds was, by any measure, a "hair trigger." But even a hair trigger required something to exert the force on it. That thing was usually a finger.

The experts were in agreement that the conditions necessary for the possibility of an accidental discharge of this type were hammer cocked back, finger on the trigger, or at the very least inside the trigger guard. SDPD firearms expert Gene Wolberg held up the .38 revolver and pulled back the hammer. "When you are in this condition in a single action or on the verge of shooting, it is ready to go; the gun is ready to be fired," he said. Silverman asked if he was aware of accidental discharges occurring with that configuration. "I handle weapons a lot," Wolberg said. "Those kinds of things can happen. I have seen them happen at firing ranges with shooters." The problem for Milt Silverman was that the only person in the trial so far to claim that Sagon Penn cocked the gun was Milt Silverman, in his opening statement. But now, at least the jury knew there did exist a scenario under which an accidental discharge of a .38 caliber revolver from a kick was very possible. Now Silverman needed to show that such a kick had taken place.

"MIKE, IS THERE any chance you can get that mannequin back out for me?" Silverman asked bailiff Mike Rodelo. Rodelo lifted Clarence out his chair, brought him to the well, and stood the life-size artificial man upright in a custom stand.

As Dr. David Katsuyama stepped down from the witness stand and approached, Clarence's remarkably lifelike face seemed to stare back at him blankly. The trim, youthful, and impeccably dressed pathologist from the county coroner's office had performed over fifteen thousand autopsies during his twenty years there, including that of Tom Riggs. Prior to his testimony, the pathologist drilled four holes into the mannequin's body in precise locations and angles based on his examination of the wounds on Tom Riggs. By sliding wooden dowels into the holes, he could illustrate the trajectory of the bullets that struck Riggs in various locations.

All of the shots that struck Riggs had been fired while Penn was still lying on his back. One of the dowels projected at a sharp, upward angle into the upper right thigh of the mannequin. The dowel representing the bullet that killed Riggs protruded straight out from the lower abdomen at a perpendicular angle as though the shooter had been standing directly in front of him with the gun aimed at that exact level. It was puzzling considering Penn was on his back when he fired.

Katsuyama slid the third dowel through a hole in the sole of the mannequin's left boot, out the top of the boot, and into the lower right chest at a sharp, upward angle. He explained that this bullet had passed between Riggs's big toe and second toe, causing minor injury, and eventually came to rest in the superficial fat and muscle above his right ribcage. He was able to match the chest wound with the bullet that went through the boot because the entry wound "was not a good oval opening. It appeared that it had been created by a distorted bullet" and that "most of its energy was expended." In other words, it had gone through something else before hitting him in the chest. The slug itself had not been found and likely fell out during CPR chest compressions.

A number of criminalists had studied the bullet holes in the sole and top of Tom Riggs's left boot. Gene Wolberg had not conducted a formal distance test to determine the proximity of the end of the gun barrel to the sole of the boot but had tested for the presence of gunpowder residue on the sole. He noted a large number of "partially burned and unburned gunpowder particles, gunshot residue, that was impacted into that shoe area." He had "just a gut feeling that it was about a six-inch shot."

Silverman's criminologist Rich Whalley had conducted the distance testing using soles taken from the exact same brand of boot worn by Riggs. "I shot into the sole at that angle at various distances from zero inches, or contact; three inches; six inches; and twelve inches," he said.

"Did you form an opinion as to how far away the muzzle of the Jacobs gun was from the boot of Officer Riggs when it hit him?" Silverman asked.

"About three inches," the criminalist answered with confidence.

David Katsuyama had also analyzed the quantity and quality of the gunpowder reside and concluded that the barrel of the gun had been within several inches of the sole of Riggs's boot when fired.

Several explanations were offered for how the underside of Riggs's boot might have become exposed to the barrel of the gun at such a close distance. One, Riggs could have raised his foot while recoiling or falling back after being struck by the first or second bullet. Or two, he could have intentionally lifted it, in a manner consistent with a motion intended to stomp directly down at the gun in Penn's hand. But for that to be true, the bullet that passed through the boot would almost certainly have to be the first to strike Riggs. Even with their substantial expertise and sophisticated testing, neither Sharon Lynch, Gene Wolberg, nor Rich Whalley felt they had enough information to venture an opinion on the order of the three shots that struck Tom Riggs. But the man currently standing before Clarence the mannequin was confident he did.

"OKAY, LET'S GET down to the sequence of these shots," Silverman said.

Katsuyama said the shot that killed Riggs by severing his abdominal aorta was the third and final shot. He explained that the perpendicular trajectory of the bullet into Riggs's abdomen was probably due to Riggs being bent over by the force of a previous bullet when Penn fired at him from his position on the ground. After bisecting the aorta, the bullet impacted the backbone and penetrated the spinal canal. The damage to the nerves would have instantly rendered Riggs paralyzed from the waist down and unable to straighten up. Based on their sharp, upward trajectory, neither of the other two bullets could have entered his body while he was in that position.

The second bullet fired by Sagon Penn, he said, struck Riggs in the upper right thigh in an acute upward trajectory, with fragments traveling into the pelvic area. The force of that impact would have pushed him backward and possibly caused him to double over. The impact of this bullet along with the fatal bullet would have been enough to propel him over the retaining wall, Katsuyama said.

By process of elimination, Katsuyama concluded that the first shot must have been the one that went through the sole of Riggs's boot. The wooden dowel in Clarence told the story of a bullet that struck the sole of a shoe positioned almost directly above the gun from which it was fired. The trajectory indicated that Riggs must have been standing immediately adjacent to Penn's head with his foot lifted at the moment the shot was fired. He felt it was unlikely that Riggs could have been in such a position had he been struck by a previous bullet, nor did he believe this bullet would have caused Riggs to double over into the position in which the fatal bullet struck him.

Silverman would argue the combined findings of Wolberg, Whalley, and Katsuyama indicated Riggs was in the act of kicking at the gun. A first kick, he alleged, had caused the accidental initial discharge that stuck Jacobs. Riggs was in the process of a second kick when Penn fired the first shot that went through the sole of the boot.

BUT NONE OF that adequately explained why Penn was justified in firing the shot at Riggs at all. The answer to that, Silverman said, went back to that single comment made by Sarah Pina-Ruiz to Detective Dave Ayers on the night of the incident: "As the gunshot went off, Officer Riggs reached for his gun." The problem was, Pina-Ruiz was now denying she ever said it, insisting instead that Riggs was holding a baton in one hand and his portable radio in the other when he was shot, leaving no available hand with which to reach for a gun.

To support Pina-Ruiz's claim, Carpenter argued that the two radio transmissions by Riggs and additional unidentified mic clicks on the radio-traffic recording strongly suggested Riggs kept the radio in his hand the entire time. Additionally, Officer Gerry Kramer recalled finding Riggs's radio out of its holster, suggesting it had been in his hand. "I remember seeing it lying next to him. I picked it up," Kramer said.

Silverman and his team spent the weekend searching for anything they might have missed that would indicate Riggs's radio was in its holster when he was shot. They went through crime scene photos and diagrams looking for any sign of a notation, image, or statement that would place the radio in Riggs's holster at some point following the shooting.

Silverman brought home a box of VHS tapes containing hours of television news footage, all of which had been combed over before for evidence related to a number of issues. That night, he and Maria sat in front of the television popping tapes in and out of a VCR, playing, rewinding, and replaying any footage that might contain a clue. They came to the graphic footage taken by a *Channel 39 News* cameraman of paramedics and officers conducting CPR on Tom Riggs.

Silverman had seen it many times, but he let the video run anyhow. It begins with shadowy figures moving hastily within the frame. Officer Kramer becomes visible. "Can you turn on your light, please," he asks breathlessly. "Sure," the cameraman says, and the scene becomes bathed in white light revealing the body of Tom Riggs, his shirt torn open and a fire department medic performing chest compressions. In the foreground, Kramer kneels in the dirt near the area of Riggs's legs. He leans forward to pull Riggs's legs out from under the black Chevelle. In that flash of a moment, Silverman saw it. He sat up in his chair, pointed the remote at the VCR, and pressed rewind and then play. And there it was again, just for an instant. Riggs's duty belt had been unbuckled, but it was still around his waist. On his right hip was the radio holster with the handy-talkie portable radio firmly inside, its stubby little black antenna giving it away.

ON TUESDAY MORNING, April 22, Silverman introduced the video into evidence during the testimony of pathologist Werner Spitz. "Now, I would like to show briefly a video tape to the jury and ask the doctor's opinion based upon the showing of the video tape," he announced. Mike Carpenter sat expressionless in his seat as Mike Rodelo wheeled the television monitor cart in front of the jury box. Spitz stepped down and stood several feet back from the monitor. The five-second clip was played, freezing on the frame showing the radio on Riggs's hip. "Dr. Spitz, are you taking note of this right here?" Silverman asked, circling his finger around the image of the radio.

Spitz leaned in and squinted. "Yes, I see this," he said in his thick German accent.

"Is it your opinion that if Agent Riggs had in fact been holding this handy-talkie in his right hand at the time that he sustained those bullet wounds, that it is unlikely that he would have gotten it back into the position that it is depicted there?"

Spitz considered it for a moment. "I think it is more likely that he would have dropped it, particularly since the minute he sustained the injury to his spine, his legs were cut off and he collapsed. So," the doctor concluded, "he wouldn't have had much time to put it into his belt."

Silverman stared for a few moments at the image of Tom Riggs on the monitor before turning it off. "All right," he said softly. "Thank you. That is all."

25

"THE QUESTION OF WHETHER PENN COULD SEE INTO RIGGS'S patrol car when he shot [Sarah] Pina-Ruiz would haunt the courtroom until the end of the trial," *San Diego Magazine* journalist Maribeth Mellin, who attended every day of the trial, wrote weeks after its completion. But that question had begun haunting investigators from both sides within days of the incident itself.

On April 2, 1985, forty-eight hours after Sagon Penn fired two shots at Sarah Pina-Ruiz, Detective Gary Murphy drove his unmarked department sedan up the driveway at 6564 Brooklyn Avenue and brought it to a stop. Murphy and fellow Team IV detective Larry Lindstrom walked around until they arrived at the bloodstains in the dirt, the break in the bushes along the retaining wall, and several sets of tire tracks. Gone were Riggs's 785 vehicle and Allen Cepeda's black Chevelle. Operating on memory, Murphy and Lindstrom picked the spot where they believed the Ford LTD patrol unit had been parked two days before. Murphy pulled his car up to the spot on the driveway, threw it in park, rolled up the driver's side window, and got out.

The kids playing and roughhousing in Carlton Smith's front yard paused for a moment and then went on with their fun. After two days of cops and reporters crawling all over their neighborhood, a couple of old guys in suits wasn't all that interesting.

Murphy positioned himself about six feet back from the driver's side door. The big, round-shouldered detective checked his watch; it was 6:00 p.m. He looked at the driver's side window and then turned around and looked west. Beyond the oleander bushes and eucalyptus trees in the foreground, and past the steeple of the Apostolic church, the sun hung low in the sky.

At 6:08 p.m., the sun disappeared behind the church and then fell beneath the hillside behind. As daylight turned to twilight, the yellow and orange tones of a Pacific sunset spread out above an area of intense white light. Murphy looked at the side window and took a few steps in each direction, studying it from different angles. He did so again at 6:11 p.m., the time forty-eight hours earlier Tom Riggs had requested a "cover now." He continued watching past the 6:13 mark, the time they estimated the shooting took place. At 6:15 p.m., Murphy and Lindstrom got back in their sedan and drove off.

"I could see that there was no glare from the sun. I could see the sky reflected behind me in the glass, but this in no way stopped me from seeing the interior of the front seat of my vehicle and the inside portion of the passenger's door," the detective concluded in his report of the window-glare investigation.

BY COMPARISON, THE work that Jim Gripp, Rich Whalley, and Al Arnson put into recreating the exact conditions for their own window-glare investigation and photo shoot had been exhaustive. Using his land survey conducted a little over three months earlier, surveyor Al Arnson had calculated their location relative to the earth, sun, and heavenly bodies in space. He then applied astronomical data to adjust those calculations to determine the position of the sun relative to the side window of Riggs's vehicle at the precise moment of the shooting.

To determine Penn's line of sight to the side window of Riggs's vehicle, Whalley began by analyzing tiny fractures spiderwebbed through a portion of what little glass remained in the window. "Those are fractures that radiate from an impact point," he later explained on the witness stand. "You can project back along those radii, and where they intersect is very close to the [first] bullet hole." Having plotted the impact point of the first bullet, he established a trajectory using the impact points of the bullets in the interior of the vehicle and physical measurements of Penn to identify with a reasonable degree of certainty the position of Penn's eyes in relation to the window at the time he fired the first shot at Sarah Pina-Ruiz.

The defense team then set their sights on the anniversary of the shooting, when the earth and sky would be precisely as they had been one year before. But when the three men arrived on the morning of March 31, 1986, they were dumbfounded. "You got to be fucking kidding me," Jim Gripp said as they stood at the end of the driveway. Sometime between their last visit and now, the owner decided to make improvements to the property, leveling the surface and raising the height of the driveway at points ranging from six inches to a foot. Considering the precision of their other calculations, it might as well have been miles.

Arnson hurriedly scribbled new calculations. "If we are going to get the correct angle, we're going to need a piece of equipment to dig up this guy's driveway," he concluded.

"How the hell are we going to get that done in six hours?" said Gripp, who had conceived and planned the whole operation.

Rich Whalley knocked on the homeowner's door and tried to explain to the baffled man why he should let them tear up his new driveway. One hundred dollars later and a promise to put it back the way they found it, they had a deal. Now it was a race against time to return the terrain back to its original configuration, set up their equipment, and begin photographing by 6:00 p.m.

By late afternoon, Rich Whalley had used a rented tractor to scrape away the layer of decomposed granite and dump it into a six-foot-high pile in the Paraderos' front yard. When Arnson declared the land back to its original configuration, Gripp pulled a rented 1985 Ford LTD, the same make, model, and year as Riggs's unit, and positioned its front wheels within an inch of their location at the time of the shootings. In the passenger seat was Audrey Acosta, Gripp's office manager, chosen because of her similar hair color and skin complexion to that of Sarah Pina-Ruiz. The ivory-colored knit sweater she wore, bought at a local thrift store, had been matched to Pina-Ruiz's using a color chip. Whalley studied a photograph of the crime scene, noticed the branches of a nearby oleander bush had grown out, and clipped them back.

Professional photographer Charlie Colladay set up his tripod and

Hasselblad camera with an 80-millimeter lens, which provided the most accurate approximation of what is seen by the human eye. Gripp set up next to him with a Canon F1 and 50-millimeter zoom lens to shoot color slides as a control image. Videographer Roger Holtzen aimed his camera at the window, prepared to hit "record" and to let it run throughout the whole process.

But as the time approached, a cloud cover moved in, and the team was forced to pack up their equipment, leaving the rented skip loader and a pile of dirt and crushed granite. It was not until April 3 that the weather cleared. Al Arnson calculated the simple two-minute adjustment to the time of sunset and location of the sun to match that of March 31.

With the Smith children and other neighborhood kids playing in the next yard, the team prepared to snap a set of photos at one-minute intervals leading up to the adjusted 6:15:45 time of the shooting and for several minutes thereafter. When the sun set at 6:10 p.m., the 6500 block of Brooklyn Avenue entered what astronomers call "civil twilight," the twenty-to-thirty-minute period when "Earth's atmosphere scatters the sun's rays to create the colors of twilight."

"Fifteen seconds," Rich Whalley alerted the team and then counted down: "fourteen, thirteen, twelve . . ." The cameras began clicking two shots a second for ten seconds straight. "The time now is 6:11 and forty-five seconds," Whalley announced to mark the time on the video recording. In the window was the reflection of a pale western sky in the background and the dark silhouettes of the oleander, trees, and roof of the Apostolic church in the foreground. But the stand-in for Sarah Pina-Ruiz remained sufficiently visible through the reflection. Periodically, Whalley instructed her to lean forward and reach out toward the center of the dashboard as though grabbing for something—a radio mic perhaps. The movement had the strange effect of making her more visible yet harder to identify.

"The time now is 6:13 and forty-five seconds," Whalley called out two minutes later. During that time, an orange glow formed behind the shadow of a tree at the bottom left edge of the reflection, along with a swath of bright white that made it increasingly difficult to identify

Audrey Acosta's white sweater. "Looks brighter," someone commented. "The white here is really white." But from the neck up, Acosta remained visible and identifiable.

Charlie Colladay viewed the glass through the lens of the Hasselblad and then dropped one f-stop to adjust for the changing light. "Ten, nine, eight . . ." Whalley counted down until there was the flurry of camera clicks again. The reflection of the western sky and objects in the foreground were becoming even more pronounced each minute. The silhouettes of the objects reflected in the window—which one year earlier included Sagon Penn himself—darkened significantly. "It's now 6:14 and 45 seconds," Whalley remarked.

"The next minute is the critical one," he said, the urgency in his voice noticeable over the sounds of children playing in the background. There was the sharp sound of someone banging on what sounded like the hood of a car. "Okay, fifteen seconds. Ten, nine, eight, seven . . ." The cameras clicked rapidly. "The time is 6:15 and 45 seconds," he called out, marking the exact moment Sagon Penn fired two shots through the side window of Thomas Riggs's police car.

They paused, silently staring at the window. In the final seconds of Rich Whalley's countdown, it had completed a final metamorphosis into a glass canvas crowded with darkened objects, the orange glow of light refracting off the atmosphere, and a swath of sky above the horizon bathed in bright white. The woman in the passenger seat had become a ghostly image moving behind the light and shadow. "Holy shit," said videographer Roger Holtzen.

Two weeks later, Milt Silverman called Al Arnson, Jim Gripp, and Rich Whalley to the witness stand to explain the lengths they had gone to recreate the exact environmental conditions that existed at the moment of the shooting on March 31, 1985. The difference between their scientific calculations and the guesstimates and lack of photographs by Lindstrom and Murphy was stark. Over the protests of Mike Carpenter, Milt Silverman presented a single photo representing the results of their effort to prove their contention that Sagon Penn would have had a very difficult time identifying Sarah Pina-Ruiz before shooting into the vehicle. He motioned to the photographic image he had projected onto a movie screen. "Ladies and gentlemen," he said, "we charted the heavens and moved the earth."

ON THE DRIVEWAY at 6564 Brooklyn Avenue, a young Black man in a white long-sleeve, button-down shirt and blue jeans lies on his back in the dirt. Straddling him is a blond-haired uniformed police officer, a .38-caliber revolver holstered on his right hip. Standing above them, just to the right of the young man's head, is a black-haired uniformed officer holding a PR-24 police baton. With the children at school on a Tuesday afternoon, the neighborhood is uncharacteristically quiet. The adults who are home stay inside; few of them want to see this again. "Ready?" says a voice outside the frame of the video camera. The blond officer cocks his arm back and makes a fist. He waits. "Three, two, one . . ." The scene is over seconds later. "Getting very close," the voice says encouragingly. "Let's do it again."

It is the afternoon of January 7, 1986, and while Al Arnson goes about his business conducting the initial land survey of the area, the actors prepare to repeat their roles in a movie that will last no more than ten seconds. An actor whose height, build, and closely cropped hair is remarkably similar to Sagon Penn's lowers the gun and lies down again on the spot marked on the driveway. The blond man in the role of Donovan Jacobs stands up from where he fell on his side on the previous take and dusts himself off. The actor hired to play Tom Riggs did not show up, so Jim Gripp put on the uniform as a stand-in. He steps up the retaining wall he had pretended to fall over after the fourth gunshot. The videographer from Seacoast Multimedia resets the three video cameras aimed at different angles, including one representing Sarah Pina-Ruiz's point of view from inside the vehicle.

Rich Whalley waits for his actors to resume their places before beginning the countdown again. When they finally get the timing right, down to the fraction of a second, the video tape will be edited, and the live audio replaced by the version of the Angela McKibben 911 call with Fausto Poza's muted beeps inserted to represent the gunshots. Silverman knew the jury would never be allowed to see the tape, but that was okay. Mostly, he wanted to prove to his defense team, and himself, that their version of events could have actually played out in real-time.

"You guys ready? Three, two, one . . ." The cameras begin recording again.

With punches and baton strikes raining down on him and fearing for his life, Sagon Penn makes a desperate grab for Donovan Jacobs's gun, easily retrieving it from the holster. In a panic, he pulls back the hammer and his finger slides inside the trigger guard. He presses the barrel to Donovan Jacobs's chest. "Please, please stop," he begs. "I have got your gun. Please stop." Tom Riggs sees Penn holding the gun, lifts his boot, and stomps down to disarm him. Instead, the boot strikes Penn's upper arm. The gun, now in the single-action, hair-trigger position, goes off. Bang! Jacobs falls off to the side. Riggs reaches for his gun as he lifts his left boot to kick at Penn's hand a second time. When it comes within three inches from the barrel, the next shot rings out, going through the sole of the boot. Bang! Riggs steps back and begins to double over at the waist. Bang! Bang! He stumbles backward, dropping the batons before going over the retaining wall into the neighboring yard.

It takes Penn 2.3 seconds to get to his feet, leaving four-tenths of a second during which he spots movement behind the bright sunset and dark shadows reflected in the side window of Tom Riggs's vehicle. Believing it is another police officer holding a gun, he shoots before the cop can shoot him. Bang! Bang!

And that, according to Milt Silverman, is how the whole thing went down.

26

A WEEK OR TWO BEFORE MILT SILVERMAN BEGAN HIS DE-
fense case, the two attorneys had their final showdown over the
months-long battle by Silverman to access the police-employment
file of Donovan Jacobs, and the degree to which the defense could introduce incidents of alleged misconduct into the trial. Carpenter's position
was that Jacobs's past was irrelevant to the Penn case. He told Hamrick,
"Donovan Jacobs and maybe Agent Riggs will be defendants in the case,
and the whole thing will be turned around. I submit to you, that would
be playing right into the hands of Milt Silverman, who is famous for this
type of defense."

"You know, I bristle a bit when someone says I am famous for putting the victim on trial," Silverman responded. "I would hope that my
reputation is one in which I seek to elicit the truth of what happened."
Hamrick decided in favor of Silverman but limited the number of incidents he could present. "Pick out your best two or three of recent origin," Hamrick told him. The result was allegations against Jacobs by
three men: Anthony Fields, Terry Garrett, and Edward Serdi.

AGENT DONOVAN JACOBS and rookie officer Anne-Marie Tyler were
on the 1700 block of Plover Street in Southeast San Diego looking for
a teenager carrying a rifle. It was 2:45 p.m. on the afternoon of March
31, 1985, almost three and a half hours before Jacobs would be shot in

the neck on Brooklyn Avenue, one mile to the south. Jacobs and Tyler spotted a young Black man fitting the description of their suspect standing in the front yard of a house. Fifteen-year-old Anthony Tyrone Fields eyed them warily as they got out of the patrol unit and approached. Jacobs asked his name and if he owned a gun. "Just a toy gun," Anthony told him.

The young man's mother, Marguarite Fields, and father came out the front door of the house. Tyler spoke with them while Jacobs stayed with Anthony Fields. At some point, Jacobs recognized Fields's name having been mentioned at the shift briefing in connection with a burglary. "Turn around," Jacobs said, taking the boy by one arm while reaching for his handcuffs at the same time. "What for?" the kid protested as Jacobs cuffed his wrists behind his back. Jacobs told him as he escorted the prisoner into the back cage of the police car. The arrest report written by Anne-Marie Tyler documented the routine and uneventful apprehension of Anthony Fields.

When Marguarite Fields took the stand for the defense on April 23, 1986, she had quite a different story to tell about the arrest of her son. Fields said Anthony, who they called Tony, was in his bedroom, not the front yard, when Tyler and Jacobs came to the door. Tyler informed her and her husband they had a report that their son was walking down the street with a rifle. They asked if they could speak with him. "Jacobs for some reason left and went and got in his car," Fields said. "I don't know where he went, but he told the female officer that he would be right back."

Less than five minutes later, Jacobs returned. Fields offered her version of what happened next: "Well, he got out of his car, telling Tony to come to him. Tony was walking down toward the car when he grabbed my son, twisted his arm behind his back very roughly. As a fact, more roughly than he should have—Tony was not a very big child at the time." Barely five feet tall and one hundred pounds, she said. "He had his arm behind his back, bending it so he could handcuff him very tightly, and then pushed [him] in toward the car."

Fields said she was still with Officer Tyler near her front door at the time this happened. "She was standing next to me, and she said, 'I don't know what's going on.' She said, 'What's he doing?' She said, 'What's happening?' You know, just very surprised." Marguarite Fields described it as a very upsetting incident.

"AS I WAS putting out the trash, he spotted me and backed his car up," Terry Garrett said of Donovan Jacobs, testifying the same day as Marguarite Fields. "He came over where I was, then asked me what I was doing. I told him I lived here. He wanted to see my arms, and suddenly he jerked my arm over the fence."

"To look for perhaps track marks?" Milt Silverman asked.

"Track marks, or whatever," Garrett said.

In his late thirties, six foot three and 180 pounds, Terry Garrett had returned home from a fifteen-month combat tour in Vietnam with a battle scar on his forearm and a heroin addiction. His life in San Diego was a revolving door of narcotic arrests, warrants for missing court dates related to those arrests, and then arrests related to the warrants issued on the previous arrests. The street cop most responsible for keeping him in the revolving door was Donovan Jacobs, whose favorite target for "contacts" were known drug addicts like Garrett.

"I took my arm back and I got up and I ran inside my house," he continued. "He came behind me and kicked my door in. He was very aggressive. He was trying to pull me out the door. I asked him what was the reason for all of this? He hit me with a stick. Then I sat down on the steps to catch my breath, and that is when he told me, 'I will beat your Black ass if you don't come out.'" Garrett's roommate, Paul Watts, recalled that Jacobs "rammed the end of his nightstick into Garrett's solar plexus and said something to the effect of 'I ought to kill your Black ass.'"

"Were you resisting?" Carpenter asked on cross-examination.

"Yes, you could say I was resisting. I didn't want to be arrested," Garrett conceded.

On cross, Carpenter showed Garrett was giving inaccurate and evasive testimony related to previous arrests by Jacobs. Garrett denied using heroin at the time of the arrest, but test results showed otherwise. Through the questioning, Garrett seemed unable to keep straight the details of the multiple arrests by Jacobs and subsequent trips to jail for failure to appear and probation violations. "Is it a fair statement to say that you don't like Donovan Jacobs?" Carpenter asked.

"I have nothing against him," Garrett shrugged.

"Despite the fact that he has arrested you four times?" Carpenter asked.

"Despite the fact, yes, sir," Garrett said.*

ON SEPTEMBER 5, 1982, a twenty-year-old short-order cook named Edward Serdi was riding his motorcycle to his job at a Denny's restaurant when a San Diego Police car coming in the opposite direction made a left turn in front of him as he approached the intersection of Imperial and Sixty-First Street. Officer William Mahue hit the brakes when he caught sight of Serdi, who swerved slightly to avoid the vehicle that had partially encroached upon his lane. "Don't you know the law?" Serdi called out as he continued through the intersection.

When Serdi looked back, there were two cop cars speeding up behind him. Serdi knew what was coming, so he pulled over before the units turned on their overhead lights.

When Ed Serdi got to work fifteen minutes later, he was holding a traffic ticket for two minor violations. He called the San Diego Police Department to file a complaint against the issuing officer, a D. Jacobs.

"Well," the fidgety and slightly hyperactive Serdi said when asked by Milt Silverman to explain what happened. The first officer he spoke with was William Mahue: "I stopped the bike. I got off the bike. He asked me if this was my motorcycle. I told him, yes. He asked me to get on it, start it up, check the blinkers and all this. I asked him why he was stopping me, and he said, for the remark of me telling him that at the intersection. He didn't like it or something like that."

After Mahue put Serdi through a vehicle inspection, the second officer, Donovan Jacobs, ran a check and found Serdi's license did not include authorization to operate a motorcycle. "He started to write me a ticket and I was a little upset. I said, 'Go ahead, you asses have been giving me a bunch of hassle all week.' He [Jacobs] didn't like what I said, so he

---

* In a postscript to his testimony, Terry Garrett's fortunes improved four months later when he hit the $1 million jackpot in the California lottery.

came up to me and pushed me up against an embankment and he took out his billy club, and he was standing right next to me and said, 'You little shit, tell me what you just said so I can beat your ass up and down the street with it.' I didn't look up at him," the five-foot-tall, 110-pound Serdi related. "I said, 'No, I know when to shut up.'" Silverman asked Serdi if he was sure all of it had happened that way. "I would not say that if it wasn't true."

In his cross-examination of Serdi, Carpenter picked apart inconsistencies between the report of his original verbal complaint and current testimony, implying Serdi's real motive for the complaint was to get his tickets dismissed. A week after Serdi's testimony, Carpenter called to the stand the patrol officer who had been in the lead vehicle that accidentally cut off Serdi. Officer Bill Mahue admitted the mistake. "As I started to make the turn, I realized the motorcycle was there and I stopped partially into his lane. He passed me. He yelled something. I turned the car around and I followed him."

On cross-examination, Milt Silverman asked him why he followed Serdi.

"The way he yelled at me," Mahue answered. "I wanted to make sure that everything was all right."

"What do you mean that everything was all right?"

"That his welfare was all right; that he understood what happened if that was the case."

"That's right," Silverman said almost mockingly. "Turned around to make sure that his welfare was all right. That's what you're telling the jury is the reason you turned around?"

Silverman had no doubt that Mahue and Jacobs had subjected Serdi to a classic "attitude stop," in which some "punk," "puke," or "asshole" who has committed no crime is pulled over and hassled anyhow just to teach him a lesson over some perceived act of disrespect or defiance. In the world of law enforcement, there was another name for it: a "chickenshit stop."

27

THE MAN WHO ENTERED THE COURTROOM ON APRIL 24, 1986, was in his mid-thirties, solidly built, with a neatly trimmed mustache, thick black hair, and a quiet intensity about him. He unbuttoned the coat of his conservative suit as he took his seat on the witness stand, his dark eyes scanning the courtroom warily before settling on the defense attorney.

"Mr. Wheeler," Milt Silverman began. "Prior to joining the police department, were you in the service?"

"I was in the United States Army. I served in South Vietnam and Fort Riley, Kansas, and Germany," Doyle Wheeler answered in his deep, resonant voice.

"Did you see combat?"

"Yes, sir, I did."

"A lot of combat?"

"Yes, sir. I did short- and long-range reconnaissance patrols."

"Did you see people killed?"

"Yes, sir."

"Were you decorated in Vietnam for heroism, bravery, and that sort of thing?"

"I received a bronze star, I believe four army commendation medals—one with a "V" device for "valor"—three purple hearts, the Vietnamese cross of gallantry."

"During the period of time that you were on the San Diego Police

Department, were you advanced to [the rank of] lieutenant faster than anybody else that you know of that was ever on the police department?"

"I believe I was."

Wheeler recited a long list of awards and citations received during his meteoric rise through the department ranks, including Narcotic Officer of the Year from the California Narcotic Officers' Association.

"While you were at Northern Division, did you become familiar with the police officer by the name of Donovan Jacobs?"

"Yes, sir, I did," Wheeler said, adding he had "numerous occasions to observe Donovan Jacobs in the performance of his duty."

"Over that period of time, did you form an opinion as to Donovan Jacobs's propensity to engage in violence, or a propensity toward any kind of undesirable racial attitudes?"

"My opinion is that he is hardheaded," Wheeler said. "I found him to be cocky. I found him to be overly aggressive. And I felt that having observed his contact in dealing with some Black suspects that he had in custody, that he used unnecessary force."

"Tell the jury what you saw," Silverman said.

"Officer Jacobs had brought a Black male that he had in custody, handcuffed, in and had him facing the wall . . . As I came down the hallway, the suspect had looked over his shoulder. Officer Jacobs grabbed him at the base of the neck and slammed his head into the wall and indicated that he had told him to face the wall. I immediately told him to knock it off."

Wheeler said he was suspicious of Jacobs's famously high contact and arrest numbers while a member of the Narcotics Street Team. When a Narcotics training detective told Wheeler he wanted to award Jacobs for the high numbers, "I advised him right then that I had some concerns," Wheeler said.

As a Narcotics Street Team sergeant, it was Wheeler's job to review heroin and PCP arrest reports. "Having reviewed thousands of [narcotics] arrest reports, I was, for lack of a better term, somewhat suspicious of 'probable cause' and 'reasonable suspicion' for contact, the way the reports were written," Wheeler said. "The reports appeared to have been stamped out. Everything read the same on nearly every report with the exception of the name of the suspect and where he was arrested."

"Are you saying that in reviewing his reports, all of the contacts that he allegedly had with the people that he was arresting were essentially the same sort of a cookbook approach?"

"Yes, sir. I had occasion to see this kind of thing before and initiated an investigation." Wheeler said he pulled the files on twenty people arrested by Jacobs for being "under the influence" of heroin or PCP. "I took them to the lab and asked them to do a check for me and give me back a list of all those who had tested positive. Over 50 percent of the arrests tested negative." Wheeler suspected Jacobs was stopping, searching, and arresting whoever he wanted and then retroactively plugging in boilerplate "reasonable suspicion" and "probable cause" justifications. "I submitted the report to his command, Sergeant Jim Duncan, regarding what I had found."

Wheeler developed such a negative opinion of Jacobs that he tried to block his admission onto the SWAT squad. "I addressed it to a sergeant and to a lieutenant," Wheeler said. "I advised both that I felt he was a hothead and that I believed that he had some problems with bias and racism." Again, the sergeant was James Duncan. The lieutenant was John Morrison. "He indicated to me that he, being Lieutenant Morrison, had a lot of relatives in South Africa and Rhodesia. And he also indicated that anybody who hated niggers was okay in his book."

Although never divulged in court, Wheeler was the mysterious "former SDPD lieutenant" who had been feeding information about Jacobs to news anchorman Michael Tuck and the Penn defense team within days of the incident. He was Silverman's unnamed source of the subsequently unproven allegations that Jacobs was a member of white supremacist groups.

Silverman paused before opening a door he knew would be at the heart of Mike Carpenter's cross-examination of Doyle Wheeler. "After the McDonald's massacre, did you experience or begin to experience a mental health deterioration?"

No one in the courtroom needed to be told what Silverman meant by "the McDonald's massacre."

On the morning of Wednesday, July 18, 1984, a forty-one-year-old unemployed security guard and former funeral home embalmer named James Huberty took his wife and two young daughters to the San Diego Zoo. After stopping off for lunch, the family returned home to their apartment in the San Ysidro community of San Diego, a mostly Hispanic suburb pressed up against the border with Tijuana, Mexico. Huberty rolled some items up in a checkered blanket and kissed his wife goodbye. "I'm going hunting," he told her. "Hunting for humans."

At 3:56 p.m., Huberty entered the McDonald's fast-food restaurant on the 400 block of West San Ysidro Boulevard carrying a 9mm Browning semiautomatic pistol, a Winchester 12-gauge pump-action shotgun, and a 9mm Uzi high-powered semiautomatic rifle, along with hundreds of rounds of ammunition loaded into high-capacity magazines. Inside the restaurant were forty-five employees and customers, including many young children in the restaurant's play area.

By the time he was finally taken out by a single bullet from an SDPD SWAT sniper, James Huberty had killed twenty-one people—customers, employees, adults, children, and an infant—in the worst mass shooting in American history to date. In the opinion of one member of the San Diego Police Department, they did not all have to die.

As the first lieutenant on scene, Doyle Wheeler assumed incident command and immediately told arriving SWAT team sniper units they had the green light to shoot Huberty if they saw him with a weapon either inside or outside of the McDonald's. But with sniper units in place and a shot developing, SWAT commander Jerry Sanders came over the radio to countermand Wheeler's order. "They don't have a green light if he's somewhere inside the building with the hostages," Sanders said. "If he comes outside alone, they have the green light. If he's inside with the hostages, they have a red light."

Wheeler was dismayed. Sanders was not even on scene yet. The red light remained on, during which time gunfire could be heard coming from inside the building. When Sanders arrived on scene and was briefed, he immediately put the green light back on. Minutes later, a .308-caliber bullet traveling at 2,600 feet per second struck James Huberty just below the sternum, bisecting his abdominal aorta and severing his spinal cord.

Doyle Wheeler was convinced Huberty would have been taken out much earlier had Jerry Sanders left the green light in place, sparing the lives of anyone who died from delayed medical care or additional gunfire after that point.

Wheeler hesitated for a moment after Silverman's question about his mental health issues following the massacre. He took a deep breath before answering. "Yes, sir."

"And is that ultimately what led to your being medically retired from the San Diego Police Department?"

"Yes, sir."

"Would it be fair to say that as an outgrowth of that incident that you developed some hostility toward the San Diego Police Department?"

"Yes, sir."

"And do you to this day still harbor some hostility [toward] the San Diego Police Department?"

"Yes, sir."

"You knew Tom Riggs?" Silverman said as he came to the close of his direct examination of Wheeler.

"Yes, I did," said Wheeler, who had been his superior in a training program.

"You liked Tom Riggs?"

"Yes, I did."

"You felt Tom Riggs was a good cop?"

"Yes, I did."

Silverman pointed a finger in the direction of Sagon Penn sitting upright and motionless at the defense table. "You realize that the man that is sitting over there, whom I represent, killed him?"

"Yes, I do," Wheeler said.

"MR. WHEELER, ISN'T it true that you hate everything about the San Diego Police Department?" Mike Carpenter asked in opening his cross-examination.

"No, that is not true," Wheeler responded calmly.

"Isn't it true that you hate the city of San Diego for the way you are treated?"

"No, I don't hate the city of San Diego."

"Isn't it true that you will do anything and say anything that will hurt the San Diego Police Department?"

"Absolutely not."

"You are bitter toward the police department?"

"I am not happy with some things that occurred with the police department."

"Do you think that you were treated unfairly by the police department?"

"I don't know that I would view it as being treated unfairly. We have some differences of opinion."

In an earlier ruling, Hamrick placed strict limitations on how far the attorneys could go into the details of the McDonald's incident and resulting disagreement between Wheeler and the department. Carpenter decided not to test the judge's restrictions and switched subjects, adopting a less aggressive tone toward the witness.

"You became a San Diego Police Department officer and in 1977 you had to kill somebody," Carpenter said, referring to a heroin addict Wheeler shot when the man tried to run him over with a car, "did you have feelings of remorse about that?"

"Certainly."

"The killing that you had participated in and witnessed in Vietnam, was that dredged up at that time when you were involved in that [1977] killing?"

"Yes, I believe it was."

"After that you were involved in the Brenda Spencer thing?" Carpenter asked, referring to the teenager who shot children and faculty at an elementary school because, she told police, "I don't like Mondays." "Did you have a feeling of helplessness beginning about that time about your inability to save lives?" Carpenter asked.

"I remember I was bothered considerably by that, yes," Wheeler said, his voice cracking at the end. He swallowed, and his eyes began to tear up.

"You also had a situation where you came across a four-year-old girl and you had administered CPR. That was a very traumatic experience, wasn't it?"

Wheeler nodded. "Yes," he said in almost a whisper. He began to cry.

"I understand. I understand," Carpenter said sympathetically. "You felt that you had saved her life and you found out later that she had died, is that right?"

"Yes," Wheeler said, tears running down his cheeks.

"You saw your daughter in her, didn't you?"

"Yes."

"Again, this inability to save lives was very traumatic for you?"

"It bothered me, yes."

"And finally, the McDonald's incident in the summer of 1984. San Ysidro. As a result of that, you felt an overwhelming trauma and inability to save lives because of the number of people that were affected by the situation, didn't you?"

"Yes," Wheeler said, wiping his eyes. "I guess so."

IT HAD TAKEN a lot to break Doyle Wheeler, but when he finally did, he crashed fast and hard. Four months after McDonald's, Wheeler was referred to a psychiatrist for treatment after telling a supervisor he had put his gun in his mouth with the intention of pulling the trigger. Dr. Steven Buchanan prescribed Xanax for anxiety, a medication that came with the warning, "Combining with other substances, particularly alcohol, can slow breathing and possibly lead to death." On March 1, 1985, Wheeler combined a lot of Xanax with a lot of alcohol and sat in a hot tub hoping that it would lead to death. Instead, he ended up in intensive care followed by three days at the Mesa Vista psychiatric facility.

In July 1985, Doyle Wheeler was granted psychiatric-disability retirement after eleven years with the San Diego Police Department. "The patient is felt to be permanently disabled as regard to police work," Buchanan concluded. He was given a workers' compensation lump-sum settlement of $22,000 along with a recommendation he seek further psychological treatment.

"Isn't it a fact that you and Donovan Jacobs had a personality conflict?" Carpenter asked, moving away from the issue of Wheeler's psychological condition.

"I didn't care for Donovan Jacobs, if that's what you mean, yes," Wheeler said.

"And you don't care for him today, do you?"

"He's not a friend of mine. No, I don't care for him."

"You know the importance of your testimony in this case, don't you?"

"Yes, I do."

"And isn't your testimony based on nothing other than your dislike and your hatred for the way you were treated by the San Diego Police Department?"

"Absolutely not, Mr. Carpenter."

CALLED TO TESTIFY later in the trial, psychiatrist Alan Abrams, who had evaluated Wheeler in relation to a workers' compensation claim, offered his assessment of the man. "He viewed the San Diego Police Department as his nemesis and at times would think that they'd go out of their way to make his life very unhappy. I wouldn't say 'hatred' so much as a feeling that they had hurt him in an unnecessary way, and he was very angry about that." Abrams said Wheeler "at times exhibited elements of paranoia" and was "very preoccupied with the department retaliating against him" for his criticism of their handling of the McDonald's massacre.

"I am going to ask you a question, sort of the bottom line," Silverman said. "Is Doyle Wheeler a liar?"

"I don't believe he would consciously lie," Abrams replied. "He's very angry. He feels very disillusioned. But Lieutenant Wheeler has an enormous respect for the concept of law, and I would not imagine that Lieutenant Wheeler would come into a courtroom and say anything he believed wasn't true."

"Everything in his background, his whole life going back to when he was a ranger in Vietnam, was devoted to doing his job as best as it could possibly be done?"

"Yes, exactly," Abrams agreed.

"And expecting others to do the same?"

"Yes."

"Those that worked for him?"

"Yes."

"Being devoted to the principle of truth?"

"Fairness."

"Fairness?"

"Justice, yes," the doctor said.

"Doing what's right?"

"Yes."

"All of those things?"

"Exactly."

"That is Doyle Wheeler in capital letters?"

"Yes, it is," Abrams answered unequivocally.

DOYLE WHEELER WOULD remain one of the most controversial figures in the trial, with observers and participants sharply divided over his motives and the veracity of his testimony. Mike Carpenter did not believe Doyle Wheeler had been honest on the stand but felt compassion for him nevertheless. "I feel Lieutenant Wheeler is an extremely tragic individual," he said. Homicide lieutenant Paul Ybarrondo, who had been deeply involved in both the San Ysidro and Penn investigations, was far less charitable: "Doyle Wheeler is a lying piece of shit," he said. Milt Silverman had a far different appraisal of the man: "Doyle Wheeler is a goddamn hero."

28

MARY JACOBS WAS SICK OF PEOPLE SAYING BAD THINGS about her kid. "Mother Speaks Out in Defense of Jacobs" ran the May 1 headline in *The San Diego Union*, three days after Milt Silverman rested his case in chief. Instead of an interview, Mary sent the paper a five-page document written in the form of a letter to her son. "If it were your wish that I not say anything, I am sorry," it read. "But when they start attacking your honesty, integrity, and character, your mom no longer will be quiet."

She wrote of their own welcoming of the first Black family to move into their Spring Valley neighborhood, when few others did. "All you children learned the lesson well, to judge people by what they do and never on how they looked."

She said her son requested a transfer to the Southeast so he could make a difference in the lives of the people who lived there. "Dammit, mom, those people need our help." After the shooting, he apologized to her from his hospital bed for allowing his gun to be taken away: "Mom, I'm sorry; I'm just no match for karate." But mostly, Mary Jacobs's letter was an unabashed defense of her son. "I am his mother," she wrote. "I know my son—and I know the truth. Your name will be cleared, Donovan!"

MILT SILVERMAN'S ATTACK on the character of Donovan Jacobs allowed Mike Carpenter one last chance to do just what Mary Jacobs hoped during his rebuttal case.

He called over a dozen former and current supervisors and fellow officers as well as people from Jacobs's personal life, including four who were Black, to testify to Jacobs's professionalism, effective policing, and absence of racial bias.

Some of those who took the stand to praise Jacobs also offered their opinion of his greatest detractor, Doyle Wheeler. "I have always disliked Sergeant Wheeler," said Sergeant Ed Petrick, who served beside Wheeler in the Northern Division earlier in their careers. "I never felt that he was very truthful with me," said Sergeant James Duncan, who denied Wheeler ever told him about excessive use of force, negative PCP test results, or suspicious arrest reports by Jacobs. Silverman had a deep distrust of Duncan, who was Jacobs's supervisor much of his time in the Southeast. He was sure the sergeant knew about all of Jacobs's alleged misconduct and was covering up for him on the force and in the courtroom, observing the age-old "code of silence," by which cops always protect other cops from anything or anyone outside the department.

Three psychiatrists testified that the inaccuracies in Jacobs's memory of events was not a case of consciously lying but subconscious distortions as the result of physical and psychological trauma. Seventy-five-year-old psychiatrist Wait Griswold outraged Silverman and Black Penn supporters in the courtroom by consistently expressing doubt about the veracity of the eyewitnesses' statements, even about universally agreed-upon facts. "I would be more inclined to accept the opinion of the police officer rather than the individuals in the truck," Griswold said, regarding Jacobs's claim the truck made a U-turn. The reason he gave for his distrust of eyewitness testimony was even more inflammatory. "I think the culture role and ethnic reason; they would tend to support the defendant," Griswold said. "It still seems odd to me they all tell precisely the same story." "Do they really?" a dumbfounded Silverman asked. "When you say *precisely* the same story, like they have got it down in a script?" Even Mike Carpenter would do his best to distance himself from Griswold's comments in his closing argument.

ON THE AFTERNOON of May 7, on the last day of prosecution rebuttal, Donovan Jacobs was called to the stand to address the allegations made against him during the defense case. He refuted the testimony of Terry Garrett, Marguarite Fields, and Edward Serdi. "Without a doubt, I didn't touch him," he said of Serdi's allegations. "I didn't take my baton out and threaten him or anything." He was asked about Doyle Wheeler's accusation that he slammed a Black prisoner's head against a wall. "I have never done that, and I never would." He summarized his relationship with Wheeler: "I didn't like him and he didn't like me."

With Mike Carpenter wrapping up his rebuttal case, Milt Silverman ended speculation over whether Sagon Penn would take the stand in his own defense. "What is he needed for?" Silverman told reporters about his decision not to have his client testify. "If we didn't have thirty-nine eyewitnesses at the scene who could testify impartially and objectively about what they saw, then certainly it would be a different story."

The exclusion of Penn's recorded statements from the night of the incident and the decision for him not to testify assured that the stoic, unreadable figure seated at the defense table day after day would remain a silent enigma to the jurors.

NEWS CENTER 39 reporter Doug Curlee had a feeling Milt Silverman was not going to let the trial end quietly. "We still don't know what defense attorney Milt Silverman knows about a conversation ride-along Sarah Pina-Ruiz had with a Navy housing worker," Curlee said, reporting from in front of the courthouse during his evening broadcast, as he had most nights during the trial. "One can't help but get the feeling Silverman still has one or two more rockets left to fire at the prosecution, and that those rockets will fly tomorrow."

What Curlee was referring to was the unexpected testimony of the defense's final major witness, a Navy housing worker named Carolyn Cherry. When Sarah Pina-Ruiz was released from the hospital on April 4, 1985, she returned to her apartment on Stork Street, three blocks from the sight of her shooting four days before. The mother of two Black children had taken two rounds from a .38 at point-blank range but suddenly found herself unwelcome in the neighborhood. "Police say Pina-Ruiz's welcome home hasn't exactly been a pleasant one," a *Channel 8 News* reporter told viewers while standing in front of a two-story stucco apartment building. The reporter said the general reaction to her return ranged from indifference to overt hostility. "Apparently, some people in the area say they don't want her around. Some have suggested she should have died too."

Police were concerned enough for her safety that they contacted the Navy to have the family moved up the waiting list for alternate military housing. On April 17, Sarah and her husband, Rocky, went to the Navy housing office to finalize the paperwork on a new rental home outside the Southeast. As they waited for a form, they had a casual conversation with the manager of the office, Carolyn Cherry.

Carolyn Cherry took the stand on Thursday, April 24, 1986, with testimony that would prove to be some of the most controversial and sensational in the whole trial. "Did you discuss with her what she had seen or not seen on March 31, 1985, when she had been shot?" Silverman asked of her conversation with Pina-Ruiz.

"I asked her, could she have ducked or ran or tried to get away, and she stated that she couldn't see anything at all, it all happened so fast."

"Did she tell you that she didn't actually see the shooting itself?"

"Yes, she did," Cherry said. "Her exact words were that it all happened so fast, and she was not able to see anything." Cherry added that she found Pina-Ruiz's behavior to be inappropriate and not consistent with someone who was a victim. "The radio station was on 92.5 and she danced there in the chair, and she was just very talkative. She kind of joked about that she wasn't going to go anyplace and leave her husband here to collect a $25,000 life insurance policy."

When Mike Carpenter began his cross-examination, he was as irritated with Carolyn Cherry as he had been with any witness before her. "At the time you spoke with Miss Pina-Ruiz, did you feel sorry for her, being that she had been shot?" he asked.

Cherry said she did at first. "But my opinion changed when I saw her sitting there dancing and making jokes about that."

"What did your opinion change to?"

"That she wasn't as much of a victim as the media had painted her out to be."

"Did you take notes of the discussion with her about the shootings?" he asked.

"I documented it," Cherry said.

"How did you document it?" Carpenter asked with obvious skepticism.

"I wrote it down," she said. "I wrote down the exact words because I went home and told my husband about it."

Mike Carpenter had little choice but to recall Sarah Pina-Ruiz to the stand to refute the allegations made by Carolyn Cherry. "There has been evidence that you said that you didn't see the shooting, or something like that," Carpenter asked. "Did you say anything like that to this woman?"

"I never told her or anyone else that I never saw anything. I saw everything very clearly," an impatient Pina-Ruiz said.

On cross-examination, Silverman strayed off the primary subject of whether she told Cherry she did not see the shooting, asking her whether she had said other, seemingly unimportant parts of the conversation as reported by Cherry. "Did you discuss Donovan Jacobs's involvement at all in the incident?"

"No."

"Are you sure?"

"I am positive."

"And did you tell her that if you jumped out of the car, he would have killed you?"

"No."

"Are you sure?"

"I'm sure," she answered.

"Do you know why I'm asking you these questions?" Silverman asked after several more similar questions, all the while prowling back and forth in front of the witness stand.

Pina-Ruiz shrugged. "Obviously you want some kind of answers from me."

SILVERMAN CALLED CAROLYN Cherry back to the stand two days after Sarah Pina-Ruiz. "Mrs. Cherry, do you generally put that religious music on and play it off a tape recorder that's right next to your desk?" he asked.

"Yes, I do."

"And on the date that Sarah Pina-Ruiz came into your office there, did you have a tape entitled 'Prayer Changes Everything' in the tape recorder?"

"Yes, I did."

"After she had made these comments to you about not seeing the shooting itself, and it all happened too quickly, did you reach down with your two fingers to that tape recorder and push the record and play buttons?"

"Yes, I did," Cherry said.

Silverman held up a cassette tape. "And did you hand this cassette to that man over there, Mr. McDaniel, on or about July 31, 1985?"

"Yes," Cherry said.

Before allowing Silverman to play the tape, Hamrick wanted to hear it himself. "Where on this tape did she say she didn't see the shootings?" Hamrick asked when it was over, flipping through the pages of a transcript of the virtually inaudible recording.

"I know!" said Mike Carpenter, who was also hearing it for the first time. "It's not there."

Silverman acknowledged that Pina-Ruiz never made the statement during the recording, but rather that comments on the tape indicated she had said it just prior to Cherry pressing the "record" button.

"This tape would not add anything to her previous testimony," a disgusted Mike Carpenter said in protesting its admission.

But Hamrick reluctantly ruled to allow the tape to be played for the jury. "I feel that it could well be [a] reversible error not to allow the tape to come into evidence," he said.

When the jurors were reseated, they heard the "Cherry Tape" for the first time, following along with transcripts provided by the defense.

"Are you sure in your mind that Pina-Ruiz told you she did not see the shooting before you turned that tape recorder on?" Silverman asked Cherry.

"I am positively sure," Cherry answered.

It was not a strong argument and Cherry was not a strong witness. But Silverman had set up another way to make Sarah Pina-Ruiz look like a liar. It had to do with the seemingly random questions he asked about other things she may or may not have said in the conversation with Cherry. She denied saying any of them, yet they were all on the tape.

CARPENTER WAS LIVID that Silverman was allowed to use a recording that contained no incriminating statements and had no evidential value for the purposes of concocting a scheme to discredit a witness. "This is a classic, classic example of sandbagging," he said. "I have been sandbagged."

"Isn't it true that you decided to record her before she ever came into your office?" Carpenter asked Cherry at the beginning of his cross.

"No, that is not true," she replied defensively.

"Isn't it true that you decided to record her in order to become a witness in this trial?"

"No, that is not true," an indignant Cherry repeated.

Carpenter held up the audio cassette tape of the conversation. "Were you told not to mention the tape unless directly asked when you testified?" he said, strongly implying the defense had urged her not to reveal its existence.

"No, I was not," she said. "I only answered questions I was asked."

He brought up his earlier question to her about whether she had documented the conversation. "Didn't you think I might have been referring to a tape recording or something?" he asked her.

"No, I didn't."

"You didn't feel compelled to tell me about the tape recording at all?"

"You didn't ask me about a tape recording."

"I said, 'How did you document it?'"

"I said I wrote it down."

"Could you have mentioned a tape recording at that point in time?"

"I could have mentioned it," she conceded.

"You didn't, did you?" Carpenter said, controlled but clearly dismayed with the woman.

"You didn't ask me."

Carpenter slowly closed the transcript binder from which he had been reading and walked away from her in disgust.

The impact the Carolyn Cherry tape had on the trial was debatable, but the splash it made in the media was not. "Milt Silverman had the tape!" one television newscaster giddily announced on the evening news. The media came up with a name for the episode: "Silverman's Cherry Bomb."

With the witness stand empty at last, Judge Hamrick addressed Milt Silverman: "Do you want to say the magic words?"

"Your Honor," Silverman announced, "the defense rests."

29

"WE'VE COME A LONG WAY," MIKE CARPENTER SAID TO BE-
gin closing arguments on the morning of May 12, 1986. "We
have heard a number of witnesses. We have seen an awful lot
of exhibits. You have seen my colleague Milt Silverman get on the floor
so much that he's going to have to put patches on the pants of his suit.
And," he paused, "you've seen me at times make a jerk of myself." He
motioned to the jury box, where a very pregnant juror number three,
Vernell Hardy, sat in the second row. "If you are here long enough, I
think you are going to see the birth of a child."

Mike Carpenter would have preferred to go about his job quietly
but now found himself under the hottest spotlight in San Diego. The
responsibility for delivering justice on behalf of Tom Riggs was crushing. And on top of all that, he had a nasty cold that sapped his strength,
stuffed up his head, and went into his chest. The body of the triathlete
had held up almost to the end before finally giving in to the prolonged
stress of the trial. His scratchy throat made it hard to talk, which was
exactly what was expected of him now.

Errors in memory about the U-turn notwithstanding, Jacobs's stop
of Penn's truck was completely justified under the circumstances, he
asserted. Penn repeatedly refused a lawful request by Jacobs that he remove his driver's license, and then unlawfully attempted to walk away
from the officer while legally detained. "Unfortunately for the fact that
Sagon Penn took umbrage of what was going on, it would have been
nothing but a thirty-second detention and they could have determined

that the Crips were not there, and they could have gone on their way, and people in the truck would have gone on their way."

He dismissed the idea Jacobs and Riggs used excessive force. "They played it by the rules. Professionally. Did what they were trained to do." He displayed the photographs of Penn and reviewed the examination reports of Dr. Barbara Groves and nurse Elaine Hilliard to assert Penn had not received injuries consistent with a "beating." "If he had been hit numerous times in the face and head with a baton, we would have seen evidence of that," he declared flatly.

He rejected the idea that Penn had willingly gone to the ground in an act of submission. "Donovan Jacobs grabbed and hung on. And through upper-body strength or whatever, Jacobs was able to get on top."

"They were in a hostile situation," Carpenter said of the officers. "It was a situation that was rapidly deteriorating and getting out of control." He described the crowd as threatening and, "in the case of Carlton Smith and several others, encouraging Penn to resist." He cited testimony of others that the crowd encouraged Penn to "give up." "But he wouldn't," Carpenter said sharply. "He wouldn't. He wouldn't let himself be handcuffed. He got the gun for a reason. He shot the gun for a reason, and that was to kill Jacobs."

Carpenter said the most accurate eyewitness version of the shootings came from Sarah Pina-Ruiz. "Did she see? Yes. Was she able to see? Yes." Riggs never kicked Penn's arm or reached for his gun, he continued. He would not concede the presence of the handy-talkie radio in Riggs's holster was evidence he was not holding it at the time Jacobs was shot. "It was 1.7 seconds between shot number one and shot number two. Certainly, the handy-talkie can be put back in the belt in much less time than 1.7 seconds."

He dismissed the idea that a reflection in the side window of Riggs's vehicle prevented Penn from identifying Pina-Ruiz as an unarmed female dressed in civilian clothing. He cited the testimony of James Harris, an expert witness in the field of "human visual performance" who said the reflection was only one factor in how Sagon Penn would have perceived what he was looking at. Despite the flawed testimony of Junius Holmes and Dwayne Williams, Carpenter maintained Penn announced his intentions by shouting, "You're a witness!" before firing.

Carpenter characterized Penn rearming himself with Tom Riggs's gun as a clear indication he had every intention to kill again if needed. He reviewed a scene diagram and measurements that showed there was room on the passenger side of Riggs's vehicle for Penn to escape without running over Donovan Jacobs. "There is absolutely no justification for running over Donovan Jacobs," he said. "How can anyone justify that?" Carpenter was reserved and relatively brief in his argument, holding back for his rebuttal argument to Silverman's closing, in which he would be allowed to address all of the defense theories and contentions.

MILT SILVERMAN TOOK to the courtroom floor impeccably dressed as usual in a white shirt, gold cuff links, and red suspenders hitched beneath his fitted suit. Speaking without the use of notes, he traversed the carpet in front of the jury box. "I was thinking of Sagon Penn getting up in the morning. His granddaddy is going to let them use his truck. I'm going to take my brother's friends to the park and show them a good time. The only thing they didn't take with them is the American apple pie. When he made [his] bed, we can wonder if he thought he would not sleep in it that night. I wonder if he thought that at the end of the day, he would have blood over him, and he would have shot three people, and killed one of them."

"There are three main characters involved in this case," Silverman said. "Sagon Penn was looking for a quiet Sunday in the park. Riggs was looking for a man with a gun. Donovan Jacobs was looking for trouble. Donovan Jacobs is a fellow that has put a uniform on, who has pumped his muscles up, and who thinks he can take anyone on, anyone in the world, and beat his ass."

As he moved through the incident, Silverman prowled the well, growled menacingly when playing the role of Jacobs, barked racial slurs, gestured expansively at exhibits, rattled handcuffs, threw punches and slashed batons at the air in front of him, and spent copious amounts of time kneeling and lying on the carpet. He quoted prophets, poets, preachers, and presidents from memory. Albert Camus, Aristotle, H. L. Mencken, Alfred Hitchcock, and the Oakland Raiders made appearances in his oratory.

"What Sagon Penn was faced with was the fact that there was an officer in front of him saying things to him, doing things to him that he didn't understand and that he couldn't believe. And his brain tried to adjust to the reality of what in the world was happening to him."

"What is going on here was a power deal, a control deal," he said of Jacobs's demands for Penn to remove his license. "And Donovan Jacobs is the kind of guy, if you don't look at him just right, he's going to take his club out and hit you over the head with it." He talked about Penn's ability to defend himself: "It must have enraged Donovan Jacobs. Can you imagine how maddening this must be to somebody taking a stick as hard as you can and swinging it against someone's head and it goes off his arms like butter? Penn wasn't trying to show this officer up. [He] was trying to keep his skull from getting caved in." He added that "[Jacobs] knew that he had no cause to pull that club out and try to take Penn's head off with it. Knew it was wrong and that's why he lied about it, and you don't need a psychiatrist to tell you about it."

Silverman came to the point in the altercation when Penn and Jacobs fell to the ground: "You've got somebody like a Doberman pinscher, what is it other than a snarling animal, on top of Sagon Penn beating his face in and telling him he's a nigger and he's going to beat his Black ass." He asked the jurors to put themselves in Penn's place. "You can talk about hearing the pounding of your heart in your temples and seeing the world not upright but [while] on your back with clubs coming down on you and begging somebody to stop. 'Please stop! Please stop! Please stop!' And them not stopping, them not quitting, them not letting up. And them saying things that let you know why they are not going to let up." His voice rose into a loud growl. "'You think you're bad, nigger? I'm going to beat your Black ass.'"

"And Penn thinking, 'God, is this a police officer on top of me? Is this a man with a badge? Is this the law? Is this guy nuts? Is he crazy? Is he going to kill me? Why doesn't he stop?' People don't measure their lives, ladies and gentlemen, in minutes in situations like that. You don't measure it in terms of minutes. You don't measure it in terms of seconds. He had a few heartbeats to decide what he was going to do."

He went back through all his evidence and testimony to support his case about the shootings themselves and Penn fleeing the scene out of fear he would be shot by the police officers closing in on him. He defended Doyle Wheeler: "Doyle Wheeler is everything a good cop should be. He understands duty, and honor, and truth, and integrity. And it hurt him to the bone, and almost killed him to get up here and tell you the truth." He assailed the San Diego Police for inaccurate eyewitness statements and misleading testimony. He defended the residents of the 6500 block of Brooklyn Avenue: "If you want to find people that are more responsible, God-fearing, Christian, American people, this is quite a good street to be on, isn't it?"

Silverman walked to the defense table and held up a document containing the list of charges against Sagon Penn. "A reasonable man could debate whether there is a manslaughter here or a justifiable self-defense. I don't think any reasonable person would spend any time on the concept of murder," he said. "I could ask you to look at this information and count the victims." He folded back a page. "Look at page two, and remember there is a blank space there. The fourth victim? Sagon Penn, because he was a victim too. And he will be a victim regardless of what your verdict in this case is."

He motioned to the American flag on a stand beside the judge's bench. "You and I have shared one thing every morning. Facing the flag of our country, the emblem of the constitution, and remembering the principles for which it stands. Like the document that gave us life, 'We hold these truths to be self-evident, that all men are created equal, that they are endowed by their creator with certain unalienable rights, that among these are life, liberty, and pursuit of happiness.'" He paused and faced the jurors. "Did you think about that? I bet you did. Or maybe you remembered [1963] when the words rang across the Washington Monument, and an American man said, 'I have a dream that one day this nation will rise up and live out the true meaning of its creed; that all men are created equal.' Or perhaps you thought of the words, 'I have a dream that my four little children will one day be judged not by the color of their skin, but by the content of their character. I have a dream today.'

"Well, Dr. King, the dream is here. We may not have reached the promised land yet, but we have, as Americans, turned our backs on bigotry, and hatred, and race prejudice, and the image of a police officer sitting on top of a Black man, beating him in the face, telling him he is a nigger, and that he is going to beat his Black ass. We have turned our back on that."

Silverman fell silent as he resumed pacing back and forth, providing an almost hypnotic rhythm to his words. "I look at your faces, and I see America," he said to the jurors. "Not a Black America, not a white America, not a brown America, not a yellow America, not a Protestant America, not a Catholic America." He motioned to the prosecution table. "Mr. Carpenter here says, '*the People* call so and so; *the People* say such and such; *the People* this, *the People* that.'" He shook his head. "They ain't the People. You are the People. You are the custodians of justice, and this community. That is a big responsibility. And it is a great honor."

He turned to the judge. "I would like to thank you, Judge Hamrick, for giving Mr. Penn a fair trial." He faced the jury again. "I would like to thank you for listening to what I have had to say. You will ask [of me], 'What is your goal?' and I will answer in one word, 'Justice.' Not a narrow, parochial justice, but a justice that means giving each man that which is his due. If he's due punishment, conviction, retribution, give it to him. But if he deserves to be acquitted, give him that. I will ask you for no more. Society demands no less. As the prophet Micah said, 'What does the Lord God ask of you but to do justice, and to love mercy, and to walk humbly with your God.' May he guide you in your task."

The courtroom was silent as Silverman returned to the defense table. He used a handkerchief to wipe beads of sweat from his flushed face with a trembling hand. Some of the jurors looked stunned by what they had just heard. Several, along with Silverman's wife, Maria, had tears in their eyes. Penn supporters in the spectator gallery hung their heads. Some wept softly. But the young man seated beside Milt Silverman sat upright, staring straight ahead with no indication he had heard anything at all.

"Mr. Carpenter?" Judge Hamrick said without any pause in the proceedings.

AS HE BEGAN his rebuttal closing, there was something Mike Carpenter felt he should address right away: "I want to say something about things that Mr. Silverman said about the fact that I am going to get up and say all the Blacks got together and have conjured up the stories, and things like that. It is really difficult to say anything to that because it is so far from the truth. I didn't mean to mislead you in my opening statement when I said the victims received no aid until the officers responded to the scene. That is of no importance. No, I'm not going to argue anything like that. I don't think it's appropriate."

Carpenter was far more animated and impassioned than in his first summation as he attempted to discredit Silverman's theories, assertions, and accusations one by one. But much of his time was spent coming to the defense of the man Milt Silverman had just argued was responsible for the entire incident.

"Something has to be said about Donovan Jacobs. Donovan Jacobs is a hero. The attempted character assassination on Donovan Jacobs didn't work. It would appear as though they used the wrong tactic and they used the wrong guy here. I mean, this is just overwhelming evidence that he's an outstanding individual, an outstanding police officer, a superior police officer on a superior police force." He addressed the errors in Jacobs's version of events: "Is he lying? No, he's not lying. That is a defense mechanism. We all do that when we have these painful things to remember."

"Let's talk about the testimony of Sarah Pina-Ruiz," he continued, beginning his defense of the woman upon whose testimony his case depended most. "Did she see the shootings? She *had* to. How did she know that it was Jacobs's gun and not Riggs's gun?" he said, referring to details in her statement the night of the incident. "Or Penn pulled out the gun? How did she know that? How did she know that Jacobs got hit in the neck if she didn't see the shootings? Nobody told her; she was in surgery. These are things that simply couldn't be made up because they *did* happen."

He shook his head. "What was she? She was a shooting victim. She had been shot by Sagon Penn. What did she do to have her character vilified? What did she do to deserve that? She was shot. She was there and she was shot," said Carpenter, as animated as at any other time in the trial. "What did she do to have somebody surreptitiously tape-record her? What did she do to have somebody call her a liar? What did she do?" He paused. "She was shot."

He turned his attention to the motivations behind the actions of the person he alleged bore absolute responsibility for the shooting of three people. "It wasn't the batons, it wasn't the punches, it wasn't the scuffle, it wasn't anything that was said. You know why he pulled that gun out and shot? The handcuffs that came out. He saw them. He was determined at that point in time to do everything in his power to avoid that arrest."

He paused and lowered his voice. "It was a request for identification and cooperation. Sagon Penn refused the smallest intrusion into his life. And all over a license. Such a small thing." He shook his head. "We all grieve over what happened," he continued. "It's difficult to go back in time. It's difficult to put yourself in this situation. I'm not saying it wasn't unfortunate for Mr. Penn. Certainly if he was at Cedric Gregory's for thirty more seconds . . . they never would have seen him. They never would have stopped the truck. I wish it would have happened that way. We all do. Not just for Tom Riggs, and Donovan Jacobs, and Sarah Pina-Ruiz, but for Sagon Penn as well."

"I join Mr. Silverman when he says that I want a verdict. The community wants a verdict. The community deserves a verdict. I am asking for the twelve of you to work together to arrive at verdicts in this case. You are the conscience of the community. Your verdicts will signal, yes, that problems can be solved. Yes, there is a future and hope. Ladies and gentlemen, let right be done here. Find justice; it's there. Assess Sagon Penn's guilt and tell the community."

AFTER EIGHT WEEKS, the trial, and fate, of Sagon Penn was finally in the hands of the jury. Bailiff Mike Rodelo cleared the courtroom of grocery bags of evidence, cabinets of documents, Clarence the mannequin, the door to Tom Riggs's vehicle, and Jim Gripp's wall-size diagram, which took three people to lower. Journalists filed their stories from pay phones, TV reporters filmed their remotes in the hallway, and cameramen tore the duct tape off their cables.

Vernell Hardy prepared to have her baby within a week or two. Coleen Riggs packed a bag and flew to Sacramento for the dedication of a law enforcement memorial upon which her husband's name would be etched. Once out of the presence of the jury, Penn quietly thanked

Silverman, knowing that they might not see each other again until the verdict. "I love you, Milt," he said, as a bailiff set a hand on his shoulder and led him from the courtroom.

That day, Mike Carpenter drove home with tears in his eyes and, for the first time in his life, wept openly in front of his wife and two children. After being interviewed by the media in the corridor outside the courtroom, an exhausted Milt Silverman leaned heavily against a window ledge holding a Diet Coke. "I'm relieved it's over," he said of his role in the trial.

But for anyone involved in the trial, it was far from over.

30

"THE WORD *HOMICIDE* MEANS THE KILLING OF ONE HUMAN being by another, either lawfully or unlawfully," Judge Hamrick said, working his way through a thick set of jury instructions. "The word *homicide* includes murder and manslaughter, which are unlawful, and the acts of excusable and justifiable homicide, which are lawful." The latter, he said, included self-defense.

"Now we are going to get into the more specific instructions that apply to the specific crimes charged as well as all lesser included or related offenses applicable," Hamrick said. There were six criminal counts pending against Sagon Penn. If the jury were to determine Penn's actions were "unlawful" on a specific count, they then must decide the appropriate offense, or charge, related to that count. The counts and related offenses were as follows:

Count 1: Murder of Thomas Riggs: first-degree, second-degree, voluntary manslaughter, involuntary manslaughter.

Count 2: Attempted Murder of Donovan Jacobs—with a Firearm: first-degree, second-degree, assault with a deadly weapon (with or without great bodily injury), resisting arrest.

Count 3: Attempted Murder of Donovan Jacobs—with a Police Car: first-degree, second-degree, assault with a deadly weapon (with or without great bodily injury).

Count 4: Attempted Murder of Sarah Pina-Ruiz: first-degree, second-degree, assault with a deadly weapon (with or without great bodily injury).

Count 5: Auto Theft.

Count 6: Grand Theft—Riggs's Gun.

Judge Hamrick explained the two degrees of murder. First-degree is "*deliberate and premeditated* murder . . . a cold, calculated judgment." Premeditation, he said, does not require a "lapse of considerable time." For instance, any decision by Penn during the physical altercation that he was going to take Jacobs's gun the next chance he got and use it to kill the officer would meet the definition of *premeditation*.

Second-degree murder is intentionally killing *without deliberation or premeditation*—for instance, if Penn had acted on impulse and opportunity to grab Jacobs's gun but did so with the intent to kill Jacobs once he had it.

Manslaughter was unlawful murder *without malice aforethought*, Hamrick instructed. "There is no malice aforethought if the killing occurred upon a sudden quarrel or heat of passion." Rather than two *degrees* of manslaughter, there were two *types*. Voluntary manslaughter required intent to kill, whereas involuntary manslaughter did not.

Just before noon on the morning of Thursday, May 15, the six men and six women of the jury filed out of the courtroom to begin their deliberations. With two older jurors having been replaced with alternates earlier in the trial, the age skewed even younger than before. Five were still in their twenties. Troy Axe was an x-ray librarian and softball enthusiast. Glen Coahran was a computer programmer who rode his bicycle to the courthouse each day. David Shipley was a forklift operator who lived at home with his parents. Rossie Cruz worked at a Safeway supermarket. She said her boss thought Penn was guilty, but that would not influence her. "All I owe him is to do my work."

Georgia native and PacBell employee Gerald Webb had nearly been killed fighting in Vietnam. Laraine Diaz was a clerk at an auto-parts store, bowling alley bartender, and mother of two from an Italian neighborhood in New York City. Sally Naley liked to fish and worked at a photo-finishing store. Postal worker Gil Padilla was born in the Philippines and served in the U.S. Navy. Lynn Decker had a master's degree in computer science. In his mid-forties, he was the oldest member of the jury.

Kimberly McGee, one of the two Black members of the jury, was a postal worker in her mid-twenties who worked evenings and weekends as a hot dog cook at Jack Murphy Stadium. Either attorney could have found reason to exclude her. She termed herself a casual acquaintance of Sagon Penn's uncle and had once dropped twenty dollars into a Sagon Penn Defense Committee collection bucket. However, her boyfriend was a San Diego Police officer who worked the same Southeast beat as Riggs and Jacobs.

The other Black member on the panel was thirty-seven-year-old Vernell Hardy, a phone-company employee originally from Arkansas. Hardy admitted to knowing quite a bit about the case but had formed no opinion, calling the incident "an unfortunate situation all the way around." "Let me just ask you flat out," Silverman said. "You are not pulling for either side in this thing?" She said she was not. The biggest impediment to having Hardy sit on the jury was the June 1 due date for her baby. Carpenter expressed reluctance to include a juror expecting a baby in less than three months, but Hamrick said it was unlikely the trial would take that long and they would accommodate Mrs. Hardy in the event it did.

Douglas Bernd served in the First Air Calvary in Vietnam; the confident thirty-nine-year-old was a logical choice for foreman.

After just three hours of deliberation, Judge Hamrick received a note from Foreman Bernd. "We have a verdict on count three," it read, referring to the charge of attempted murder of Donovan Jacobs with the police vehicle. "The instructions are unclear whether we should deliver it or wait until we have the others," it read. "I don't want to rush you on this," Hamrick instructed. "If you have partial verdicts, hold on to them until all issues are resolved." Among all of Penn's actions, the hardest to justify was running over a wounded Donovan Jacobs with his own police car. That the jury had so quickly come to a decision on that particular count was ominous for the defense. Silverman and Penn were now left to wonder what it portended for the other charges.

After two more days of deliberation, Hamrick called the court in session the morning of Tuesday, May 20. "Mrs. Hardy is now in labor," he informed the attorneys and remaining jurors. "What I'm going to do is recess the jury deliberations until Thursday of next week." He addressed Bernd. "Now, I want to know if you have arrived at verdicts on any counts?"

"Yes, we have," Bernd answered, reiterating they were still decided on count three.

Hamrick surprised observers by announcing he would accept the verdict related to count three after all, even though the other counts were still outstanding. He was trying to avoid the possibility that Hardy would not be able to return and therefore would be replaced by an alternate, thus requiring the jury to redeliberate the charge. After the verdicts were read, he would "poll the eleven jurors here in open court to determine whether that was and is their verdict. And thereafter when Mrs. Hardy is able to communicate and receive visitors, we will take her individual poll in her hospital room in the presence of both counsel and the defendant."

"I am going to ask the clerk to read the verdicts," Hamrick said. Although it was only one count, each came with the associated lesser offenses, making it possible for multiple verdicts on the same count.

At the defense table, Silverman rested an arm on the back of his client's chair and fixed his eyes downward, listening. Mike Carpenter stared straight ahead at a point on the far wall.

Clerk LaRue Slaugh read out the verdict: "In the Superior Court, State of California, in and for the county of San Diego, Department Twenty-Five. The people of the state of California, plaintiff, versus Sagon Penn, defendant. Verdict: We the jury in the above entitled clause find the defendant Sagon Penn not guilty of the crime of attempted murder."

Neither attorney nor Penn betrayed any emotion. For Carpenter, the impact was profound. If that was not attempted murder, what was?

"Verdict," Slaugh continued. "We the jury in the above entitled clause find the defendant Sagon Penn not guilty of the crime of attempted and voluntary manslaughter." As despair crept in on Mike Carpenter, Silverman worked to keep his growing optimism in check.

Slaugh read the jury's decision on the final lesser offense related to count three. "Verdict: We the jury in the above entitled clause find the defendant Sagon Penn guilty of the crime of assault with a deadly weapon, a lesser included offense of the crime of attempted murder as charged in count three. Victim, Donovan Jacobs." Carpenter leaned back slightly in his chair as Silverman stroked his mustache. "And we further find that in the commission of the above offense, the defendant did personally inflict great bodily injury upon Donovan Jacobs. Dated May 16, 1986. Signed, Douglas M. Bernd, Foreman," Slaugh concluded.

"Do either counsel wish to have the jury polled?" Hamrick asked.

Carpenter declined. "Yes," said Silverman. "Just the one on which there was a guilty verdict." Silverman barely paid attention to what was no more than an administrative formality, as his mind churned over the consequences of the verdict. With the conviction and associated finding, Penn was facing the probability of nine years in prison, with five more counts still in the hands of a jury who believed his client bore at least some responsibility in the events of March 31, 1985.

"Troy Axe," the clerk began. "Correct," the young lady in juror seat number one responded.

"David Shipley?" "Correct."

Silverman moved a hand to Penn's shoulder, but his immutable client stared straight ahead, looking as though the proceedings did not involve him.

"Kimberly McGee?" "Correct."

"Lynn Decker?" "Correct."

At the opposite table, Carpenter was equally expressionless, although the verdict represented a victory for the prosecution. He had expected an attempted-murder conviction, but at least he had one conviction locked in and was no longer facing his worst nightmare that Sagon Penn would walk free.

"Sally Naley?" "Correct."

"Glen Coahran?" "Correct."

"That's eleven out of the twelve," Hamrick said when the remaining jurors had affirmed their votes. "And we will poll Mrs. Hardy as soon as she becomes available." Hamrick then excused the jurors for the coming week. Penn was led from the courtroom by bailiff Steve Sharp without having spoken a word to Milt Silverman following the verdict.

Seven hours later, Vernell Hardy gave birth to a healthy baby boy she and her husband named William. The hospital announced to the media that "both are doing fine."

The story of the first Penn verdict fronted every evening television news broadcast, dominated talk radio chatter that evening, and headlined page one in *The San Diego Union, Evening Tribune*, and *Los Angeles Times*. "First Penn Verdict: Guilty of Assault," read *The San Diego Union* headline, with the subheading, "Baby delays deliberation of jury on five other counts."

Silverman did not comment on the verdict to the media, and Carpenter said little. But just about everyone else had plenty to say. Thomas Penn said he was still processing the news: "Right now, I can't believe it." Yusuf Abdullah was concerned and somewhat confused by the layers of lesser offenses. "I don't know too much about the law or how it works," he told a reporter. "I think he's innocent all around." Coleen Riggs was at Bible class when the verdict came in. "I would have preferred, of course, it was attempted murder, but I'm glad at least the guilt is there." Donovan Jacobs was contacted at home by Glenn Bunting of the *Los Angeles Times*. "The guy ran me over; what defense is there for that?" He added that he felt vindicated by the verdict. "I think it's great. Convict him on all of 'em."

At 10:30 a.m. the following morning, the two attorneys, a court reporter, clerk LaRue Slaugh, Judge Ben Hamrick, and Sagon Penn accompanied by U.S. marshals rode to Kaiser Permanente Hospital in a county-jail van with wire mesh covering the windows. They stopped along the way for flowers to present to the new mother. In the maternity ward, they huddled around Vernell Hardy, still dressed in a hospital gown, but absent baby William.

After a round of congratulations, the judge explained that he had asked for the partial verdict, what the results had been, and the purpose of their visit. "So I am going to have the clerk read that verdict to you now as it was read in court; then I want to ask you a question." Slaugh read the guilty verdict on the assault-with-a-deadly-weapon charge, including the finding of great bodily injury. "Was that and is that your verdict?" Hamrick asked Hardy.

"Well," Hardy began slowly, "it was."

Silverman, head lowered in concentration, looked up at the woman when he heard it. Carpenter's jaw tightened.

"I would like to say this," Hardy went on. "On Friday, when we all voted on this, we all voted that's the way it would be. When we came into the court [on Friday], it was told to us that we were not to turn in one [verdict] at a time. On Monday, we all decided that was what our vote was. But, some of us were not sure and we were going to talk about it . . . to decide clearly what we were going to do with that." When she was admitted to the hospital early Tuesday, Hardy said she was still under the impression the verdicts were not going to be entered. "So at this point, I would say I would like to talk about it more before I am sure."

Before Milt Silverman left for the hospital that morning, he told Maria only a miracle from heaven could help them now. When Hardy stopped talking, he raised his eyes to the ceiling and mouthed a silent thank-you. Carpenter leaned back against the wall, feeling as though the blood were draining out of him.

"All right," said Hamrick. "That's why we came out here. So we will not record this verdict, and we will wait until Tuesday and we will give it back to the jury along with all the other charges," he said, referring to the counts for which they had not returned verdicts. "You are still part of the jury now, so you are still admonished not to allow anybody to talk to you," he added in closing.

"A lot of people have tried," Hardy said to the judge.

The final comment from Hardy did not go unnoticed by Mike Carpenter, who could not help wondering, What people are those?

WITH THE COURT in recess until the following Tuesday, May 27, Hamrick instructed both attorneys not to discuss the meeting at Kaiser Permanente, or even acknowledge that it had taken place. "I can't tell you whether we went to the hospital or whether we're going to the hospital," Carpenter told a reporter. "I can't comment." For an entire week, life went on in San Diego under the assumption that Sagon Penn had been found guilty of assault with a deadly weapon.

Upon the return of Vernell Hardy to the courthouse on Tuesday, they found out differently. "Good morning, ladies and gentlemen," Hamrick addressed the jury. "Let me bring you up to date on the developments." As startled reporters scribbled furiously in their notepads, Hamrick explained to the jurors what the negative vote by Hardy meant to them. "So, I am going to send in a clean blank verdict form as to count three involving the lesser offense of assault with a deadly weapon, and ask you to again discuss that verdict as well as continue your deliberations on all the other matters." The jurors stared back at him, trying to conceal their shock. "All right, so go to work."

31

I N THE SUMMER OF 1986, NOTHING LOOMED LARGER OVER
the prosecutors in the San Diego District Attorney's office than the
prospect of having an entire case sabotaged by a "lone wolf" holdout juror who decided in advance that the defendant is not guilty. Just
months before the start of the Sagon Penn trial, the DA had experienced
exactly that in one of the highest profile cases in the city's history. San
Diego mayor Roger Hedgecock was charged with multiple counts of
conspiracy and perjury related to campaign contributions. The evidence
against the mayor was overwhelming, but the jury ended up hung, on all
thirteen counts, eleven to one in favor of conviction. The lone holdout
was a city sanitation worker who proudly proclaimed his belief from the
start that the DA was out to get the Republican mayor for political purposes. During the Penn case, Carpenter had questioned each prospective juror whether they had already formed an opinion or would hold
out over allegiance or for publicity, as had happened in the Hedgecock
case.

Two weeks into his prosecution case in the Penn trial, a special
agent with the IRS named Dennis McCarthy had contacted Mike Carpenter with some information. McCarthy had "a source" who told him
that one of Carpenter's jurors had expressed to a coworker long before
the trial that Sagon Penn "is just a victim of racial prejudice and should
be set free." The juror was Vernell Hardy.

When Carpenter brought the information to the attention of
Hamrick and Silverman at the time, Hamrick proposed that "some

confidential undercover investigation should be initiated." Milt Silverman was firmly against it. "I am frankly not in favor of skulking around with jurors," he said. "I'm not going to get involved in it, Judge." Carpenter did not disagree. "I wanted to avoid that very thing, to offend her by us skulking around," he said. "I don't want to be in the position of doing that." The issue was dropped.

Now, after his visit to the maternity ward at Kaiser Permanente two months later, Mike Carpenter feared that Vernell Hardy might indeed be a lone-wolf juror.

WITH CONTINUATION OF deliberations upon Hardy's return and assurance from foreman Douglas Bernd that the jury was nowhere near verdicts on the remaining counts, Judge Ben Hamrick departed for a five-day visit with family in Indianapolis. Judge William Todd would preside in the event the jury had questions or issues during his absence. During the noon recess on his first full day of coverage, bailiff Mike Rodelo located Judge Todd in an adjacent courtroom and delivered a handwritten note that read, "Need to talk to judge." It was signed by Vernell Hardy.

Todd sent word to the attorneys to come to his chambers immediately. Mike Carpenter had taken advantage of the expected lull to attend a weeklong seminar for criminal prosecutors in Houston. It was Carpenter's second chair, Bob Phillips, who arrived to represent the prosecution. "I read the note from Mrs. Hardy," Phillips announced, "and I thought that before she comes in, I might inform everybody that I have got a good guess what she wants to talk about."

Phillips seemed nervous and unsure of himself, clearly relating information about events in which he was not involved. After delivering a convoluted, stammering backstory related to him by Carpenter, Phillips revealed that DA investigators were at that very minute interviewing Vernell Hardy's coworkers at the small PacBell installation repair center where she worked. "As I understand now, as of right now, there's been at least eight, maybe nine coworkers of hers interviewed. And I just talked to the investigator an hour or so ago, and he found out that Mrs. Hardy had been told he is out checking her and [that] it is, in fact, the DA's office. And I think that's what she probably wants to inform the Court about." There was a long pause. "So this is no secret to anybody anymore, and this is as good a time as any to inform the Court and Mr. Silverman about what we were doing."

When Phillips was done, the apparently speechless Judge Todd looked at Milt Silverman. "Well, I'm a little shocked that this late in the game that has occurred," Silverman calmly said. "I guess what we should do is find out what Mrs. Hardy has to say."

"Okay, the problem is," Vernell Hardy began, after entering the room, "I understand that someone has been at my job asking questions, someone from the DA's office asking about me pertaining to this case, and I was a bit concerned about it."

"It will stop immediately," Judge Todd said, "and it will not affect in any way your deliberations on this case. You should go on with your work as a juror and don't give it another thought. Because if it has occurred, as I think it may have, it has ended as of now, I assure you."

When she was gone, Todd turned to Phillips. "That will be my order, that there be no further attempt to talk about anything in connection with Mrs. Hardy without further showing it to the Court," he said firmly. He ordered Phillips to have the investigators immediately type up reports of the interviews already conducted. "Be here in court with it at eight o'clock tomorrow morning, right in these chambers," Todd directed firmly.

THE FOLLOWING MORNING, Silverman came to the courthouse and read through the interview reports put together by investigators of the district attorney's pretrial division. The original source of the information told to IRS Agent McCarthy was a PacBell worker named Robin Campbell. She reported overhearing another PacBell employee named Michele Bishop engaged in a "heated argument about the guilt or innocence of Penn," in which Hardy expressed her belief that Penn was not guilty. But Bishop, who had expressed to Hardy her belief that Penn was guilty, told the DA investigators it was a "casual conversation" in the lunchroom in which "Ms. Hardy was trying to make a point there are two sides of the story." The DA interview report added, "She did not hear Mrs. Hardy make any statements saying Penn was innocent or not guilty."

The investigators interviewed seven coworkers of Vernell Hardy at the PacBell offices. According to Claire Willkom, Hardy once commented to her that Penn "looks so sweet and innocent." Murial Bryant said Hardy told her, "The whole thing is police harassment, he is innocent, his actions were justified." Others had never heard Hardy discuss it at all, or reported she had not decided about Penn's guilt. Marsha Lewis's desk was next to Hardy's. "When she was picked as a juror, she said that she would try to hear both sides of the story and decide what was right after she had heard all the testimony and evidence." Candace Hooker said Hardy told her "she would judge the case on the evidence produced in court."

At 8:00 a.m., the two attorneys were in Judge Todd's chambers. "Have you seen these yet, Mr. Silverman?" he said, holding up copies of the interview reports.

"Yes, I have read them," Silverman replied.

Todd turned to Phillips. "Do the People have any comment, first of all?"

"I wanted to clarify a few things," Phillips began. "Not only about this, but all the surrounding circumstances, mainly because I was taken aback yesterday." Phillips wanted to make it clear that he was not involved in the investigation, had been given little information, and was not happy about being the one left to answer for it. "I walked out of here embarrassed yesterday because, on the face of this, it looks like an unfair, bad situation. I am embarrassed by it, and I have indicated to my superiors I'm embarrassed being here." His frustration with Mike Carpenter was obvious. "I attempted to call Mike in Houston after work, and I left him a message to call me. So he either went back to Gilley's or didn't pick up the message." ("Gilley's" was the massive country-and-western music, dancing, and mechanical-bull-riding roadhouse owned by singer Mickey Gilley, made world-famous in the movie *Urban Cowboy*.) "He didn't call me back. We were left rudderless yesterday when all of this was going on." As for the Hardy investigation, Phillips had little to add. "All I can say is that we are just attempting to make sure that both sides get a fair trial in this case."

"Judge, I have a few things to say," Silverman said when Phillips was through. "I cannot conceive of somebody doing this. This is a direct violation of the canons of professional ethics. It is an obstruction of justice. It is jury tampering of the worst kind. It is coercive." He shook his head. "It is a mess. For all Miss Hardy knows, she's being investigated for some crime. Right now, at a time when she is in there deliberating Mr. Penn's fate, the district attorney's office is contacting at least eight of her coworkers, and if you hadn't stopped them, probably ten of her coworkers at work. It is the most outrageous thing I have ever seen in my life. There's really only one remedy left to me, and that's a motion to dismiss the case for prosecutorial misconduct."

Silverman expressed his belief that it was no coincidence Carpenter left town just hours before the investigation began and now apparently could not be located even by the attorney covering for him. Todd looked at Phillips with apparent wonder at the man's predicament. "Are you in charge of the case?" he asked.

"The term around the office that has been used is *babysitting* the case in that respect," Phillips said sheepishly.

"I'm not trying to demean your situation," the judge said. "I don't know what it is exactly."

"I'm not sure I know either," Phillips said.

When the attorneys convened the next morning, it was before Judge Ben Hamrick, who had returned the previous evening and been briefed by Judge Todd. Silverman was surprised to find the prosecution and Bob Phillips were not retreating from the issue. Hamrick held up a five-page document. "I have this motion that has been filed by the district attorney's office for the removal of Vernell Hardy."

The justification for the motion written by Phillips was stated on the first page: "It is alleged by the People that juror Vernell Hardy was untruthful in some of her responses on voir dire; that she purposely failed to reveal certain prejudices concerning relations between the police and Blacks in general; and that she failed to reveal that she entertained certain preconceived opinions on the guilt or innocence of the defendant, Sagon Penn." As supporting evidence, Phillips offered only quotes taken from the PacBell interviews.

"Why don't we start with what brought this to the surface," a stern Ben Hamrick instructed.

Phillips explained that Mike Carpenter initiated the investigation after Hardy "reneged on a verdict" in the hospital. "It disturbed Mr. Carpenter considerably when she made some comment indicating that somebody or some people had been trying to get to her," he said. The reference was to Hardy's hospital-room comment that "a lot of people have tried" when Hamrick admonished her not to allow people to talk to her about the case. "And that's what bothered him," Phillips said. "He felt somebody got to her."

"The only thing wrong with that is Carpenter wasn't investigating any recent conduct of third parties attempting to communicate with Mrs. Hardy while she was in the hospital," Hamrick said of the PacBell interviews. "What Carpenter has done is just dig up all these old fellow employees that may have had discussions with her before she was impaneled. Not one of them has anything to say about her in deliberations."

Phillips's defense of Carpenter was half-hearted. "He had to start somewhere."

"I disagree," Hamrick said bluntly. "I don't think he had to start at all."

Milt Silverman offered his own assessment of the prosecutor's actions. "The reason, Your Honor, that the prosecution in this case went out and investigated Mrs. Hardy was not because of the concerns expressed [in March]. It was because the prosecution wanted to secure a conviction. Rather than coming in here and boldly proclaiming that they think you should kick poor Mrs. Hardy off of the jury, they ought to be in here asking that you do not find the district attorney's office and its supervisors in contempt and refer the matter to the attorney general of the state of California for investigation of violation of the criminal law, which is jury tampering. I dare say, Your Honor, if I did this—and I would never dream of doing it even in my worst nightmare—I would expect myself to be calling you from jail." He added, "I am not going to make a motion for a mistrial. I am going to make a motion to dismiss this case and all of the charges against Mr. Penn on the basis of outrageous governmental misconduct."

"All right," Hamrick said. "The motion to discharge juror Vernell Hardy is denied." He added that the denial of the prosecution motion was "with prejudice," meaning, final, never to be brought up again. "In my opinion, they don't reach the strength of any evidence that would warrant my finding that Mrs. Hardy would not be able to perform her duty," he said of the PacBell interviews. "The motion of defendant to dismiss all charges is denied," he said of Silverman's motion. Hamrick then sealed everything related to the Hardy investigation and proceedings, hoping he had contained the situation and put it behind them.

It was too late.

The first thing the following morning, Thursday, June 5, *Channel 39 News* reporter Doug Curlee got word to Hamrick that his station received an anonymous call from a PacBell worker informing them of the Hardy investigation. He also informed Hamrick that a woman claiming to be a PacBell coworker had phoned in to former mayor Roger Hedge-cock's conservative talk radio show to reveal the investigation of the juror who, a week before, had "switched her vote." And that very moment, he said, reporters were descending on the PacBell installation repair center attempting to interview Hardy's coworkers. Company security had been forced to lock the doors to keep them at bay.

An hour and a half later, Hamrick addressed the jury and attorneys in the courtroom. "Good morning, ladies and gentlemen. I made an important decision which I wanted to inform you about," he began. "In an abundance of caution so that this jury will not be influenced in any way by what may be appearing in the newspaper or on the radio or on television, I am going to sequester the jury for the balance of the deliberations." He told them they would be transported back and forth from the Sheraton Harbor Island hotel each day, deliberate from 8:00 a.m. to 6:00 p.m. seven days a week, have a box lunch in the deliberation room and other meals at the hotel, and have one phone call in the evening to family. He advised them to bring a chess set or deck of cards "because you are not going to be watching TV at night."

"I am going to make special arrangements for a marshal to accompany Mrs. Hardy to her home each evening so that you can have a brief visit with your youngster, perhaps an hour," he said to the mother with the sixteen-day-old infant.

Hamrick said he hoped it would not be too much of an inconvenience for them all, but the looks of dismay told him otherwise. One by one they raised their hands to voice their concerns: "I am supposed to pick up my kids today." "I am supposed to sign papers at the car dealership tonight." "I have nobody to pick up my daughter from school every day." "I did want to visit my mother Friday." Then Vernell Hardy began to sob uncontrollably. Mike Rodelo escorted her to the rear of the courtroom while fellow juror Kimberly McGee tried to comfort her. Hardy's whole body began to shake. "Why don't you ladies and gentlemen stay right there," Hamrick said to the other jurors. "Give us ten minutes to work out some details."

In chambers with Hardy and the two attorneys, Hamrick tried desperately to accommodate the woman whose presence on the jury he had preserved only a half day earlier. He told her she could have the baby with her at the hotel overnight. Or part of the night. Or whatever she wanted. "I have made the decision, and I am going to live with it," Hamrick said. "But the sequestration, if it is an unbearable burden, the choice is yours. If you tell me you can't continue to serve as a juror under these circumstances, then we will just have to excuse you and put an alternate in." A few minutes later, Hardy had calmed down somewhat. "I have to do what I can do," she said optimistically. As the jurors filed out of the courtroom, some glared accusingly at members of the media, assuming they were to blame for their impending hotel incarceration.

With the courtroom cleared of jury and spectators, Silverman was as livid as he had been earlier. If Hardy could not continue due to sequestration caused by the prosecution's actions, it would be a case of "the prosecution by its malfeasance achieving indirectly what it could not achieve by its unconscionable jury tampering," he said. "What we have here is a conspiracy."

WHEN HE ARRIVED at the courthouse on the morning of Monday, June 9, just four days into the sequestration, Judge Hamrick got broadsided by a written request from Vernell Hardy and Kimberly McGee to speak with him. The two women had finally had it. "Your Honor, I have given a lot of consideration to everything that is going on," Hardy told the judge. "I am scared, and I feel bad, but I can't live with it. I can't live with what has been requested. It is too much of a hardship on me and my family. I cannot go on."

"I feel pretty much the same way," McGee said. "I can't function. I go to bed at night with knots. I wake up with knots. I come here and I cry. I am wondering if I am going to make it to my wedding."

With the choice between losing the only two Black jurors or lifting the sequestration, Hamrick took the only option he could. He summoned the jury to the courtroom and announced his decision to end the sequestration, along with a firm admonishment not to discuss the case or expose themselves to news reports or reporters. "We're not going to try this case in the newspaper," he said. "We're going to try it with the evidence right here in the courtroom."

With the sequestration issue seemingly under control, Hamrick turned his attention to a new crisis, one that would soon make everyone forget about Vernell Hardy.

32

June 2, 1986
The Honorable Ben W. Hamrick
Judge of the Superior Court
Department 25

Dear Judge Hamrick:
Please find a document that was found in the manner described in Officer Castro's attached declaration. We received it on May 21, 1986. After discussions with supervisors in this office we have decided to forward it to you so you can decide whether it's discoverable or not. We think it is not discoverable for the reasons listed below but recognize the possibility of reasonable minds differing, ethical considerations, and difficulties which may arise if a court disagrees with us . . .

Respectfully,
Michael G. Carpenter
Deputy District Attorney

M ILT SILVERMAN SET THE COVER LETTER ASIDE AND READ the header on the document provided to him by Judge Hamrick. It was a San Diego Police Department "Officers Report" issued by three sergeants at the police training academy, dated August 4, 1978. The text of the document was a transcript titled "Interview with Donovan Jacobs."

Silverman would later learn the circumstances of what turned out to be a counseling session of Jacobs by the three training sergeants, Tom Hall, Dave Hall, and Dick Bennett, while he was a cadet at the academy. Cadet Jacobs had been asked to critique the actions of two officers in a simulated interaction with two gay men in a car parked in an area of a public park where men frequently came to engage in sex. In the simulation film titled *Protecting Rights & Dignities*, the officers were aggressive and disrespectful, using anti-gay slurs while ordering the men to leave the area. Tom Hall, the training sergeant leading the exercise, found Jacobs's assessment of the scenario made before the class worrisome enough to call for an immediate counseling session and took the highly unusual step of tape-recording it. What Milt Silverman had before him was a raw, eleven-page verbatim transcript of the session.

"What is your first name, Jacobs?" Tom Hall asked to start the session.

"Donovan."

"They call you Don?"

"Yes."

"Okay, Don. I am very much concerned, as we all are, about some of the comments you made in class today. What I would first like to do is for you to explain to me why you feel that scenario was proper on the part of the officers, okay, the discussion we just had in class."

"You mean the way the homosexuals were handled?" Jacobs said.

"Yes."

"Okay. As far as I know, the point of the stop was to keep them out of that area. The way that was handled by that officer gave such a, I guess, a negative effect on the homosexuals that they were not going to return. And, if that was the purpose of the stop for them not to come back, then I think he got his point across very well."

"Do you believe in the methods the officer used, the profanity, calling people 'faggots' and things like that?" Hall asked.

"Okay, in reality, no. I personally wouldn't use that. Like you said, it's degrading. I didn't bring that out when I was up in front of the class but, like I said, he got his point across . . ."

"Okay, but what you said was as long as he got the job done then it was okay, as long as he didn't stimulate complaints . . ."

"Well, sometimes you've got to resort to that, I feel, if that's the way the job can get done. Like I said, I personally wouldn't do it. And I really don't agree with it, but if [it] does the job."

"Okay, the same with the question that was raised to you about minorities: What if you are using derogatory terms against minorities? Your same response was?"

"That they got the job done . . . Okay, I know of situations where . . . 'professional profanity' is used in order to get the point across. Like, you got a crowd of people and you're asking them to disperse and they've got a negative attitude toward you and they are not moving. If you came across with some professional profanity and they started to move, I think that's very effective." He was asked for an example. "I would say something like, 'Listen, God damn it, I'm going to tell you one more time . . .'" Jacobs paused. "Am I shooting myself downhill or what?"

"Well, I am very concerned," Tom Hall said. "We have talked a lot of hours about the type of professional conduct that we want from our officers. And then you come right back at us here and you're talking about using profanity, using derogatory terms or, as you say, whatever is necessary to get the job done. Now, don't you feel that you're maybe a little bit different than the rest of your classmates?"

"I don't think I'm that different than anybody else, it's just that I'm saying it."

"Okay, what you're saying is that you're being more honest than the others?" Hall asked.

"I feel I am. If you can do that by using foul language then I can't see anything wrong with that."

"What if you had a group of Blacks, do you think you could use the word *nigger* or some word like that, a trigger word?"

"No. Like you said, it's a trigger word. Maybe I was wrong in saying that using derogatory remarks, like racist remarks, stuff like that, maybe that would be wrong. But I don't know, maybe there would be a situation where it wouldn't be, but I doubt it."

"However, if all else fails do you think it would be something that would be resorted to?" Hall asked.

"If all else failed and I thought that it would be effective, yes."

Hall asked if the reason Jacobs was not opposed to the treatment of the gay men in the video was because "homosexuality" conflicted with his "personal feelings and values."

"I personally don't accept it," Jacob said.

"Well, nobody is asking you to accept homosexuality," Hall said.

"I know I would not use the term *faggot*," Jacobs responded. "I just know I wouldn't because I know, like I said, I know I wouldn't do it. I don't do that; I don't usually use racial—" Hall inadvertently cut Jacobs off with another question before he completed the sentence.

Jacobs said perhaps he was not expressing himself correctly in class and felt he would be "perceived differently on the street."

"The problem with that, Don, is that if you are doing that here in the academy, you're going to do that very same thing in the street," Hall replied.

The three trainers informed Jacobs how they felt about his answers, his attitude, and his chances of graduating from the academy. "Professional conduct is our number one priority, and you're standing out as not accepting that, Don. I wonder just how much thought you've really put into what it takes to be a police officer on the San Diego Police Department?"

"If you can't deal with it," another said, "you're only going to cause yourself some harm as well as other people . . . It's going to manifest itself somewhere, in stress, in a fight, or in a situation that really ticks you off and the next thing you're going to have the community coming all over you as well as the department."

Sergeant Dick Bennett issued cadet Donovan Jacobs a final warning: "Unless you show some considerable changes or at least some more consideration for others and can change your behavior along those same lines, we don't want you because you are going to do nothing but create problems for yourself, for the public, and for the department."

"I HAVE BEEN, since the day I got on this case, without pause, without stopping, trying to find this very thing, and here it is," Milt Silverman said, jabbing a finger at the front page of what would become known as "the academy transcript." Silverman was standing before Ben Hamrick, pleading with the judge to pause jury deliberations and admit the academy transcript into evidence for the jurors. "This report is the most significant thing that there could conceivably be in this entire case. It is a devastating document. A devastating document. This document establishes the very heart of the prosecution's case is founded on a lie. It shows that when Donovan Jacobs was in that academy, he held these racial attitudes. It shows that he lied under oath on the stand." He singled out Bennett's final warning. "The prophecies in here are chilling," he said emphatically.

"The community isn't going to stand for it," he continued. "If Mr. Penn is convicted, and the jury doesn't know about this document, no right-minded citizen is going to like it, and no right-minded person is going to abide it. It will put a blemish on our justice system. It will never go away. It will never go away."

If at all possible, there was something about the academy transcript that outraged Silverman even more than its contents, and it had to do with the third document referenced in the cover letter and contained in the file given to Silverman. The two-page document was dated May 30, 1986, and titled "Declaration of Jenny Castro." It read:

> I am a police officer employed by the city of San Diego. I have been so employed for over seven years. My present assignment is service coordinator at the San Diego Police Academy.
>
> Eight or nine months ago I was cleaning out an unused office at the academy when I came across the transcript mentioning Donovan Jacobs from August 4, 1978. This transcript was in an old basket with numerous other unrelated papers which I threw out.
>
> I kept this transcript because I wondered whether it was standard operating procedure to record such scenarios, and did Jacobs know it was being recorded.
>
> I put it in my desk at that time with intentions of reading it later.
>
> About a month ago I cleaned out my desk and found the transcript.
>
> I put the transcript in my car in order to give it to Chief Kolender because Donovan Jacobs was mentioned and because of his connection to the Sagon Penn case.

I thereafter gave the transcript to Assistant Chief Bob Burgreen on May 20, 1986.

Silverman checked the dates referenced in the cover letter to form a quick timeline of the document's journey from discovery to his desk. "Son of a bitch," he thought.

"How does Jenny Castro have this for eight months and not mention it to anybody?" he said to Hamrick with utter dismay. "It must have been in the newspapers night and day that the defense was claiming that Donovan Jacobs had the very character traits that are in these eleven pages that the police department had. She says the reason she held on to it, she wanted to know if in 1978, which is seven years earlier, it was standard routine practice to tape-record these sessions. She wanted to find out if Jacobs knew he was being tape-recorded. It is so preposterous and absurd."

"Do you know when she finally gets around to giving it to Chief Kolender?" he continued, noting the significance of May 20. "The very day the jury returns a verdict [on the ADW (assault with a deadly weapon) charge] in this case, which would have precluded me forever from making a motion with respect to this document. Of course, what happens on May 21 is Mrs. Hardy says, 'No, that is not my verdict.' So now we are back at the point in time where I could then make this motion [to reopen]." He held up the cover letter, which stated the DA's office received the transcript on the same day as Hardy's decision, May 21. "They had this document!" he boomed. "What do they do on the twenty-second? Do they come down and say, 'Judge Hamrick, we don't know if you have this, but here it is. We think you ought to look at it right quick'? No, sir. They waited until June second . . . until they knew that you were leaving and wouldn't be back until the fourth. They wait, and they wait, and they wait, and they wait. And why do they wait? They were holding on to that thing because they wanted the jury to come back and say, 'Guilty,' and [then] say, 'By the way, here is this other thing; and now [it] doesn't matter anyway.' I think that what we have here is deliberate suppression of evidence."

"I know I am arguing uphill, but it burns my soul that they can get away with this stuff," Silverman said in his final plea for the document to be entered into evidence. "Judge, you have to right this wrong. I am asking, give them the document. Give them the document. I want this jury to hear this. I ask you to take it in your hands and to do justice in this case. Do the right thing. I *plead* with you to do that."

"Your Honor," Mike Carpenter responded, "Milt Silverman has this case exactly where he wants it to be: somewhere between a rock and a hard place. And if you do anything else he requests you to do, it's going to get in deeper."

Hamrick allowed the prosecution overnight to write a response to Silverman's motion to pause deliberations and reopen the trial. When they returned the next day, they found Hamrick had ordered the bailiff to cover the courtroom windows and duct tape the cracks in the doors so reporters could not eavesdrop on what was going on inside. Still, the arguments became so heated that marshals had to move members of the media down the corridor so they would not overhear.

Despite "grave reluctance," Hamrick said, "I am inclined to grant a motion to reopen." As long as both attorneys stipulated to the authenticity of the transcript, he would have it read to the jury by the court reporter.

"No, Your Honor, we will not stipulate," Carpenter said flatly. "We will never stipulate to this going in front of the jury at this time. You have to take into consideration where this was taking place. This was a session at the academy—"

"I have heard all the argument," Hamrick interrupted. "I don't want to hear the merits. I am going to reopen the case for that limited purpose. It is a question of how we do it with the least possible disruption."

If Carpenter refused to stipulate the authenticity, Hamrick said he would do whatever necessary to bring in the academy trainers who were in the counseling session to do it. By the end of the day, Hamrick had done just that. Tom Hall and Dave Hall both took the witness stand, but, under questioning from Hamrick, each said they had no recollection of the counseling session and could not authenticate the transcript. Now it was Carpenter who had Hamrick "somewhere between a rock and a hard place." With a jury already in near mutiny and on its way to the longest deliberation in San Diego history, allowing witnesses and arguments to authenticate the transcript would take days more of their time.

After considering his options, Hamrick made his ruling. "The prejudicial effect and problems created by its introduction far outweigh the probative value. Accordingly, the motion to reopen is denied."

BY THAT TIME, reporters were able to piece together enough shards of information to determine the controversy involved the counseling of Jacobs at the academy over his behavior in a training exercise of some sort. "I have no idea what you're talking about," Donovan Jacobs said when told of the possible existence of the evidence. "I didn't get in any trouble while I was at the academy. I'm as clean as a newborn babe, just what the prosecution showed you."

On Wednesday, June 11, the day after Silverman's motion was denied, the original declaration by Jenny Castro, with her name redacted, was released, revealing to reporters the shocking news that the mysterious transcript had been discovered eight months earlier. Mike Carpenter downplayed the delay by his own office in handling the transcript, telling reporters they had "acted with what we believe to be reasonable diligence and speed." He pointed out that the twelve-day gap included two weekends. "I'm not like Milt Silverman," he said. "I don't work on weekends."

ON JUNE 13, the ruling on an appeal by Silverman came down from the Fourth Court of Appeals. The justices in the majority, Howard Weiner and Edward Butler, neither agreed nor disagreed with Hamrick's ruling, only that he, not them, was best qualified to assess the relevance of the transcript within the context of the "lengthy, complex and emotionally charged trial." Therefore, they stated, "We will accordingly deny this position." However, the dissenting opinion of Justice Donald Work was scathing of Hamrick's ruling and concurred almost entirely with Silverman's argument. It came with a blunt warning that "a denial of the motion to reopen to allow the jurors to evaluate this evidence so affects the fairness of this trial as to raise the serious probability a motion for new trial would be granted in the event of convictions."

Hamrick took Judge Work's warning seriously. He pleaded with

Carpenter to drop his opposition to the motion and allow the evidence in. "It seems to me that the prosecution could avoid a new trial, or a motion for new trial, or mistrial by agreeing to have the document read to the jury. If you were a betting man, I think you could lay odds on the outcome," he added, referring to what he called "the handwriting on the wall from the Fourth Court" decision.

Carpenter would not change his position. "I believe your decision of last week will [with]stand a motion for a new trial," he responded.

"We are pleased," Carpenter commented to reporters on the final ruling, after which the text of the transcript had been made public. Of Jenny Castro, he said, "It will be shown that she was innocent in whatever she was doing." He added that a "full and fair hearing" would also exonerate his office of any alleged mishandling of the process. "It didn't seem much of anything to me," Chief Kolender said of the transcript content. Donovan Jacobs also declared exoneration. "A bunch of garbage," he labeled the transcript. "This is just another attempt by the defense to throw smoke up in the air." Milt Silverman had a simple answer for their dismissiveness: "If it doesn't mean anything, why don't they read it to the jury?"

The ruling also compelled Silverman to tell Judge Ben Hamrick, a man he admired and a judge he respected, something he had hoped he would not have to say: "I no longer believe Sagon Penn received a fair trial."

33

WHILE THE STORM OVER THE ACADEMY TRANSCRIPT raged outside their presence, the jury disappeared into their little deliberation room day after day, while the attorneys, media, and public waited, on the lookout for any sign of which way they might be leaning. On June 13, the judge asked Foreman Bernd for a status. "We're still talking. There's no black eyes on anybody yet," he replied. On June 18, he told Hamrick, "Maybe a week or two more, in all fairness."

On Tuesday, June 24, the twenty-fifth day of deliberations, the jurors had another handwritten request delivered to Hamrick. It read, "Please define 'intent' as used in CALJIC 9.0." Section 9.0 of the standard *California Jury Instructions, Criminal*, or CALJIC, relates to the charge of "assault on a peace officer." Just after 2:00 p.m., the judge read the text of CALJIC 9.0 in open court. He provided further clarification of the instruction for the jurors: "To find the defendant guilty of assault you must find that he had general *intent* to commit the act. A conviction of assault may not be grounded upon mere reckless conduct alone." A juror raised her hand with a question for the judge. "Does that mean that is what has to be in his head at the time?" she asked, pointing to her own head. "Yes," said Hamrick.

What made the seemingly mundane procedural action so remarkable was that Milt Silverman had fought all the way up to the Fourth Court of Appeals for those exact instructions to be given the jury, only to be denied at every level. Due to what he referred to as "a momentary lapse in focus" on his part, instructions related to the requirement of intent for ADW guilt had been omitted from jury instructions by Hamrick. Silverman had not realized the error until clerk LaRue Slaugh read the guilty verdict on the ADW charge the day Vernell Hardy entered the hospital. He pleaded with Hamrick to halt deliberations, have the intent portion of CALJIC 9.0 read to the jury, and instruct them to reconsider the ADW conviction. Hamrick refused and the appeals failed. Silverman had long since given up on the issue, haunted that his client still might be convicted in part due to his own error. But now an unexpected jury request to define a single word had resulted in Hamrick reading them the entire instruction. Following the earlier verdict reconsideration by Vernell Hardy, it was the second miracle Milt Silverman had received on the ADW charge.

AT 10:45 A.M. on the morning of June 26, the handful of reporters covering the trial every day were languishing on benches in the corridor when bailiff Mike Rodelo opened the door to the courtroom and began setting up the walk-through metal detector. It was a ritual performed anytime members of the public were expected inside the courtroom. "It's not a verdict," Rodelo had assured them on all the previous occasions. This time he was quiet. The reporters and several die-hard spectators perked up. "Is it a verdict?" someone asked breathlessly. "No comment," Rodelo said. An instant later reporters were sprinting down the hall toward the bank of pay phones to alert their newsrooms to activate the prearranged coverage teams. The verdict was in.

Within minutes, television and radio news crews arrived wearing headsets, hoisting video cameras, staking out spaces for their remotes, and running transmission cables out a window four stories down to the news vans parked at the curb with their antennae extended upward. Additional reporters from *The San Diego Union*, *Evening Tribune*, and *Los Angeles Times* arrived to cover all angles of the breaking story. The corridor was soon choked with reporters representing over two dozen news organizations from across the country.

Mike Carpenter and Bob Phillips walked from their offices on the other side of the building and sat at the prosecution table. Ben Hamrick had been several blocks away but hustled to the courtroom when no-tified. When Milt Silverman arrived, he went to a pay phone to call Thomas Penn. "Tom, there's a verdict," he said. "Better hurry."

"I may need a sword to fall on," Silverman commented with a ner-vous smile as he passed reporters on his way into the courtroom. Inside he stood beside the defense table, restlessly pacing a step or two in each direction or shifting his weight from foot to foot in anticipation. Maria leaned over and handed him a colored index card with a handwritten quote from the Old Testament: "Fear not for I am with you. Do not be dismayed. I am your God. I will strengthen you."

It was 11:30 a.m. by the time family members had taken their usual seats, along with whatever media could be accommodated. Coleen Riggs and two of Tom's sisters were in the back row, the strain of the moment evident beneath their composed exterior. Thomas Penn and other fam-ily members arrived, helping Yusuf Abdullah to his chair. The corridor outside filled with members of the public drawn by radio and television reports of the impending verdicts. Two speakers wired to the courtroom audio system were placed in the hallway so the overflow crowd could hear. Five additional U.S. marshals were stationed at the courtroom door and positioned along the corridor.

At 11:55 a.m., Sagon Penn entered wearing his navy blue suit, walked straight to the defense table without looking at the spectator gallery, and assumed his usual position staring straight ahead. Silverman sat beside him and rested a hand on his shoulder, as he had so many times during the trial. "Whatever it is, take it like a man," he whispered to his client. Penn nodded almost imperceptibly.

At high noon, Judge Hamrick entered the courtroom. He admon-ished spectators about their expected conduct during the proceedings. Moments later, the jurors entered, taking their seats while avoiding eye contact. Foreman Doug Bernd passed the verdict forms to Mike Rodelo, who handed them up to Hamrick. Hamrick looked through the forms and handed them to LaRue Slaugh to be read.

"We the jury in the above entitled cause find the defendant, Sagon Penn, not guilty of the crime of first-degree murder as charged in count one of the information. Victim: Thomas Riggs."

"We the jury in the above entitled cause find the defendant, Sagon Penn, not guilty of the crime of second-degree murder as charged in count one of the information. Victim: Thomas Riggs."

Slaugh read only charges for which the jury had reached a verdict, not those which had ended in a deadlock. When she moved on from count one to count two without further verdicts, it was understood that the jury had deadlocked on the next lesser charge of manslaughter in the death of Riggs.

"We the jury in the above entitled cause find the defendant, Sagon Penn, not guilty of the crime of attempted murder as charged in count two of the information. Victim: Donovan Jacobs."

Count two was the attempted murder of Jacobs with a firearm. The absence of an additional verdict on the count meant the jury was deadlocked on manslaughter.

Slaugh announced no verdict associated with count three, attempted murder of Donovan Jacobs with a police vehicle. The not-guilty verdicts on first-degree and second-degree attempted murder had already been recorded as part of the partial verdicts taken when Vernell Hardy entered the hospital. The absence of any verdict now meant they had remained deadlocked on the assault-with-a-deadly-weapon verdict Vernell Hardy had declined to affirm at the maternity ward.

"We the jury in the above entitled cause find the defendant, Sagon Penn, not guilty of the crime of [auto theft] as charged in count five of the information."

"We the jury in the above entitled cause find the defendant, Sagon Penn, not guilty of the crime of grand theft—firearm, as charged in count six of the information."

Conspicuously absent from the announced verdicts was count four, the attempted murder of Sarah Pina-Ruiz. That meant the jury had been unable to decide whether Sagon Penn intended to murder an unarmed thirty-two-year-old housewife and mother of two when he fired a gun at her at point-blank range. The attempted-murder charge would remain available, along with the other deadlocked charges, should the DA choose to retry Penn.

Included on each verdict form was the date the jury had come to their final decision. For the attempted murder of Donovan Jacobs with a vehicle, the first- and second-degree not-guilty verdicts were dated May 16, the first full day of deliberations. The next verdict reached was not until May 27, when they decided Penn was not guilty of attempted murder of Donovan Jacobs with a firearm. The decisions on the auto and gun theft had been reached on May 30. It was not until June 18 that they decided the shooting of Thomas Riggs did not satisfy the legal definition of murder.

They spent the last week unsuccessfully trying to break the deadlocks on the remaining counts. Hamrick asked Bernd how many votes they had taken on each of the deadlocked counts. At least a dozen, Bernd said. "Would you tell us which way you were divided?" Hamrick asked of the deadlocked counts. The numbers offered by Bernd were almost as startling as the verdicts.

Count one, voluntary manslaughter of Thomas Riggs, ten to two in favor of not guilty. Count two, attempted voluntary manslaughter of Donovan Jacobs with a firearm, ten to two in favor of not guilty. Count three, assault with a deadly weapon on Jacobs, vehicle, eight to four in favor of not guilty. That final deadlock was dated June 25, the day after Hamrick instructed the jury that intent was required for an ADW conviction. The attempted murder of Sarah Pina-Ruiz was deadlocked eleven to one in favor of not guilty.

"The jury is excused and discharged," Hamrick announced. "The Court will declare a mistrial on the charges not resolved."

HAMRICK SCHEDULED A bail-review hearing for the following week, but Silverman spoke up asking for an immediate determination because his client would be in danger from "neo-Nazi and Ku Klux Klan types" in the county jail who had been threatening Penn throughout the trial. After hearing brief arguments, Hamrick reduced Penn's bail from $250,000 to $25,000 "in view of the finding of the jury heavy toward acquittal." Silverman was satisfied. The bail money was put up by Si Casady, the newspaper publisher who hosted the fundraiser at his La Jolla home attended by Muhammad Ali. Penn was led from the courtroom by a bailiff to wait for the administrative process to be completed. At no time had he expressed happiness, relief, or any other emotion at the verdicts. There were no smiles exchanged with family or supporters and only a few whispered words from his lawyer.

When the doors to the courtroom were finally opened, the crowded corridor was a cacophony of conversation, debates, arguments, and expressions of disbelief from stunned supporters and spectators who had not gotten a seat inside. As the now-familiar main characters in the drama departed, they were met with a sea of television news cameras, photographers, and microphones pointed in their direction.

The jurors escaped down stairwells or were escorted to their cars by court personnel. Those who exited the building at street level were intercepted and followed by reporters waiting for them outside. Glen Coahran unchained his bike from a lamppost, ignoring reporters' questions. He showed that the pressure of deliberations had not diminished his sense of humor by slipping on a Groucho Marx combined glasses, nose, mustache, and bushy eyebrows "disguise" before riding away. As he passed Doug Bernd speaking with reporters, he tossed one of the disguises to him.

Mike Carpenter expressed his disappointment as he walked briskly in the direction of his office followed by reporters. Milt Silverman, who paused briefly to answer questions, said what many were feeling after the verdicts: "There's no victory celebration here. This is a terrible thing that has happened to Officer Riggs, his family, his widow, his children, and to Sagon Penn."

PART 4

34

"**H**OW CAN A GUY KILL A COP AND WOUND OTHER PEOPLE, shoot an unarmed civilian, and nothing happened to him?" an indignant Donovan Jacobs said to reporters at police headquarters several days after the verdict. "This isn't the first time justice hasn't been served. He's guilty as sin and should be punished." Jacobs was bitter about a lot things—the failed justice system, Milt Silverman, the unfairness of life—but he had reserved most of his wrath for the jury he accused of allowing themselves to be manipulated by Silverman. "How could people be so naive to believe what was said. In a nutshell, the jury has said it is okay to murder a police officer."

It took the city of San Diego several days to assess the damage from the Sagon Penn story being laid bare before them over a three-and-a-half-month trial. With some serious charges left unresolved, the trial had failed to produce a final resolution on the question of guilt. Nobody was happy about it, and the people they were most unhappy with was the jury.

"I have lost faith in the justice system," Coleen Riggs said sadly of the verdicts that held no one responsible for her husband's death. "It sounds like the jury did everything in its power to ensure that Mr. Penn would be given absolutely the lightest sentence, if any at all," said Coleen's sister Cynthia. "It's just one of many injustices that takes place in this city," Chief Bill Kolender said during a moment of frustration. "This verdict gives new meaning to the expression 'getting away with murder,'" said one patrolman who, like most, preferred to remain anonymous. "They ought to give badges to each of the jury members and let them patrol the streets tonight," remarked another. Thomas Penn and other Sagon Penn supporters voiced displeasure in the jury because they had not declared him innocent of all charges, leaving him open to a second trial.

It was several days before jurors responded to the criticism. Their decisions had been variously attributed to cowardice, stupidity, bias, ignorance, and gullibility. But their comments showed it had been anything but that. As directed, they stayed faithful to Judge Hamrick's jury instructions and legal definition of the offenses. They decided against the murder charges, they said, because Penn's actions did not meet the strict legal definition of the crime. "To me, none of it was murder," thirty-six-year-old juror Sally Naley said. "It was just a bad situation that got worse, tragically, and ended with somebody losing their life." They were careful to point out that they had not absolved Penn of all responsibility, as evidenced in the charges remaining, and not just those hung at eleven to one and ten to two. Several said they were inclined toward guilt on lesser charges. "It wasn't one person's fault," Laraine Diaz said. "Penn could have given him his license."

Donovan Jacobs's insults and condemnation of their decision had not gone unnoticed, causing some jurors to publicly voice what had been implicit in their finding Penn not guilty of murder or attempted murder of Riggs and Jacobs. "There was a general feeling Jacobs handled the whole thing very badly," said Naley, the daughter of a retired Oakland police sergeant. "I would say he's the one who started it." Glen Coahran felt that "Jacobs was the defense's best witness. He came across as a guy who did not mind knocking people around." Twenty-six-year-old Troy Axe was even more direct in her assessment. "Jacobs was an asshole and caused it all," she later said. "It was a power thing. He couldn't be in control and it made him enraged." She said Jacobs "put Riggs in danger" with his actions. Naley agreed. "Riggs was doing his job. I think if he was alive today, he'd be very upset with Jacobs."

For those who sought to attribute the absence of guilty verdicts to bias on the part of the two Black jurors, Vernell Hardy and Kimberly McGee, the final vote count showed that there had been no lone-wolf holdouts blocking any conviction. The final vote count of eight to four in favor of acquittal on the ADW charge suggested Hardy had been correct in putting the stops on the guilty verdict in the hospital, saying the charge deserved more discussion. Both women also demonstrated a willingness to consider guilt—Hardy by initially casting a guilty vote on the ADW in deliberations, and McGee by carrying it all the way through to her ballot.

Because jurors are not polled on deadlocked counts, nor are their votes recorded by name, the identity of the lone eleven-to-one holdout against acquittal on the attempted murder of Sarah Pina-Ruiz would never be known unless the juror revealed it himself. "I was the lone holdout, and I'll always be the lone holdout," jury foreman Douglas Bernd volunteered to a reporter who caught up with him while he was repairing a horse stable on his property. He and Lynn Decker, the oldest member of the jury, were on the short end of the ten-to-two deadlocks in favor of acquittal on manslaughter charges related to the shooting of Riggs and Jacobs. He rejected the idea that he had his mind made up from the start, noting that he voted for acquittal on many of the charges. "The decisions were based on listening to every witness, and not emotions," he said. He had no harsh words for those who disagreed with his vote. "I think it would be a pretty crappy society if we all walked in and all had the same opinion." His fellow jurors were complimentary of the way he ran the deliberations. "We worked hard," Bernd said. "We didn't play around in there." The six-foot-two, 250-pound foreman had a message for those in the city who were critical of the jury and their verdicts. "We were twelve people that gave a hell of a lot. They have no right to crab at us."

The trial and its outcome only further polarized the ardent and vocal supporters of law enforcement as the commentaries, editorials, radio talk show chatter, and letters to the editor became vitriolic. One editorial staff writer for *The San Diego Union* went for a wide-eyed ride-along in the Southeast the night of the verdicts, concluding that "it's clear to anyone that the cops are the only thing preventing the community from slipping into outright anarchy." "People of color, especially poor people, take note . . . next time there's a stabbing and the criminal is not caught," a former city council aide lectured the people of Southeast. One editorial cartoon in *The San Diego Union* featured an ink rendering of Riggs captioned "The other verdict . . . Thomas Riggs: Innocent. Sentenced to death." Another depicted a blindfolded "Madam Justice" grieving over the tombstone of Tom Riggs.

Reiko Obata, the very visible and active head of the Sagon Penn Defense Committee, commented on the reactions: "It's a whole lynch type atmosphere. It's an atmosphere that gives green lights to racists in this city."

At *Channel 10 News*, anchorman Michael Tuck continued to voice opinions more in line with the young, college-educated, and multiracial population that made up "the new San Diego." He offered conciliatory words in his "Perspective" segments but expressed sharp opposition to a second trial on the unresolved counts. For Tuck, trial one had decided it all, and any further prosecution would represent pure maliciousness on the part of the district attorney and police. This time, the backlash toward his editorial pieces was even more volatile, resulting in a torrent of threats expressed on talk radio and calls to the station. The recent cold-blooded gunning down of controversial liberal talk show host Alan Berg by an enraged listener in Denver was never far from his mind.

A deeply troubling development for the Black community had unfolded during the Penn trial, reminding them that despite the influx of a more progressive demographic, the city was still a stronghold for some very regressive attitudes toward race. In January 1986, the majority-Republican San Diego City Council voted to change the name of a five-mile stretch of Euclid Avenue to Martin Luther King Jr. Way. They called it the city's way of honoring 1986 as the first year the civil rights leader would be recognized with a national holiday. The council was blindsided by the reaction of the residents and store owners on the section of Euclid that lay outside the Southeast. It was not subtle, with some of those opposed loudly voicing objections to "Dr. King's methods and mission."

In April, the council backed down, announcing it would now rename a section of Market Street stretching from the San Diego Bay to Encanto instead. The uproar shifted to the retail-store owners of Market Street who hastily formed the Keep Market Street Committee to oppose the name change, saying it was a matter of preserving history. "For me and our group, it's not a racial issue," said chairman Tod Firotto. "I certainly would like to see something named for King. I don't think it should be Market Street." "They can sugarcoat any way they want," prominent Black business owner Willie Morrow responded. "What they are saying is 'Dr. King was a great person who should be honored as long as it's not in my neighborhood.'"

With some of the King Way signs already up, the city council met in July to decide whether to add the issue of the name change to the November ballot. The Keep Market Street Committee brought the results of a research poll showing 65 percent of San Diegans opposed the name change. Members of the Black community spoke against the idea of the ballot measure, adamant that the effort to rescind the name was racially motivated. Reverend George Walker Smith said it was indicative of the "negative attitude that white folks here have toward King and other things." A city council member lamented the opposition happening less than two weeks after the verdict in the Sagon Penn trial: "We had hoped at the time to bring San Diegans closer together. God knows this city needs it, especially right now." In a four-to-three vote, the council kept the question off the ballot, and the renaming effort continued.

The Keep Market Street Committee was not ready to give up, and efforts began in earnest to collect the required number of signatures to put the referendum on the 1987 ballot.

"I think it's a crisis now," Chief Kolender's deputy chief and community fixer, Norm Stamper, said of the acrimony being expressed throughout the city and the growing rift between the Black community and police. Stamper held urgent face-to-face meetings with community leaders from the Southeast to address grievances and solutions, but what little progress they had been making in their discussions was wiped out by an incident in early November.

Patrolling the mostly Black Mountain View neighborhood of the city on November 4, 1986, two white patrol officers on horseback approached a man for having his dog off-leash. After giving the officers false information, the man was put under arrest. To deliver him to a patrol vehicle for transport, the officers elected the antebellum method of handcuffing the man's hands in front of his body, tethering a rope between the cuffs and the saddle of a horse, and leading him twelve blocks through crowded streets and a public park to the waiting police car. It was a public relations disaster. "My first thought was, my god, this guy looks like he just got off the slave ship and was going to the slave market," said Neil Pettis, the area parks director. The police quickly ended the practice, raising the question of how such a thing could have been procedure in the first place.

PRETRIAL MOTIONS FOR the second trial began in January 1987. The offenses and charges on which Sagon Penn would be retried were voluntary manslaughter of Tom Riggs with a firearm, attempted voluntary manslaughter of Donovan Jacobs with a firearm, and attempted murder of Sarah Pina-Ruiz with a firearm. Each included lesser charges for which Penn could be convicted.

Penn could never be retried on the higher charges of murder and attempted murder on the counts, which would be forever recorded as not-guilty verdicts as decided in trial one. It had not always been that way. The California law requiring such "partial verdicts" be upheld was established in the 1982 landmark case of *Stone v. Superior Court*. The attorney who successfully argued the case before the California Supreme Court on behalf of his client Clifford Lee Stone was Milton Silverman.

Prior to the start of the second trial, Silverman won another victory for his client when the court of appeals ruled to dismiss the lesser remaining assault-with-a-deadly-weapon charge for running Jacobs over with a vehicle. Because the first jury had found there was no intent on the part of Penn, they ruled, it should have resulted in a not-guilty verdict. With that, Penn was acquitted of all charges related to the count.

During a break on the first day of preliminary motions, associate attorney Carl Lewis was seated at the defense table when he looked up at the judge's bench and saw a curious sight. Youthful and dark-eyed Judge J. Morgan Lester was pouring over a document while taking notes, the eraser tips of two pencils moving back and forth. It took Lewis a moment to realize the judge was writing with both hands.

J. Morgan Lester was an eccentric among the sensible and sober world of San Diego judges. From a low-income Detroit neighborhood plagued with violent youth gangs, he was stationed with the army in San Diego and then remained. He was a prosecutor for eight years, at one point sharing an office with Mike Carpenter. He was an elected municipal court judge before being appointed to the superior court by Republican governor George Deukmejian. Lester had a reputation among local attorneys for fairness and impartiality, and was known to be calm under pressure with an almost supernatural level of concentration. Darkly complected with angular features, Lester was one-quarter Iroquois. He provided pro bono legal support to the Rincon Indian Reservation near his home in rural inland San Diego, where he "sweated" with members, participated in tribal ceremonies, and was bestowed with an honorary Native American name, "Golden Owl."

Not without ambition, he readily accepted the assignment to commute to the downtown courthouse to preside over the high-visibility Penn case. Having worked alongside Carpenter and having been involved in cases against Silverman, he made sure both attorneys were aware of his history with the other. "I want you both to know, I don't care who wins this trial," he said. Both attorneys were satisfied with him presiding over the case.

Pretrial proceedings opened on January 20, 1987, and quickly turned to arguments over the admissibility of Jacobs's academy counseling transcript. The prosecution again refused to stipulate the authenticity of the transcript, with their motions-and-appeals expert Bob Phillips even suggesting Jenny Castro had forged it herself.

Silverman was outraged that the prosecution would continue to block the transcript over authenticity, but it was the responsibility of the defense to prove the document was legitimate. After testimony from an amnesic Jenny Castro, academy-trainer Lieutenant Richard Bennett, and Jacobs himself, Lester came out firmly on the side of Silverman. "It is almost inconceivable that this could have arisen from any other source than a transcript of a tape-recorded counseling session," he said in his ruling.

"Nobody compliments us for giving it to the Court," Mike Carpenter lamented over the transcript fiasco afterward. "What I should have done is burn the thing."

MIKE CARPENTER MOSTLY ignored the press during the first trial, but an article by Glenn Bunting in the June 29, 1986, edition of the *Los*

Angeles Times titled "Penn Prosecutor Met His Match in Veteran Defense Attorney" stung. "What began as a gentlemanly battle between two legal gladiators escalated into a bitter confrontation that included harshly worded personal attacks, accusations of ethical misconduct, and emotional outbursts," wrote the journalist, who had covered every day of the trial. Both attorneys were interviewed extensively for the piece and expressed lingering bitterness toward the other. Silverman called some of Carpenter's actions "unfair, misleading, and cheap." He said he was so confident of his case by the end of the trial, he had no reason to risk putting Sagon Penn on the stand. "When you're a touchdown ahead in the Super Bowl, you don't give the other team the ball."

Carpenter singled out Silverman's use of Carolyn Cherry: "The other side is jumping around thinking they pulled one over on us. I thought, you know, it would be easy for me to get up and rip him a new one." Going into trial two, Carpenter was less inclined to pass up any opportunity to rip Silverman a new one or allow him to pull anything like the Carolyn Cherry episode again. His superiors at the DA's office felt the same and intended to do something about it. That something walked into the courtroom on the first day of jury selection.

"Milt Silverman needs to be controlled. He needs to be made to play by the rules," Deputy District Attorney Wayne Mayer announced to the press after being assigned to assist Mike Carpenter in the second trial of Sagon Penn. "His courtroom flamboyance and drama have to be eliminated." Forty years old, over six feet tall, tanned, fit, blow-dried, and mustachioed, Mayer was ruggedly handsome with the self-confidence to go with it. The presence of Mayer signaled a new, significantly more aggressive approach to trial two, which had been endorsed all the way up to DA Ed Miller. It was felt that Carpenter had let Silverman get away with too many courtroom shenanigans the first time around. Mayer was going to use the power of the objection to put a stop to that. From now on, they would fight the defense on everything and prosecute their case more forcefully.

Silverman, a renowned counterpuncher when challenged, was bemused by Mayer. When Carpenter asked prospective jurors if they would be swayed one way or the other by the performance of a particularly charismatic and theatrical attorney, Silverman began asking female prospective jurors if they would be similarly swayed by Mayer's good looks. "Mr. Mayer is a handsome fella, all muscle and sinew, and he walks like a panther," he said. He relentlessly needled Mayer in open court over his handsomeness and "*Magnum P.I.* smile," a reference to the television detective heartthrob Tom Selleck, to whom Mayer bore a strong resemblance. On another occasion, he referred to him as "that handsome devil over there with the long arms."

Jury selection stretched to almost three weeks. Carpenter asked each juror if the presence of a gallery of all-white or all-Black courtroom spectators would impact their judgment. Silverman asked about their feelings toward police and the institution of law enforcement. And again, he engaged them in the question of loyalty versus truth.

Although the two sides fought hard over acceptance or rejection of certain candidates, it was not until their efforts to fill the final jury seat that emotions boiled over. With no Black jurors yet seated, both sides accepted Southeast-area Baptist minister Matthew Cornelius Frazier Jr., only to have Carpenter reverse his decision with a peremptory challenge to have him removed. Silverman argued the decision was purely based on race. Lester took the unusual step of rejecting the prosecution's request, expressing "absolute astonishment" at the effort. Silverman celebrated the ruling. "What this means is that the prosecution is not going to be able to bleach that jury all white." Carpenter bristled at the characterization, noting he had not used peremptory challenges against prospective Black jurors in either trial without cause and that he had other reasons for not wanting Frazier on the panel.

Once again, Sagon Penn was a motionless, expressionless, immaculately dressed enigma seated at the defense table during the proceedings. But outside the courtroom, his psychological condition worsened as he tried to resume a life in which everything had changed. The strain of the trial and terrifying prospect of spending the rest of his life behind bars had exacted an emotional toll. He stayed with his grandfather for a time, then with a family friend, but changed his location frequently in fear of retribution from members of the police or public. The media dogged him for interviews and stalked him for photographs. Strangers and organizations wanted to meet him, host him, interview him, have him join their causes, and appear at their functions.

Penn received no mental health care during his incarceration, and whatever he was receiving afterward was not nearly enough considering his previously existing fragile psychological state and traumatic experience of the incident and trial. He had been desperate for the DA to drop the remaining charges and be freed of the crushing fear that he would have to go through another trial after what the first had done to him. But when District Attorney Ed Miller quickly announced his intention to try him a second time, the full weight of the possibility he might yet spend decades in jail descended on him again.

35

"WHEN SAGON PENN WAS APPROACHED BY DONOVAN JA-cobs and Thomas Riggs, he was just a time bomb waiting to be detonated." Mike Carpenter's more aggressive approach toward the prosecution was on display in his opening statement on the afternoon of March 9, 1987. He portrayed Penn as overtly defiant and hostile, eager to get into a fight, and loving it when he did. He said Penn "lost his temper," was "uncontrollable," and was "totally impossible to deal with." "He didn't want to be shown up in front of his friends and younger brother." When Penn shot Jacobs and the others, the prosecutor said, he was "setting an example for his younger brother." By contrast, Carpenter characterized Donovan Jacobs's attitude during the interaction as "polite, positive, and inquisitive."

Milt Silverman wasted no time reprising his attack on the character and actions of Donovan Jacobs, calling him "a bigot, hothead, and a racist from the day he went to the police academy." His approach to Sagon Penn that day was "hostile and aggressive, like a Doberman pinscher." He called the altercation a racially motivated beating, made worse when Penn effectively blocked his baton strikes. "Jacobs was enraged. He was trying as best he can to crack this young fella's skull, and he can't do it . . . This is what caused him to press his savage attack," he said. "He couldn't bear to see himself not dropping this 'nigger.'"

Unlike trial one, this time the jury would not have to wait long to see the man one attorney referred to as a Doberman pinscher and the other characterized as "polite, positive, and inquisitive."

DONOVAN JACOBS LOOKED healthier and more confident as he took the stand as the first witness in the second trial of Sagon Penn. It signaled a big change in strategy by Carpenter from having previously called Jacobs and Sarah Pina-Ruiz at the end of his case. This time, his most important eyewitnesses would be the ones to establish the baseline narrative. He was also determined to get a stronger performance out of Jacobs, who the jurors in trial one called off-putting and "his own worst enemy." Jacobs spent twenty hours prepping with the prosecution team and reviewing his past statements and testimony. He was calmer and more accessible this time, often turning in the witness chair to speak directly to the jury "so they can look at me, look in my eyes, and determine whether I'm telling the truth."

Jacobs said he was "hazy" on certain events of March 31, 1985, and acknowledged he might be mistaken on some details. "I know all the accusations about me lying about what happened that day. I know I'm not lying." He was unwavering in his assertion that he and Riggs had done nothing wrong. "To this day, there is no doubt in my mind that I did exactly what I was supposed to do."

Under cross-examination by Silverman, Jacobs denied he approached Penn aggressively, saying he remembered he was in a good mood at the time because he was still "jazzed" about the arrest of fifteen-year-old Anthony Fields hours earlier. He said he may have asked Penn, "What do you claim, Blood or Cuz?" and conceded it was possible he grabbed Penn by the arm: "I'm not denying touching him, I'm just telling you what I remember." Silverman asked him whether he was sure he did not spin Penn around and punch him in the face. "I'm not going to break my hand on somebody if I have a baton," he replied.

Silverman questioned Jacobs at length over the file containing photographs of alleged gang members Jacobs was maintaining. It was Silverman's contention the file showed Jacobs was engaged in a personal war against minority street gangs for whom he harbored an intense hatred. Jacobs denied targeting young Black men for the project. He said the file was maintained at the Southeast station and approved by superiors. He described the filing system as three cardboard boxes, each about a foot long and eight inches wide, and "each designating white, Mexicans, or Blacks, and then alphabetized by their last name."

"Okay. What were the white gangs?" Silverman asked.

"There wasn't any," Jacobs said.

"So there were no photographs of any whites?"

"That's correct."

When Silverman introduced the academy transcript of Cadet Jacobs's 1978 counseling session, Jacobs stood by his assertion that "professional profanity" was still acceptable "to keep something from getting out of control." He had apparently disregarded the warnings of the academy trainers and used it on the street. "It may not be what all the citizens out there want us to do, but we've found it to be effective," he said.

Silverman asked if he felt the same about the use of "derogatory terms" and "racial slurs." "No," he replied, "because I've come in contact with a lot of people since then, and I've discovered there is no situation where using racial remarks would deescalate the situation." Silverman asked him about the specific racial slurs some witnesses alleged him to have used in the altercation. "That is something that is so totally out of line with my character that I can say without a doubt I would never do it," Jacobs responded.

Jacobs's testimony was lengthier but followed much the same course as before. As he concluded what Mike Carpenter called five days of "brutal cross-examination," Silverman asked Jacobs about his preparation for the trial. Jacobs said it had been extensive, mostly in preparation for cross-examination. "Well, I hope I didn't disappoint you," Silverman said.

"Mr. Silverman," Jacobs replied, "you have met my expectations."

"SLIM AND ANGULAR, with aquiline features and a thinly veiled anger," was how *San Diego Magazine* writer Maribeth Mellin described Sarah Pina-Ruiz as she entered the courtroom following Donovan Jacobs's testimony. Her testimony marked Wayne Mayer's trial debut questioning a witness. She repeated that the altercation that moved down the driveway was no more than a "scuffle" in which Penn was effectively blocking what few baton blows there were, striking back, and getting the best of the officers. She again claimed she saw the shootings in detail: "I watched his finger go, and then the hammer going back, and then the shot, and blood splattered." Pina-Ruiz displayed more emotion than she did before, covering her face and sobbing as the radio-traffic tape of her cries for help was played.

On cross, Silverman again highlighted the differences between her testimony and her statement to Detective Dave Ayers the night of the incident. He tore three-by-two-foot sheets of paper from an easel pad and stuck them to the courtroom wall. He went through every one of her previous statements, recording each on the paper using different colored markers: green for those she agreed with, red for those she denied ever saying, and purple for those which she could not remember. The coding system resulted in a tricolor mural of inconsistencies. Pina-Ruiz was combative over these discrepancies: "That's what I said last year; this is what I am saying this year."

Silverman spent hours addressing the tape-recorded conversation with Carolyn Cherry. Pina-Ruiz said she had been confused in the last trial over what she might have said to Cherry, because she thought Silverman was referring to someone else. "I can say this being very positive—I didn't tell her or anyone else I didn't see the shooting."

Silverman challenged Pina-Ruiz over her positioning of Penn and Jacobs outside the driver's door of Riggs's vehicle and her ability to see the shootings. He took the clear-plastic overlays upon which she had marked the location with stick figures on three separate occasions during trial one and laid them over each other, revealing how her positioning of Penn had migrated over the course of her testimony. Silverman's parking garage demonstration had been a dramatic moment in trial one, but this time it was the prosecution who requested the proceedings be moved outside the courthouse for a reenactment.

AT 10:30 A.M. on the morning of March 30, 1987, the twelve jurors and four alternates boarded two San Diego County Sheriff's vans and headed east on the 94 freeway. When they arrived at their destination twenty minutes later, the prosecution and defense teams, defendant,

witness, judge, three armed marshals, and court personnel were waiting for them on the driveway at 6564 Brooklyn Avenue. On the gravel-
covered driveway was Tom Riggs's patrol unit 785 parked in the same
place it had been on the evening of March 31, 1985.

Once all the jurors had stepped into the bright sunlight, Lester led
them on a forty-five minute tour of the crime scene, as they scribbled in
their notebooks and checked out various vantage points. The attorneys
followed along silently while neighborhood residents watched from a
respectful distance. Sarah Pina-Ruiz remained with investigator Guy
Johnson and SDPD criminalist David Parker, who had drawn up the
crime scene diagram used by investigators.

When the jurors returned to the area of Riggs's vehicle, Pina-Ruiz
was seated in the same police car she had been in two years earlier.
Mike Carpenter lay on his back in the dirt beside the vehicle with Guy
Johnson atop him in the role of Jacobs. Parker, as Tom Riggs, stood beside Carpenter's head. Pina-Ruiz lifted herself up on the center console,
looked out the window, and instructed their movement. When she was
done, Carpenter was almost perfectly parallel to the vehicle, his head
up the driveway. The jurors took turns viewing from the passenger seat.

The moment they were done, Jim Gripp and Milt Silverman took
out a measuring tape and their own maps and diagrams of the scene and
began marking off points in the dirt. When they were done, they took
up positions perpendicular to the vehicle, as reported by most of the
eyewitnesses. Gripp lay on his back, with Milt Silverman in his green
mechanic's overalls straddling him and Parker standing as Riggs. The
jurors took their turns in the passenger seat once more.

By noon, the group was back in their vans headed westbound toward the superior courthouse. On Brooklyn Avenue, residents were left
staring at the image of San Diego Police patrol unit 785, a haunting reminder of when their neighborhood suddenly erupted in violence.

36

ON THE MORNING OF MARCH 31, 1987, MIKE CARPENTER called to the stand Patrol Officer Richard Lundy, who along with his partner, Officer Sylvester Wade, were the first personnel to stand guard over Sagon Penn after his surrender. With Penn handcuffed to a chair in the commander's office, Lundy testified he had set a cassette tape recorder on the table at 6:59 p.m. and let it run while his prisoner went on an unbroken monologue about the incident that occurred just forty-five minutes earlier.

In the courtroom, Mike Carpenter placed "people's exhibit ninety-two" into a cassette machine wired to a pair of speakers and pressed play. After unsuccessfully fighting so hard to get the recordings of Penn's statements entered into the first trial, Silverman was shocked when Carpenter unexpectedly made the major strategy change to play the tapes in trial two. Exactly two years to the day he initially made the statement while handcuffed to a chair in police headquarters, the voice of Sagon Penn was heard by a jury for the first time.

Lundy: "Testing, one, two, three . . . March 31, 18:59 hours, interview with Sagon Ames—"

Penn: "Aahmes."

Lundy: "Sagon Aahmes Penn."

Penn: "Um, a confrontation occurred in Encanto and Sagon was stopped by a police car," he began, speaking in the third person. "He got out and he asked the officer what was going on because he hadn't been speeding; he had just pulled up into a, uh, a driveway to drop some neighbors off at their house. And the police, they got out of the car and came up to me and . . . he said something about, 'So what's going on, Blood?' or 'What's happening, Blood?' or something like that." He switched to the first person. "And I said, I don't know nothing about that kind of stuff. And then he just looked at me like, 'You ain't stupid, you know what that is.' And he said, 'You claim?' and I said, 'I claim? If I claim anything, I claim myself.'"

On the "Lundy tape," as it became called, Penn spoke rapidly and without pause, often stammering and repeating words, his mind racing as he tried to explain his actions. After the twenty-five-minute tape was played, Detective Alfonso Salvatierra took the stand, and Carpenter played a much longer recording made while Salvatierra and Detective Robert Lopez sat with Penn in their office in the street-gangs unit while waiting for the Homicide detectives to arrive.

The "Salvatierra tape" began with a long, disjointed monologue on the subjects of numerology, photosynthesis, acting classes, Buddhism, world peace, boxing, high school teachers, and Penn's pending application with the San Diego Police Department. Thirty minutes into the tape, Penn paused for a few seconds before launching into a full statement. "The incident that occurred today was very unique and very unusual and I never ran into an incident like that with a policeman ever in my whole life," he said. "Never. It was like, I didn't break no laws or nothing, you know?" The two recorded statements were consistent in their details and contained no contradictions. Between them, they provided the jury with almost two hours of Sagon Penn's version of events, what was going through his mind, and why he did what he did.

"I said, 'Wow, you makin' a mistake. I'm not even like that,'" Penn said about Jacobs's accusation he was a gang member. "For some reason, he didn't want to hear that. I guess he was just in a bad mood . . . And then after that, he said, 'Okay, just hand over your license.' In my wallet all I had was the license and a picture, right? So I hand it over to him. He said, 'I don't want your wallet.' I said, 'That's my driver's license. Everything is on the front.' He said, 'I don't want to go through your wallet.' I said, 'That's okay, it's all right,' because I want to be, you know, be fully cooperative [and] I'm not trying to hide anything from him.

"And then he started talking all mean to me and stuff," Penn continued. "And then I said, oh man, I can't deal with this, and I just started walking away. And then when I was walking away, he acted like I did something wrong or something, and he just, 'Foom!' grabbed me real hard, and I just got scared. I said, 'Please, don't do that. Don't grab me. What did I do?' And then he just started saying, 'Just turn around, just turn around.' I said, 'Turn around for what?'

"The other one [Riggs] started coming over just telling me to shut up. I couldn't understand, why's he telling me to shut up, I wasn't even doing nothing? Next thing you know, they started grabbing on me and stuff. And then he [Jacobs] just said, 'Boom! Boom!' He punched me. I couldn't believe it. He just hit me in my face. And then the other one with the black hair, he reached down into his holster and he pulled out the billy club. And I said, 'Wow, I can't believe this.' He started coming at me and I said, 'Please, please, don't. Why are you guys doing this? I didn't do nothin.' He swung at me. My hands didn't come up fast enough. It could have hit me in the head, so I moved my body up, and it hit my back. I said, man, he's trying to kill me.

"I couldn't believe all their negativity, their evilness, and [they] just kept coming at me. And it wasn't no use, I couldn't stop it, you know. Seemed like they was trying to kill me, but they wanted me to feel a lot of pain first, or something. And the blond-haired [Jacobs], he was already into some type of higher consciousness where he was just going at me. He was throwing his billy club at me full blast and then I just kept blocking it. I just started backing up real fast. I said, 'Please don't do it . . . We can talk, whatever you wanna do.' And he just kept coming. Then I just hit him, just to try to slow him down."

Penn described striking back at Riggs and Jacobs several other times to keep them away from him. "It was actually making me do something I really didn't want to do, so I just started fighting back." And then, "They just both rushed me at the same time. I made both of them repel. I just backed both of them off . . . I just kept trying to talk to him while he was doing all this. And the next thing you know, I just had to start inflicting pain back on them, 'cause I couldn't get through to them. I couldn't even communicate with them." When Jacobs came at him with the baton, he said, "I just started kicking him and moving him back. They both got in rhythm. Their timing was just right, and they just thrashed me."

Penn said when Jacobs charged him without a baton and grabbed him, he was relieved. "When he grabbed me, I didn't try to do nothing. The reason why I didn't try to resist was because he wasn't doing nothing to hurt me. But the other things that they was throwing at me was trying to hurt me," he said of the baton strikes. "Then he just started trying to swing me around. And all of a sudden, he threw me to the ground. I just relaxed and then I said, 'What's the matter?' And then he just said, 'Boom! Boom!' He hit me. I said, 'Wow, why did you just hit me like that for?'

"And then he [Jacobs] was just hollering at me and then he said, 'Turn around, turn around.' And then he's holding me down. You see a line right here on my neck somewhere?" he asked Salvatierra. "Well, that's where he was grabbing me real hard, and he was, like, choking me. And then, all these people, they're looking, and then they're telling the cop, 'Why don't you leave him alone?' 'cause they knew I wasn't doing nothing . . . I was just getting tortured and tortured," he said.

As he continued to call out "Stop" and "What's the matter?" Jacobs told him to shut up and "just busted me in the face a couple of times. It tripped me out, and I said, 'Don't do that.' And then I was just holding his hands." He said Riggs knocked one of this hands away with a kick. "I had my hand on the ground, and he just started stomping on my hand. I said, 'Wow, you don't have to do that. Why are you doing that?'" He said Riggs pinned his hand to the ground with his boot. "And he just looked at me real mean. And then he pulled out his club and he was looking at me like, *goodbye.* [He] was ready to hit me with his billy club, so I snatched my hand from under his shoe, and I blocked the billy club, and I just grabbed the gun real quick, and I said, 'Hold it, don't, please, please.'"

Penn said he "kept giving warnings and warnings," but Jacobs seemed to ignore them. "'You see I got this gun in my hand. It's loaded, isn't it?' He acted like I didn't even have no gun on him. It was like he didn't even care or something, you know?" Penn said it was when he saw Riggs was "ready to start again" that he pulled back the hammer on the gun. "I told him out loud, 'It's cocked, it's cocked. Please, don't do nothing. Don't hurt me. Just leave me alone and I'll give you back this gun and everything, and you can go ahead and see my ID like you was gonna do and, you know, go ahead and check on me.'"

But no matter how much Sagon Penn might have wanted to turn back the clock, it was too late. "Then he kicked me. The one that was standing up. He kicked me in my arm where I had the gun on him [Jacobs]. That gun, it went off when he kicked my arm. That's when the whole incident just got worse. I said, 'Man, now it's gonna seem like . . .'" His voice trailed off. "He wouldn't have never even got shot if he wouldn't have kicked me in my arm like that.

"I was just scared to death," he went on. "Then I was just firing the gun because he [Riggs] was gonna get ready to shoot me. I was scared he was gonna kill me. I don't know what was going to happen right here, you know, just trying to protect my life.

"And then, the one in the car," he said, referring to Sarah Pina-Ruiz, "he or she was gonna kill me. I couldn't see in that good because the light was flashing on the window. And I thought, you know, it seemed like something might have been pointed at me. And the next thing you know, the gun's empty.

"I got the gun off the other police holster and got into the car. I left in the car because the natural reaction of the law [when] something like that happens, just straight kill me and stuff because they don't know what's going on . . . I just drove off, and I was real scared. I drove the car to my grandfather's house and told him what happened. I said, 'Daddy, I'm gonna have to turn myself in.' And then he drove me, you know, down here." He looked at the two detectives. "And that's, you know, that's what happened."

THE FOLLOWING DAY, Carpenter called to the stand Detective Larry Lindstrom for the purposes of introducing into evidence the third recording: Penn's statement made to the Homicide Team IV detectives responsible for the investigation. From the moment Lindstrom read Penn his Miranda rights at 11:42 p.m., five and a half hours after the altercation in Encanto, it was obvious to him and his Team IV partner Detective Gary Murphy they were dealing with an extremely naive young man.

"You said anything you say can and will be used against you?" Penn asked about his Miranda rights. "When you tell the truth, then they can't really use that against you. I can't see how they can use it against you unless they twist it around, which is going to be impossible."

"As long as you tell the truth," Lindstrom assured him.

Penn thought about it. "I mean, they say like *against you*, right? That might mean if you tell a lie then, huh? That's what they [are] talking about, like if you tell a lie?"

"If somebody, say, in the district attorney's office or a court of law ask us, 'Well, did you ask Sagon this question, what answer did he give you?' we can tell them," Lindstrom explained.

Penn did not appear any closer to understanding the issue or his right to an attorney when he enthusiastically waived his Miranda rights. "I'm willing to talk to both of you," he said. "I'm willing to tell you guys everything that happened."

Lindstrom led the questioning. "Well, what happened this evening?"

"This is the first time that anything like this has ever happened with a police officer. I couldn't believe it," Penn began. When he talked about striking the officers to keep them back, Murphy tried to pin him down.

"He kept throwing punches at me, and junk, and then I just block and then I tagged him a couple of times to try to slow him down."

"What do you mean by 'tagged him'?"

"Like, you know, trying to keep him off me, because I really didn't want to hurt them."

"You keep saying 'tag'; what do you mean by that word?"

"Like a tag, like this," Penn demonstrated, thrusting a hand forward. "That's a tag. Like it ain't full force."

"You hit him with your fist? Is that what you mean by 'tag'?"

"I was, like, defending myself," Penn said, growing frustrated.

Penn added several important details he had not mentioned in the previous statements. When describing the scene with Jacobs on the ground, he quoted Jacobs as saying, "You think you're bad, huh? You think you're bad, huh?" As he had with Salvatierra, he said he warned Jacobs he had the gun in his hand, and only pulled the hammer back when they kept beating anyhow. At the same time Riggs was striking the final baton blow, "somebody was saying, 'They're gonna kill you. They're gonna kill you,'" he said, echoing the words that several eyewitnesses would later attribute to Carlton Smith.

He held up his hand to show Lindstrom and Murphy how he was holding the gun before Riggs kicked him. "I had my finger up here because I didn't really want to hurt nobody. Way up here away from the trigger."

"Did he know you had the gun?" Lindstrom asked.

"Yeah, he knew I had it. I told him. I said, 'I got your gun.' And this one right here [Jacobs], he hit me in my face, and this one [Riggs] kicked my arm . . . When he kicked my arm, the sound went off—the blast."

"How many times did you shoot the officer that was on your chest?" Lindstrom asked.

"See . . ." Penn paused, seeming to understand the subtle inference of guilt if he were to answer the question as asked. "I couldn't say that I did [shoot Jacobs] because this guy right here kicked my arm. And the gun went off, that's all I could say." He said he shot Riggs because "he was reaching for his gun."

He was more detailed in his description of shooting at Sarah Pina-Ruiz through the side window. "I looked and the sun was shining on the window; it was like a reflection. I was real scared, you know. I saw something moving, something black in there. I said, somebody's there grabbing a gun [and] trying to kill me . . . and then I just—'Toom! Toom!'" he said, simulating the noise of two gunshots. "And then it was empty."

"How did you know it was empty?" Lindstrom asked.

"Because I was still pulling the trigger."

Penn explained that he retrieved Riggs's gun because he thought he might still be alive. "I pulled his gun out of his holster 'cause I didn't want him to look at me and shoot me and kill me." It was also the first time Penn acknowledged running over Jacobs with the patrol car. "I was real scared and I just wanted to hurry up and get out of there 'cause I just knew I was going to get killed. And I just drove right over—" Penn halted.

"Drove right over what?" Lindstrom prompted him.

"The one that was on top of me beating—" Penn paused again, seemingly overwhelmed at the thought of it. "Right over him," he said. "I wanted to, like, move [him] real quick, but then I heard these other sirens and stuff coming already and I said, 'Man, by the time I move him over then I'm just going to get killed.'"

When Penn was done explaining the incident, Detective Murphy took over and painstakingly walked Sagon through the details once again. When Murphy asked how Riggs fell over the retaining wall, Penn hesitated. "Oh, man," he said. "See, I don't like doing it like this."

Penn began challenging the way Murphy was phrasing his questions more aggressively than Lindstrom.

"Was the fight going on up here?" Murphy asked, referring to a diagram.

"It was not a fight," Penn corrected. "I was just getting beat right there on the ground."

Murphy ignored the correction and asked, "So the fight actually started up here? The physical fight?"

"Where they was just throwing billy clubs and fists and stuff?" Penn responded, refusing to accept Murphy's characterization of the altercation as a "fight."

"And you shot which officer first?" Murphy asked.

Again, Penn avoided responding to a question phrased in the form of a confession. "The one standing right there kicked my arm," Penn corrected. "The blast went off."

"Okay," Murphy said dismissively. "Which one did you shoot first?"

"The *blast went off* on the one that was on top of me when the one kicked me."

"Okay, so you got the cap on him first?"

"Don't put nothing like that," Penn said.

"Well, you say blast, I say shot. We're going to have to agree on what it is."

"I'm just agreeing on what I just said, that's all," Penn countered, backing Murphy off.

"Right after the blast went off, what did you see him do?" Murphy asked about Riggs's reaction to the first shot.

"I just saw him—" Penn demonstrated with a reaching motion toward an imaginary holster on his hip.

"Did he have a gun in his hand?"

"His hand was on it," Penn said.

Midway through Murphy's questioning about the shooting of Sarah Pina-Ruiz, the cassette tape came to the end and shut off. No one noticed to flip it over, so whatever was said beyond that point was not recorded, transcribed, or ever heard by a jury.

Throughout the three recordings, Penn was preoccupied with the shooting victims, whose condition was unknown to him. He often paused to chant his Buddhist mantra "nam myoho renge kyo." "I have the power to help them and make them better just from chanting," he explained. "My life force chanting to their life force, and it's going to make things better for them. I want them to live, and I want them to really recover, because it means a lot to me. People, and human beings, and life is very important to me. I want them to be alive, no matter what."

37

MIKE CARPENTER HAD ALSO RECONSIDERED HIS STRAT-
egy on eyewitnesses. He dropped some of his least productive
and problematic ones and gave up on persuading a jury that Penn
had called out, "You're a witness!" before shooting Sarah Pina-Ruiz.

He eliminated other witnesses who had fared poorly under cross-
examination, notably nurse Elaine Hilliard and Dr. Barbara Groves,
relying solely on photos to show the extent of Penn's injuries. Instead
of spending days and having multiple psychiatric experts arguing the
cause and nature of Jacobs's faulty memory, he simply introduced one
opinion that it was far more likely due to physical and emotional trauma.

He cut back on the use of expert witnesses. One notable addition
was Special Agent Bruce Koenig, who traveled from FBI headquarters
in Virginia to testify as an expert in magnetic tape analysis. Koenig
came with impressive credentials and was the prosecution's response to
acoustic expert Fausto Poza and his analysis of the gunshot "impulses"
on the Angela McKibben 911 tape. According to Koenig's analysis, Penn
had an additional one full second to decide whether to shoot Riggs a
third and fatal time after already shooting him twice. The additional
time could indicate intent and premeditation and the difference between
self-defense and manslaughter. After five hours of highly technical testimony and excruciatingly detailed cross-examination by Silverman,
both sides asserted their expert was correct.

Trained in evidence collection, Officer Patrick "Gil" Padillo was
assigned to Homicide Team IV to identify, collect, and index crime

scene evidence the night of March 31, 1985. Although it was not standard practice, the young officer decided a crime scene video would be of help to investigators. On April 9, Padillo took the stand for the prosecution to introduce the tape. But first, he needed to explain how his seventeen-minute crime scene video had been misplaced for eighteen months—preventing its inclusion in trial one—before being discovered during an office move. He never personally had the tape, he said. "It was in the possession of the cameraman."

Mike Carpenter planned to play the video for the purposes of identifying the location of evidence at the scene. Silverman had no objection. Carpenter asked him if he wanted the tape stopped at any point. "No, let's go ahead and play it all the way through," Silverman said.

"This is going to be a video tape of the death of Officer Tommy Riggs at 6552 Brooklyn Avenue in the city of San Diego." Padillo's narration on the video was halting and precise, as though he was nervous about getting everything right. Recorded on a consumer-grade VHS camera, it was a slow crawl through a grim tableau of medical waste, bloody clothing, and scattered police equipment. "Officer Riggs was found lying on the east side of a black Chevelle," Padillo announced as the camera settled on the uncovered body of Tom Riggs lying sprawled in the dirt face up between the retaining wall and the black Chevelle, exactly where emergency responders left him. Padillo fell silent as the camera lingered for a very long time on the dead body of Riggs. Like everything else on the video, Thomas Riggs had become just another piece of crime scene evidence.

Milt Silverman was stunned when the image appeared on the monitor. He glanced over at his client, who remained expressionless as he stared at the screen, but something in Penn had changed. By the time the lights were turned back on, Silverman knew he had made a terrible mistake.

"I'm going to make a motion in open court today for mistrial based on my own incompetence in representing Mr. Penn," Silverman told Judge Lester when the attorneys met in chambers. "I did not remember that Agent Riggs was on that tape. I don't blame Mr. Carpenter for that, I blame me. I let the tape play through to its conclusion. That was a very serious mistake on my part. The prejudice that I see is very profound to Mr. Penn in that the camera lingered, it seemed forever, on Agent Riggs.

I should have asked the Court for a ruling on this tape, and I didn't, and the jury has seen it, and I think Mr. Penn has been substantially prejudiced by it."

Lester was not about to let Silverman off the case despite the self-flogging. "It's true the tape lingered probably a few seconds longer than necessary. I don't view it as anything on the nature of granting a mistrial. I deny the motion, and we should be willing and ready to proceed."

But Silverman was not quite ready. "Your Honor, my client is extremely emotionally distraught at this moment. He's crying and sobbing in grief in the jury room at what he witnessed. I feel that I need an additional several minutes to try to calm him down."

Lester granted the request. Silverman joined his client in an empty jury room. "I made a mistake," Silverman said, telling him he asked to have himself removed from the case. Sagon said he did not want another attorney, that he still had confidence in him. They prayed before entering the courtroom and resuming their positions at the defense table.

On the morning of Thursday, April 23, 1987, the prosecution rested its case in chief. Although Mike Carpenter and Wayne Mayer trimmed the witness list down from eighty in the first trial to forty-eight, their case had taken two weeks longer due to more detailed questioning and lengthy cross-examinations by Silverman. "I was pleased with the way the evidence came in," Carpenter told reporters afterward. "The chronology and the people we involved were effective. Jacobs being first tells the jury what he's doing there to begin with, rather than having them wonder like they did last time." Carpenter was relaxed and upbeat. "I felt really good last time at this stage," he joked. "I feel really good this time. Maybe I'm just a cockeyed optimist."

Milt Silverman felt very differently about Mike Carpenter's case in chief. He interpreted the significant change in approach as an indication that the prosecution did not believe in their case and were simply determined to get Sagon Penn one way or another. He had no intention of changing his defense. "I believed in my case from the start, so why would I change it?"

38

"FORGIVE ME, OFFICER CASTRO. IT STRIKES ME AS QUITE EX-traordinary that your memory is that frail."

On the witness stand, the young woman with sharp facial features and jet-black hair pulled back tightly in a bun looked down. "It is," she said softly.

"How long have you had this kind of memory problem?"

"Long time."

"Has this memory problem ever manifested itself in any of your police work?"

"There could have been instances."

"But you have forgotten them?"

Jenny Castro paused, realizing she was being made fun of again. "Yes," she said sternly.

Milt Silverman smiled. "I should have known."

Officer Jenny Castro entered the courtroom with an air of dread about her as she prepared to defend her baffling story about the discovery and handling of the academy transcript. Although the content of the transcript had been covered word for word during the testimony of Donovan Jacobs, making the jury aware of its suspicious journey was almost as important to Silverman. He found no sport in humiliating Castro, but he was determined to show the jury just how far he felt the cops were willing to go to convict his client.

"To me it doesn't even look like evidence," Castro said in explaining how she could have put the document in her desk drawer and forgotten it for six months. "At one point in time, I thought about throwing it away." She stuck to her story that she never read beyond the second page of the report until Silverman informed her he had the document checked for fingerprints and hers were on every page.

Silverman questioned her decision to take it directly to Chief Kolender herself when she rediscovered it six months later rather than turn it over to a superior up the chain of command. "I figured the less people whose hands it went through, the better," she said. "There have been instances [when] documents have gotten to newspapers. I didn't want that to happen." That was a lot of importance to place on a document she thought so insignificant she considered throwing it away, Silverman pointed out.

Silverman told her that her supervisor at the academy at the time, Sergeant James Duncan, testified he did not believe her story about having found the document, saying he thought she intentionally removed it from Jacobs's academy file. "You didn't just make up a story about finding this document in an unused file cabinet in order to cover up the fact that you had gone into a file and pulled this document out of the file, did you?"

"No, I didn't make up that story," the beleaguered Castro answered. She did not try to disguise her dislike of her former boss. "You didn't trust him to give him this?" Silverman said, holding up a copy of the transcript. "No," she said sharply.

"I FOUND HER to be unreliable and disloyal," Sergeant James Duncan said of Jenny Castro, the woman he had directly supervised for the entire time Castro claimed to have had possession of the transcript. Duncan was short in height with a full head of dark hair, crisply ironed uniform, and an air of authority about him. He made it clear he did not feel Castro was qualified for such a desirable assignment. "The department was eager to push minorities into positions of command and training," he noted.

Silverman was suspicious of Duncan's proximity to the academy-transcript incident. He had not ruled out that someone else removed the transcript from Jacobs's personnel file and intentionally "misplaced"

it in an unused room at the academy long enough for the trial to finish. "Now, you realize that she has testified that she found this academy
transcript in the office that you once occupied?" he asked Duncan.

"Yes," Duncan said.

"And I think you have previously testified that you don't believe
Jenny Castro's story about finding that document?"

"I find it hard to believe that that document was in that office for
any period of time laying in the open area and no one else found it or
saw it but her."

"How many times in your [employee] evaluations of Jenny Castro
have you noted any difficulty that she has had with the truth?"

"I have never [noted] that during any of my evaluations of her."

"Is it something that she just developed, you think, suddenly?"

"I don't know," Duncan said. "Maybe she doesn't remember where
she found the document."

"Of course, if someone else did find it," Silverman asked, "or someone else did know about it, they would be in trouble too, wouldn't they?"
Silverman's insinuation of who that "someone else" might be was clear,
but a sustained objection from Carpenter prevented Duncan from
answering.

Lieutenant Richard Bennett was the senior academy trainer in the
room during the counseling session and the one who warned Jacobs
that his current attitude would "create problems for yourself, for the
public, and for the department." Bennett confirmed he felt the issues for
which Jacobs was counseled to be serious and numerous. "In your experience as a San Diego police officer, had you ever been in a counseling
session where so many issues were addressed in one setting?" Silverman
asked. "I can't remember a session similar to this," Bennett said. "Did
you mean it?" Silverman asked of the stern advice and warning given to
Jacobs at the time. "Of course," the lieutenant answered.

AS THE FIRST three eyewitnesses to testify, Patricia Ann-Lowe Smith,
Demetria Shelby, and Cynthia Clantion were once again Donovan Jacobs's most vehement accusers, alleging he used racial slurs while he
and Riggs inflicted a vicious beating on Sagon Penn. Wayne Mayer was

particularly aggressive in confronting the women with their inconsistencies, improbable details, and doubts about their ability to hear anything said by the officers or Penn considering their locations at the time.

Bryan Ross reported hearing Jacobs say, "I'm going to ask you one more time, boy, to take the license out." Silverman compared it to a statement made by Jacobs during the 1978 academy counseling session in defense of "professional profanity": "I would say something like, 'Listen, God damn it, I'm going to tell you one more time.'"

Carpenter was openly disdainful of Ross's motives. "You just know that the defense is based on dirtying up Officer Jacobs, don't you, so you want to dirty him as much as you can?"

"Why should I have to do that?" Ross said, taken aback.

"To help your best friend, Sagon Penn."

Penn's longtime tae kwon do instructor, Master James Wilson, took the stand in a three-piece suit. Silverman asked him if Penn would have gone on the offensive, would he have been able to overpower two police officers attacking with batons. "It would take [a] mere fraction of seconds to be done," he said. After testifying, Wilson donned his white martial arts uniform and reprised his hallway exhibition of tae kwon do blocking and counterattacks as Silverman struck at him full force with a police baton. After performing his graceful flowing and striking kata movements, he bowed in respect as onlookers once again applauded his efforts.

CAROLYN CHERRY DEFENDED her tape recording of a conversation with Sarah Pina-Ruiz at the Navy housing office shortly after the incident. Wayne Mayer did not hide his utter disbelief of her story, doubted her truthfulness, and expressed disdain for her actions. When "a friend" of Sarah Pina-Ruiz took the stand to substantiate Pina-Ruiz's claim she had confused Cherry with another woman in the housing office, things got strange even by Sagon Penn–trial standards. Patsy Phillips presented a photocopied page from her personal diary to prove she had spoken with Pina-Ruiz about her possible mix-up of the two women. When Silverman pointed out that the date on the document had clearly been altered, Judge Lester ordered Phillips to bring in the original diary the following day. When Phillips did not appear, Lester sent word that she was under contempt unless she returned. When she appeared two days later to claim the diary had been stolen from her car, a miniature gold police badge dangled from a chain around her neck.

MILT SILVERMAN FELT that the San Diego Police Department had been engaging in misconduct since the moment they began collecting evidence at the crime scene and interviewing witnesses the night of the incident, all the way through to perjuring themselves under oath on the stand. He clashed openly in both trials over the issue with detectives, officers, evidence technicians, and even representatives of organizations under contract with them. His message to the jurors was clear: You can't trust these guys. An unexpected phone call to his law offices by a woman during trial two only confirmed his suspicion that the department would stop at nothing to convict his client.

Arguments over the validity of window-glare photographs and the visibility of Sarah Pina-Ruiz inside Tom Riggs's patrol unit had been just as fierce in the second trial as they had been in the first when Mike Carpenter called Milt Silverman's photo "one of the biggest frauds ever perpetrated on a court and jury." The prosecution entered into evidence their own window-glare photo, taken days after they became aware of the defense's "heavens and earth" photo. Theirs also showed a swath of white light obscuring the view through the bottom half of the window, but a woman wearing civilian clothing sitting in the passenger seat was still clearly recognizable.

To discredit the prosecution photo, Milt Silverman called to the stand thirty-one-year-old Sue Marvin, the woman who called the law offices of attorney Milton Silverman several weeks earlier to express her concern.

"Miss Marvin, where do you work?" Silverman asked when the woman took the stand in the final days of witness testimony.

"At Master Photo."

"Have you in the past done work, crime scene photos and the like, for the San Diego Police Department?"

"Yes." She said she remembered processing and enlarging the

prosecution window-glare photograph displayed on an easel in the courtroom, along with smaller prints in which the woman in the car was significantly less visible.

"Now, please tell the jury what the instructions were that you received regarding the development of those photographs," Silverman said.

"They had at least two or three pictures in there that they asked to make darker when we did the enlargements so they could see through the reflection."

Police evidence technician Gary Avery took the stand on the last day of witness testimony to defend the photo that he had taken and was responsible for having developed and enlarged. By then, the prosecution was convinced the defense had in their possession the original envelope given to Marvin by Avery with his instructions written on it. This was due to a ruse Silverman pulled by pretending to read instructions off a multicolored envelope instantly recognizable as the type used by retail photo shops to hold prints. But the envelope was not the original, and there was nothing written on it. There was no indication Avery planned to deny he had given the instructions, but if so inclined, he certainly could not risk it now. "What request did you have made at the time that you had [the] photograph blown up?" Silverman asked.

"I asked that the photographs be printed slightly darker so the person inside the vehicle could be seen," Avery answered. "That's what I wrote on the envelope."

"So, you knew when you went out there that you wanted to get a picture that showed that the sun was not shining on the window?" Silverman asked.

"We were going out there to photograph it at the particular time to show that the sun was not reflecting in the window. That is the only reason I was out there at that time." After two hours of ferocious cross-examination, Avery would still not budge from his position. "I was just doing my job, and doing it accurately."

Mike Carpenter was livid over the photo-darkening issue. "There's no reason for Mr. Silverman to call this lady to testify as to the request of the police department for development of those pictures or blowups," he argued to Lester. If Carpenter did not like getting into the issue of photo tampering, Silverman said, he had no one to blame but himself. "They sought to introduce this into evidence," he said of the darkened photograph. "And, you know, 'He who sows the wind shall reap the whirlwind.'"

SILVERMAN AGAIN CALLED witnesses for the three incidents in which civilians complained about hostile interactions with Donovan Jacobs. Marguarite Fields recounted the rough treatment her son Anthony received while being handcuffed by Jacobs in the arrest made several hours before the Penn incident. Jacobs's partner on the call, Officer Anne-Marie Tyler, remained as remarkably forgetful about the details as she had been in the first trial but insisted it was an uneventful and routine arrest. She was so openly hostile and combative with Silverman this time that Judge Lester later nicknamed her "Miss Charm School." In one exchange, Tyler recalled Anthony's father to be "an average-sized man" in height. "What would average size be to you?" Silverman asked. "Taller than you," the five-foot-ten-inch Tyler responded acerbically.

Motorcyclist Edward Serdi was quirky and sometimes inconsistent in his recollections of being stopped by Jacobs and Officer William Mahue but remained adamant about the bogus reason for the stop and Jacobs's insulting and threatening behavior. When called to the stand after Serdi, Mahue repeated his claim that he pursued and pulled Serdi over simply out of concern for the young man's welfare, rather than the unjustified "attitude stop" it clearly appeared to be. Silverman focused his withering cross-examination not on proving the real reason for the stop but rather his contention that the ridiculous claim by Mahue was just another example of a San Diego Police officer lying under oath. "You didn't turn around because Mr. Serdi yelled at you, did you?" Silverman asked accusingly after cornering Mahue. "I don't know, sir," the officer answered weakly. "I don't either," Silverman shot back in disgust.

When Sergeant James McGinley testified about the investigation he conducted into the Serdi complaint, he appeared ill informed and disinterested in the details of the incident. "What initiated this whole thing?" Silverman asked, referring to the reason for the traffic stop.

"Violation of right of way," McGinley said, reading from the report.

"Who violated whose right of way?"

"Well, I would assume that the motorcycle violated the right of way. All I know is that he got a ticket and was angry about it." Silverman pointed out that according to McGinley's report, Serdi told him it was the officer who obstructed *his* right of way. "That's just his side of the story, that the officer violated his right of way," said McGinley, consistently dismissive of Serdi's claims. "I don't know who violated whose because I wasn't there." Well, Silverman said, Officer Mahue was there, and that's what he said too. McGinley was unmoved by the new information. "You have heard of 'attitude stops'?" Silverman asked.

"I don't know exactly what 'attitude stop' means," McGinley answered, maintaining the reason for the stop was not his concern. Silverman made it clear he thought McGinley had decided not to make the reason for the stop his concern because he knew it was obviously bullshit and would reflect badly on the officers.

McGinley's final report cleared Jacobs of the serious allegations based solely on accepting the word of the officers over that of Serdi. Silverman read a line directly from McGinley's report: "Officer Jacobs was advised that it was necessary for him to tell the truth so a complete investigation could be conducted." He lowered the report. "Do you feel that it is necessary to tell officers of the San Diego Police Department that it is necessary to tell the truth?"

"Yes, or I wouldn't do it," McGinley replied.

Silverman had another witness he wanted to ask about the Serdi incident. "Sergeant Duncan, did you ever hear of any complaint about some little fella, five feet tall, that Officer Jacobs stopped for a traffic citation?" Again, James Duncan was somehow connected to a complaint about Donovan Jacobs, this time in his capacity as Jacobs's supervisor at the time of McGinley's investigation. "[He] allegedly took this five-foot fella and stood over him and glowered at him and said, 'You know, I ought to beat the shit out of you and break your arms.' Did you ever hear anything about anything like that?"

"No, I didn't," Duncan said.

"If some citizen had complained that Officer Jacobs had said that to him, that's something you would have heard about, isn't it?"

"I would think so."

"But you never heard of it?"

"I didn't, no."

Silverman held up a copy of the Serdi complaint. "Well, I got a 'Complaint Control Form' here that has you down there as the 'Investigating Supervisor.' Can you explain that for me?"

"I cannot explain that to you."

"Why does it have your name, Sergeant Duncan, where it says, 'Investigating Supervisor'?"

"Mr. Silverman," Duncan interrupted. "I have never seen this report. I have never read this report. I just don't know anything about this report."

For Silverman, the Edward Serdi incident illuminated abuses of power and misconduct at every stage, from the unjustified stop, physically threating a civilian, retaliating with a citation, an investigation intended only to clear the officers, and everyone involved willing to lie on the stand to cover up the misconduct of a fellow officer. "Have you heard of the code of silence?" Silverman abruptly asked Duncan.

"Yes, I have heard of the code of silence," Duncan replied.

"Have you heard of the code of silence in connection with San Diego Police officers, or officers in general?"

Duncan studied Silverman warily. "I have heard something similar to that, yes."

39

FTER TWENTY YEARS ON THE SAN DIEGO POLICE FORCE, Bob McDaniel knew the code of silence was going to be a big problem in investigating Donovan Jacobs's reputation inside the department. The code was the unspoken loyalty oath among cops that demands one never turn in or turn against a fellow officer, especially to outsiders, which McDaniel most certainly was now.

By doggedly running down any lead, McDaniel discovered a number of officers felt Donovan Jacobs was an overly aggressive cop who had issues with minorities and believed he had contributed to escalating the Penn incident into a physical confrontation. But the only ones willing to speak with McDaniel, it seemed, were no longer on the force or on their way out. "I was not surprised when I learned that Jacobs was one of the officers involved in this incident," Jesse Navarro, a cop with nine years on the force, told McDaniel. "I have seen him on the street and would judge him to be what I would call 'overly aggressive.' As soon as I heard this incident went down, I thought, how unfortunate, but I bet Jacobs started it. He had a shitty attitude toward everyone, but especially toward minorities." McDaniel's notes indicated Navarro apparently did not realize he had been speaking with a defense investigator and that he immediately notified the DA's office that he had inadvertently passed along the information about Jacobs to the wrong side.

According to McDaniel's interview notes, San Diego Police sergeant Connie Zimmerman "expressed her personal belief that Jacobs probably just let things get out of hand after stopping Penn for no good reason, overreacted when Penn turned around, and was primarily responsible for Riggs's death." Zimmerman was near retirement, embroiled in an unrelated dispute with the department, and did not want to get involved with "the Penn thing." Former officer Sheila Brandon said she "had heard from sources that the general feeling around the police department was that the wrong officer died." None of the three qualified as viable witnesses.

McDaniel continued chipping away, but heading into the last two weeks of their case in chief, the defense still had only one witness with any association with the San Diego Police Department willing to testify about Donovan Jacobs.

WHEN DOYLE WHEELER took the witness stand on May 8, 1987, he appeared stronger and healthier than the year before but no less wary. Under questioning by Silverman, he repeated his allegations that Donovan Jacobs was a "hothead and had a chip on his shoulder." He said, "When his authority was challenged, he became aggressive," and he "had a problem dealing with minorities." He again accused Jacobs of slamming a Black prisoner's head against a wall and writing cookbook arrest reports with false information, and he said that most of his PCP arrests tested negative for drugs. Wheeler said he reported all of this to Jacobs's superiors, including Sergeant James Duncan, and warned others in the department about Jacobs's misconduct.

This time on cross, Mike Carpenter displayed no sympathy for Wheeler's traumatic past. He highlighted Wheeler's mental collapse from post-traumatic stress and his suicide attempt while serving a five-day suspension for sexual harassment. He questioned the validity of Wheeler's claims to have saved lives while off duty and accused Wheeler of being the one who slammed a prisoner's head against the wall, not Jacobs. "Absolutely not," replied Wheeler. Wheeler denied using the Penn trial as a soapbox to air his grievances over the McDonald's massacre.

In response, Wheeler made a flurry of new allegations against the San Diego Police Department for misconduct and coverups, including unnecessary deaths at the McDonald's massacre, destroying unseemly video tapes found at the home of a murdered officer, and failing to report a SWAT sniper who sighted his scope on Vice President George H. W. Bush during a security detail.

When Carpenter pointed out that he was the lone police officer in the trial making accusations about Jacobs, Wheeler cited the code of silence and described incidents of retaliation against those who violated it. To testify against a cop was to risk one's life, he said, alleging that a dead rat was left on the hood of his own car for testifying in the first Penn trial. He had already moved his family out of state for fear of reprisal.

If Jacobs was such a violent and racist cop, why weren't there more citizen or officer complaints in his file? Carpenter asked. Wheeler described "Maytag artists" who cleanse an officer's file of all incriminating documentation during investigations. Carpenter said he would be producing a dozen or more members of the SDPD who will testify to Jacobs's unblemished conduct. "I don't care what your witnesses come up here and testify to," Wheeler replied. "I'll let the jury decide who is telling the truth in this case."

In a hearing outside the presence of the jury, Carpenter asked Wheeler to allow the prosecution access to his police employment files. "His [Wheeler's] character is not a relevant issue in this case," Lester reacted sharply. "He is not on trial. I am not going to permit this to be dragged on ad nauseam."

ON TUESDAY, MAY 19, 1987, Milt Silverman called what was expected to be his last witnesses in his case in chief. Billy Anderson was Black, in his fifties, with slightly graying hair and a pencil mustache.

"Mr. Anderson, where do you work?" Silverman asked.

"I work for San Diego Community College," Anderson said in a deep and confident voice. "I'm an officer there."

"What kind of officer?"

"Peace officer."

"About three weeks before March 31, 1985, were you in the area of Southeast San Diego in the area of the Greene Cat Liquor store?"

"Yes I was."

Silverman held up a photograph of Donovan Jacobs. "Did you see that human being around the Greene Cat Liquor store?"

"Yes," Anderson said. "He was in a police uniform commonly worn by the San Diego Police officers."

"Would you tell the jury what you saw?"

"I was parked in the Greene Cat Liquor store parking lot" while his wife was inside buying a couple of sodas, he said. "I saw a police vehicle made a U-turn and parked approximately five to six feet from me. I saw the officer get out of the car, he took his microphone and hung it out of the window. He leaned with his right arm propped on the door itself." Anderson demonstrated how Jacobs was standing in the open V of his door, with one foot on the ground and the other on the threshold of the door. "At this time there was a young Black male walking on the same side we were parked on. As the young male reached the rear of my car, the officer turned his hand up with his finger. He said, 'Come here, boy.'"

"Is there any doubt in your mind that the words that left the officer's lips were 'Come here, boy'?" Silverman asked.

"There is no doubt in my mind, no."

"Did the young man say anything?"

"He said, 'I ain't your fucking boy.'"

"In response to the statement, did Officer Jacobs do anything?"

"He left his police car, walked over, grabbed the youth, and pulled him roughly over to where his car was, where he slammed him over the hood."

Anderson said the young man was probably fourteen or fifteen years old and had been eating some tacos. When Jacobs grabbed him, his tacos spilled over the ground. Jacobs said something Anderson could not hear, and the young man responded, "You ain't gonna do shit to me."

"After the officer slammed the kid's head down," Anderson continued, "I spoke up and said something to the officer. I told him there was no need to slam that kid around like that. He hadn't done anything." Silverman asked what Jacobs's response was. "He told me, quote, 'Get your Black ass out of here or you'll find yourself over this car.'"

"What did you say to him?"

"I told him he was a liar; he wasn't man enough to put me over the hood of that car."

"What happened next?" Silverman asked as the jurors sat riveted.

"I told him that as long as I had been an officer, I had never seen people treated like that. And he responded, 'Are you a cop?' I told him, 'I'm not with San Diego anymore, but I'm still in the field.' And with this, his whole demeanor changed. He seemed like he wanted to be friendly."

"Did you mention this thing about being a San Diego Police officer because you had been a San Diego Police officer?"

"About eight years," Anderson said.

"What about the young man, did he arrest him and put him in the patrol car?"

"Let him go on his way. He [the young man] started walking half-way across the street. He told him he was going to sue his ass, and somebody was going to pay for his tacos that he threw all over the street, and he started running."

Anderson acknowledged he did not testify in the first trial and had not contacted the defense. He said Bob McDaniel had been his sergeant for a few years but was not sure how the investigator learned of the matter.

Carpenter's most effective rebuttal against Anderson was Cheryl McKinnie, a supervisor in the SDPD payroll department. Anderson was adamant that he witnessed the incident at Greene Cat Liquors on a Saturday within three weeks prior to the Penn incident. McKinnie was asked what Donovan Jacobs's work status was on the three Saturdays in March 1985 leading up to the weekend of the incident. "Twenty-third, vacation. Sixteenth, vacation. And ninth, vacation," she said, reading from a printout. Carpenter said Anderson must have his cops or his story mixed up. Silverman dismissed the conflict in schedule, saying that Anderson probably just had the date or the day of the week wrong, but he certainly did not have the wrong cop.

AFTER AN HOUR of cross-examination of Billy Anderson by Wayne Mayer, Judge Lester recessed the court for the day, guaranteeing there would be at least one more day of the defense surrebuttal. At 4:00 a.m. the following morning, Milt Silverman pulled his Toyota Supra into the parking lot of Greene Cat Liquors at the intersection of Imperial and Euclid in the heart of the Southeast. The Green Cat was the location of Billy Anderson's alleged confrontation with Donovan Jacobs, but that was not why the defense attorney was there. Several minutes later, Bob McDaniel pulled up, locked his car, and got into the passenger seat of the Supra. McDaniel was armed. They were, after all, at the intersection gang members called "the four corners of death."

Silverman pulled out of the lot and into the residential side streets of the Southeast. He had received a tip that the man eluding them for weeks would be getting off his graveyard shift somewhere around 5:00 a.m. He pulled the Supra to the curb among a row of parked cars on the side street where they believed the man lived. Experienced in stakeouts, McDaniel was calm. Silverman was fidgety. With one day remaining, he was out of witnesses, so this was his last chance to find this guy.

In the predawn dark, a car turned onto the street and cruised along slowly, looking for a parking space. When it drew parallel to the Supra, the man behind the wheel made eye contact with Silverman and took off. "Go!" McDaniel said. Silverman raced down the street as the tail-lights of their target disappeared down another side street. When they turned onto the street, the car had disappeared. Silverman stomped on the accelerator, and the Supra shot forward. As they passed a side street, McDaniel suddenly yelled, "Stop!"

Silverman slammed on the brakes. "Go back," McDaniel said. Silverman reversed the Supra. "Down there," McDaniel instructed, pointing to what appeared to be an empty side street. As Silverman moved slowly down the street, they spotted the vehicle nestled among others parked against the curb with its engine and lights off, and the man they had been looking for sitting behind the wheel. With the Supra blocking any escape, Silverman grabbed the folded document off the dashboard, threw open the door, and approached the open driver's side window. "Nathanial Jordan," he said, breathing heavily from the excitement of the pursuit.

"Yeah?" the man said in resignation.

Silverman handed him the documents. "Consider yourself served to appear in the trial of Sagon Penn."

Jordan looked at the subpoena without any sign of surprise. "When?"

Silverman looked at his watch as the first sliver of sunlight appeared over the Southeast. "Four hours from now. Will you be there?"

"If I'm subpoenaed," the ex-cop said, "I'll be there."

————

THIRTY-FIVE-YEAR-OLD NATHANIAL JORDAN cut an imposing figure. He was powerfully built at five foot ten inches tall and 250 pounds,
with close-cropped hair and a mustache. He had played on the SDPD
football team and was medically retired from the department in 1986
after being struck by a drunk driver. He worked as a security guard at
Rohr Industries aerospace company in Chula Vista, was a lay minister at
Mount Zion Missionary Baptist Church, and had a third job counseling
young people about drug and alcohol abuse.

Silverman opened by asking him if he wanted to testify in this trial.
"No, I don't," Jordan declared. "I haven't been a snitch in the past. I don't
wish to be that today."

Did he fear reprisals from San Diego Police officers for testifying? Silverman asked. "Absolutely. I know how police officers feel about snitches,"
he said.

Did he fear for his life as a result? "Absolutely," Jordan answered
without hesitation.

Silverman asked Jordan to describe an incident in 1983 during
the time he and Jacobs were part of the special Narcotics enforcement
team focusing mostly on PCP. He said they were in the shift briefing, or
"lineup" room, reviewing a team operation conducted the day before
and he said something critical about Jacobs.

"What happened then?" Silverman asked.

"I guess he made a mistake," Jordan said. "He called me a nigger."
Jordan, who outweighed Jacobs by almost seventy-five pounds, went after him. "I turned the lineup table over."

"Did you come to blows with him?" he was asked.

"I wanted to."

"Were you restrained by other people?"

"My sergeant."

"Duncan?"

"Yes."

Jordan was questioned about his opinion of Jacobs. "I had a lot of
qualms about his police techniques," he said. He felt Jacobs was "very aggressive and overzealous," particularly with young Black men. "He was
very angry. It seemed it was a problem to arrest those people. It was 'boy'

this, 'nigger' that." He said it was common for Jacobs to draw fellow cops into dangerous situations: "Just about everybody on the team was involved in some confrontation Jacobs started." He noted instances when Jacobs undermined or ruined carefully planned enforcement-team operations. "Jacobs would go out on his own and do what he wanted to do."

In one instance, Jordan said, Jacobs blew the cover of an informant who was about to identify a murder suspect. The suspect was not apprehended. Another time, members of the team were preparing to raid a house they believed contained a PCP lab when Jacobs spotted two known PCP users unrelated to the operation. "He chased these other two guys into a house we were not interested in," Jordan said. "It was a dangerous situation." With the operation blown, other members of the unit followed to back up Jacobs. Inside, they found that Jacobs had forced an eighty-five-year-old disabled woman out of her wheelchair to search the built-in commode for hidden drugs. There were none. "That's what I went to the sergeant about," he explained. He said he told Duncan, "We didn't need those kind of flare-ups. We've got enough stuff dealing with someone on PCP." It was not the first time he and others on the team had gone to Duncan about issues with Jacobs, Jordan claimed.

Jordan said he met with Duncan immediately after the incident with Jacobs at the briefing. The result, Jordan said, was "I was transferred, he [Jacobs] remained in Southeast San Diego." He claimed Duncan ordered the transfer to what he considered a backwater assignment. "He knew all about Jacobs," Jordan later said. "But I guess when it came down to it, he chose him over me anyhow."

DUNCAN TESTIFIED HE had not observed nor was aware of any incidents of aggression, racism, or misconduct on the part of Donovan Jacobs, and no one, including Doyle Wheeler and Nathanial Jordan, had ever brought any such incidents to his attention.

Of Nathanial Jordan, he said, "I thought he was a very honest, straightforward-type person . . . a highly satisfactory police officer." However, Duncan did not agree with any of Jordan's allegations, and said he had no idea what would have caused him to make them. "Can you state, under oath, categorically that that did not happen?" Carpenter asked about the alleged altercation between Jordan and Jacobs.

"It did not happen."

"There is testimony to the effect that you had to separate these individuals."

"That is baloney."

"Would you have any motive to lie about the incident?" Silverman asked Duncan on cross.

"No, I would not."

"How would it reflect on you as a sergeant, if in fact this incident had occurred in your presence and it came out that you did nothing about it?"

"I think it would make me appear as though I were not doing my job."

"How would it appear if it came out publicly that not only Officer Jordan, but a number of other individuals in the team there had come up to you and had said these things to you, and you hadn't done anything about it?"

"It would appear that I hadn't done my job," Duncan repeated coldly.

Silverman believed Duncan cared a lot more about Penn being convicted than he did about him receiving a fair trial. "Did you have any feeling as to the verdict in the first trial?" he asked, nearing the end of two hours of questioning.

"I was disappointed," the sergeant replied.

"You felt Mr. Penn should have been convicted of murder?"

"Yes."

"Did you feel that the system had gone astray?"

"Yes, I did."

"And who do you blame for the system having gone astray?"

"I think that you had a very major role in that problem," Duncan said flatly.

JORDAN'S TESTIMONY ALLOWED Mike Carpenter to call rebuttal witnesses. Three officers testified they were assigned to the same shift as Jordan and Jacobs and never witnessed any altercation during a lineup briefing. Silverman countered with Officer William Green, who testified that he witnessed the confrontation and that Duncan was in the room at the time and met with both Jacobs and Jordan afterward.

Milt Silverman took the opportunity to call a last rebuttal witness of his own. Bob McDaniel had originally contacted former San Diego Police officer Drew MacIntyre prior to trial one while looking into reports of a disturbing incident involving members of James Duncan's Southeast enforcement team, including Donovan Jacobs.

On the afternoon of March 30, 1983, a man named Rodney Jackson was inside the Texan Café on the 3600 block of Ocean View Boulevard when he heard some commotion outside. "There were several police officers around this guy," Jackson later explained. "One officer was on his chest with the officer's back toward this guy's face. There was an officer on each side of the guy holding his arms, and there was one officer holding his feet. The officers were beating the guy on the ground in the area of the knees and legs with their clubs. All of the officers were white, and the man was Black." McDaniel had reason to believe the two officers striking Harold Martin in the legs were Donovan Jacobs and James Stevens.*

One of the other three members of the Southeast enforcement team involved in the incident was Drew MacIntyre, who spoke with McDaniel at the time out of respect for his former supervisor. McDaniel's summary report of his conversation with MacIntyre on October 12, 1985, was brief:

> *Mr. MacIntyre disclaimed any knowledge of any complaint involving him and Officer[s] Jacobs, Stevens, Moran, and Tryon. He observed that as far as "complaints" are con*

---

* Officer Mike Moran, who was involved in the arrest, confirmed it was Jacobs who continued to strike Martin after the suspect had been controlled. "I had to pull Donovan Jacobs off the guy because it was obvious he was not going to stop hitting him," he later said. Moran had an overall low opinion of Jacobs. "I didn't like Jacobs; I didn't like the way he treated Black people." Moran testified in both trials in his capacity as the first officer to arrive on scene at Brooklyn Avenue but was never asked about the Ocean View Boulevard incident.

cerned, "someone was always complaining about something when you arrest people." He acknowledged he knew Jacobs through the department, but had no information of value relative to Jacobs's demeanor or approach to his job.

No subpoena was issued.

When Nathanial Jordan was asked by Mike Carpenter who on the Southeast enforcement team might have witnessed the confrontation with Jacobs in the lineup room, one of the names Jordan mentioned was Drew MacIntyre. This time, McDaniel issued a subpoena to MacIntyre at his home in the east-county mountain town of Alpine.

"Sir, what is your current occupation?" Milt Silverman asked MacIntyre when he took the stand on Friday, May 29, 1987, as the defense's final surrebuttal witness.

"I'm senior pastor of Calvary Chapel of Alpine," MacIntyre said, referring to the evangelical Christian ministry headquartered in Orange County. MacIntyre was asked what prompted the change in occupation. "The Lord called me into the ministry full-time," he said with the clear and confident voice of someone accustomed to speaking before a room full of people. MacIntyre had been a San Diego Police officer for four and a half years, including a year and a half on the Southeast enforcement team with Donovan Jacobs.

"Did you have an opportunity to observe Donovan Jacobs in the field?" Silverman asked.

"Yes, I did."

"And did you formulate any opinion or see any incidents relating to racial bias or prejudice with respect to Donovan Jacobs?"

"In my opinion, Donovan Jacobs is one of the most prejudiced white people I've known," MacIntyre said. "And if there were an ideal candidate for the Ku Klux Klan, he would be one."

"I object," Wayne Mayer called out sharply. "It's nonresponsive. Move to strike."

"Overruled," Lester responded.

"I would like to ask you for the record, sir, are you a white person?" Silverman continued.

"Yes."

"Did you form an opinion as to whether Donovan Jacobs possessed character traits of aggression and the use of excessive force?"

"Donovan Jacobs on a number of occasions did use excessive force in arresting various people in the area that we worked."

"In connection with incidents involving excessive force that involved Black citizens, was it accompanied by any racial slurs that he might utter?"

"He used on a number of occasions the term 'boy' and 'nigger.'" MacIntyre was aware of the lineup-room incident between Jordan and Jacobs but said, "I believe that took place before I came on the squad."

"And, sir, were you aware of any situations in which Donovan Jacobs would escalate the situation into a conflict when it was unnecessary to do so?"

"Yes," MacIntyre answered.

"Were you aware of complaints that were made regarding Donovan Jacobs's use of excessive force and racial slurs, complaints formal or informal, being made to his supervisors?"

"Yes, about his overaggressiveness," MacIntyre said. "No, I was not aware of any about the racial slurs." He was asked who those supervisors were. "The first one when I came on was Sergeant Jim McGinley. The second was Sergeant James Duncan."

THE WITNESS PHASE of the second trial of Sagon Penn ended the next day with the type of utterly mundane procedures that take up more time in criminal court cases than anyone would like to admit. Silverman's investigator and courtroom exhibit designer Jim Gripp was the last, testifying to technical matters related to the window-glare photographs. Silverman said he wanted to take the stand himself to testify to the timeline of some other photographs but that it would require another attorney be assigned to Penn to question him. Lester looked over at Silverman. "I deny the motion," he said. By that point, everyone just seemed tired.

40

"HE'S GOT THESE PROBLEMS WITH AUTHORITY FIGURES; HE'S not going to comply with their request for the license because they are telling him what to do."

Mike Carpenter knew he could not put on the same case as he had in the first trial and expect a different outcome, and that extended to his summation as well. The feeling around the DA's office was that his efforts in trial one had been overwhelmed on summation by Silverman's passion, persuasiveness, compelling storytelling, and utter conviction in his arguments. Carpenter had no intention of ceding that terrain to Silverman this time.

"So he's going to avoid abiding by their request in front of his friends, going to avoid being shown up there," the prosecutor went on, offering his theory of what was going through Sagon Penn's mind at the time of the altercation. "He's going to set an example for his half brother that you don't have to kowtow to 'The Man.' You don't have to kowtow to these authority figures, these police officers. And you get into this big dispute of the wallet and the license. What a trivial thing to get blown out of proportion by an immature, insolent, arrogant individual, Sagon Penn."

"I'm not going to kowtow to you, Mr. Authority," he continued as though Penn were speaking. "I'm not going to follow your request. I'm going to walk away from you." At that point, Carpenter argued, Jacobs had no choice. "He's got to control the situation. He would have controlled this so easily had it not been for karate expertise and the things that go along with that karate expertise, the arrogance, the brazenness, the insolence that Mr. Penn showed during this contact."

"That's where the whole thing starts. He violated the law there. All [Jacobs] did was grab him, trying to turn him around to keep him from walking away. Mr. Arrogance here, Mr. Penn, would have none of it, yanked his arm away, turned around with his hands in the knife position," Carpenter said, his hands frozen in flat, vertical planes in front of his body.

He spoke for Tom Riggs, who could no longer speak for himself. "If Tom Riggs had lived, what would he say to you people? It is reasonable to assume that he would have said something along the lines as follows: 'I saw the situation and we had more than we could handle. So I . . . what? I called for help.'" The prosecutor hit the button on a cassette tape player, and the room was filled with the real voice of Tom Riggs: "Four-fourteen, cover now." Carpenter stopped the tape and continued. "Two and a half minutes before he is killed: 'Four-fourteen, cover now; officer needs help.' That's him talking to you, ladies and gentlemen. If that doesn't decide the case . . ." He shook his head, voice trailing off.

"Jacobs made one mistake, and that was not recognizing the explosive personality he was dealing with. A person with an insurmountable attitude problem based on his skill in karate, based on what the evidence shows in this case, his problem with authority. You see, the expertise in karate adds to your arrogance. It adds to your confidence to deal with authority figures. That's what makes his attitude problem a lot more difficult to deal with."

"They try to get the guy to give up," Carpenter said, regarding the two officers pulling their batons on Sagon Penn. "He won't do it." Carpenter used Sagon Penn's own words against him. "Let's talk about Penn's statements: 'I hit him to try to slow him down, and he slowed down.' 'I had to repel him.' 'I just backed both of them off.' 'I had to start inflicting pain back on them.'"

He went after Silverman's case: "Make no mistake about it, ladies and gentlemen, the defense in this case is not based on the facts or the law. The defense in this case is based on emotion. The defense in this case is based on the specter of Mr. Penn being beaten by two police officers wielding batons, when in fact the evidence indicates that he was in total control of that situation." He said the eyewitnesses were simply mistaken about what they were watching. "The eyewitnesses were not aware of the extraordinary ability Penn possessed to block a police baton without incurring injury. None of you believed it yourself until you saw Master Wilson in the hallway," he told the jurors.

Carpenter stressed that because the officers were never able to arrest Penn, they could not have used an unreasonable amount of force. "The use of this baton on me would be excessive force," he said before slamming the nightstick against a metal filing cabinet. "The use of this baton on Sagon Penn is nowhere near excessive force." He offered his assessment of Penn's attitude during the altercation: "He's in his element. He's having a great time. He's showing off. He's loving it. He was laughing at those officers."

Once on the ground, "Jacobs uses reasonable force. He hits him, even hits him in the face. Doesn't have any effect on him . . . What does Penn do? He locates the gun, he grabs it, he pops the holster, pulls the gun out of the holster, turns the gun around, points it, and pulls the trigger, shoots Jacobs."

To describe the shooting of Tom Riggs, he again assumed the dead officer's point of view. "The first I knew that he had the gun, I heard the shot. I was surprised. The gun was pointed at me. I put my foot in the air. I was shot through my foot. It hurt, it seared. It went through the foot and into my chest, staggered me backward. The next shot hit me in the thigh, doubled me over. The pain was overbearing. There was a period of time, a second and a half, I tried to get out of there. I couldn't. I was incapacitated. He shot me the third time in my breadbasket as I was bent over. I had no time to react to the first two. The third one, I was incapacitated and it killed me."

He concluded the first of his two summations by characterizing the shooting of Sarah Pina-Ruiz as a cold-blooded attempt to murder a witness. "He perceived a person in there who was a threat to him. Not a physical threat, but a threat in the legal sense. He made up his mind he was going to take her out, eliminate that witness . . . You shoot somebody from five to six feet away and you bracket their chest cavity, you mean to kill."

"when you review the evidence in this case," Milt Silverman began, "you have to decide, what did Sagon Penn intend? What did Sagon Penn believe? What did Donovan Jacobs intend? And what did Donovan Jacobs believe? I say to you that the first place to look is the heart. Was there a heart of darkness or was there a heart of light? Was there evil in his heart? Was there hatred in his heart? Was there racism in his heart? Was there destruction in his heart, or was there not?"

Silverman retrieved a large posterboard and carried it across the room. "Now, we are going to examine, because Mr. Carpenter invited us to, the character and attitudes that are in the heart and in the soul of Sagon Penn and Donovan Jacobs." He set the posterboard on an easel facing the jurors. "I want to start with Sagon Penn because I listed here the things that were said about him: arrogance, brazenness, insurmountable attitude problem." He took a felt-tip marker. "The glimpse that you have into Sagon Penn's soul is what he said when he spilled his guts out to the police department over a four- or five-hour period."

He began reading through the transcripts of Penn's statements. "He talks about the Buddhist organization he's attending: 'We had Hispanics, African Americans, Blacks, Caucasians, Orientals, all of us. We was all family and stuff, chanting, helping each other, and we all trust each other.' He was chanting for the officers to make them feel better. He talked about starting an anti-alcoholism program. He explained that his grandfather is a real beautiful person." Silverman paused and stepped back from the posterboard. "Well, that's sort of a sample of what Sagon Penn spilled from the depth of his soul when he was sitting there handcuffed to a chair. There is an awareness at a young age, twenty-two,* of his place in the universe, and of morals, and ethics, and truth. And wrong, good, and evil. That's what spills out of him."

"I want to go to Jacobs's character," Silverman said, picking up the academy transcript. He noted that Jacobs was twenty-two years old when he attended the academy, similar to the age Penn was at the time of the incident. "We know that in 1978 when he walked into the police academy that he thought it was okay to use professional profanity, call people 'faggots.' We know he said he wouldn't really agree with using racial slurs and profanity and that sort of thing, but it would be okay if it 'got the job done.' 'We're not out there to beat people; we're just there *to get the job done.*'"

"The training officers told him, 'Donovan Jacobs, we don't know if you understand what it means to be a San Diego Police officer. We don't

---

* Penn's actual age on March 31, 1985, was twenty-three.

think you understand what is expected of you in dealing with members of the general public.'" He addressed Jacobs's apparent defiance of the warnings received from the academy trainers: "I think you're telling me this stuff because it's written in the book somewhere. But, man, let me tell you, I, Donovan Jacobs, know how to police this city. I, Donovan Jacobs, know how *to get the job done.* You don't like it, tough." Silverman reminded the jury of the particularly ominous warning from academy trainer Richard Bennett. "And if you don't understand that, Donovan Jacobs, then one day you're going to go too far, and you're going to get yourself hurt, or you're going to get your partner hurt, or you're going to get a citizen hurt." He paused and shook his head. "H. L. Mencken said, 'There are two things wrong with being a prophet: one is being proven wrong, but far more terrible is being proven right.'"

"You, ladies and gentlemen," he said to the jury, "have been presented with a lie. A lie about Donovan Jacobs, a lie about his character, a lie about his qualities as a police officer, a lie from him on the witness stand under oath as to whether or not he harbors any racial prejudice, as to whether he's hostile and aggressive, whether he escalates the situations. And that lie almost held. They almost pulled it off because you might have been there thinking about Wheeler. You might have been thinking, well, Wheeler has had these psychiatric problems. Maybe he's trying to get back at the San Diego Police Department. Remember all those hits that came in on Doyle Wheeler, who was the only guy last time to stand up and say something about Donovan Jacobs? But this time, ladies and gentlemen, this time you have Nathanial Jordan, don't ya? And this time you have Drew MacIntyre, don't ya? This time you have Billy Anderson, who saw him two weeks before doing exactly what the character traits show from 1978, from the day that he was in the San Diego Police Department to two weeks before this incident when Anderson saw him slam that kid up against a car."

"When he testified to that," Silverman said of Wheeler's accusations against Jacobs, "no one had ever heard of Nathanial Jordan or Drew MacIntyre. It's his word against the array of the San Diego Police Department. And you know what he said? 'I don't care if you believe me, Mr. Carpenter, because the jury is the one that decides that.' You want to talk about heroism? He was out there alone at that point. There was nobody to corroborate him about Duncan. There was no one out there to make a liar out of Duncan."

Silverman addressed the alleged code of silence among police. "Someone said that the cruelest lies are often told in silence. Penn was being beaten on March 31, 1985. The beating that he got on March 31 didn't stop there. It's gone on to this day, mostly by silence." Silverman paused. "I wonder, if you knew how many Wheelers, and how many Jordans, and how many MacIntyres there were out there who had sealed their tongue, I wonder if you might not go mad."

Silverman read extensively from transcripts of Penn's own statements about what occurred and why he acted as he had.

"So Penn is describing [Jacobs]: 'He was all negative and everything at first, he just pissed off. He probably just want to give me a hard time.'

"He's putting this down on a tape recorder, not knowing one thing about Donovan Jacobs, and he is describing everything that you have heard over three months of testimony that we know to be true.

"'I know he wasn't angry at me, 'cause he didn't have nothing against me, 'cause I didn't do nothing to him.'

"There was one thing that Sagon Penn *had* done to him: Sagon Penn had been born with Black skin. And Donovan Jacobs, who is the most prejudiced white person that Drew MacIntyre ever met, came face to face with him." Silverman roamed the well in front of the jury box. "And everywhere that Donovan Jacobs goes, there is *danger*," he growled. "Whether it is there when he starts or not. If it ain't there, he will make it. He will make it 'a hot time in the old town tonight,' because he's out there *getting the job done*, wearing that badge, representing you.

"When he went up to that truck, if he knew they were Crips, why does he ask, 'Are you Blood or Cuz?' Why does he say, 'What's up, Blood?' Because that's a Piru. I submit to you he didn't know what he had in the truck. He didn't have a real strong belief that there was a gun in it, or he would have approached it different, and so would Riggs.

"And we have got Penn, who doesn't have the slightest idea what's going on. We know that Donovan Jacobs is one of these 'let me get up in your face and kick your ass up against the car and push you around' types. And he has an audience, with Sarah Pina-Ruiz sitting there looking on."

Silverman said there was a reason why Penn did not specifically mention racial slurs in his statements. "Keep in mind the kind of person Penn is from what you have seen on these tapes. We say 'nigger,' we say 'boy' in here because we have to. There are people that would never say it. But he does say, not once, but several times: 'And then all of a sudden, you know, [he is] saying all kind of negative stuff, and then he went to grab me. And I said, 'Wow, I'm just going to walk away from this thing right here.'

"Now, I wonder what some of those 'negative things' might be?"

He approached the jury box. "It's hard for most of you to put your-self exactly in Mr. Penn's spot because you're not Black. You may be a minority. You may be Italian, Hispanic, you may be a woman, you may be Oriental appearing. Put yourself in his spot, okay? You're a woman, you're out of your car, some police officer comes up, coming on mean, something's wrong: 'Listen, bitch, I'm gonna tell you one more time.'" He paused and looked at several of the female jurors. "How'd that feel when I said it? What did you feel in your stomach? We can pick others—wop, chink—and it hits you in the gut because that's you. What would you feel at that point? And how is it likely that you might react?"

Silverman said they knew how Penn reacted. "So, he turns and he starts to walk away. Jacobs grabs him real hard." Jacobs pulled the baton and began swinging, he said. "Anybody else with Donovan Jacobs here, he'd have had an arm broken, or head caved in, or nose bloodied, and he'd have been hauled to the car like some sort of prize game in front of Sarah Pina-Ruiz, and she would have seen how our police department works, how to *get the job done*. But Penn has been trained to defend himself, and that's what he does.

"I don't think from the evidence, ladies and gentlemen, that it can be concluded Donovan Jacobs wanted to arrest Sagon Penn. Donovan Jacobs is a certain kind of guy. He's had this fella block his blows, and he's had his ego ruffled, and he wants to beat his Black ass. Would he have killed him? There *have* been people that have been killed by police officers.

"What we have here is Mr. Carpenter telling you with a straight face, without getting purple, that Mr. Penn was loving this combat with the officers, that he was in his element. And I'm wondering if perhaps he can tell you when he gets back up who it was that said this, or who testified to this, or what facts even would point toward that inference being made? He told you that the evidence in the case shows that 'Mr. Penn ain't going to kowtow to "The Man."' Now, put that in your mouth and roll it around a while and see if you can swallow it. This isn't a plantation here, folks."

But Donovan Jacobs was not the only villain in this story, Silverman said. The San Diego Police Department had been out to get Sagon Penn from the start and had committed gross misconduct at every point along the way. He took the jurors back through his litany of allegations—the detective notes destroyed, inaccurate eyewitness-statement reports, the violation of Penn's Miranda rights, turning the tape machines on and off during Penn's statements, the "misplaced" Padillo crime scene video, the darkening of the window-glare photo, the academy transcript, perjury, Maytag artists, evidence tampering, the code of silence. Silverman pointed at his client. "Folks," he said, "they want him bad.

"There is one person who has not been able to tell his side of it, and that's Tom Riggs," he said. "And Donovan Jacobs is the kind of guy that is willing to lay this off on Tom Riggs. He's the kind of guy that is willing to come in here and look you in the eye and say, 'I didn't start it; Riggs got into it with Penn.' Donovan Jacobs comes in here and he boldly proclaims, 'I have a clear conscience about everything that happened. I did exactly what I was trained to do.' And who is it that shows remorse? Who is it that feels sorry? Penn. The remorse you hear on that tape is the remorse that must live with Sagon Penn for the rest of his life, that he killed a man, that he took someone else's life.

"There has been a lot of talk about victims in this case. I'd like you to consider *that* victim," he said, pointing at Penn. "This is not a fight he spoiled for. This is not a fight he looked for. This is not something he wanted to do. This is something he *had to do* because Jacobs didn't give him any options." He continued, "This thing was sparked, and caused, and created, and fueled by racial prejudice, wasn't it? And they may try to cover it, throw dirt on it, and make it hide, but it won't do that. Because the truth has a force of its own. Truth may come a little slow, as it did here, but it came in time."

WHEN MIKE CARPENTER returned for his rebuttal summation, he was even more fiery and aggressive than before. He attacked Milt Silverman for his "confusing, baiting, accusatory, deceitful, bluffing, trapping cross-examination" of Donovan Jacobs, who he noted "never once lost his temper, never once got out of hand" while on the stand.

He pointed out contradictions and inconsistencies among eyewitnesses in the descriptions of the actions of the officers, their use of force, and the alleged racial slurs. He attacked what he saw as fatal flaws in Silverman's version of events and what he saw as illogical conclusions. He made good use of his leaner roster of expert witnesses to counter the testimony of Silverman's. But he was not his usual, disciplined self in his attempt to address all of Silverman's points and evidence. He often jumped rapid-fire from one witness to another, from one out-of-sequence moment to the next, drowning the jury in a tsunami of information and weaving a narrative that was at times difficult to follow. He attacked everyone and everything that did not support his version of events, often mockingly so: "Angela [McKibben] comes in and says, 'Oh yeah, police brutality and they were beating him and blah, blah, blah.'" He called former academy trainer Lieutenant Richard Bennett "that holier-than-thou instructor." When at his most strident, Carpenter's voice rose to a pleading falsetto, as though it was simply impossible to believe any other explanation than his.

Carpenter overreached in his efforts to make Penn look as bad as possible. His extreme characterization of Penn's personality and motivations had been formed in large part by information that never made it before the jury—the 1983 arrest, psychiatric evaluations, Safeway interviews. His hyperbole on the subject in the absence of supporting testimony or evidence made it appear as though he was just guessing or making it up. It certainly contrasted sharply with the Sagon Penn heard on the almost three hours of tapes.

He concluded by imploring the jury to come back with a verdict. "You people have not been chosen to waffle. You have been chosen to make up your mind, all twelve of you together, unanimously." In response to Silverman, he invoked the Gettysburg Address for his own purposes: "We highly resolve that these dead shall not have died in vain." His ending was a triumphant proclamation lacking only the swelling of cinematic soundtrack music in the background: "Let the word go forth from this courtroom that, *yes*, there is a system of justice in San Diego. *Yes*, there is guilt in the Sagon Penn case. And, *yes*, Sagon Penn is guilty."

41

N O ONE KNEW WHERE TO START. ON JUNE 10, 1987, THE JU-
rors in the second trial of Sagon Penn found themselves locked
inside a small room with a table and twelve chairs, almost four
hundred pieces of evidence, VCR and cassette tape players, a one-inch-
thick copy of the jury instructions, and a buzzer to summon the bailiff
Gary Van Housen should they need anything. After three months of
being tightly managed in a courtroom, they now had to fend for themselves to resolve charges a previous jury had been unable to. They looked
around the table at each other with blank faces. They shook their heads,
shrugged, began sentences that trailed off into nothing, muttered familiar phrases of despair. "Maybe we should begin with a vote on the
charges?" someone suggested half-heartedly. Juror Michael Alexander
laughed to himself. "How could I?" he thought. "I have no idea where I
stand." Neither did anyone else.

Someone proposed they go back to the broadest-reaching jury instruction of all, the one that defined the jury system going back to English common law. It was read aloud: "Reasonable doubt is defined as
follows: It is not a mere possible doubt, because everything relating to
human affairs and depending on moral evidence is open to some possible or imaginary doubt. It is that state of the case which, after the entire
comparison and consideration of all evidence, leaves the minds of the
jurors in that condition that they cannot say they feel an abiding conviction, to a moral certainty, of the truth of the charges."

There was a collective exhale of relief. They found the passage wise and comforting, and an offramp from the emotional burden of "passing judgment" on a fellow human being, which, for those who believed, was the sole province of God Almighty himself. Now, at least they had somewhere to start. Someone took a green felt-tip pen and wrote on a blank piece of posterboard: "Beyond a reasonable doubt; To a moral certainty." The sign was hung on the back of the door, where it stayed for the remainder of the deliberations.

Howard McDowell was in his mid-thirties, a Navy veteran with a master's degree in psychology and a job in inventory control for Xerox. The patient, easygoing, and supremely organized McDowell was an easy choice for the role of foreman.

The jury of eight men and four women skewed young, all but three under the age of forty, and five age thirty-one or younger. There were three Hispanics: Belinda Stallworth worked for Pacific Gas & Electric, Debbie Trujillo worked in the personnel office at UCSD Medical Center, and Emmett Cruz was a grocery store manager who began the trial as an alternate. The youngest and only juror of Asian descent, Richard Bunaun, worked retail but aspired to becoming a music producer. Michael Alexander was an army veteran and regional manager with the city's Parks and Recreation Department. John Vickery was a bishop in the Mormon church. Assistant Baptist minister and electronics inspector Matthew Frazier was the only Black juror. There was a bank cashier, a supermarket clerk, a postal worker, and a full-time mother of two.

After deciding not to take an anonymous vote on the charges for fear it would force members to stake out a position they might then feel a need to defend, they stuffed Clarence the mannequin in the closet, moved the seat and door from Tom Riggs's vehicle into the adjoining bathroom, and then got to work on the evidence. They discussed the motivations and credibility of witnesses, accepting none at face value, and feeling some eyewitnesses were more outspoken than believable. They were skeptical of police officers and the code of silence. They listened to the McKibben 911 call until they had it memorized, and they played the Penn tapes exhaustively. McDowell, the foreman, made sure everyone was allowed to speak without interruption. Any anticipation on the part of the attorneys and the public of a quick verdict faded fast.

The first casualty of the Sagon Penn trial came four days after commencement of jury deliberations when prosecutor Wayne Mayer was spotted and subsequently arrested for stealing power tools out of the back of a pickup truck in the parking lot at De Anza Cove. Mayer's swagger in the courtroom belied a far more sensitive nature. The father of four later said the pressure of the Penn trial had unleashed a previously controlled alcohol problem immediately following its conclusion, and the indiscretion had occurred during a blackout. Mayer did not appear in the courtroom of the Penn trial again.

Judge Lester recessed the court at the end of Friday, June 19, and departed to serve his two-week military-reserve commitment as a military judge. His interim replacement was Judge Ben Hamrick. On Thursday, June 25, twelve days into deliberations, the jury asked to have the two-and-a-half-hour testimony of eyewitness Demetria Shelby read back to them. On Monday, July 6, Lester returned, but both attorneys left town, Silverman to Colorado to lead a weeklong training in trial advocacy, Carpenter to begin two months of accumulated vacation days.

When the jurors finally cast their first vote on the charges on July 10, they saw they were getting close. Foreman Howard McDowell sent a handwritten note to Judge Lester with a highly unusual request. "The feeling among the group is to have us sequestered," it read. "[We] would like to know if the weekend is enough time to take care of personal matters and be fully prepared on Monday." Some would later say the purpose was to sharpen their focus to get over the finish line. Others revealed that it had been impossible to entirely avoid the opinions of others in their out-of-court lives. "I didn't want to hear another person telling me to 'hang the nigger,'" one said.

At the Sheraton Harbor Island, marshals unplugged TV sets, sat next to jurors while they spoke to family members once a night, kept other guests away, and shuttled them back and forth to the courthouse for deliberations. At the end of the day on Wednesday the fifteenth, they took a vote, tallied the ballots, and decided they were done. That night, while marshals looked on, several slipped into the cool waters of the hotel pool, contemplating the enormity of their decisions.

AT 10:00 A.M. on Thursday, July 16, San Diegans who had their televisions tuned to one of the network game shows were surprised to see their local newscasters appear on the screen. All three networks were tapping into a single live feed from the courtroom in Department 34 of the downtown superior court building.

Notified first thing in the morning that the jury had reached verdicts, the court contacted a list of family members and others associated with the trial. Thomas Penn, Peggy Barnes, and Yusuf Abdullah took their usual seats behind the defense table, surrounded by other family, friends, and supporters. Coleen Riggs entered the courtroom for the first time since her only appearance, which had been for the testimony of Donovan Jacobs. She sat between her mother and Tom's sister Kathy Ruopp, squeezing a hand of each. Sarah Pina-Ruiz and a friend slipped into the row behind them.

Milt and Maria Silverman entered, joined by Carl Lewis and Bob McDaniel. Absent from the prosecution table was Wayne Mayer or Mike Carpenter, the latter notified by phone in Michigan that a verdict was imminent. In their place was another deputy DA, James Pippen, who had been covering since Carpenter's departure ten days earlier. Sagon Penn entered wearing his usual blue suit and took a seat beside his defense attorney, who whispered something to him. Penn then assumed his position seated erect in the chair, staring ahead expressionless as McDowell passed the verdict forms to Judge J. Morgan Lester. Silverman rested an arm on Penn's shoulder and studied his client for a moment. Lester himself read out the verdicts, with the citizens of San Diego watching on all three networks.

"We, the jury in the above entitled cause, find the defendant Sagon Penn not guilty of the crime of voluntary manslaughter. Victim: Thomas Riggs."

Shouts and cries of outrage and elation could be heard coming from the hallway. A NOT GUILTY graphic appeared on television screens. There was no visible reaction from Silverman or Penn, but the attorney placed his other hand on Penn's forearm and held it there. Coleen Riggs's eyes began to tear up. Beside her, Riggs's sister Kathy Ruopp looked stricken.

"We, the jury in the above entitled cause, find the defendant Sagon Penn not guilty of the crime of attempted voluntary manslaughter. Victim: Donovan Jacobs."

Both verdicts were dated July 10, the date of the very first vote taken among the jurors.

"We, the jury in the above entitled cause, find the defendant Sagon Penn not guilty of the crime of attempted murder. Victim: Sarah Pina-Ruiz."

This verdict was dated July 13, the first day of sequestration.

"We, the jury in the above entitled cause, find the defendant Sagon Penn not guilty of the crime of attempted voluntary manslaughter. Victim: Sarah Pina-Ruiz."

The date of the verdict, the last reached, was the previous day, July 15, 1987, or two years and three and a half months since the incident on Brooklyn Avenue.

McDowell affirmed to the judge that they were deadlocked on three lesser charges and no additional deliberation would change that. He said they were hung eleven to one in favor of acquittal on involuntary manslaughter of Thomas Riggs and that they were deadlocked ten to two for acquittal on assault with a deadly weapon in the shooting of Donovan Jacobs. On assault with a deadly weapon for the shooting of Sarah Pina-Ruiz, they had stalemated at seven to five in favor of conviction. Like the first jury that deadlocked on attempted murder of the ride-along, the majority of the jury felt Sagon Penn bore some responsibility for shooting the unarmed woman.

"This is probably one of the most controversial cases in the history of this city, if not the most," Judge Lester said to the jury. "Each of you by being here has shown a high degree of courage." Several of the jurors had tears in their eyes as they filed out of the courtroom.

Wearing a blue plaid sports coat and bright-red shirt, a subdued Thomas Penn paused as he exited the courtroom. "I can't rejoice in something like this," he said. "Everybody is scarred and hurt. A man's dead, another wounded, a boy is hurt. How can you see a victory in that?"

Sarah Pina-Ruiz walked quickly down the courthouse corridor flanked by two female friends, as camera crews backpedaled to keep up.

She held up a hand to shield her eyes from the camera lights. "The jury is blind," she snapped as she left the building.

Coleen Riggs and Kathy Ruopp spoke to reporters in a conference room minutes later. Coleen, who had just turned thirty, remained composed, but there was an edge to her voice, as she expressed her frustration that the issue of race had been made central to the case by Milt Silverman. "I feel that justice was not served," she said. "Those two officers would have handled the situation in exactly the same manner if Sagon Penn were a white man. Because Sagon Penn is a Black man, he is free today. If he were white, I think he would have been found guilty of all the crimes committed."

Donovan Jacobs received the news while at his desk in the Narcotics unit at police headquarters. For one of the few times in the case, he had no comment.

It was the lunch hour in Michigan when Mike Carpenter received word of the verdicts. The outcome did not shock him, but he would never understand it. "If I was little Adam Riggs and I grew up without a father, I'd have a great number of questions about what happened to my father," he said. He was asked about a retrial. "It might be futile to try the remaining charges," he said wearily. "It wouldn't make much sense for the community or for Mr. Penn or [his] family."

A METAL DOOR leading from a delivery entrance to the superior court building swung open, and a U.S. marshal in a green uniform stepped out onto the sidewalk, instructing reporters to stay back. A burly man with a brown-and-tan beard, an open collar, and a handgun holstered beneath his sports coat scanned the area as he exited with Sagon Penn just behind him. Beneath his immaculate dark-blue suit, Penn wore a bulletproof vest. "Any word, Mr. Penn?" a reporter called out. "How do you feel?" Penn said nothing. Following with a hand on Penn's back was another armed bodyguard hired by Milt Silverman, who ushered Penn quickly into the back of a waiting Chrysler sedan. "Let's go," he told the driver as he followed Penn inside. A television-news cameraman circled around to the driver's side and aimed his camera at the side window as the car pulled away, but all that could be seen was a reflection in the glass.

The Chrysler moved through the surface streets of downtown San Diego, eastbound on A Street and then south on a numbered street in the direction of the 94 freeway. Anyone following the Chrysler would now feel certain Sagon Penn was headed back to the Southeast via the 94. But the Chrysler crossed the onramp at G Street and abruptly made an evasive maneuver and turned east in the direction of the offices of M&W Investigations in the South Bay area. While his family members and supporters convened at the Quartermass-Wilde House exchanging hugs, Sagon was brought into the offices for safekeeping from anyone looking to harm or interview him.

One of the bodyguards offered Penn a comfortable chair in front of a picture window overlooking a golf course and got him a soda. The young man immediately reassumed his familiar courtroom position, sitting perfectly erect and staring straight ahead out the window, as though the posture was now hardwired into his brain, along with everything else put there over the last seventeen months. As hours rolled by, Sagon Penn just stared, as though even with the verdicts, there was no such thing as freedom anymore.

PART 5

42

I T DID NOT TAKE LONG FOR THE CORONATION OF MILT SILVERMAN to begin. "This city can add a name to America's pantheon of legendary defense lawyers: Milton Silverman. It eventually may be listed with the likes of Lloyd Paul Stryker, Clarence Darrow, Earl Rogers, and F. Lee Bailey," read the July 20 editorial in the *Evening Tribune* written by nine-term San Diego congressman Lionel Van Deerlin. A major profile in the *Tribune* reviewed his previous stunning trial exploits, his skills, and his legendary work ethic, interspersed with laudatory comments from San Diego's most prominent attorneys. Mike Carpenter was gracious in his comments. "He's the expert in cross-examination," Carpenter said. "He has epitomized the highest and best standards that lawyers in California can achieve."

F. Lee Bailey himself weighed in with a lofty assessment of Silverman's victory. The legendary criminal defense attorney who represented Patty Hearst, Dr. Sam Sheppard, and the Boston Strangler hailed Silverman as "the top shelf of trial lawyers. If I made a list of the ten best defense lawyers alive today, he would be near the top." The always-provocative Bailey, however, had this to add: "The burning question is, did this guy get away with murder and did Milt Silverman get him off?"

That was a question leaders in the Black community wanted to make sure the people of San Diego were not asking themselves. For them, the real message was that Penn was found not guilty based on *the facts* of the incident as determined by the jury, not that America's new "legendary" and "top-shelf" defense attorney "got him off." *The facts* as they saw them were that white police officers in the Southeast savagely beat an innocent young Black man. They wanted white San Diego to understand that such things really do happen there. "The difference in this case was that juries have never before been confronted with the facts like this," said J. T. Smith, who was active in Southeast business groups.

Silverman said he hoped that as a result of the trial, the belief among those in the Black community that they "will get chewed up and spit out by the system has changed." Some thought it was a little premature to believe much had changed in a justice system they felt seldom worked for Blacks. "We thought the boy was already in the electric chair, so it was astonishing for us to see Penn receive a fair trial," said Hartwell Ragsdale, a prominent Southeast business owner. "It's something I've never seen in America before in my life."

THE DAY AFTER the verdicts, police chief Bill Kolender attended the weekly lunch meeting of the Catfish Club, a loose-knit group of Black civic and business leaders working to better life in the Southeast. Prominent community members had directed some harsh words about Kolender over the previous two and a half years, some calling for his resignation. "I should have followed my father into the jewelry business," he joked dryly of the experience.

Kolender had come to the Catfish Club to listen, but in brief remarks he struck an optimistic tone. "The case has created some very serious strains between the police department and particularly the minority community," he told the group. "I think we have all learned from what has happened. At this point things are looking up."

Just prior to Kolender's visit to the Catfish Club, it was announced that there would be no retrial of Sagon Penn. "We've been through two years of this," District Attorney Ed Miller said. "I think it would be wise at this point on our part not to go forward for a third time." Kolender's message to the city was that it was time to move on. "We want it over," he said. "We want to move forward." Editorials and letters to the editors in *The San Diego Union* conveyed a similar message. Everybody seemed ready to move on. But there was one person in the city who was not quite ready to do that.

"THE ZEAL TO get Mr. Penn at all costs caused major problems and they came back and haunted the prosecution and the police department repeatedly in the trial," Judge J. Morgan Lester said. "It is something absolutely new and was flabbergasting to me. I've been in the legal business twenty-one years, and I have never seen a case where this type of thing was going on." Lester was not making the comments in a private conversation; he was speaking on the record to *Los Angeles Times* reporter Glenn Bunting four days after the verdicts in the trial. He was troubled by Chief Bill Kolender's statement that there was no evidence of misconduct on the part of Jacobs. "There's too many witnesses for the department to ignore the reality of what was going on," Lester said. "To get an officer so carried away in beating someone that they don't even know their gun is being tugged at or taken away proves that the jury believed there is a real beating going on here." Jacobs was responsible for escalating the situation into violence by demanding that his "authority win at all cost when it wouldn't have mattered whether the license was out of the wallet or not." The officers chose to engage in a violent confrontation "when nothing is going to happen except caving someone's head in." Judge Lester referred to their actions as "nightstick justice."

"The code of silence that was brought out by the defense was preeminent in the minds of several officers," he said of police personnel who he believed lied, claimed amnesia, or withheld information while on the stand. "I see too much ingrown loyalty that came forth in this case for an objective presentation, and I think the department looked very embarrassed at times." He said the academy transcript "was purposely withheld" and the police should "stop hiding and stuffing exhibits in desk drawers that bear on an important case."

He criticized the attitude of police and even segments of the public toward the case. "I have run into people who want to make the conclusion that there is a dead officer and someone has to pay. They are almost happy to be ignorant of the real details and what was going on." Lester then emphasized, "The concerns I've voiced are from one who sat through the trial on a completely impartial basis."

For a sitting judge to offer such posttrial criticism was unheard of, and Lester's comments shook the city. The morning the article appeared on July 20, Norm Stamper found Kolender fuming in his office, a copy of the *Los Angeles Times* on his desk. After enduring one of the chief's prodigious outbursts of profanity, Stamper read through his proposed press release. In it,

Kolender and DA Ed Miller announced they were requesting that California Attorney General John Van de Kamp conduct a full investigation into the judge's allegations of misconduct by members of the San Diego Police Department. "What else can we do?" the chief said to Stamper. Despite Stamper's urging, Kolender refused to remove criticism of the judge. "Judge Lester's comments, whatever motivations may underlie them, are inappropriate, irresponsible, and disregard the best interest of the community."

"I am further personally convinced that nothing at all would have been done if some of my comments had not been made public," Lester said in response to Kolender's remarks.

Several jurors reluctant to voice these same concerns now spoke up. "I think his observations are absolutely accurate," Debbie Trujillo said of Lester's remarks. "I support the judge and his statement," said John Vickery. "I think there were police officers who lied. Their goal while testifying was to observe the code of silence and not let the truth be known." Jury foreman Howard McDowell said, "They weren't interested in the truth." Jurors named several police witnesses they believed had lied under oath, including Jenny Castro and William Mahue, who conducted the Edward Serdi stop. They were virtually unanimous in their negative appraisal of Sergeant James Duncan. "He's a very scary man," Trujillo said. Another referred to Duncan as "a weasel." The other individual singled out was Donovan Jacobs. "There was definitely some excessive force used that night," Trujillo said. "I don't think we ever got the truth out of Jacobs," one felt. "If it hadn't been for Jacobs, none of this would have happened," said another.

THE CRITICISM, RAGE, and even threats directed at Michael Tuck for over two years for his position on the Sagon Penn story had taken their toll on the Channel 10 news anchorman. During the trials, the Penn case had often been the subject of several of his "Perspective" segments a week. They were frequently critical of Kolender, the police department, the attorney general, Ed Miller, and *The San Diego Union* editorial staff. The day after Judge Lester's comments, Tuck took aim at his detractors in one of his final "Perspective" pieces on the Sagon Penn story.

"It seemed like a rather curious but convenient turn of events to me how so many of the very people who were screaming for Sagon Penn's scalp for two years were suddenly so eager to, quote, 'put the whole thing behind us,' once the facts were out and the verdict was in," he said, standing in front of a desk in shirtsleeves and tie.

"You see, some of those facts had been disturbing. It said something that two juries had concluded Penn was the victim of a brutal beating, so brutal he was justified in defending himself with the shooting which followed. If that was true, and that's what the juries which heard all the evidence concluded, then there must be something wrong in a police department which allows a hothead like Agent Donovan Jacobs in a sensitive job. Or, one so concerned with its own image it would apparently alter evidence and would send cops to the witness stand to tell what many jurors thought were pure lies. All of it to get Sagon Penn.

"Well, it all began to come unraveled. It became painfully obvious this police department has serious problems. So obvious, in fact, some of the jurors refused to speak out after the trial for fear, they said, that police might retaliate against them. Despite those problems, though, everybody, from the police chief to the editorial writers for *The Union* to civic leaders, were saying it was time to, quote, 'put this whole thing behind us.' Which to me is just another way of saying, 'Let's sweep the whole thing under the rug.'

"And that's what would have happened had it not been for Judge J. Morgan Lester. Judges have their own little 'code of silence.' So, when Lester spoke out as strongly as he did, it may have been about the most gutsy move that courthouse has ever seen. No, Judge Morgan Lester does not need to be investigated. He ought to be applauded. Nor is it time yet to, quote, 'put this whole thing behind us.' Not till we've figured out some way to make sure it never happens again.

"I'm Michael Tuck, and that's my perspective."

The formal request to the Office of the Attorney General of California—the agency empowered with the ultimate authority to investigate and prosecute law enforcement agencies and personnel within the state—came from DA Ed Miller. It said Lester's accusations "raised the specter of perjury by law enforcement officers" and the possibility both officers involved in the altercation had engaged in "the grossest form of police brutality."

The man heading the investigation, Deputy Attorney General Bob Foster, was careful to point out that the objective of the investigation was limited to determining whether sufficient evidence existed to pursue criminal prosecution. "It's going to take a long time," he cautioned. Within days, agents at the San Diego field office of the FBI launched an investigation into possible civil rights violations by the San Diego Police Department against Sagon Penn. In a communication to the attention of the FBI director, the investigation was designated a "significant case" due to "wide media coverage; much community controversy."

ON THURSDAY NIGHT, July 23, exactly one week after the verdicts, Donovan Jacobs was at Diego's nightclub in Pacific Beach with seventeen of his fellow police officers and about two hundred women very excited to meet them. Most of the cops were in tuxedos, and the women were lined up five deep to get their "1988 San Diego's Finest" beefcake calendars autographed by this year's pinup boys. "I've always tried to avoid policemen," a giddy thirty-three-year-old hairdresser told a reporter, "but they look pretty good out of uniform."

Jacobs appeared relaxed and in good spirits. He had sold five thousand copies of the 1986 edition at nine dollars a copy and hoped to sell at least that many this year. Part of the profits were earmarked for the Police Memorial Scholarship Fund in the name of Thomas Riggs. He answered a few questions about his future on the San Diego Police force. "If I don't feel I'm adequately contributing to law enforcement or if I get bored with what I'm doing, I'll leave," he said. "But right now I plan on staying with the department and continue doing some private enterprise work."

Jacobs had returned to limited duty before the end of 1985 as a fitness trainer and teacher at the academy. He transitioned to full-time and was enjoying the work. Jacobs claimed Norm Stamper told him in June 1986 they did not want him there anymore. "He said it didn't look good to the recruits," in reference to his partially paralyzed left arm. "He didn't want the recruits being influenced by the fact that they could be shot and disabled, and he didn't want them to see the black side of police work."

Jacobs was moved to a desk job in the Narcotics investigation unit and received glowing performance evaluations and a special commendation for helping to break up a cocaine ring, resulting in seventeen federal indictments. He was making $36,000 a year with benefits plus a little extra beefcake money on the side. And then Norm Stamper showed up again around Thanksgiving 1987, this time to inform him he was going to be medically retired on 50 percent annual salary for life due to his injuries.

Jacobs resisted the move. "Why are they making such an effort to get rid of me?" he said. "Maybe it's [because] when anything controversial has come up, somebody drops my name. They feel that it comes back on them."

Jacobs was correct. The deputy chief was still on the front lines of repairing divisions with an angry Southeast community outraged at Jacobs's continued presence on the force. Publicly, Chief Kolender stood firmly behind Jacobs, but privately, he and Stamper felt Jacobs had brought all of this down on the department by making a bad stop and then letting it get out of hand.

"That is absolutely ridiculous," Kolender responded to the suggestion that the move to retire Jacobs was unrelated to his injuries. "The man can't be a police officer. I'm sorry to say that." This time, Jacobs retained an attorney to fight the move.

Six weeks after the end of the trial, the first public rift in the Riggs family's opinion of Donovan Jacobs surfaced in an article in the *Los Angeles Times*. "My personal opinion is that [Jacobs] killed him, not Penn," twenty-five-year-old Michael Riggs said of his older brother's death. "I would like to see him drummed off the face of the department." Riggs's distrust began shortly after the incident when he learned of Jacobs's statements to Detective Manis at Mercy Hospital. "The first thing he did was blame my brother. It was the first thing that came out of his mouth, but they couldn't get any of the witnesses to back that up." He accused the police department of knowing about Jacobs's reputation. "They must have all the scuttlebutt on him," he said. "I know that my brother didn't speak very highly of [Jacobs]. He was not thrilled about the fact that they were going to have to work together because of the areas they were working in, and his attitude."

EVERYONE IN SAGON Penn's life warned him that despite the not-guilty verdicts, he could no longer stay in San Diego. "He's got to realize that he can be nothing in this town now," Thomas Penn said. "Although he is a free man after two trials in the case, Sagon Penn cannot stay in this, his hometown," wrote longtime *Tribune* columnist Ozzie Roberts. But no one tried harder to convince Penn than his former attorney. "I told him his life was in danger if he stayed," Milt Silverman related. "I knew the type of people we were dealing with," he said, referring to members of the police force. Milt and Maria went to Penn's family members: "We begged them to send him to a relative in some far-away state." Sagon Penn's answer to all of them was the same: "Where am I gonna go?"

Penn had another reason to stay. Donna Parks was in her early twenties and working as an operator for a telephone company when she came into contact with Sagon Penn while he was incarcerated in the county jail. Parks recognized Penn's name while providing him operator assistance on an outgoing collect call. They chatted, and she soon began visiting him in jail. By June, they had built enough of a relationship that Donna was seated with the Penn family when the verdicts were read in the first trial.

The shy and fearful young man with no experience in intimate relationships walked out of the county jail and straight into an all-consuming one with Parks. "It seemed they clung to each other and only needed each other," Penn's sister Subrena said. Parks all but moved in with Sagon at his grandfather's house. Some days when Sagon was not in court, they never left the bedroom except to eat.

The relationship could be rocky. Blowups between the two sometimes went on for days. Penn did not seem to know how to process the conflicts, often coming out the other side emotionally damaged. He was distrustful and afraid of the outside world, avoiding it whenever possible. He was as recognizable among San Diegans as any local celebrity and was loathed by half of them. He lived in fear of reprisal from the police and, with the second trial looming, in terror at the prospect of being found guilty on the remaining charges.

One day in March 1987, Subrena stopped by Yusuf's house. "You're going to be an aunt," Parks told her. She wondered aloud to Subrena if the baby would have Sagon's nose or long fingers but hoped it would not have his temper. Sagon seemed thrilled about having a real family and the stability it implied.

Sagon and Donna moved out during the pregnancy, staying several months at the home of godmother Barbara Cornist and several weeks with Subrena. Sagon took some community college classes, registering under the name MeeCee Parks to avoid recognition. MeeCee was a name of affection he had been called since he was a small child.

Although the two did not marry, he chose Parks because it made him feel they were more like a family. He began using the name in his daily life and planned on having it legally changed. On November 9, 1987, four months after the acquittals in trial two, Brittany Sheree Parks was born. Sagon was listed as the father on the birth certificate.

Sagon showered the baby with love. Fearful that anything could be taken away from him at any moment, he was afraid Brittany would be snatched away by crib death. He slept with her on his chest, he said, so she could hear him breathing and remember to breathe herself. When Donna went to her job at the phone company, Sagon looked after Brittany, proving to be a very capable parent. But his temper became shorter, his tirades more volatile. He had episodes of extreme paranoia. In early February 1988, three months after Brittany was born, Donna Parks broke up with Sagon, took the baby, and moved into her own apartment five miles away.

Subrena later said the breakup triggered something inside her brother. On February 9, 1988, just days after Donna and Brittany moved out, employees of the San Diego Police Department were stunned when Sagon Penn appeared at the information counter earnestly requesting a job application. "He was serious, deliberate, and polite," a department supervisor reported. He said Penn's application would receive the same consideration as any other. Many around Penn felt the bizarre move was a desperate attempt to show Parks he was serious about making a career. Others felt it was an attempt to pretend March 31, 1985, never happened, and a misguided belief he could go back to the way things were before.

IT TOOK MONTHS of negotiation with Milt Silverman and an assurance of immunity to persuade Sagon Penn to meet with Department of Justice agents involved in the attorney general's investigation of the San Diego Police Department. On March 12, 1988, Deputy AG Bob Foster, along with two seasoned DOJ agents, flew to San Diego to speak with the now-twenty-six-year-old Sagon Penn. With Penn was Silverman and another attorney for what would become a five-hour interview. It was immediately clear to the DOJ investigators something was not right with Penn.

"All I wanna know is, why am I here?" Penn asked at the beginning of the meeting. "Like, is it to prosecute Donovan Jacobs, is that what it's for? Because if it is, I don't want to play any part in prosecuting no one because I don't believe in prosecuting people," he said. "I just believe that God has something in store for him and he needs to be given a chance because even though his attitude was evil, and hateful, and angry, and everything for no reason, I still feel that he should be granted mercy."

"Just tell them what happened, Sagon," Silverman urged.

"I didn't get a chance to meditate to God," Penn announced instead. "First of all I want to say to God that, that I love him, I love the Lord, I love Jesus Christ and that, that the people here you know, I just wanna say this prayer to God because I didn't get a chance to say it this morning because I've been in this rush getting ready to get here, so I didn't know what was going on. I don't even know what's going on here." Long minutes of prayer followed.

Penn could not hold a train of thought, spoke rapidly, addressed multiple subjects within each answer, and was maddeningly unresponsive.

Penn, now converted to Christianity, called Jacobs a "victim of Satan." "The devil was trying to take my life through Donovan Jacobs so that I would go to hell," he said. He said the officers were "like two vicious wild dogs . . . just breathing real hard and trying to take my head off . . . I should have just gone ahead and let them just blow my head off." He became so carried away acting out the struggle with Jacobs that investigators told him to stop. He grabbed an investigator's hand in an attempt to have them pray together. They took breaks so Silverman could read the Bible with him to calm him down.

"I gotta tell you this," he said as the interview limped on. "I really feel uncomfortable in this whole thing because, you know, it's not pleasing to me. There's more important things that should be done in our society besides just prosecuting this officer because he tried to take my life." Only Silverman's constant intervention kept him anywhere near a coherent answer. But even that was not enough.

Investigators told Van de Kamp that Penn's statement was useless and that his mental condition would not allow him to be a witness in a trial against Jacobs or anyone else. "If he is subpoenaed, I think he would leave the area or do harm to himself," Bob Foster said. "After this interview, it was the unanimous view of the investigating team that Penn would not be a credible witness."

THE SUMMARY OF findings leading off the attorney general's April 11, 1988, final report of the investigation stated that "serious questions were raised about the conduct and testimony of some officers." As to the nine specific allegations against the department and individuals, including Jenny Castro, William Mahue, and James Duncan, however, "in each instance there was either no evidence or insufficient evidence to justify criminal proceedings. It was determined on March 24, 1988, that no charges would be filed."

The most serious was "Allegation One: San Diego Police agents Jacobs and Riggs used excessive force in their contact with Sagon Penn on the evening of the shooting incident." The "finding" exonerated Riggs but stated that "there is evidence that Agent Jacobs used excessive force during the confrontation with Penn." The problem in pursuing prosecution against Jacobs and others was not just Penn. "Given the conflicting statements by eyewitnesses, proving such a charge beyond a reasonable doubt and to a moral certainty would be extremely difficult. Given Penn's lack of credibility as a witness and his reluctance to be involved in any prosecution of Jacobs, the filing of criminal charges is inappropriate."

To support their conclusion, the agency released the entire 154-page transcript of the meeting with Penn. Silverman felt the only purpose was to embarrass and discredit Sagon. "Interview Offers First Glimpse into Sagon Penn's Inner World," headlined an article in the *Los Angeles Times*. For readers, it was the inner world of a very troubled young man.

Chief Kolender and the San Diego Police Department claimed vindication from the investigation, even though it had concluded, in the words of the attorney general himself, "there was legitimate cause to question the conduct and the testimony of some officers," and alleged one officer had used excessive force in an ultimately deadly altercation. "It is gratifying, but not surprising, that the truthfulness and professionalism of members of this department have been upheld," Kolender announced, to the astonishment of many.

Some questioned the attorney general's willingness to prosecute any law enforcement agencies or personnel. "It was a whitewash," said Daniel Weber, president of the local chapter of the NAACP. "The attorney general has elected not to pursue a case that should be prosecuted." That suspicion appeared to be supported by a questionable track record on the part of the agency. Asked how many convictions of law enforcement personnel they had secured among the fifty investigations conducted during the Van de Kamp administration, division director Jerry Clemens answered that he could not remember a single one. After reviewing the conclusions of the Attorney General's report, the FBI quietly closed its investigation into civil rights violations without pursuing any action.

THE ATTORNEY GENERAL'S assessment of the state of Sagon Penn's psychiatric condition had been accurate, and it was only getting worse as he became increasingly desperate to win back Donna and Brittany. On May 12, 1988, police were called to Donna's apartment at about eleven thirty at night. SDPD officer Fausto Gonzalez reported seeing "a light-skinned Black male without his shirt pushing a female into an apartment." When Gonzalez and his partner entered, Penn was breathing hard. He gave his name as MeeCee Parks. Donna was seated on the couch holding Brittany and crying. She wanted to go to the hospital and bring the baby with her. The officers observed a red mark and swelling on the left side of her face. She thought her jaw might be broken.

When Gonzalez followed her to the bedroom to collect some baby items, Penn stepped between them and began shouting at the officer not to look around the apartment. Gonzalez told him to "be quiet and shut up because we were trying to solve the problem, not make it worse." Penn thrusted a finger at Gonzalez, who pulled his baton and held it at his side. Penn screamed that Gonzalez was going to hurt him with the "stick" but backed down.

They accompanied Parks down the outside stairs. When they reached the bottom, "the male came face-to-face with me and told me that I was a minority son of a bitch and that I reminded him of someone from a time ago." Penn stared intently at Gonzalez's name tag. "I took a better look at his face and recognized him as Sagon Penn, but there was something different about him," Gonzalez wrote. Penn was wearing blue contact lenses.

Donna's mother later told police that Penn "continuously harasses her [Donna] and shows up at her apartment" and that "this was not the only time he had hit her." Donna refused to file a domestic violence report or press charges, saying she did not want it to be in the newspapers and on television. She just wanted to protect him and was trying to help him, she said.

After police left, Penn called his grandfather from a pay phone and asked for a ride home. Driving on El Cajon Boulevard, Sagon suddenly leaned his body out the passenger window and began shouting at a passing police car. When the officers stopped Yusuf Abdullah's car at 1:30 a.m. and asked Penn for identification, he reportedly lay in the road and began wildly kicking and screaming. According to a police spokesman, "The grandfather indicated he was having flashbacks and having a nervous breakdown." No arrest was made.

Thomas Penn told the press the incident was a "love quarrel" and that Sagon was "unstable and edgy" of late. He advised his son to hold a press conference "to discuss his feelings." But other family members interceded to prevent Sagon from making his first-ever remarks to the media during what appeared to be a significant mental health crisis.

The following day, Assistant Chief Bob Burgreen issued a safety alert to SDPD subdivisions that read, "All personnel are advised to USE CAUTION when encountering Sagon Penn or being dispatched to locations where he resides or visits." The memo warned that "Penn's emotional behavior indicates he could be mentally unstable and a threat to our officers."

There did not seem to be anything anyone could do to help Penn. He obsessed over Donna, called her constantly, and appeared unannounced on her doorstep. On August 16, 1988, he stormed into her Idaho Street apartment at ten o'clock at night in a rage. He pushed and threatened her brother Wayne and a friend of his. When he demanded to have "the baby," Donna fled with Brittany to a neighbor's apartment. Sagon followed, pushed his way in, and shoved and threatened the neighbor when the woman stood between him and Donna to protect her. He finally left, driving off in Donna's car. When police arrived, all five victims gave similar reports, and all five told police they did not want to prosecute. Several days later, Wayne Parks reported to police that Penn was harassing Donna with phone calls and threatening to kill her and Brittany.

On October 2, 1988, the *Los Angeles Times* featured a lengthy article based on the first media interview ever given by Sagon Penn. Penn said he lived in constant fear of retaliation by police. "Some of them will do anything to get you. Some of them will plant dope on you," he said. He

described a peripatetic existence, moving from location to location, changing his routines, disappearing for days at a time. Journalist Richard Serrano said Penn cycled through a wide range of abruptly shifting emotions,
his speech alternating between slow and thoughtful to rapid and manic.
Sometimes he would break into a wide grin; other times he'd settle into a
look of deep anguish. At one point, Penn suddenly became very serious,
telling Serrano he did not trust reporters because they turn their notes
over to the police. Moments later, Penn grabbed Serrano's cassette tape
machine, ejected the tape, put it in his pocket, and ran out of the house.

For several months, Penn stayed out of the news and away from
contact with the police, but it only created the false hope that his emotional state might be improving.

In May 1989, police were called for two incidents in which Penn
forced his way into Donna's apartment and threatened her. According to
one report, Penn "goaded the officers to shoot him." No arrest was made
after he stormed out of the apartment. By then, the late-night visitations
were increasingly alcohol-fueled, gin being Penn's preferred intoxicant.

The third incident that month was even more serious, with Penn confronting twenty-two-year-old Roger Worshim as he was leaving the Idaho
Street apartment at 5:30 a.m. on his way to work. "What are you doing
with my woman?" Penn screamed before attacking and choking him until
Donna's brother, Wayne, pulled Penn off. Worshim ran for his life, calling police from a pay phone three blocks away. Again, Penn left before
police arrived, taking some items from the apartment and vandalizing
Worshim's motorcycle on his way out. When arrested, the charges against
Penn were burglary, misdemeanor vandalism, and attempted murder.

Bail was set at $10,000. This time, no benefactor stepped forward
to bond him out. In court a week later, Roger Worshim asked that the
attempted murder charge be dropped. On June 14, Penn pleaded guilty
to the vandalism charge while the other charges were dropped. He was
sentenced to the fifteen days in jail already served and agreed to eighteen months of weekly psychological counseling at the urging of family
members. He was placed on three years of probation. Judge Frank Brown
voiced his concern about Penn's current psychological state. "Love can
be transformed into violent acts," he said, "and there's no question that
Mr. Penn is still in love with Donna Parks, and that's eating him alive."

43

"I THINK FEAR IS EMBEDDED IN EVERY ONE OF US," JUROR DEB-
bie Trujillo said shortly after the conclusion of trial two in July 1987.
"That is the reason why there was a lot of 'no comment' after the verdict was given." Trujillo and the other jurors had been spooked by the
testimony of Nathanial Jordan and Doyle Wheeler about alleged police
retaliation. "These were ex-officers, and *they* were afraid to say something about the police department," one said, asking not to be named.
Foreman Howard McDowell said he was careful not to give the police
any excuse to pull him over while driving. John Vickery said he felt his
house was being "stalked" by SDPD patrol units. "Our street was patrolled by what we felt was about half the policemen in San Diego, which
is an extremely scary situation because of the outcome of this particular trial." When asked why he had not reported the issue to the police,
Vickery responded, "When they are the ones doing the stalking, where
do you turn?"

TWO ALLEGATIONS OF police reprisals received significantly more
attention. Driving her car in the early morning hours of Saturday, August 8, just four weeks after the trial two verdicts, Reiko Obata, chair of
the Sagon Penn Defense Committee, was approached by an officer at
a makeshift sobriety checkpoint. The fiery and charismatic Obata had
been a highly visible defender of Penn for over two years. "It was obvious to me they knew I was with the Sagon Penn thing," she said of the

encounter. She was ordered to exit her vehicle and perform a field so-briety test. The police report of her arrest alleged Obata "exhibited belligerent and arrogant behavior" and "was so intoxicated that she could have been a danger to herself or to others." She was handcuffed and transported to the local substation, where a breathalyzer test registered 0.01 percent alcohol level, one-tenth the legal limit for intoxication. She was held overnight at the Las Colinas jail for women anyhow. When her mother arrived at the jail the next morning, she was told her daughter had "an attitude about police." "We've grown up in Southeast San Diego, and we've seen plenty, and you're not all nice guys," Donna Obata told the officer tersely. "That may account for something she said."

The incident appeared in the news a week later. At first the police defended their actions, but they quickly began backpedaling when the results of the breathalyzer test were revealed and Obata became vocal over the incident. The story lingered in the media and was joined by another less than two weeks later.

On August 21, Nathanial Jordan, who testified that Jacobs called him a racial slur in the briefing room, stopped at an ice cream shop on the way back from a Pop Warner youth football game so his nine-year-old son and a teammate could run in for a cone. With all the parking spots taken, Jordan pulled into a handicapped space and waited in the car with the engine running while the kids hurried to get their ice cream. A plainclothes detective with whom Jordan had once worked came out of a bank and ordered him to move. There would be sharp disagreement between the two sides as to what happened next. Jordan said the detective and a uniformed officer called to the scene insulted, assaulted, and unsuccessfully attempted to put him in a choke hold before placing him under arrest.

The officers' version of Jordan's actions bore a striking, and Jordan felt intentional, similarity to those attributed to Sagon Penn. The arrest report stated Jordan was uncooperative, refused requests to produce his license, walked away from the officer, and then reacted aggressively when the officers attempted to stop him.

"I was really shocked and surprised, and then I wasn't," Jordan said of the confrontation. "After testifying in the Penn case, I was almost certain something like this was going to happen. And it did." When released, Jordan walked directly to the front desk of the police station and filed a citizen complaint for harassment and excessive use of force. When he appeared to address charges of misdemeanor resisting arrest and battery on a police officer, the last person the San Diego Police Department wanted to see walked into the courtroom with him. "I feel morally obligated to represent him because he didn't want to testify and he told me there would be retaliation," Milt Silverman told reporters. "I told him if there was, I would represent him." He said a civil suit against the department and city would be filed shortly. A week later, Reiko Obata filed a civil suit of her own. But the most serious accusation, and one of the strangest episodes related to the Sagon Penn case, occurred eight months later and one thousand miles away.

JUST BEFORE TWO o'clock in the afternoon of April 19, 1988, a man in Stevens County, Washington, just north of Spokane, called 911 to report he had been attacked and shot by intruders and was currently tied up in his basement. When the Stevens County sheriff's deputies and emergency medical personnel arrived, they found Doyle Wheeler hog-tied with rope, his old police badge pinned to his shirt, and blood around the area of his left ear. Wheeler explained to investigators that he was repairing a leak in his refrigerator's ice maker when two men in their late twenties came up the basement stairs and rushed him. One of the men stuck a revolver in his face while the other wrapped a rope around his neck from behind. They forced him into an adjacent room and demanded he write a note. When he refused, they burned him with a cigarette on his chest and back and threatened to kill his children when they came home from school. "So I wrote the note," Wheeler said. The assailants dictated the contents of the letter.

"To the San Diego Police," it read, "I lied in the trial about Donovan Jacobs and the San Diego Police Department. I'm sorry. I make this statement of my own free will."

It was signed, "Doyle F. Wheeler."

He said he was then dragged down the stairs to the finished basement room and tied up. A third man, who Wheeler believed had ransacked his bedroom, appeared and roughly pinned Wheeler's old police badge to his shirt. He said he was forced to kneel in front of a sofa and had his head shoved down onto a cushion. He felt the cold barrel of the revolver placed behind his left ear, just before a pillow was placed over his head. Wheeler jerked his head to the right as the gun went off. The bullet grazed the side of his head, piercing the flap of skin on his ear. He felt blood and stayed very still with his eyes closed as the pillow was pulled off. He sensed the men watching to make sure he was dead.

He heard footsteps ascending the stairs and a vehicle engine start up outside and then fade away. He lifted his head. "There was blood everywhere," according to Wheeler. Still bound hand and foot, he wriggled to a nearby rotary phone, knocked it to the floor, and used his nose and tongue to dial 911.

After Wheeler was cut loose and transported to the hospital by paramedics, sheriff's detectives scoured the house for clues. When they discovered Wheeler's handwritten note of apology to the San Diego Police Department, they made a call. A high-ranking member of Chief Kolender's staff who listened to their description of the incident offered an alternative explanation. He said Doyle Wheeler was unstable and probably staged the attack himself. The detectives went through the crime scene again but found nothing to indicate the attack had been staged.

After being treated and released from the hospital, Wheeler told a Spokane journalist the attack was reprisal for his testimony in the Sagon Penn case and that he recognized at least one of his assailants as an informant for the SDPD Narcotics unit, where he'd once been a detective and of which Donovan Jacobs was currently a member. "If Jacobs isn't responsible for this," he said, "then somebody is framing Jacobs, and it's not me."

When told about the incident, Donovan Jacobs shook his head in disbelief. "If you knew Doyle at all, you would not find that hard to believe that he would set something up to get the kind of attention he likes to seek."

Assistant Chief Bob Burgreen called Wheeler "a fellow who is really disturbed" and said the story was hard to believe. "I gotta tell you, if something smells like a fish, it's a fish." Others in the department disparaged and mocked Wheeler both on the record and off.

The following day, Wheeler responded with a press conference held on the front lawn of his trilevel home overlooking the Spokane River. Wearing a denim suit and cowboy hat, Wheeler faced local, San Diego, and Associated Press reporters and camera crews. "I didn't stage this. I didn't shoot myself, didn't pay to have somebody shoot me," he said. He then launched into a string of accusations of massive corruption and misconduct throughout the San Diego Police Department, including an allegation that Chief Bill Kolender kept "intelligence files" containing incriminating information on journalists, politicians, and perceived enemies within the department. Kolender shook his head wearily when told. "That's absolute nonsense," he responded. "He's got a lot of problems."

About the same time, a local Spokane ABC affiliate reported that Wheeler had shown up at their newsroom two months before. "He said he just wanted somebody to hear his story because, if he turned up dead, it wouldn't be what it seemed to be." Michael Tuck revealed that Wheeler called him two weeks prior to the attack to warn him of "another in a long line of death threats" by a group of SDPD officers "involved in a small conspiracy who were out to make an example of him and me."

The San Diego *Evening Tribune* released psychiatric assessments of Doyle Wheeler that concluded he had a "preoccupation with anger and paranoia toward the police department." Stevens County sheriff Richard Andres questioned parts of Wheeler's story and said investigators had not ruled out the possibility that Wheeler staged the event himself or with the help of others.

Just when most following the case were concluding a mentally ill ex–San Diego cop had staged a fake attack on himself to get back at his old department, evidence surfaced to support Wheeler's story. EMS personnel first at the scene believed it would have been impossible for Wheeler to tie himself up in the position they found him and did not believe the cigarette burns at the center of his back could have been self-inflicted. They said they observed rope burns around his neck and wrists and cuts on his face.

A neighbor reported to police he heard a sharp "bang" minutes before Wheeler's white station wagon sped away from the scene, and that a "suspicious" dark-blue Toyota Celica hatchback had been parked just off the road at the bottom of the street. A resident of the area contacted police a short time later to report seeing a blue Celica in a parking lot twelve miles away earlier that same day with four suspicious men he did not recognize standing around it. A day later, Wheeler's white Toyota Tercel station wagon was found abandoned in the same location.

Sheriff Andres also revealed that according to phone records, a call had been placed during the time of the attack from Wheeler's house to the recorded main phone line of the San Diego Police Department. The caller asked to speak with Donovan Jacobs in the Narcotics unit. After being put on hold, the caller hung up. When informed, Jacobs said the only explanation was Wheeler made the call himself.

Investigators asked Wheeler to take a lie detector test. Wheeler declined, saying he did not trust their reliability. Sheriff Andres told reporters he felt Wheeler would have failed, but an eventual analysis of the recorded phone call by federal officials concluded the voice was not that of Wheeler. After dedicating two thousand man hours to the investigation, a frustrated Andres said his office was out of leads and pulled investigators off the case. Wheeler took a parting shot at the sheriff and his team: "If I were to say they were incompetent, it would be too kind."

But the case would not go away. The Office of the Attorney General of California again found itself investigating the San Diego Police Department in relation to the Penn case, this time for possible involvement in the attack on Wheeler. Their investigation found no evidence of such involvement, but they also sent Wheeler a letter notifying him, "We have uncovered no evidence to discredit your statements that your injuries were not self-inflicted and that two other men were involved in the incident." The FBI got involved but could not solve the mystery either.

The final word in the bizarre saga came from SDPD Internal Affairs investigators looking into the possible mishandling of money seized in a drug bust by the Narcotics Street Team unit and team sergeant Dennis Sesma, who had abruptly quit the department when suspicion over the missing money first arose. During the investigation, a drug addict and informant used by the Narcotics Street Team named Leslie Wardwell said Sesma offered him and another man $3,000 to rough up Doyle Wheeler. He alleged Sesma, one of Jacobs's superiors in the Narcotics unit, told him, "We don't want him dead. We just want him hurt, messed up, scared, to shut him up." Wardwell, who was living in Washington

State at the time, said they turned Sesma down because it was too much risk and not enough money. The alleged attack on Wheeler occurred three days later.

The $3,000 amount alleged by Wardwell caught the attention of SDPD Internal Affairs investigators. The amount missing from the Narcotics Street Team's drug seizure was $2,900. Wardwell's phone records for the period revealed dozens of phone calls from his home to the direct line of the Narcotics Street Team unit. The Narcotics unit attributed them to his work on an unrelated investigation.

When a *San Diego Union* reporter looking into the story tried to reach Wardwell, his roommate said he had not heard from him in months. The last contact had been when Wardwell called the roommate from a phone booth in Lemon Grove, the city bordering Encanto to the east, claiming "somebody was trying to kill him." Without more information from Leslie Wardwell, no link between the Wheeler incident and Dennis Sesma, the Narcotics Street Team, or the missing money was ever proven.

DRINKS WERE FLOWING at the Camel's Breath Inn, a well-worn drinking, darts, and pool table joint in Mission Valley. The place was a favorite hangout for cops, and on an evening in early June 1989, at least fifty of them and their friends were crowded into the bar area for an event called "The Third Annual Doyle Wheeler Wake."

The event was well-planned and promoted by the organizers. Teaser leaflets were the first to appear several weeks prior, passed around among the SDPD officers. "Never has a man been Missed More!" it read, in dual reference to Wheeler's departure from the force three years before and the bullet that allegedly grazed the side of his head one year earlier. "Don't Miss a Chance to Sharpen your Skills!" Fliers promoting the event appeared shortly after, prominently posted in break rooms and locker rooms throughout the department. Attendees were promised a chance to enter a "sharpshooting/ear-piercing contest" and to "practice your knot tying." T-shirts for sale showed up around the same time. On the back was emblazoned MEMBER OF DOYLE WHEELER HIT TEAM surrounding a large drawing of an ear with a bullet hole through it. On the front it read MARKSMAN, SDPD '88, SPOKANE. The price tag was eight bucks a shirt. A reported seventy-five were sold, many of them worn by members of the San Diego Police Department at the Camel's Breath.

Standing in the middle of it all, wearing a DOYLE WHEELER HIT TEAM shirt himself, was the man rumored to be responsible for the design and sale of the shirts. "Cops have a good sense of humor," Donovan Jacobs told a reporter. Not everyone felt the same. "I think it's one of the poorest examples of a joke I've seen in a long time," a fellow bar patron not associated with the group said. "It's absolutely bizarre." One reporter termed it, "A gathering that conjured up images of law enforcement officers mocking a former officer who might indeed be a crime victim."

Jacobs disagreed. "It's so ludicrous for us to believe we would send a hit team," he said. "Anybody who knows him would have the sense to know he did it himself." Asked by a reporter to confirm the rumor that he was the man behind the "The Third Annual Doyle Wheeler Wake," Jacobs demurred with a knowing smile. "You can write I have a good sense of humor."

THE BLACK COMMUNITY of San Diego could not help feeling that it was being retaliated against by the rest of the city in the aftermath of the second trial. After failing to stop the street renaming in 1986, the Keep Market Street Committee gathered eighty thousand signatures to put an initiative on the November 1987 ballot to repeal the name of Martin Luther King Jr. Way and return its original name. "It doesn't have anything to do with the Black community. The initiative was a reaction to the loss of heritage," committee president Tod Firotto persisted, referring to the Market Street name, which held no particular significance to the city. He added that the new name was hard for his "Mexican customers" to pronounce or remember in Spanish.

"The initiative is racism. We can't avoid that," said Reverend W. E. Manley, president of the local Baptist Ministers Union. Councilman William Jones warned the referendum would split the city on racial lines. Reverend Robert Ard said, "Do you know what it will look like, not only to the city, but to the world?"

In November 1987, Proposition F passed in a landslide, and San

Diego joined Anchorage, Alaska, and the state of Arizona as the only areas in the entire country to rescind an official recognition of Martin Luther King Jr. Urban League CEO Herb Cawthorne called it "a wound that will continue to bleed for a long, long time."

ON JANUARY 14, 1989, a team of special agents for the Drug Enforcement Agency smashed in the front door of an apartment on Logan Avenue in Southeast San Diego. Inside was what they considered very dangerous members of a drug ring including career criminals, street-gang members, and a notoriously violent Mexican national tied to a drug cartel.

The raid was conducted moments after completing an undercover buy of 6.6 pounds of crack cocaine with an estimated street value of $200,000 from the alleged ringleader.

In addition to arresting five members of the operation, agents seized cash, more cocaine, and two handguns.

Even in a border city used to huge drug busts, this one attracted attention, but mostly because of the identity of the man alleged to be at the center of the operation, Thomas Penn. The father of Sagon Penn had surrounded himself with people he thought he could trust. The supplier, Clyde Spears, was his son-in-law, married to daughter Subrena. His twenty-one-year-old nephew, Raphyal Crawford, was termed "his drug trafficking confederate." Also arrested inside the apartment was a man listed as Carlton "Smitty" Smith. Locked up in the Metropolitan Correctional Center, Penn, Smith, and the others were facing ten years to life on charges of conspiracy to manufacture and distribute crack cocaine. When federal prosecutors discovered Penn's apartment and crack-cooking operation was located within one thousand feet of an elementary school, those sentences were automatically doubled.

Few rallied to support Thomas Penn, who had already been openly accused by the Sagon Penn Defense Committee and Black leaders of holding fundraisers and then pocketing the money himself. "There isn't going to be any community marching over this arrest," said Reverend George Walker Smith. Penn pleaded guilty and was sentenced to twelve years in federal prison. His son-in-law Clyde Spears received a ten-year sentence. Carlton Smith, the father of six young children and key eye-witness in the Sagon Penn case, received eight years.

Sagon felt betrayed and bitter toward his father over the arrest. He later told a reporter he was grateful for his father's support during the trial but could not forgive him for abandoning him as a child after the divorce. Now the man had abandoned him again. "I want to give my daughter something that I never had," he said, "a good father."

DONNA PARKS WAS granted a domestic violence restraining order against Sagon Penn on July 14, 1989. It forbade Penn from contacting her and granted her primary custody of Brittany. But Parks had included in the request that she had no objection to Sagon having Brittany for visits. The weekly therapy ordered by the court, the threat of parole violation, and the chance to be with his daughter appeared to stabilize Penn. He saw Brittany once a week, with her occasionally staying overnight at his grandfather's house, where he was living again. The child adored him. Penn had her name tattooed on his chest, thought of her constantly, and began each meal with a prayer for her.

The man now legally known as MeeCee Parks had looked for employment off and on since being released, hoping to find something to develop into a career. There was bartending school, installing carpeting in downtown office buildings, four months at a Kentucky Fried Chicken, several months at a wire-manufacturing facility. He was still handsome and was in good physical shape, but a journalist noticed the contrast to the immaculately dressed, unfailingly disciplined, and ultimately unknowable Sagon Penn the public had seen in the courtroom. He let his hair grow out to shoulder length, wore jeans and T-shirts, and appeared more gangly and loose-limbed. Women pursued him, drawn to his good looks and, some, to his local celebrity and folk-hero status, often overlooking the obvious emotional issues.

He enrolled in cosmetology school, which made use of his artistic talent and sensibilities, where he had perfect attendance and was recognized in a local competition. At the school, he met Annilie Ganon, a woman of Philippine descent ten years his senior who worked in administration. She was loving and protective of him, and he adored her and got along well with her children. But these periods of stability and calm never seemed to last long.

On March 11, 1990, police were called again, this time by a hysterical Annilie, who said Penn had become enraged during an argument, grabbed her by the arm, and threw her to the ground in front of her children. Penn would not utter a word to the police responding to the domestic-disturbance call. When they began to handcuff him, he sprung up from the couch and struck a martial arts pose, screaming that he would not be taken alive. Officers attempted to calm Penn in a forty-minute standoff, during which he called Milt Silverman and screamed he was being shocked with a Taser.

Afterward, Annilie changed her story, denying any physical confrontation or threats toward her children. Two weeks later she called 911 again, this time requesting paramedics to save Sagon, who was unresponsive on her sofa after intentionally overdosing on alcohol, muscle relaxants, and sleeping pills from her medicine cabinet. Penn was kept overnight at the hospital for observation and released.

Annilie blamed Donna for much of Sagon's decline, saying she was fiercely jealous of their relationship, harassing them both through phone calls in which Parks insulted her and used control over access to Brittany to taunt and torment Sagon. Two days after Penn's suicide attempt, Annilie was granted an injunction against Parks ordering her to stop the alleged harassing calls.

The next day, Sagon checked himself into the Mesa Vista psychiatric facility for twenty-two days. There he wrote to Brittany constantly, calling her his "pumpkin," telling her how much he missed her. He tried to see his daughter after he was released, but Donna refused.

The previous incident with Annilie triggered a parole violation for Penn. Upon sentencing, he was taken directly into custody to begin serving sixty days in the Vista jail. Once again, Sagon Penn heard the sound he had grown to fear the most in his life: the sharp metallic locking of a jail-cell door.

44

AFTER SUCCESSFULLY FIGHTING OFF FORCED RETIREMENT, Donovan Jacobs continued to excel at his job in the Narcotics unit. On December 6, 1988, it was announced that his extraordinary investigative work had been instrumental in one of the largest drug arrests in the city's history, involving large amounts of methamphetamine, cocaine, marijuana, cash, and weapons with a street value of $850,000.

Five months later, Jacobs announced his voluntary retirement set for August 1, 1989. It was reported the thirty-three-year-old with eleven years on the force would be receiving $1,639 a month for the rest of his life. He threw himself a going-away bash cruising and boozing around San Diego Bay on a rented sightseeing boat with two hundred guests aboard.

After leaving the force, Jacobs began law school and was admitted to the State Bar of California in August 1992. Much of his practice developed into representing police officers involved in Internal Affairs investigations and in civil actions. This included bringing civil suits for damages against the assailants of police officers injured in line-of-duty altercations. His own such lawsuit against Sagon Penn was dismissed with prejudice, prohibiting it from being refiled in the future.

That same year, Jacobs published *Street Cop: Innovative Tactics for Taking Back the Streets*, his guide to "aggressive, proactive-type police work" for ambitious young patrol officers. The book was scenario-based and well-organized, with plenty of photographs and a clever, informal "from one cop to another" narrative voice. Chapter titles included "Learning to Play the Legal Game by the Rules," "Vehicle Pursuits," and "Street Gangs." It offered tips for identifying, contacting, searching, and arresting individuals. "This is a hard-core philosophy directed at a hard-core criminal element," Jacobs declared. "I am not apologetic about it, and neither should you be."

Jacobs never mentioned or alluded to the terrible events of March 31, 1985, other than a note that the author "retired due to injuries from a gunshot wound." The only other reference was the dedication: "To Tom, a good street cop."

WHEN DONNA PARKS left her apartment on her way to work the morning of July 26, 1990, she was surprised to see colorful balloons tied to the railing of her balcony. As she drove out of her parking lot, telephone poles throughout the neighborhood had posters pinned to them reading "Brittany, I Love You, MeeCee" in bold letters. For Donna, it was an ominous sign that the trouble was starting all over again.

When Sagon Penn was released from his sixty-day sentence for parole violation in the Annilie Ganon incident, he had not seen two-and-a-half-year-old Brittany in months. By then, Donna was blocking all contact between the two. Although he was still under a restraining order not to contact her, he knocked on her apartment door unannounced in an effort to see his daughter. This time, a new man answered the door. Maurice Bell told Sagon that Donna wanted nothing to do with him ever again. The following morning, the balloons and posters showed up.

It got worse three weeks later when Maurice and Donna heard someone outside the apartment yell, "Fire!" Outside, Bell's car was ablaze. He was able to put the fire out, which appeared to be caused by a flammable liquid poured onto the surface of the vehicle. Later that evening, there was a pounding at the door. Bell opened it and told Penn he could not enter and warned him he would press charges if Penn got physical. Penn struck him in the chest with an open hand. "See, no bruises. You don't have nothin' on me," he said. When Bell tried to go back into the apartment, Penn dragged him out onto the landing. A neighbor heard Penn shouting, "You think you're God? Well, you're not. I'm God." When Maurice tried to record the license plate number on Penn's vehicle at the instruction of police, Penn opened the trunk and tried to force him inside. Penn fled before officers arrived.

"I fear for my life and for the lives of my daughter Brittany and Maurice, my fiancé," Parks wrote in her request for an extended restraining order two days later. "He needs to be stopped." In complaints and arrest reports involving Sagon, Donna had never referred to Brittany as "our" daughter. It was always "my" daughter or "my" baby. In the August 16 request, she made her meaning explicit: "Brittany is my daughter and since Sagon was in the delivery room with me when she was born, he claims he is her father."

Penn's response was to obtain a domestic restraining order enjoining him and Donna from contacting each other. But that was not his intention in obtaining the order. Before filing the document with the court clerk, he altered it in his own handwriting to indicate that Maurice Bell was also to have no contact with Donna Parks. In doing so, Penn had committed the serious felony of altering an official court document, and he had done it while on probation.

The September 1 hearing for Donna's restraining order was held in the same courtroom in which Sagon Penn had been declared not guilty at his second trial a little over three years before. Penn tried to present the judge with an exhaustive written response to Donna's request, but the judge refused to take the packet, saying it should have been submitted earlier.

When a dejected Penn left the courtroom, he was met in the hallway by two DA investigators and courthouse marshals, who placed him under arrest for two felonies related to the altered documents. Penn contacted Milt Silverman from jail, asking to be saved one more time. "Sagon, I have already given you all I have to give. I cannot do it again," Silverman told him.

Nine days after Penn's arrest, Maurice and Donna were married, moving up their original plans to position themselves better for the hearing on their request for an extended restraining order. Two days later, a judge granted their request, extending the existing restraining order to prohibit Penn from having any contact with Donna, Maurice, or Brittany for three more years. During the proceedings, Donna Parks—now Donna Bell—reportedly stated outright that Sagon was not Brittany's biological father.

On December 12, Penn was found guilty of altering the document and of battery on Maurice Bell and sentenced to six months in jail. When his parole was extended to five years, the order to have no contact with Brittany and the others was extended to five years as well.

When Sagon Penn walked out of jail six months later, in the middle of 1991, Annilie Ganon was gone. By then, Yusuf Abdullah was showing signs of Parkinson's disease, which was slowing his movements and speech. Sagon could sense the only man he had ever considered his "daddy" was beginning to slip away from him too. He got a job in the hair salon at JCPenney, but when the store manager realized who MeeCee Parks was, she let him go. He worked in a salon in La Jolla where the owner found him talented, but other stylists worried that he was costing them business among their mostly older, wealthy, and white clientele. The owner did everything he could to accommodate the situation, but after news of his employment appeared in *The San Diego Union*, Sagon chose to leave.

His renewed efforts to have contact with Brittany became a wilderness of court filings, appearances, pleas, appeals, parole restrictions, and a labyrinth of legal jurisdictions that he was nowhere near equipped to negotiate.

He tried to move on. On his birthday in January 1992, he married Debra Hackley, a young woman in her twenties whom he first met in December 1988. Debra had a previous child, and together they eventually had two more. He was so devoted and capable in taking care of them, Debra called him "Mr. Mom." But the anger and pain over losing Brittany never went away, nor did the mental health issues. In an argument in October 1992, Sagon threw a brick at Debra's pickup truck as she drove away, shattering the back window and showering Debra and her three-year-old daughter with broken glass. The sentence this time was two years in jail.

The arrest and sentence triggered something else even more devastating for Penn. Donna filed a "petition to terminate the rights of alleged natural father, Sagon Aahmes Penn, to his daughter Brittany Sheree Parks," stating that he had effectively abandoned the child by not having contact with her or paying child support in over two years. In it, she stated Penn was "likely" the biological father. Donna and Maurice did not want to involve Brittany in the process. "They feel she does not remember him, and she is better off not knowing about him until she is older," an associated document read.

Penn tried to fight the petition from jail while an attorney collected testimonials and evidence that Penn had tried desperately to see his daughter during that time but was prevented by restraining orders and Donna's refusal to allow him access. He wrote long, pleading letters to judges and others involved in the process. A review by a Department of Social Services representative concluded, "There does not seem to be clear and convincing evidence that the father intended to abandon his child." It recommended Donna's petition be denied. But on October 21, 1993, the court declared "Brittany Sheree Parks free from the custody and control of her father, Sagon Aahmes Penn."

Penn would never see his daughter again. During the petition, his attorney asked him about the last time he saw her. He said it was April 29, 1990. Restrained from stepping on the property of the apartment building, he had stood on the other side of a chain-link fence looking in. He saw Maurice holding Brittany, but he was not able to speak with her. He remembered "getting a glimpse of her for the last time. Her hair was in a ponytail."

AFTER EIGHTEEN MONTHS of psychotherapy sessions with Sagon Penn—MeeCee Parks—the court-ordered clinical psychologist announced she was giving up. "Mr. Parks has made considerable gains during therapy, however, no longer appears to be benefiting from psychotherapy," psychiatrist Judith Meyers wrote to the presiding judge, Charles Patrick, in a status report. "The fact that I am his court-ordered therapist, he is having difficulty differentiating me from the system. He is withholding information from me. I can no longer serve the purpose the Court originally intended." She noted that "Mr. Parks carries a primary diagnosis of borderline personality disorder with narcissistic, histrionic, independent features. Also a major depressive episode and post-traumatic stress disorder." In other words, Penn had psychiatric problems to begin with and then a traumatic experience on top of that. The events of March 31, 1985, months of incarceration, and stress of two trials in which his life hung in the balance had all contributed to a catastrophic collapse of his mental health. But losing Brittany forever may have been the most damaging of all, the one event from which he would never recover.

SAGON'S RELATIONSHIP WITH Debra remained in shambles, with outbursts of anger and allegations of violence. They split up, and Debra eventually filed for divorce. He often just drifted quietly about town and among acquaintances and friends, disappearing for months and then reappearing, sometimes to stay for a few days. Milt Silverman had periodic contact with Penn after his release on the two-year sentence. He would appear unannounced at the Quartermass-Wilde offices, once dressed exactly like Silverman with a blue suit, cufflinks, red suspenders, and blue contact lenses. He sometimes came to the Silvermans' house, where Maria would sit with him for hours, but that happened less and less and then not at all anymore. Sagon sometimes attended the Church of the Nazarene near their house, sitting silently in the front pew.

Penn earned income only sporadically, amid episodes of psychiatric crisis and severe despondency. Friends and family claimed he would be periodically harassed by police during this time. The instance that raised the most suspicion was a 1997 physical altercation between Penn and five officers who stopped him after he made "an obscene gesture at a U.S. Immigration officer," an act that was not against the law. In November 1999 he was approached by security at a women's basketball game at the San Diego Sports Arena when he was spotted walking around the perimeter of the court near the players' benches. He appeared disoriented and refused their instructions to leave the area. He was arrested but never prosecuted. He was thirty-seven years old. The last time Maria Silverman encountered him was outside the courthouse one afternoon around that time. Penn appeared shabby and downtrodden. He asked Maria for money to buy shoes. She went to a nearby ATM, but when she returned, he was gone.

ON THE MORNING of Thursday, July 4, 2002, the city of San Diego was preparing for a long Independence Day weekend, the first since the September 11, 2001, terrorist attacks. American flags were raised throughout the city, and there would be parades and a fireworks show over the Navy fleet in San Diego Bay. By six thirty in the morning, hikers were on the trails at Torrey Pines, the sportfishing boats were on their way out to sea, and surfers were bobbing on the blue swells at Black's Beach.

About that same time, Peggy Barnes came into the living room of her Spring Valley apartment in East County and found her son asleep on the couch. A moment later, she spotted the empty wine bottle, the empty pill containers, and the note. Paramedics worked to save Sagon Penn before pronouncing him dead at the scene at 7:00 a.m.

Family members arrived at the apartment of Sagon's mother, some in time to watch as his body was wheeled out by personnel from the San Diego County Medical Examiner's office. "He was angry, very angry, because he couldn't have a life," his mother said. "Everything was hard for him. Everything was difficult," said his godmother, Barbara Cornist. "We think he was just tired."

Others were less charitable. "I have always felt he was guilty of killing a police officer," Bill Kolender said. "I think his conduct and his behavior after his release shows there is some validity to what I'm saying." Bill Farrar, president of the San Diego Police Officers Association, offered his thoughts: "As far as the Police Officers Association is concerned, the world is better off without him." Frank Morgan, who had befriended Penn and introduced him to the Church of Nazarene, lashed back at both men and the department in a letter to the editor: "I'm sad, disappointed, and ashamed to hear these community leaders taking pleasure in the fact that Penn has finally been driven out of our world."

"Everyone in the community saw Sagon Penn as their own son or nephew," Black community leader Vernon Sukumu said. "His case was the epitome of our sorrows and suffering." Milt Silverman said Penn had been an innocent young man "thrust into a vortex of circumstance who did his best to survive, endure, and persevere," but from which he had never recovered.

There was another person who seemed to have recognized that as well and understood where it was all headed. A year after the second trial, Sagon Penn sat in a friend's living room speaking with a reporter. "I might have made something of myself," he said, reflecting on his life before the evening of March 31, 1985, when everything had gone so terribly wrong. "Sagon Penn was killed that night too," he said. "He no longer exists."

EPILOGUE

O N THE AFTERNOON OF JULY 12, 2002, MOURNERS FILLED the pews inside the stately Christ United Presbyterian Church in Southeast San Diego. The overflow crowd stood against the white plaster walls of the large chapel. At the front lay the body of Sagon Penn, dressed in a blue suit, his open casket surrounded with flowers. Not among the mourners that day was Sagon's father, Thomas Penn, who died in prison several years earlier while serving out his term for the crack cocaine arrest. Nor was his daughter Brittany, who would not learn the identity of her father until years after his death.

After Reverend George Walker Smith offered his prayers of remembrance, others were allowed to offer their own words. One man called him a "warrior" who refused to let himself become another casualty of police violence. Another recalled him as so gentle he could not bring himself to hit an opponent in the boxing ring. Milt Silverman stood before the crowd and spoke of an idealistic young man who in 1985 saw the world not as it was but as it should be. He said that in the face of all the notoriety, Sagon had become "like a leaf floating on the water during a hurricane." As he spoke, he began to punctuate his remarks with a preacher's call of "Can I get a witness?" but received only scattered responses of "Amen." It was indicative of the Black community's unwillingness to ever embrace him fully, fearing that affording him credit for the not-guilty verdicts would somehow detract from what they saw as the facts of Penn's innocence. When he was finished, Silverman walked to the casket and kissed Sagon Penn on the forehead.

Outside the church, a dozen snow-white doves were released, flying into a clear blue San Diego sky. "It represents freedom," said his godmother, Barbara Cornist. "Nobody can hurt him anymore."

THERE WERE TIMES Coleen Riggs felt as though she were drifting in a canoe on a river. It happened to her a lot back then. "I have lost the oars," she explained. "I see them floating on the surface, but the current is slowly and quietly taking me away from where I want to be." Where she wanted to be was with the love of her life, who walked out the door on March 31, 1985, and never returned. Today their son, Adam, is almost forty, and Coleen has been happily remarried for decades. When she thinks of Tom these days, it makes her happy. But with that comes another feeling: I miss you.

"I moved on from having anger at Sagon Penn a long, long time ago," she says. Her religious faith has helped her shed past bitterness and resentment of a system that failed to deliver any justice for her or for Tom. She resisted indulging in vindication over Penn's later troubles. Word of Penn's death brought no closure, only the feeling that she was once again in a canoe, drifting helplessly on a river of grief. "It made me think of Tom and how special he was to the family and that he is still missed."

WHAT DONOVAN JACOBS lost on March 31, 1985, was his lifelong dream of a career in law enforcement. He still has a successful law practice, but he never really stopped being a cop. In 1995, Jacobs's follow-up to the book *Street Cop* was published. *Street Crime Investigations: A Street Cop's Guide to Solving Felony Crimes* was targeted at the "five-percenters" who wanted to go beyond "aggressive and proactive-type policing" to initiate "active felony street crime investigations" while on patrol. Both books carried a decidedly adversarial "us against them" tone, with "them" being everyone other than a street cop. Both books reveal a lingering bitterness. In *Street Crime Investigations*, he refers to an imaginary defense "weasel of an attorney" in his advice for testifying in trials, and he writes about an "unappreciative public" and "politicians and police administrators" who "work to sap this motivation from the enthusiastic officer." In *Street Cop*, one whole section is titled "Everyone Lies to a Cop," with five pages dedicated to "The Lying Citizen."

The predator-versus-prey theme is prevalent: foot pursuits are "Man Tracking" in which the pursued are "rabbits" and lead to the "Capture." Having provided the new patrol officers with his formula for aggressive and proactive policing, Donovan Jacobs offers them his best wishes for success on the streets: "Good luck, good hunting, and be careful out there."

ACTOR ROBERT STACK walks slowly down the wood-paneled corridor in the direction of the camera as a room full of detectives wearing shoulder holsters buzzes with activity in the background. The baritone host and narrator of NBC's hit television show *Unsolved Mysteries* introduces the segment on the November 8, 1989, episode:

> *Our next story concerns a former San Diego police officer, Doyle Wheeler. After Wheeler retired he was shot in the head by unknown assailants who attacked him in his own home. Amazingly he survived. Wheeler believes many he had worked with on the San Diego force engineered this brutal attack. When we contacted the San Diego Police Department, they declined the offer to participate officially. However, a recently retired member of the force acting on his own agreed to the interview. There are strong accusations made by both men. Who is telling the truth? You be the judge.*

In the segment, Doyle Wheeler wears a royal-blue button-down shirt and looks directly into the camera as he repeats the allegations leveled at Jacobs in the trial. When the "recently retired member of the force acting on his own" appears on camera to respond, it is Donovan Jacobs. "I think Doyle Wheeler definitely needs some psychological help. He's obviously involved in a lot of self-destructive behavior," he says. The segment ends with a plea to viewers to contact the Stevens County Sheriff's Department if they have any information that may be helpful to law enforcement. Few calls were received, and none were helpful. The Doyle Wheeler incident remains an unsolved mystery.

In 2008, a comment appeared on a video-hosting website where a faded copy of the 1989 *Unsolved Mysteries* episode was posted. Below it was another post: "Anyone know if this guy is still alive?" The next comment read: "Yes, I'm alive. It ruined my life and kept me from getting any decent work for years. All I did was stand up and tell the truth and for that I paid an extremely high price, as did my family. I have no trouble looking in the mirror each morning and know that my honor is intact. I wonder if Jacobs and his buddy [Narcotics sergeant Dennis] Sesma can do the same thing." Doyle Wheeler and his wife live on a ranch in Texas.

WITH ALL THE controversy surrounding her during the trials, many people forgot that Sarah Pina-Ruiz had been guilty of nothing more than an interest in law enforcement when she was shot at point-blank range with two slugs from a .38-caliber revolver. While some jurors questioned parts of her story, most remained sympathetic toward the girl from Cuttyhunk Island. "She didn't want to believe the police were wrong," one said. She never spoke publicly about her experience. In her civil suit, Pina-Ruiz settled for $11,000 from the city of San Diego and $100,000 from an insurance policy that covered Penn. Her marriage to Rocky ended, but at age forty, she finally found the man who her son Joshua called "her soul mate." Sarah Pina-Ruiz died of breast cancer at the age of forty-four.

AS THE 1987 Christmas holidays approached, Mike Carpenter was five months removed from the exhaustion and heartbreak of the Sagon Penn trials and was on to new cases. But he could not escape the feeling that he had let people down and wondered how his peers perceived him and his handling of the case. He got his answer at the regional Deputy District Attorneys Association annual Christmas dinner dance when association president Carlos Armour offered some remarks: "Mike's performance during the Penn trials was an eloquent testimony to his professionalism, but this award is in no way recognition of him simply because of that trial." As Michael Carpenter walked to the podium to accept the award for "San Diego County Prosecutor of the Year," his colleagues rose to their feet in applause that continued as he stood holding the award. "I am deeply touched and humbled," a visibly moved Carpenter said.

"I was just in the wrong place at the wrong time and I got the case," Carpenter said earlier that year. But looking back on the assignment decades later, he cited the words of U.S. Attorney General Robert H. Jackson in a 1940 speech: "If the prosecutor is obliged to choose his cases, it follows that he can choose his defendants. Therein is the most dangerous power of the prosecutor: that he will pick people that he thinks he should get, rather than pick the cases that need to be prosecuted." Mike Carpenter had not picked the Sagon Penn case, but he still believes it was a case that needed to be prosecuted. He remains physically fit and can be found captaining his sailboat in the inland waterways and open seas of the Atlantic Ocean near where he lives with his wife.

THE JURORS WHO spoke about their experience years later said that knowing of Sagon Penn's prior and subsequent behavioral and psychiatric problems did not change their belief that they had reached the correct verdicts. "I don't see how any of that would have affected how Donovan Jacobs acted that day," one said. They continued to have immense compassion for Coleen Riggs and understood her criticism of their decisions. "I would have been shocked and disappointed if she hadn't reacted like that," Michael Alexander said. "The emotion of love is blinding. It takes over everything." Jurors in the first trial felt vindicated by the verdicts reached by the jury in the second. "It seems these jurors came to the same conclusion as the majority on our jury," said Troy Axe. "Twenty-four people thinking the same way." For some, there remained one lingering frustration about the case. "I would like to see him admit it," Vernell Hardy said of Donovan Jacobs. "I would like to see him say, 'I know I was wrong.'"

WHEN JUDGE BEN W. Hamrick passed away in 2007, his obituary noted his love of animals and involvement with the local Humane Society, along with some impressive numbers: age eighty-three, thirty-five bomber missions in World War II, twenty-two years of private law practice, eighteen on the bench, and fifty-seven years of marriage to his wife, Madeline.

Judge J. Morgan Lester never regretted going public with his concerns about the conduct of the San Diego Police Department after the second Sagon Penn trial. "I would not want to look in the mirror and see nothing but a coward for the rest of my life," he said. After serving as a superior court judge, Lester received a prestigious appointment to the court of appeals. "Golden Owl" continued to volunteer legal services to the Native American tribes near his home and to participate in some of their ceremonies as an honorary member. He died in 2023.

THE SAN DIEGO Police Department implemented important changes as a result of the Sagon Penn incident, but it was soon reminded that some things remained the same. Five months after the second Sagon Penn trial, twenty-four-year-old rookie patrol officer Jerry Hartless was chasing a group of suspects near "the four corners of death," when he was shot between the eyes with a .22 revolver. The death of Officer Hartless meant that police officers in San Diego remained more likely to be murdered in the line of duty than those of any other big city in the country.

In July 1988, Chief Bill Kolender retired from the San Diego Police Department after thirteen years at its helm to take a position as assistant general manager at the Union-Tribune Publishing Company. The Sagon Penn case was considered a dark episode in an otherwise successful administration. Upon Kolender's retirement, his assistant chief, Bob Burgreen, became chief of the San Diego Police Department. Deputy Chief Norm Stamper, who dedicated much of his career to ridding the department of bad cops, went on to become the chief of the Seattle Police Department.

THE WEDDING INVITATIONS came in the form of subpoenas. Defense investigator Bob McDaniel married his investigation partner Suzanne Berard on a weekend during the second trial. McDaniel and Milt

Silverman, the two men who had been so wary of each other at the start, had grown so close that Silverman acted as best man. Maria Silverman served as the matron of honor. Carlton Smith's daughter Krystal Smith was the ring bearer. Milt Silverman would later say of his "Old Clydesdale" McDaniel, "I never would have won this case without him." Jim Gripp continues to operate Legal Arts, the premier litigation graphics and multimedia presentation specialists in San Diego. Rich Whalley remained the top criminologist in the city and spent thirty-six years in the business before passing away in 2003. A *San Diego Union* obituary reminded readers of his motto: "Physical evidence doesn't lie, but people do."

IT DID NOT take long for Hollywood to swoop in on the Sagon Penn story. In late October 1987, two television writers representing a Hollywood production company showed up in town gathering information with which to develop a screenplay for a miniseries tentatively entitled *The Sagon Penn Story.* "We're researching to prepare for a major network, which is NBC, a miniseries based upon the incident," said one of the writers. "God, I hope not," Bill Kolender said when told about the possibility of a miniseries. "Jesus, let it go."

When the screenplay was complete, anchorman Michael Tuck revealed in a "Perspective" piece that the main character in *The Sagon Penn Story* would be anchorman Michael Tuck. The plot, he said, would "parallel" his involvement in the case. Tuck revealed to viewers that he had encouraged the Penn family to retain Milt Silverman. "As the story unfolded and we heard from witnesses what had gone on down there, I began to feel that something wasn't right and to have serious concerns about whether he'd be able to get a fair trial. I felt I had no moral choice but to become involved." He later acknowledged the mostly negative public reaction to his actions. "There is a [journalistic] boundary and I crossed it."

The Sagon Penn Story was never made. Michael Tuck died in 2022.

"THE NEIGHBORHOOD FELT haunted after that," Krystal Smith said of the 6500 block of Brooklyn Avenue. The Smith family moved out of the neighborhood after they lost her father, Carlton Smith, to a decade in prison on the Thomas Penn crack bust. The families with young children were the first to leave. The Taylors, the Alexanders, the Williamses . . . "Nothing was the same after that," said Charles Alexander, who was twelve at the time he witnessed the incident.

For some of the witnesses, being part of the Sagon Penn incident remained the defining moment in their lives. Cedric Gregory wrote a memoir about growing up in the Southeast and his experience in the Penn incident titled *1985 Back of the Truck: My Ride with Sagon Penn.*

On July 21, 1988, a thirty-minute documentary titled *I Claim Myself: The Sagon Penn Incident* premiered to a full-capacity crowd at St. Stephen's Church in Southeast San Diego. In the film, Anthony Lovett, Junius Holmes, and Ricky Clipper stand before a graffitied wall rapping a song about the Penn incident written mostly by Lovett: "They was beatin' him, beatin' him, beatin' him down. Something happened that wasn't expected; he grabbed that gun and got self-protected." Anthony Lovett still regrets giving up on a career in music but said everything seemed to fall apart soon after the incident, including his rap group and marriage to Angie McKibben. "I still ask myself, why did that truck have to come up my driveway that day?"

Angela McKibben had been waiting for thirty-five years for someone to write about the Sagon Penn story. "Dude, I was wondering when someone was going to call me about this," she said when contacted by a writer. She now manages a modest-size apartment complex. In a rush to clean one of the units, she sprays Fantastik cleaner on countertops as she talks about her experience decades before.

"For a little while, it was kind of exciting," she says. Television reporters knocked on their door, their names were in the papers, she and Lovett were featured in the documentary film. But that initial rush was gone by the start of the first trial, replaced by terrible memories she still cannot get out of her head. The only time Angie McKibben stops her cleaning is when asked if there had ever been any disagreement among the witnesses in the neighborhood about what happened that day and who was to blame. "Oh, no," she says, slowly shaking her head. "If you saw it, you knew what it was."

FOR SIX DAYS in the spring of 1992, South Central Los Angeles murdered and burned itself down after the acquittal of four white police officers in the beating, caught on film, of a Black man named Rodney King. At the same time, one hundred miles to the south, the city of San Diego remained relatively calm: a Molotov cocktail, the windows of a Foot Locker and a Radio Shack shattered by looters, attempts to pull motorists from their vehicles on Imperial Avenue, and some angry protests on local campuses. The area was quiet even compared to protests and riots in other western cities such as Oakland, San Francisco, and Las Vegas.

Among the factors contributing to the low level of civil unrest cited by both local law enforcement and members of the Black community was an incident that occurred seven years earlier. "If we had not gone through what we did with Sagon Penn, things would have been very different," a prominent community leader in the Southeast said. "We had been through our own crisis between police and the Black community years before Los Angeles did," said former deputy chief Norm Stamper. "We learned how to talk and listen to each other." "It was our Rodney King," said San Diego police chief Bob Burgreen. Most felt that had the Sagon Penn trial ended in conviction, the Southeast would have been ready to explode by the time Rodney King came along. Instead, the acquittals released a little steam out of the pressure cooker. Milt Silverman took the most optimistic of views. Unlike Los Angeles, he said, "After the Penn trials, a lot of people here believe San Diego is a place where it is possible for a Black man to find justice."

THIRTY-FIVE YEARS AFTER the Sagon Penn trials, Milt Silverman stands in the basement of his former Quartermass-Wilde House office. Gone is Rich Whalley's crime lab that used to occupy the cavernous subterranean space. Silverman is retired and rents the majestic Victorian building to another law firm. Inside the basement are stacked hundreds of cardboard boxes filled with documents and evidence from his legendary trials: Adkins, Stone, Driscoll, Neville, and Sagon Penn.

There were more stunning victories after Penn which Silverman had been given little chance of winning. "I never take cases just because I'm going to win them," he once said. "I take tough cases." Some cases were civil actions, some criminal defense, but most had one thing in common: powerful and trusted institutions who conspired to victimize unempowered individuals. His adversaries included the University of California, the United States Navy, the Pueblo, Colorado, county school system, and, most often, law enforcement agencies who Silverman accused of conspiring to unjustly convict the innocent. Dale Akiki, a church volunteer falsely accused of ritualistic child abuse, was put on trial by the district attorney over the objections of his own prosecutors. Fourteen-year-old Michael Crowe was harshly interrogated by Escondido Police Homicide detectives into a false confession for stabbing his ten-year-old sister to death. Jim Wade spent years in prison wrongly convicted of raping his eight-year-old in a trial his original defense team called "the worst case of injustice we have seen in our entire lives." Silverman won all of their cases.

But the case Milt Silverman is most proud of, and believes will be his legacy, is the trial of Sagon Penn. "Never before in American history had a young Black man admitted to killing a police officer and been found not guilty by a jury for having acted in self-defense," he says. But there is only anger in his voice as he stands amid the boxes of old documents reflecting on the fate of his client. "There was nothing to celebrate. This story began as a tragedy, and it ends as a tragedy."

NOTES ON SOURCES

This book is the result of four years of research and writing. Documents and materials were located in news archives, microfiche reels, courthouses, libraries, museums, private collections, scrapbooks, Facebook pages, and just about anywhere else you can imagine finding documents, video, audio, photos, maps, and physical evidence from a forty-year-old event. Trial transcripts ran over sixty thousand pages. Police reports and investigation materials, well over ten thousand pages. One archive alone exceeded thirty boxes of documents, trial exhibits, unedited recordings of police radio traffic, 911 calls, interrogations, and hundreds of hours of video.

Over fifteen hundred news articles were included in the research. Journalists Glenn Bunting, Mike Konon, George Flynn, Jim Schachter, Jennifer Warren, Eddy McNeil, and Kathleen Jackson provided excellent daily trial coverage for *The San Diego Union*, *Evening Tribune*, and *Los Angeles Times* newspapers. Maribeth Mellin's multipart feature piece in *San Diego Magazine* was invaluable. Television-news video exceeded one hundred hours. Dozens of websites and books of all types and subject matter were referenced. The project benefitted immensely from the generous help of specialists, experts, local historians, and writers on events and subject matter involved.

The most important part of any story is the experience of those who lived it or were directly impacted. During the course of writing this book, I located and spoke with as many as possible and from all areas of involvement. Eyewitnesses, police officers, members of the Black community, attorneys, family, friends, members of the media, and jurors were just some. Over 150 people were interviewed, some multiple times. Others could not be located. Some declined to participate or preferred not to be acknowledged here; both decisions should be respected. For those who revisited their experience even though it would have been easier not to, I am grateful.

In an incident of this nature and in criminal trials, there are differing and opposing opinions, contentions, and versions of events. I have tried to make clear to the reader which are disputed, and by whom, and to fairly represent all sides of contested facts and events. Errors, contradictions, and inconsistencies in witness accounts, documents, evidence, and reports were not uncommon. I attempted to resolve these by referencing multiple sources. When concerning incidental details, I chose the most reliable. When unable to resolve those of more importance, it is noted in the text, the details are attributed to their source, or each account is represented.

The overwhelming majority of dialogue was taken verbatim from trial transcripts, news articles, and recordings. Dialogue related to the author in personal interviews is recreated as faithfully as possible. In the event that one or more participants were not available, I used secondhand accounts I considered reliable. Some trial transcript text is condensed and edited for flow, context, and clarity, but never to alter meaning.

Notes on the subject of race and ethnicity: I attempted at all times to be respectful to all individuals and groups in this writing. I also felt it was important to be faithful to the common and accepted terminology of the era and that used by individuals in the story, which might not always be consistent with current use. There are racial slurs in this book. They are included only when critical to the story and spoken by individuals at the time. I do not use them in my narrative, and their inclusion is as limited as possible. The capitalization or non-capitalization of words related to identity, ethnicity, and race follow the guidelines of *The Chicago Manual of Style*, used by the publishing industry.

I apologize for any offense; it is entirely unintentional.

ACKNOWLEDGMENTS

I would like to thank the following people and organizations for their help and cooperation in the making of this book:

Alex Alonso Villega, Andrew Monti, Angela McKibben, Anthony Lovett, Arman Sedgwick-Billimoria, Bernadette Smith, Beverly Wight, Billy Moore, Billy Papenhausen, Bob Boyce, Bob Strahan, Carl Lewis, Cedric Gregory, Charles Alexander, Chuck Apostolas, Chuck Sevilla, Coleen Riggs, Cory Smith, Dan Smetanka, Dani Simson, Daniel White, Dave DeCaro, Don Boughton, Doug Curlee, Doyle Wheeler, Ed Quinn, Emmett Cruz, F. Lee Bailey, Frances Veeder, Frank Morgan, Fred Dreis, Gary Schons, Gary Murphy, Glen R. Coahran, Glenn Bunting, Judge J. Morgan Lester, J. W. August, Jack Mullen, Jack Schaffer, James and Olivia Houlahan, Jeff Ourvan, Jill McDaniel, Jim Gripp, Joaquin McWhinney, Joel Zwink, John Stoll, Jon Sternfeld, Joshua King, Judith Farkas, Judith Weber, Judy Houlahan, Junius Holmes, Keith Taylor, Kevin Ruddy, Krystal Smith, Laraine Diaz, Larry Avrech, Dr. Linus Abrams, Maria Silverman, Maribeth Mellin, Matt Nye, Dr. Maurizio Zanetti, Mia Bendixsen, Michael Appelman, Michael Nacar, Michael Carpenter, Michael Moran, Michael Tuck, Milton Silverman, Mychal Odom, Nancy Riggs, Nathanial Jordan, Neal Panish, Norm Stamper, Orned Gabriel, Paul Ybarrondo, Paul Krueger, Pauline Repard, Pete Cohen, Rachael Cianfrani, Raphyal Crawford, Reiko Obata, Renato Rodriguez, Richard LeVine, Richard Louv, Richard Huffman, Richard Thwing, Robert Coons, Robert Phillips, Robert Ottilie, Roberto Rivera, Roger Holtzen, Roger Showley, Sean McDaniel, Sean McDowell, Sheila Marten, Steve Fiorina, Steve Willard, Theodor Whalen, Susan Manis,

Tony Perry, Tony Doubek, Troy Axe, Vern Lovett, Vernon Sukumu, Wayne Mayer, and William Jeffers.

California Office of the Attorney General, Federal Bureau of Investigation, *Los Angeles Times*, NAACP, San Diego History Center, *San Diego Magazine*, San Diego Police Museum, San Diego Police Officers Association, San Diego Public Library, San Diego Superior Court, *The San Diego Union-Tribune*, Stevens County Sheriff's Department, University of California San Diego.

Thank you also to all who preferred not to be acknowledged here.